SLAVERY, ABOLITIONISM, BIBLICAL SCHOLARSHIP

The Bible in the Modern World, 38

Series Editors
J. Cheryl Exum, Jorunn Økland, Stephen D. Moore

Editorial Board
Alison Jasper, Tat-siong Benny Liew,
Caroline Vander Stichele

Slavery, Abolitionism, and the Ethics of Biblical Scholarship

Hector Avalos

Sheffield Phoenix Press

2013

Copyright © 2011, 2013 Sheffield Phoenix Press

First published in hardback, 2011
First published in paperback, 2013

Published by Sheffield Phoenix Press
Department of Biblical Studies, University of Sheffield
45 Victoria Street, Sheffield S3 7QB England

www.sheffieldphoenix.com

All rights reserved.
No part of this publication may be reproduced or transmitted in any form or by any means, electronic or mechanical, including photocopying, recording or any information storage or retrieval system, without the publishers' permission in writing.

A CIP catalogue record for this book
is available from the British Library

Typeset by Forthcoming Publications
Printed by Lightning Source

ISBN 978-1-909697-18-8 (paperback)
ISBN 978-1-907534-28-7 (hardback)

ISSN 1747-9630

TABLE OF CONTENTS

Acknowledgments	xi
Abbreviations	xiii

Chapter 1
INTRODUCTION 1
    Basic Elements of the Argument 4
    Defining Slavery 5
    Biblical Scholars and Slavery 7
    The Historiography of Abolition 13
    Ethics and the New Atheism 16
    Organization 17
    Summary 18

Part I

SLAVERY AND BIBLICAL SCHOLARSHIP

Chapter 2
UNETHICAL HERMENEUTICS 23
    Representativism 24
    Trajectorialism 27
    Reinterpretation: Does Original Intent Matter? ... 29
    Communitarian/Analogical Reinterpretations 30
    Summary 36

Chapter 3
NEAR EASTERN ETHICS AND SLAVERY 38
    Mesopotamian Beginnings 39
    Egypt and Divine Care for Humanity 43
    Hittites and *Lex talionis* 45
    Greece and the Bonds of Freedom 48
    Rome: Home of Slavery and Freedom 55
    The *Imago Dei* and Universal Inequality 57
    Reversing Comparative Ethics 59
    Summary 61

Chapter 4
SLAVERY IN THE HEBREW BIBLE/OLD TESTAMENT 62
   Lexicographers as Apologists 62
   Genesis 1.26: Let Dominion Begin 65
   Genesis 3.16 and Female Subjugation 67
   Genesis 9.19-27 and Noah's Curse 69
   Genesis 16: Rape of a Slave Woman? 70
   Genesis 17.12 and Genital Mutilation 71
   Genesis 17.23: Abraham, the Blessed Slavemaster 72
   Exodus 1–15: A Liberationist Paradigm? 73
   Exodus 20.10/Deuteronomy 5.12-15 and the Sabbath 75
   Exodus 21.1-6 and Term Limits 76
   Exodus 21.16 and 'Manstealing' 77
   Exodus 21.20 and Killing Slaves 80
   Exodus 21.26-27: Beating Manumission 80
   Leviticus 25.42: Who's your Master? 83
   Leviticus 25.35-43: Jubilee Manumission 84
   Leviticus 25.44-46: Enslaving Outsiders 86
   Deuteronomy 15 and Inner-Biblical Progress 87
   Deuteronomy 23.15: Fugitive Slaves 88
   1 Samuel 8: Exclusive Service to Yahweh? 90
   Ezra 2.64-65 and Slave Societies 92
   Job 31.13-15 and Justice for Slaves 94
   Joel 2.28-29: Possessing Slaves 94
   Summary 95

Chapter 5
SLAVERY IN THE NEW TESTAMENT 96
   Matthew 7.12: The Golden Rule 96
   Acts 17.26 and Human Unity 97
   1 Corinthians 7.21: Better to Remain in Slavery? 98
   Galatians 3.28: A Magna Carta of Humanity? 108
   Galatians 4.7: No Longer Slaves? 112
   Ephesians 6.5: Obedience through Terror 114
   Philippians 2.4-6: Slavery as Human Destiny 116
   Colossians 3.18–4.1: The Magic of Socio-Rhetorical Criticism 119
   1 Timothy 1.10: 'Manstealing' 124
   1 Timothy 6: Honoring Christian Slavemasters 126
   Philemon: What Are You Insinuating? 127
   Why Was the New Testament Not More Vocal? 135
   Summary 138

Chapter 6
CHRIST AS IMPERIAL SLAVEMASTER   139
   Imperial Political Rhetoric 101   140
   Christ as Emperor   141
   Christ as Slavemaster   144
   Jesus and God's Plantation   149
   Christ and the Least of my Brethren   152
   Christ, the Torture Master   154
   Are Believers Friends of Slaves?   155
   Summary   156

Part II

SLAVERY AND THE BIBLE IN CHRISTIAN HISTORY

Chapter 7
SLAVERY IN LATE ANTIQUITY   159
   Parabiblical Sanctions   160
   Church Doctrine   160
   Major Theologians   161
   Clerical and Papal Acceptance   163
   Legal Sanction   164
   Gregory of Nyssa   164
   St Bathilde and St Anskar   167
   Summary   171

Chapter 8
ST THOMAS AQUINAS: A MEDIEVAL ABOLITIONIST?   172
   Does Aquinas See Slavery as a Sin?   172
   Serfdom or Slavery?   176
   When Did Racism Begin?   180
   Summary   182

Chapter 9
RENAISSANCE POPES AND SLAVERY: A WHOLE LOT OF BULLS   183
   Sicut dudum (1435)   184
   Romanus Pontifex (1454/55)   186
   Inter caetera and *Eximiae devotionis* (1493)   187
   Ineffabilis et Summi Patris (1497)   189
   Sublimis Deus (1537)   194
   Do as I Say, Not as I Do   197
   Summary   198

Chapter 10
A BRAVE NEW WORLD: LAS CASAS VS. SEPULVEDA   199
    Bartolomé de las Casas   200
    Juan Ginés de Sepulveda   202
    Basic Exegetical Principles   203
    Leviticus 19.18 and Neighborly Love   204
    Leviticus 20.4-5: Criminalizing Indians   205
    Deuteronomy 20.10-14 and Conquest   206
    Joshua 7.16-26 and Genocide   207
    Ecclesiasticus 34 and Sinful Gains   209
    Matthew 10.5-15 and Peaceful Missionaries   210
    Luke 14.16-24 and Forced Conversions   211
    1 Corinthians 5.12-13: Who's to Judge?   214
    Galatians 3.28 and Equality for All   215
    Ephesians 6.5 and 1 Peter 2.18   215
    Las Casas vs. Sepulveda: An Innovation?   216
    Summary   218

Chapter 11
THE SIXTEENTH CENTURY: PROTESTANTS UNBOUND?   219
    Martin Luther: To Hell with Equality   219
    John Calvin: I Do Mean Slaves   220
    Jean Bodin, the Pragmatist   221
    Summary   225

Chapter 12
CATHOLICISM, PROTESTANTISM, AND LOUISIANA SLAVERY   226
    The Catholic Codes   227
    Is Baptism a Sign of Humanity?   229
    Was the Spanish Black Code Better?   230
    Sex, Race and Immigration as Factors   232
    Ursuline Nuns   234
    Summary   236

Chapter 13
BRITISH ABOLITIONISTS   237
    James Ramsay   238
    Granville Sharp   239
    Thomas Clarkson   242
    Quobnah Ottobah Cugoano   245
    William Wilberforce   247
    Summary   249

Chapter 14
AMERICAN WHITE ABOLITIONISTS — 251
    John Woolman: A Quaker Hero — 252
    George Bourne: A Singular Scholar — 255
    Summary — 258

Chapter 15
AFRICAN-AMERICAN ABOLITIONISTS — 259
    David Walker: Egypt Was Better — 259
    Frederick Douglass: A Secular Humanist? — 261
    Summary — 267

Chapter 16
EXPLAINING ABOLITION — 269
    Why Stark's Thesis is Wrong — 269
    Freedom Is Inherent in Slavery — 271
    Economics: Money Matters — 272
    Non-Christian Abolition: Haiti — 275
    Demographic Imbalances — 276
    Abolition as a Military Strategy — 278
    Secularization — 279
    The Decline of Biblical Authority — 280
    Summary — 284

Chapter 17
CONCLUSION — 285

Appendix — 289

Bibliography — 290
Index of References — 319
Index of Authors — 325

Acknowledgments

I will never again complain about the labor a book demands from its creator. Despite the long days and nights that writing this book entailed, such toil pales in comparison to the labor expended by millions of slaves in sugar and cotton plantations of the New World. This book is part of my penance for ignoring the suffering of those slaves for as long as I did as a biblical scholar. I feel responsible for once trumpeting the ethical superiority of a collection of books called the Bible that actually had much to do with keeping the horrible institution of slavery alive for nearly two thousand years.

Any of my labor, however, was made easier by a crew of loving and caring assistants, and first among them is my wife, Cynthia Avalos. Not only did she attentively meet all the needs that a busy author has, but she proofread drafts of the manuscript, and acted as a good sounding board for my ideas. Whitney Hulse, Melissa MacDonald and Jessica Drobot, my diligent research assistants at Iowa State University, gathered a lot of the materials that I used and helped to proofread the manuscript. Iowa State University also provided me a year of research leave that I used to write this book.

David Clines of Sheffield Phoenix Press was patient and generous with his time as he prepared my manuscript. I am also indebted to him and others at Sheffield Phoenix for their expert suggestions on some issues.

The New Orleans Notarial Archives, which I visited to inspect slave manumission records in November of 2009, provided invaluable assistance. My thanks also to Gwendolyn M. Hall, a doyenne of the history of slavery, who graciously gave permission to obtain her database on slavery records and provided bibliographical suggestions. David Haugaard, Director of Research Services for the Historical Society of Pennsylvania, deserves my thanks for providing a copy of an unpublished letter by William Wilberforce. Dr Peter Williams, Warden of Tyndale House, was generous enough to provide me with a copy of a paper he delivered at the Annual Meeting of the Society of Biblical Literature in Atlanta in 2010. F. Rachel Magdalene of the University of Leipzig generously provided me with copies of her work on Babylonian slavery.

As usual, I must thank Rusty, our omniscient pet squirrel, and his friend, Skippy, whose antics provided needed entertainment when writer's fatigue subjugated me.

All are, hereby, manumitted from any transgressions committed within these pages.

Unless noted otherwise, all biblical quotations are from the Revised Standard Version as presented in Herbert G. May and Bruce M. Metzger (eds.), *The New Oxford Annotated Bible with Apocrypha* (New York: Oxford University Press, 1977).

ABBREVIATIONS

AB	Anchor Bible
ABD	D.N. Freedman (ed.), *The Anchor Bible Dictionary* (6 vols.; New York: Doubleday, 1992)
AHR	*American Historical Review*
ANET	James B. Pritchard (ed.), *Ancient Near Eastern Texts Relating to the Old Testament* (Princeton, NJ: Princeton University Press, 3rd edn, 1969)
BDAG	Bauer, W., F.W. Danker, W.F. Arndt, and F.W. Gingrich, *Greek–English Lexicon of the New Testament and Other Early Christian Literature*
CAD	Ignace I. Gelb et al. (eds.), *The Assyrian Dictionary of the University of Chicago* (Chicago: University of Chicago Press, 1964–2005)
CBQ	*Catholic Biblical Quarterly*
CDLJ	*Cuneiform Digital Library Journal*
CH	Code of Hammurabi
CIL	Corpus inscriptionum latinarum
CSEL	Corpus scriptorum ecclesiasticorum latinorum
DCH	D.J.A. Clines (ed.), *Dictionary of Classical Hebrew* (Sheffield: Sheffield Phoenix Press, 1993–2011)
ETL	*Ephemerides theologicae lovanienses*
HSM	Harvard Semitic Monographs
HTR	*Harvard Theological Review*
IDB	George Arthur Buttrick (ed.), *The Interpreter's Dictionary of the Bible* (4 vols.; Nashville: Abingdon, 1962)
IDBSup	*IDB, Supplementary Volume*
JBL	*Journal of Biblical Literature*
JECS	*Journal of Early Christian Studies*
JSOT	*Journal for the Study of the Old Testament*
JSOTSup	*Journal for the Study of the Old Testament*, Supplement Series
KJV	King James Version
LCL	Loeb Classical Library
LXX	Septuagint (Greek versions of the Hebrew Bible)
NAB	New American Bible
NIDB	Katharine Doob Sakenfeld (ed.), *New Interpreter's Dictionary of the Bible* (Nashville: Abingdon Press, 2006–2009)
NIV	New International Version
NPNF[1]	Philip Schaff (ed.), *The Nicene and Post-Nicene Fathers* (Series 1; 14 vols.; 1886–89; repr., Peabody, MA: Hendrickson, 1994)
NPNF[2]	Philip Schaff and Henry Wace (eds.), *The Nicene and Post-Nicene Fathers* (Series 2; 14 vols.; 1890; repr. Peabody, MA: Hendrickson, 1994)
NRSV	New Revised Standard Version
PG	J.-P. Migne (ed.), *Patrologiae cursus completus... Series graeca* (166 vols.; Paris: Imprimerie catholique, 1857–83)

PL	J.-P. Migne (ed.), *Patrologiae cursus completus...Series latina* (221 vols.; Paris: Imprimerie catholique, 1844–65)
REB	Revised English Bible
RSV	Revised Standard Version
TDNT	Gerhard Kittel and Gerhard Friedrich (eds.), *Theological Dictionary of the New Testament* (trans. Geoffrey W. Bromiley; 10 vols.; Grand Rapids: Eerdmans, 1964–76)
TLOT	Ernst Jenni and Claus Westermann (eds.), *Theological Lexicon of the Old Testament* (trans. M.E. Biddle; 3 vols.; Peabody, MA: Hendrickson, 1997)
VT	*Vetus Testamentum*

Chapter 1

INTRODUCTION

Deconstruction can be constructive when the truth is left standing. I seek to deconstruct the myth that reliance on the Bible was primarily responsible for the abolition of slavery in Western Civilization. Part of my evidence consists of detailed studies of how abolitionists used and abused scripture to make their case. Equally important is my critique of most of modern biblical scholarship insofar as it still functions as an apology for biblical slavery. Within a broader philosophical and ethical framework, my basic premise is that if slavery is not regarded as wrong, then little else can be. And if slavery is regarded as inexcusably wrong, then biblical ethics stands or falls on its attitude toward slavery. As such, this book is a critique of the broader idea that the Bible should be the basis of modern ethics.

My project actually began with a puzzling experience. If one reads almost any book on Christian ethics written by academic biblical scholars, one finds something extremely peculiar: *Jesus never does anything wrong*. Rudolf Schnackenburg's *The Moral Teaching of the New Testament* represents the view one usually encounters:

> The Early Church, and with it, Christianity, throughout the centuries was profoundly convinced that the greatest of Jesus' achievements in the moral sphere was the promulgation of the chief commandment of love of God and one's neighbour. The message of Christian *agape*, the model and highest expression of which is the mission of the Son of God to redeem the sinful human race, brought something new into the world, an idea and reality so vast and incomprehensible as to be the highest revelation of God, and quite inconceivable apart from revelation.[1]

The rest of the book finds nothing but praise for Jesus, and not a whit of criticism.

---

1. Rudolf Schnackenburg, *The Moral Teaching of the New Testament* (trans. J. Holland-Smith and W.J. O'Hara; London: Burns & Oates, 1975), pp. 90-91.

Perhaps this unrelenting praise of Jesus' ethics can be expected because Schnackenburg was a Catholic priest with an openly Christian commitment. But if we look at the work of Richard Horsley, who teaches at the University of Massachusetts, a public secular university, there is not much difference. For example, the worst thing about Jesus in Horsley's *Jesus and the Spiral of Violence* is this assessment:

> It would be difficult to claim that Jesus was a pacifist. But he actively opposed violence, particularly institutionalized oppressive and repressive violence, and its effects on a subject people. Jesus was apparently a revolutionary but not a violent political revolutionary... Jesus preached and catalyzed a social revolution... 'Love your enemies' turns out to be not the apolitical pacific stance of one who stands above the turmoil of his day, nor a sober counsel of non-resistance to evil of oppression, but a revolutionary principle. It was a social revolutionary principle insofar as the love of enemies would transform local social-economic relations.[2]

For Horsley, even when this new revolutionary principle is threatening to the ruling social order, that threat is a good thing because it will help liberate people from oppression.

So it looks as if scholars with open religious commitments and scholars with seemingly secular commitments can agree that Jesus never did anything wrong. This uniformly benign picture of Jesus' ethics is peculiar because when historians study Alexander the Great or Augustus Caesar, they note the good and the bad aspects of their actions. Even when academic biblical scholars study Moses or David, they might note their flaws.[3] From a purely historical viewpoint, Jesus is a man and not a god. He should have flaws. So how is it that most academic biblical scholars never see anything that Jesus does as wrong or evil?

The answer, of course, is that most biblical scholars, whether in secular academia or in seminaries, still see Jesus as divine, and not as a human being with faults. Such scholars are still studying Jesus through the confessional lenses of Nicea or Chalcedon rather than through a historical approach we would use with other human beings. In fact, Luke Timothy Johnson, a well-known New Testament scholar at Emory University, remarks:

---

2. Richard A. Horsley, *Jesus and the Spiral of Violence: Popular Jewish Resistance in Roman Palestine* (Minneapolis: Fortress Press, 1993), p. 326.

3. Baruch Halpern, *David's Secret Demons: Messiah, Murderer, Traitor, King* (Grand Rapids: Eerdmans, 2001). For moral evaluations of many Old Testament figures, see Mary E. Mills, *Biblical Morality: Moral Perspectives in Old Testament Narratives* (Burlington, VT: Ashgate, 2001). For some of the philosophical problems that attend moral evaluations of literature, see Wayne C. Booth, *The Company We Keep: An Ethics of Fiction* (Berkeley: University of California Press, 1988).

1. *Introduction*

We can go further and state that the basic 'historical' claims of the Nicene Creed are well supported: 'He was born of the virgin Mary, suffered under Pontius Pilate, was crucified, died, and was buried'...in essence, what the most universally used Christian creed asserts about the human person Jesus is historically verifiable.[4]

Although Johnson realizes that many of the supernatural claims about Jesus cannot be validated historically, he adds that '[t]he only real validation for the claim that Christ is what the creed claims him to be, that is, light from light, true God from true God, is to be found in the quality of life demonstrated by those who make his confession'.[5] Johnson, of course, assumes that this 'quality of life' based on imitating Jesus must be completely good.

But if Jesus is a special case, one would not know it from books treating the wider scope of biblical ethics. In general, there are few, if any, books by biblical scholars that denounce biblical ethics. Some may denounce specific actions God is portrayed as commanding or allowing, but few denounce the biblical god in general. This is admitted by R. Norman Whybray, a noted biblical scholar:

> The dark side of God is a subject that has received astonishingly little attention from Old Testament scholars. The standard Old Testament theologies, monographs, about the Old Testament doctrine of God, articles about particular passages, even commentaries are almost silent on the matter...even those that make reference to them have tended to play down such passages or sought to explain them away with a variety of arguments.[6]

However, few scholars have ever expanded or elaborated upon Whybray's frank observation.

In a previous book, *The End of Biblical Studies*, I showed how the main subfields of biblical scholarship are permeated with religionist assumptions that present themselves as objective descriptive scholarship.[7] Such fields include archaeology, history, textual criticism, aesthetics, and translation.

---

4. Luke Timothy Johnson, *The Real Jesus: The Misguided Quest for the Historical Jesus and the Truth of the Traditional Gospels* (New York: HarperSanFrancisco, 1996), pp. 126-27.

5. Johnson, *The Real Jesus*, p. 168.

6. R. Norman Whybray, '"Shall not the judge of the earth do what is just?" God's Oppression of the Innocent in the Old Testament', in David Penchansky and Paul L. Redditt (eds.), *Shall Not the Judge of the Earth do What is Right? Studies in the Nature of God in Tribute to James L. Crenshaw* (Winona Lake, IN: Eisenbrauns, 2000), pp. 1-19 (2). See also R. Norman Whybray, 'The Immorality of God: Reflections on Some Passages in Genesis, Job, Exodus and Numbers', *JSOT* 21 (1996), pp. 89-120. For a recent attempt to mitigate these negative images, see Eric A. Seibert, *Disturbing Divine Behavior: Troubling Old Testament Images of God* (Minneapolis: Fortress Press, 2009).

7. Hector Avalos, *The End of Biblical Studies* (Amherst, NY: Prometheus, 2007).

Examining those fields shows how biblical scholarship is preoccupied with retaining the Bible's relevance when its own findings paradoxically show the opposite.

The same can be said of the study of biblical ethics, which represents itself as an academic endeavor that is no less descriptive than the fields I have examined in *The End of Biblical Studies*. For example, John Barton approves of the leadership of Eckart Otto, a premier biblical ethicist today, 'in aiming primarily to present a descriptive, historical account of ethical beliefs and practices in ancient Israel as evidenced in the Old Testament...'[8] Similarly, Richard B. Hays, of Duke University, remarks that '[t]he first task of New Testament ethics is to describe the content of the individual writings of the New Testament canon'.[9]

Basic Elements of the Argument

Despite the thoroughly benign manner in which biblical ethics are often represented, the Bible endorses horrific ideas and practices. One of these horrific practices is slavery, one of the most tragic and vicious institutions ever devised by humanity. For about 1900 of the last 2000 years of Christian history, it was self-described Christians who kept slavery, in some form or another, a viable institution. Yet, many modern historians and biblical scholars still claim that the Bible was a main factor in abolition.

In contrast, the main point of this book is that reliance on biblical authority was instrumental in promoting and maintaining slavery far longer than might have been the case if we had followed many pre-Christian notions of freedom and anti-slavery sentiments. The obverse side of my argument is that abolition of slavery was mainly the result of abandoning crucial biblical principles and interpretations rather than following them. Briefly, my work has the following interrelated elements:

(1) Biblical scholarship generally functions as an apology for biblical views now deemed unethical, and slavery is a primary example.

---

8. John Barton, *Understanding Old Testament Ethics: Approaches and Explorations* (Louisville, KY: Westminster/John Knox Press, 2003), p. 173. See also Eckart Otto, *Theologische Ethik des Alten Testaments* (Stuttgart: Kohlhammer, 1994); Otto, 'Of Aims and Methods in Hebrew Bible Ethics', in Douglas A. Knight (ed.), *Ethics and Politics in the Bible* (Semeia, 66; Atlanta: Society of Biblical Literature, 1995), pp. 161-71.

9. Richard B. Hays, *The Moral Vision of the New Testament: A Contemporary Introduction to New Testament Ethics* (New York: HarperOne, 1996), p. 13. Douglas A. Knight ('Old Testament Ethics', *Christian Century* 99 [1982], pp. 55-59 [58]) says: 'biblical ethics is primarily a descriptive discipline'. *Per contra* Bruce C. Birch (*Let Justice Roll Down: The Old Testament Ethics and Christian Life* [Louisville, KY: Westminster/John Knox Press, 1991], p. 25) says: '...nor do I believe that ethics should be primarily descriptive'.

(2) Reliance on biblical ethics generally has delayed the abolition of slavery and any progress toward freedom in the manner the latter is currently conceived.
(3) Any credit to the Bible for ethical advances concerning freedom is usually the result of arbitrary exegesis of the Bible, reinterpretation, and the abandonment of biblical principles.

Each element of my argument requires a few preliminary remarks. First, the modern world contains a variety of ethical systems, and so I need to explain what we mean by modern ethics. I mean the system of ethics that is, for the most part, enshrined in the United Nations Universal Declaration of Human Rights, which has an arguable position as the consensus of most nations today. Article 4 states: 'No one shall be held in slavery or servitude; slavery and the slave trade shall be prohibited in all their forms'.[10]

For my purposes, modern Western ethics also includes the notion of equality, insofar as all human beings are thought to be equal in terms of life, liberty, and the pursuit of happiness. This idea is included in Article 1 of the Universal Declaration: 'All human beings are born free and equal in dignity and rights. They are endowed with reason and conscience and should act towards one another in a spirit of brotherhood.'[11]

Democracy or republicanism is viewed as the ideal form of government in modern Western ethics. Laws based on the consent of the governed is a key to the entire legal structure of modern society. Article 21(1) of the Universal Declaration embodies this concept: 'Everyone has the right to take part in the government of his country, directly or through freely chosen representatives'.[12] I shall demonstrate that the bulk of such principles are owed to Greece and Rome more than to the Bible.

Defining Slavery

Definitions are essential to any detailed investigation of how biblical scholars have approached the role of the Bible in promoting and/or abolishing slavery. Yet, the institution of 'slavery' has been difficult to define. I.A.H. Combes rightly notes that definitions have fallen into two types: (1) slaves as property

---

10. United Nations, *The Universal Declaration of Human Rights* (1948). Online: www.un.org/en/documents/udhr/.
11. United Nations, *The Universal Declaration of Human Rights*. For a general philosophical treatment of inequality, see Amartya Sen, *Inequality Reexamined* (New York: Oxford University Press, 1992). For a study of inequality in ancient Israel, see the collection of essays in Saul Olyan, *Social Inequality in the World of the Text: The Significance of Ritual and Social Distinctions in the Hebrew Bible* (Journal of Ancient Judaism Supplements, 4; Göttingen: Vandenhoeck & Ruprecht, 2011).
12. United Nations, *The Universal Declaration of Human Rights*.

('chattel hermeneutic'); (2) slaves as alienated persons ('social death hermeneutics').[13] In addition, legal and academic traditions have not always agreed on which part of those types to emphasize.

One of the most distinguished scholars of slavery is David Brion Davis, who spent the bulk of his academic career at Yale University. In his classic, *The Problem of Slavery in Western Culture*, Davis summarized some of the definitions as follows: 'In general it has been said that a slave has three defining characteristics: his person is the property of another man; his will is subject to his owner's authority, and his labor or services are obtained through coercion'.[14]

Legal definitions routinely emphasize the property aspect of slavery. In Alabama, there was a formal legal definition of slavery as follows:

> The state or condition of negro or African slavery is established by law in this State; conferring on the master property in and the right to the time, labor and services of the slave, and to enforce obedience on the part of the slave to all his lawful commands.[15]

The 1926 Slavery Convention, more formally known as the Convention to Suppress the Slave Trade and Slavery, was issued under the auspices of the League of Nations. That Convention defined slavery as 'the status or condition of a person over whom any or all powers attaching to the right of ownership are exercised'.[16] The Universal Declaration of 1948 is succinct and absolutist: 'No one shall be held in slavery or servitude; slavery and the slave trade shall be prohibited in all their forms'.[17]

Harvard University's Orlando Patterson, a preeminent historian of slavery, opts for a more sociological approach that focuses on alienation rather than treatment as property. According to Patterson, 'Slavery is the permanent violent domination of natally alienated and generally dishonored persons'.[18] This definition has been very popular among biblical scholars, including

---

13. I.A.H. Combes, *The Metaphor of Slavery in the Writings of the Early Church, from the New Testament to the Beginning of the Fifth Century* (Sheffield: Sheffield Academic Press, 1998), p. 21.
14. David Brion Davis, *The Problem of Slavery in Western Culture* (repr., New York: Oxford University Press, 1988 [1966]), p. 31.
15. John J. Ormond, Arthur P. Bagby, and George Goldthwaite, *The Code of Alabama* (Montgomery: Brittan & De Wolf State Printers, 1852), p. 300, as cited in **Thomas D. Morris**, *Southern Slavery and the Law 1619–1860* (Chapel Hill: University of North Carolina Press, 1996), p. 1.
16. Combes, *The Metaphor of Slavery*, p. 21.
17. United Nations, *The Universal Declaration of Human Rights*.
18. Orlando Patterson, *Slavery and Social Death: A Comparative Study* (Cambridge, MA: Harvard University Press, 1982), p. 13.

Allen Dwight Callahan, Richard Horsley, and J. Albert Harrill.[19] However, I agree with Paul V.M. Flesher, who believes that Patterson's over-emphasis of the comparative approach means that the latter 'never proves that his definition of slavery applies to even one society'.[20]

In truth, there was a wide diversity of systems that may be called 'slavery'. In fact, it may be best to visualize slavery as an extreme end of a continuum in some ancient societies.[21] There was also a related tension between the view of slaves as chattel property and the view of slaves as persons. Common chattel property, such as hammers or hoes, did not run away or rebel against masters. Common chattel property could not speak. Thus, slavery always had an inherent tension between the personhood and objectification of a slave.

Yet, Thomas Morris is correct in remarking that 'the slave as property is central to any consideration of the relationship between slavery and law'.[22] For my purposes, *slavery is a socioeconomic system centering on the use of forced laborers, who are viewed as property or as under the control of their superiors for whatever term was determined by their masters or by their society.* This definition encompasses modern and ancient situations. Within a broader social context, slavery means that human beings could be abducted from their families and be subjected to the most cruel and horrible treatment. Any mercy was completely at the discretion of the master or the broader society to which the master belonged.

Biblical Scholars and Slavery

Scholars of biblical ethics have dealt with slavery in two principal ways.[23] One is to ignore the subject. Consider the fact that Waldemar Janzen's *Old*

---

19. See Allen D. Callahan, Richard A. Horsley, and Abraham Smith (eds.), *Slavery in Text and Interpretation* (Semeia, 83/84; Atlanta: Scholars Press, 1998), p. 1; J. Albert Harrill, 'Slavery', in *NIDB*, V, pp. 299-308 (299).

20. Paul V.M. Flesher, *Oxen, Women, or Citizens? Slaves in the System of the Mishnah* (Brown Judaic Studies, 143; Atlanta: Scholars Press, 1988), p. 176.

21. See, for example, Robert McC. Adams, 'Slavery and Freedom in the Third Dynasty of Ur: Implications of the Garshana Archives', *CDLJ* (2010), pp. 1-8. Online: cdli.ucla.edu/pubs/cdlj/2010/cdlj2010_002.html.

22. Morris, *Southern Slavery*, p. 2.

23. For the historiography of slavery, see Enrico Dal Lago and Constantina Katsari (eds.), *Slave Systems: Ancient and Modern* (Cambridge: Cambridge University Press, 2008); Niall McKeown, *The Invention of Ancient Slavery?* (London: Duckworth, 2007); Richard A. Horsley, 'The Slave Systems of Classical Antiquity and their Reluctant Recognition by Modern Scholars', in Callahan, Horsley, and Smith (eds.), *Slavery in Text and Interpretation*, pp. 19-66; Moses I. Finley, *Ancient Slavery and Modern Ideology* (ed. Brent D. Shaw; repr., Princeton, NJ: Markus Wiener Publishers, 1998 [1980]), especially pp. 3-52 and 77-134.

Testament Ethics: A Paradigmatic Approach does not bear a single indexed reference to 'slavery'. The same applies to noted books on ethics by John Barton and Gordon J. Wenham.[24] The authoritative *Interpreter's Dictionary of the Bible* has no entry for 'slavery' in the New Testament in its first edition. Separate articles on slavery in the Old Testament and New Testament were included in the later Supplement.[25] *The New Interpreter's Dictionary of the Bible* does have an entry on 'slavery', by J. Albert Harrill, who comes to some conclusions similar to mine, but without elaboration.[26]

However, ignoring slavery is a minority position. Far more common is discussing slavery within an apologetic framework. That is to say, some scholars acknowledge the existence of slavery, but that acknowledgment is usually associated with claims about how biblical slavery was better or more benign than the slavery known in Near Eastern cultures. For example, Léon Epsztein claims:

> As for the Israelites, they can have foreign slaves in perpetuity… However, we should recall that even the Covenant Code prescribes the immediate liberation of male and female slaves if their master puts out an eye or breaks a tooth (Ex 21.26f)… It is clear that the protection of slaves that the Torah seeks to assure is very inadequate, but on the whole the Jewish law was much in advance of other legislation in antiquity.[27]

In this and other passages, we can reduce Epsztein's rhetorical structure to: (1) a descriptive statement about biblical slavery; and (2) a mitigating comment introduced by an adversative conjunction ('however', 'but').

When we examine the nature of the mitigation, it becomes clear that Epsztein's claim that Hebrew slavery was 'much in advance of other legislation in antiquity' is an exaggeration or a very subjective judgment. According to Epsztein, we are supposed to think that it was an advance to allow slavery in perpetuity for non-Hebrews as long as granting freedom after mutilating slaves or severing a body part is counted as an 'advance'.

---

24. Barton, *Understanding Old Testament Ethics*. Although no indexed references to 'slavery' are provided, Gordon J. Wenham (*Story as Torah: Reading Old Testament Narrative Ethically* [Grand Rapids, MI: Baker Academic, 2000], p. 92 n. 52) furnishes a footnote claiming that '[s]lavery under a benevolent lord in biblical times was analogous to employment today…'

25. George A. Buttrick (ed.), *Interpreter's Dictionary of the Bible* (4 vols.; Nashville: Abingdon Press, 1962); Walther Zimmerli, 'Slavery in the Old Testament', and W.G. Rollins, 'Slavery in the New Testament', in *IDBSup*, pp. 829-30 and 831-32, respectively. See also the comments of S. Scott Bartchy, *ΜΑΛΛΟΝ ΧΡΗΣΑΙ: First-Century Slavery and 1 Corinthians 7.21* (Eugene, OR: Wipf & Stock, 1973), p. 34 n. 88.

26. Harrill, 'Slavery'. See also Harrill, *Slaves in the New Testament: Literary, Moral, and Social Dimensions* (Minneapolis: Fortress Press, 2006), especially pp. 169-92.

27. Léon Epsztein, *Social Justice in the Ancient Near East and the People of the Bible* (trans. John Bowden; London: SCM Press, 1986), pp. 122-23.

Of course, this is not surprising given the long history of the idea of 'ethical monotheism', which began to permeate the scholarly literature in the late nineteenth and early twentieth centuries.[28] This idea was the result of seeing Israelite religion in a more evolutionary manner. Particularly popular, even today, is Edward Burnett Tylor's otherwise outdated unilineal model of religious evolution, which posited the following stages: animism > polytheism > monotheism.[29]

Within biblical studies per se, we can already see this evolutionary approach in the work of the Charles Darwin of biblical scholarship, Julius Wellhausen (1844–1918), who remarked: 'It was Amos, Hosea, and Isaiah who introduced a movement against the old popular worship of the high places; in doing so they are not in the least actuated by a deep-rooted preference for the temple of Jerusalem, *but by ethical motives*'.[30] We see it in 1949, with Isaac Mendelsohn's influential *Slavery in the Ancient Near East*, which is still cited by a diverse pool of scholars.[31] The book tried to show that the Bible represented a great advance over other systems of slavery among Israel's neighbors. In fact, Mendelsohn's conclusion is that 'this denial of the right of possession of man by man in perpetuity is as yet restricted to Hebrews only…but it is a step which no other religion had taken before'.[32]

About forty years later, we see even more blatant denials that inequality was endorsed by biblical authors. When discussing the curse of slavery imposed on the Canaanites, Ephraim Isaac says that 'in spite of the slurs,

---

28. See Theodore M. Vial and Mark A. Hadley, *Ethical Monotheism, Past and Present: Essays in Honor of Wendell S. Dietrich* (Brown Judaic Studies, 329; Providence, RI: Brown Judaic Studies, 2001). For popular expressions of ethical monotheism, see Karen Armstrong, *A History of God: The 4000-Year Quest of Judaism, Christianity, and Islam* (New York: Ballantine Books, 1993), pp. 368-69; Jack Miles, *God: A Biography* (New York: Vintage Books, 1996), pp. 110-13. For a recent treatment of justice in the Bible, see Richard H. Hiers, *Justice and Compassion in Biblical Law* (New York/London: Continuum, 2009).

29. For a famous example of a similar evolutionary scheme in biblical studies, see William F. Albright, *From the Stone Age to Christianity: Monotheism and Historical Progress* (Garden City, NY: Doubleday, 1957). For a recent critique of this unilineal view, see Fiona Bowie, *The Anthropology of Religion* (Oxford: Blackwell, 2000), pp. 14-16.

30. Julius Wellhausen, *Prolegomena to the History of Ancient Israel* (repr., Gloucester, MA: Peter Smith, 1983 [1883]), p. 47 (Wellhausen's italics). See further Douglas A. Knight (ed.), *Julius Wellhausen and his Prolegomena to the History of Israel* (Semeia, 25; Chico, CA: Scholars Press, 1983).

31. Isaac Mendelsohn, *Slavery in the Ancient Near East* (New York: Oxford University Press, 1949). It is cited by Epsztein (*Social Justice*, p. 119), Rodney Stark (*For the Glory of God*, p. 325), and David B. Davis (*Inhuman Bondage: The Rise and Fall of Slavery in the New World* [New York: Oxford University Press, 2006]), p. 338 n. 30. See also Davis, *Slavery in Western Culture*, p. 54 n. 48.

32. Mendelsohn, *Slavery in the Ancient Near East*, p. 123.

insults, and denigrating remarks that are heaped upon the Canaanites in Biblical and Rabbinic literature, there is no explicit or implicit denial of their human dignity and their equality with Israelites as human beings'.[33] Isaac leaves unexplained how biblical commands to kill and enslave Canaanites (e.g., Deut. 7; 20; 23) uphold their equality and human dignity.

About a half century after Mendelsohn, the Society of Biblical Literature, the largest organization of professional biblical scholars in the world, published *Slavery in Text and Interpretation*, an anthology with contributions from biblical scholars and historians.[34] Despite a few acute critical remarks (especially by Stanley Stowers) about biblical scholars who mitigate slavery, one still finds the bulk of the contributors putting the best face on biblical ethics.[35] Orlando Patterson, for instance, says: 'The cornerstone of my argument is that Christianity explains the nature, pervasiveness, and continuity of freedom in the West'.[36]

Indeed, Christian biblical scholars, in particular, believe that the New Testament is the culmination of ethics and offers us a clear contrast with Greco-Roman cultures. In speaking of slavery in Pauline literature, Ben Witherington tells us:

> [I]n all this material, we find Paul treating all members of the family, including the children and slaves, as moral agents responsible for their own behavior. This is remarkable in comparison with other ethical literature of the day, which treated women, children, and slaves as property or objects to be managed rather than as subjects to be related to.[37]

Yet, as we have seen, Witherington forgets that slavery always had an inherent tension between seeing slaves as property and as human beings. *The Institutes of Gaius*, which is the most pristine legal textbook we have from the Roman period, divides its subjects into 'persons, things, or actions'.[38]

---

33. Ephraim Isaac, 'Genesis, Judaism, and the "Sons of Ham"', in John Ralph Willis (ed.), *Slaves & Slavery in Muslim Africa* (2 vols.; London: Frank Cass, 1985), I, pp. 78-79.

34. Callahan, Horsley, and Smith (eds.), *Slavery in Text and Interpretation*.

35. Stanley K. Stowers, 'Paul and Slavery: A Response', in Callahan, Horsley, and Smith (eds.), *Slavery in Text and Interpretation*, p. 310.

36. Orlando Patterson, 'Paul, Slavery, and Freedom', in Callahan, Horsley, and Smith (eds.), *Slavery in Text and Interpretation*, p. 273; Patterson, 'The Ancient and Medieval Origins of Modern Freedom', in Steven Mintz and John Stauffer (eds.), *The Problem of Evil: Slavery, Freedom and the Ambiguities of American Reform* (Boston: University of Massachusetts Press, 2007), pp. 31-66. Similarly, Muhammad A. Dandamaev, 'Slavery (ANE and Old Testament)', in *ABD*, VI, p. 65: 'Christian ideology undermined the institution of slavery, declaring an equality of all people in Christ'.

37. Ben Witherington III, 'Was Paul a Pro-Slavery Chauvinist? Making Sense of Paul's Seemingly Mixed Moral Messages', *BR* 20, no. 2 (2004), p. 44.

38. Gaius, *Institutes* 1.8: 'Omne autem ius, quo utimur, uel ad personas pertinet uel ad res uel ad actiones... Et quidem summa divisio de iure personarum haec est, omnes

Slaves are placed in the section dealing with 'persons'. So, how did the New Testament differ from the 'other ethical literature of the day' in this regard?

In any case, these sorts of apologetic claims by biblical scholars eventually filter their way into popular books and even to the work of respected historians who are not biblical scholars. Rodney Stark's impressive publishing record in the study of American religion has catapulted him into being a spokesperson in areas of history in which he has done very little primary research.[39] Moreover, according to Stark: 'Slavery did not die of its own inefficiency, and emancipation was not a capitalist ploy... Moral fervor is the fundamental topic of this entire book; the potent capacity of monotheism, and especially Christianity, to activate extraordinary episodes that have shaped Western Civilization'.[40]

Such conclusions filter down to popular writers and to a wider public, who cannot evaluate critically any of the claims put forth in more scholarly presentations. Among the most popular purveyors of Christian apologetics we find Dinesh D'Souza's *What's So Great about Christianity*, which glorifies the role of Christianity in abolishing slavery.[41] D'Souza is, for the most part, dependent on the work of Rodney Stark. Others who extol the Bible's role in humanizing or abolishing slavery include Joel Panzer, a cleric who writes academic defenses of Christian slavery, and Alan Dershowitz, the famed Harvard Law professor.

So, in large part, this book is a response to historians, such as Rodney Stark and Orlando Patterson, who are not biblical scholars. It is a response to popular writers such as Dinesh D'Souza and Alan Dershowitz who were trained in neither history nor biblical studies. It is a response to clerics who

---

homines aut liberi sunt aut servi'. In the present work I make use of the following edition: Gaius, *The Institutes of Gaius* (trans. W.M. Gordon and O.F. Robinson; Ithaca, NY: Cornell University Press, 1988).

39. For example, Charles Y. Glock and Rodney Stark, *Christian Beliefs and Anti-Semitism* (New York: Harper & Row, 1966); Roger Finke and Rodney Stark, *The Churching of America 1776–2005: Winners and Losers in our Religious Economy* (New Brunswick, NJ: Rutgers University Press, 2005).

40. Rodney Stark, *For the Glory of God: How Monotheism Led to Reformations, Science, Witch-Hunts and the End of Slavery* (Princeton, NJ: Princeton University Press, 2003), p. 365. For other works that glorify the role of the Bible and Christianity in Western civilization, see Stark, *The Victory of Reason: How Christianity Led to Freedom, Capitalism, and Western Success* (New York: Random House, 2005); Stark, *One True God: Historical Consequences of Monotheism* (Princeton, NJ: Princeton University Press, 2001).

41. Dinesh D'Souza, *What's So Great about Christianity* (Washington, DC: Regnery Press, 2007), especially pp. 70-72. Other similar works include Alvin J. Schmidt, *How Christianity Changed the World* (Grand Rapids, MI: Zondervan, 2004); Thomas Cahill, *The Gift of the Jews: How a Tribe of Desert Nomads Changed the Way Everyone Thinks and Feels* (New York: Anchor Books, 1998).

write academically, such as Joel Panzer.[42] More importantly, it is a response to biblical scholars such as Allen Dwight Callahan, J. Albert Harrill, Richard Horsley, Isaac Mendelsohn, Moshe Weinfeld, and Ben Witherington.

My idea is not completely new nor a product of some atheistic radicalism. Refutation of the Bible's abolitionist stance can be traced at least as far back as John Millar's *Observations concerning the Distinction of Ranks in Society*.[43] Within the current guild of biblical scholars, Harrill wrote an important article on 'slavery' for the authoritative *New Interpreter's Dictionary of the Bible* that acknowledges the problem that abolitionists have when using the Bible:

> In the late 19th century conflict over the Bible and slavery, American abolitionists, many of whom were Christian evangelicals, ransacked Scripture for texts condemning slavery, but found few. As a consequence, they developed new hermeneutical strategies to read the Bible to counter the 'plain sense' (literalist) reading of proslavery theology... Most embarrassing for today's readers of the Bible, the proslavery clergymen were holding the more defensible position from the perspective of historical criticism. The passages in the Bible about slavery signal the acceptance of an ancient model of civilization for which patriarchy and subjugation were not merely desirable but essential.[44]

Yet, Harrill's position is a minority among biblical scholars. Later, we demonstrate how Harrill himself attempts to mitigate any pro-slavery stance in 1 Cor. 7.21.

Other notable attempts to counter the whitewashing of biblical and Christian slavery include David P. Wright's *God's Law: How the Covenant Code of the Bible Used and Revised the Code of Hammurabi*, Catherine Hezser's *Jewish Slavery in Antiquity* and Jennifer A. Glancy's *Slavery in Early Christianity*.[45] Glancy specifically comments on how nineteenth-century scholars

---

42. Joel S. Panzer, *The Popes and Slavery* (New York: Alba House, 1996).

43. John Millar, *Observations concerning the Distinction of Ranks in Society* (London: John Murray, rev. edn, 1773), p. 287: 'There is no precept of the Gospel by which the authority of the master is in any respect restrained or limited'. For a more recent and forceful articulation of this idea, see Siegfried Schulz, *Gott ist kein Sklavenhalter: Die Geschichte einer verspäteten Revolution* (Zurich: Flamberg, 1972).

44. Harrill, 'Slavery', p. 307. See also Harrill, 'The Use of the New Testament in the American Slave Controversy: A Case History in the Hermeneutical Tension between Biblical Criticism and Christian Moral Debate', *Religion and American Culture* 10 (2000), pp. 149-86.

45. David P. Wright, *God's Law: How the Covenant Code of the Bible Used and Revised the Code of Hammurabi* (New York: Oxford University Press, 2009); Jennifer A. Glancy, *Slavery in Early Christianity* (repr., Minneapolis: Fortress Press, 2006 [2002]); Catherine Hezser, *Jewish Slavery in Antiquity* (New York: Oxford University Press, 2006). See also comments on the brutality of biblical slavery by David P. Wright, '"She shall not go free as male slaves do": Developing Views about Slavery and Gender in the Laws of the Hebrew Bible', in Bernadette Brooten (ed.), *Beyond Slavery: Overcoming its*

attempted to suppress the Christian origin of slave collars by calling them 'dog collars rather than acknowledge that ancient Christians regularly bound other persons in such a manner'.[46] She also rightly criticizes scholars who have not seen the violent context of the servant parables of Jesus.[47] However, her work focuses on the treatment of slavery as an embodied experience, and does not specifically focus on systematically exposing Christian apologetics on this issue.

The Historiography of Abolition

My entire enterprise is bound up with debates over the triumph of abolitionism in the nineteenth century. That period saw the decisive overthrow of slavery in Britain and the Americas, including in the United States. Although slavery has not really disappeared, an international consensus delegitimized openly legalized slavery. By 1900, all of Western Europe and the Americas had freed their slaves.

The triumph of abolitionism in this period has raised a very important question: Why, after some 1900 years of Christianity, did abolitionism triumph then and not before? Frederick Douglass, the great American abolitionist, had already pondered this very question in 1883:

> It may not be a useless speculation to inquire when[ce] comes the disposition or suggestion of reform; whence that irresistible power that impels men to brave all the hardships and dangers involved in pioneering an unpopular cause? Has it a natural or a celestial origin? Is it human or is it divine, or is it both?[48]

Douglass's dichotomy followed the historiographical division that was already evident in the nineteenth century when explaining abolition. The Bible, as the primary document of Christianity, was at the center of it all.

On the side of Christianity was Henri Wallon, the French historian who wrote a monumental work, *Histoire de L'esclavage dans l'antiquité*, which argued that Christianity was a major force in abolitionism.[49] But those

---

Religious and Sexual Legacies (New York, NY: PalgraveMacmillan, 2010), pp. 125-42 (especially 125, 139). See also John Byron, *Slavery Metaphors in Early Judaism and Pauline Christianity* (Tübingen: Mohr Siebeck, 2003).

    46. Glancy, *Early Christian Slavery*, p. 88.

    47. Glancy, *Early Christian Slavery*, p. 103.

    48. John W. Blassingame and John R. McKivigan (eds.), *The Frederick Douglass Papers*. Series One. *Speeches, Debates and Interviews* (5 vols.; New Haven: Yale University Press, 1979–92), V, p. 137. I cite this source simply as 'Blassingame, ["Title of speech, debate or interview…date"], *The Frederick Douglass Papers*'.

    49. I have consulted Henri Wallon, *Histoire de l'esclavage dans l'antiquité* (Paris: Librairie Hachette, 2nd edn, 1879). For a similar view, see Paul Allard, *Les esclaves chrétiens depuis les premiers temps de l'Eglise jusqu'à la fin de la domination romaine en Occident* (repr., Hildesheim/New York: Olms, 1974 [1876]).

who thought the Bible was not helpful to abolition were not silent. In the nineteenth century, the pro-slavery Presbyterian clergyman, Fred A. Ross (1796–1883), ridiculed the manner in which Albert Barnes (1798–1870), an abolitionist minister, used the Bible:

> You get nothing by torturing the English version. People understand English. Nay, you get little by applying the rack of Hebrew and Greek; even before a tribunal of men like you, who proclaim that Moses, in Hebrew, and Paul, in Greek, must condemn slavery because 'it is in violation of the first sentiments of the Declaration of Independence'. You find it difficult to persuade men that Moses and Paul were moved by the Holy Ghost to sanction the philosophy of Thomas Jefferson![50]

Ross was followed by many other pro-slavery writers who thought abolitionists were fostering newfangled French and German deistic ideas about the Bible.

There are modern historians of slavery who have challenged the idea that Christianity effected the end of slavery. G.E.M. de Ste Croix, one of the most prominent Marxist scholars of ancient Greece, observed: 'It is often said that Christianity introduced an entirely new and better attitude toward slavery. Nothing could be more false.'[51] David B. Davis, another major scholar of slavery, allows for Christianity as a factor, albeit not a decisive one: 'I would still maintain that hostility to slavery, largely religious and philosophical in origin, had little chance of having any practical effect until it became incorporated into the political culture of the British governing elite'.[52]

---

50. Fred A. Ross, *Slavery Ordained of God* (repr., New York: Negro University Press, 1969 [1859]), p. 97. For a study of Ross's views, see Tommy W. Rogers, 'Dr F.A. Ross and the Presbyterian Defense of Slavery', *Journal of Presbyterian History* 45 (1967), pp. 112-24. See also Albert Barnes, *An Inquiry into the Scriptural Views on Slavery* (Philadelphia: Parry & McMillan, 1857). For comments on how pro-slavery advocates responded to challenges with the Bible, see also Lacy K. Ford, *Deliver Us from Evil: The Slavery Question in the Old South* (New York: Oxford University Press, 2009), pp. 126-27.

51. G. E.M. de Ste Croix, 'Early Christian Attitudes toward Property and Slavery', in Derek Baker (ed.), *Church Society and Politics: Papers Read at the Thirteenth Summer Meeting and the Fourteenth Winter Meeting of the Ecclesiastical History Society* (Oxford: Blackwell, 1975), pp. 1-38 (19). See also William L. Westermann, *The Slave Systems of Greek and Roman Antiquity* (Philadelphia: The American Philosophical Society, 1955). For a modern Marxist perspective sympathetic to Christianity, see Elena M. Shtaerman and M.K. Trofimova, *La schiavitù nell' Italia imperiale: I–III secolo* (Rome: Editori Riuniti, 1982), pp. 323-24. Shtaerman and Trofimova (*La schiavitù*, p. 324) call Christianity a 'new ethico-religious system' ('nuovo sistema etico-religioso'; my translation).

52. David Brion Davis, 'The Perils of Doing History by Ahistorical Abstraction: A Reply to Thomas L. Haskell's AHR Forum Reply', in Thomas Bender (ed.), *The Antislavery Debate: Capitalism as a Problem in Historical Interpretation* (Berkeley: University of California Press, 1992), pp. 290-309 (308).

Perhaps no scholar is more celebrated for removing credit from Christianity than Eric Williams, author of *Capitalism and Slavery*, who asserted that capitalism, not Christianity, was the major factor in the final abolition of slavery.[53] Wage-labor was found to be more advantageous than slavery, especially when large slave populations could also be politically and socially threatening. Moreover, Williams took every opportunity to question the supposedly pure humanitarian motives of major Christian abolitionists. Even if his thesis has been largely abandoned, he is given credit for changing the emphasis away from lofty religious motivations.[54]

Rodney Stark, who is known for his work on American sociology of religion, has responded vigorously to explanations that do not see Christianity as essential to abolitionism. As Stark phrases it: 'Just as science arose only once, so, too, did effective moral opposition to slavery. Christian theology was essential to both.'[55] Stark appeals, in part, to John A. Auping, whose statistical analysis claims to demonstrate that revivalist and experiential religious traditions were intimately linked with abolitionism.[56] Other scholars have staked intermediate positions.[57]

My thesis offers a new nuance in this debate. Both economic and biblical factors were involved, along with many other factors. However, the nature of the biblical factor is not what most scholars have postulated. Rather than abolitionism being the result of reliance on biblical precepts, it is abandoning and reinterpreting biblical precepts that were the major factors. Since I see reinterpretation of the Bible as a *de facto* abandonment of the original meaning and context of biblical texts, then what was seen as 'biblical' by abolitionists is nothing more than an illusion.

---

53. Eric Williams, *Capitalism and Slavery, with a New Introduction by Colin A. Palmer* (repr., Chapel Hill: University of North Carolina Press, 1994 [1944]).

54. For Williams's role in this historiographical shift, see Stanley Engerman and David Eltis, 'Economic Aspects of the Abolition Debate', in Christine Bolt and Seymour Drescher (eds.), *Anti-Slavery, Religion and Reform* (Folkestone, Kent: Wm Dawson & Sons, 1980), especially pp. 272-73; and David B. Davis, 'Foreword', in Seymour Drescher, *Econocide: British Slavery in the Era of Abolition* (Chapel Hill: University of North Carolina Press, 2nd edn, 2010), pp. xiii-xix.

55. Stark, *For the Glory of God*, p. 291.

56. John A. Auping, *Religion and Social Justice: The Case of Christianity and the Abolition of Slavery in America* (Mexico City: Universidad Iberoamericana, 1994).

57. See Arthur A. Rupprecht, 'Attitudes on Slavery', in Richard N. Longenecker and Merrill C. Tenney (eds.), *New Dimensions in New Testament Study* (Grand Rapids, MI: Zondervan, 1974), pp. 261-77 (277): 'The truth of the matter, therefore, lies somewhere between the romantic illusions of Wallon and Allard and the unsupported extreme indictments of Westermann and Davis'.

Ethics and the New Atheism

Recent denunciations of biblical ethics are principally found in works by non-biblical scholars, and promoters of the New Atheism. These include books such as *The God Delusion* by Richard Dawkins, *God is Not Great* by Christopher Hitchens, and *The End of Faith* by Sam Harris.[58] These manifestos have their place, but they are not scholarly critiques of academic defenses of biblical ethics. Consequently, Dawkins, Hitchens, and Harris are easily dismissed as not knowing enough about the biblical sources, Christian history, and theology to make a difference to such academics.

My book bridges the gap between the New Atheist critiques and the scholarly critiques that are still sorely lacking. I am a secular humanist. To the extent that I believe that religion is an obstacle to good ethics and general human welfare, I do identify with the New Atheism. I believe that the best ethics are not based on religion, but rather on balancing verifiable individual and group interests. I also believe that even good outcomes may be unethical when based on supernatural premises.

There is, of course, nothing really new about the 'New Atheism' but the same applies to many religious movements that claim to be 'renovationist' or 'reformational'. But an important feature of the New Atheism, and one largely missed by its critics, is the participation of *bona fide* biblical scholars.[59] Openly atheist biblical scholars are rare, and the vast majority of them have ecclesial or religionist ties. But, today, we have a few vocal and openly atheist or agnostic biblical scholars, who cannot be so easily dismissed when speaking about the religionist biases in biblical scholarship. These scholars include Bart Ehrman, Jim Linville, and Robert Price.[60] It is these scholars, and not so much the popular New Atheist writers, who pose a greater danger to the benign view of biblical ethics.

---

58. Richard Dawkins, *The God Delusion* (Boston: Houghton Mifflin, 2006); Sam Harris, *The End of Faith: Religion, Terror, and the End of Reason* (New York: W.W. Norton, 2005); Christopher Hitchens, *god Is Not Great: How Religion Poisons Everything* (New York: Twelve, 2007).

59. For critiques of the New Atheism, see John Haught, *God and the New Atheism: A Critical Response to Dawkins, Harris, and Hitchens* (Louisville, KY: Westminster/John Knox Press, 2007); David Marshall, *The Truth behind the New Atheism: Responding to the Emerging Challenges to God and Christianity* (Eugene, OR: Harvest House, 2007).

60. For example, Bart Ehrman, *God's Problem: How the Bible Fails to Answer Our Most Important Question—Why We Suffer* (New York: HarperOne, 2008); Robert M. Price and Julia Sweeney, *The Reason Driven Life: What Am I Here on Earth For?* (Amherst, NY: Prometheus, 2006).

Organization

The present work is divided into two major parts: Part I, Slavery and Biblical Scholarship (Chapters 2–6), addresses the variety of strategies used by modern biblical scholars to mitigate negative ethical implications of slavery in the Bible. Part II, Slavery and the Bible in Christian History, illustrates how the Bible was used to sustain slavery, as well as how the Bible's stance on slavery posed an enormous, and sometimes insuperable, challenge for abolitionists. Otherwise, the organizational principle is mainly chronological, with the major exception of the first two chapters, which provide an Introduction (Chapter 1) and a basic overview of the interpretive techniques used by biblical scholars to exalt biblical ethics (Chapter 2). Some themes and topics do overlap chronologically in order to provide a more coherent analysis.

Beginning with Chapter 3 I explore slavery from its earliest traces in the ancient Near East because most Christian historians and apologists give short shrift to many pre-biblical Near Eastern developments that are then credited to the Bible. Other historians exalt the Bible's advance without noticing that many of those advances were made without the help of the Bible. I demonstrate how simple lack of acquaintance with Near Eastern primary sources misleads even reputable historians into the illusion that the Bible had praiseworthy new ethical principles concerning slavery.

Since my focus is on biblical scholarship, I devote one chapter each (Chapters 4 and 5, respectively) to the Old and New Testaments. The objecttive is to illustrate how modern biblical scholarship attempts to mitigate slavery in the Bible. These chapters also help to evaluate how later abolitionists departed from the original meaning of those texts, insofar as we can determine that meaning. Jesus has a special place in Christian ethics, and so Chapter 6 is devoted to the supposedly anti-imperialist ethics of Jesus. Briefly, Jesus, as portrayed in the New Testament, is no better than other slavemasters in ancient times. Jesus was not interested in liberating any real slaves, especially because he is often portrayed as the mirror image of the Roman emperor.

Since Christian apologists often argue that Christian opposition to slavery began with the early Church, I devote a chapter (Chapter 7) to summarizing these supposed efforts against slavery in Late Antiquity by people such as Gregory of Nyssa, St Bathilde, and St Anskar. The Middle Ages are often thought to represent a Christian triumph in abolishing slavery from most of Europe, but Chapter 8 demonstrates that the Middle Ages were not as slave-free as is claimed. In particular, I examine the work of St Thomas Aquinas, whose thought becomes fundamental for later Catholic and Protestant moral

18   *Slavery, Abolitionism, and the Ethics of Biblical Scholarship*

theologians. Far from seeing slavery as a sin or as something that needed to be denounced, Aquinas had a more complex view that allowed enough loopholes to construct almost any slave system in the New World.

It was during the Renaissance that the New World slave system, which is acknowledged by most scholars to represent the most extreme form of racist slavery ever devised, began to show its horrific fruit. While many apologists credit Christian institutions, especially the papacy, with being a guiding light against slavery, Chapter 9 exposes how often those claims rest on partial consideration of evidence as well as on basic misreadings of important papal documents. I focus on a few important papal bulls in order to show the continuity of biblical ideas about slavery.

In order to confirm why we cannot credit biblical ethics with the antislavery movement, I devote six chapters to the biblical exegesis of noted abolitionists and Christian figures from the Renaissance to the nineteenth century. Chapter 10 focuses on Bartolomé de las Casas and Juan Ginés de Sepulveda, two Catholic figures who embodied the fight between slavery and abolitionism in the Catholic world of the sixteenth century. Chapter 11 explores major Protestant figures (Martin Luther, John Calvin, and Jean Bodin) in that same century.

I explore Catholic attitudes about slavery in the eighteenth and nineteenth centuries in Chapter 12, where I focus specifically on Rodney Stark's claim that Louisiana exhibited a more humane and advanced treatment of slaves because it followed a Catholic moral theology rather than a Protestant one. British abolitionists, including an Afro-British writer, are the focus of Chapter 13. White American abolitionists are featured in Chapter 14, while African-American abolitionists are featured in Chapter 15.

Although I cannot claim to resolve the heated dispute about the specific causes or set of causes that made abolition triumph between about 1775 and 1900, I do include a chapter (Chapter 16) sketching some of the possible factors that explain abolition better than any claimed reliance on biblical ethics. I include discussion of the role of non-Christian religions (e.g., African traditions in Haiti), usually ignored by Christian apologists.

Summary

Despite frequent claims to being descriptive and objective, the study of biblical ethics is still permeated by a religionist agenda intent on validating the role of the Bible in modern society. However, this programme deconstructs itself because usually we find that the role of the Bible must be maintained by following specious, selective, and arbitrary procedures. While there are instances where reliance on the Bible can be credited with some ethical advance, this study will confirm that the Bible presents such contradictory and ambiguous notions of ethics that opposing positions could easily justify almost anything by relying on it. In fact, it demonstrates that it was abandoning or marginalizing biblical argumentation, and shifting to secularized economic, humanitarian, legal, and practical arguments, that made a much greater impact on abolition.

Part I

SLAVERY AND BIBLICAL SCHOLARSHIP

Chapter 2

UNETHICAL HERMENEUTICS

It is difficult to deconstruct biblical ethics without a summary of the interpretive strategies used by Christian apologists.[1] Ignoring those interpretive strategies allows undue credit to the Bible in the abolition of slavery. If anything, pro-slavery advocates had an upper hand in any scriptural debate with abolitionists. We return to the observation of J. Albert Harrill, the New Testament scholar:

> In the late 19th century conflict over the Bible and slavery, American abolitionists, many of whom were Christian evangelicals, ransacked Scripture for texts condemning slavery, but found few. As a consequence, they developed new hermeneutical strategies to read the Bible to counter the 'plain sense' (literalist) reading of proslavery theology... Most embarrassing for today's readers of the Bible, the proslavery clergymen were holding the more defensible position from the perspective of historical criticism. The passages in the Bible about slavery signal the acceptance of an ancient model of civilization for which patriarchy and subjugation were not merely desirable but essential.[2]

However, Harrill does not elaborate how these interpretive strategies function to whitewash biblical endorsement of slavery. There are three principal interpretive strategies used by Christian ethicists:
  (1) Representativism
  (2) Trajectorialism
  (3) Reinterpretation

I examine each more carefully, and then show in later chapters how they are used in various combinations.

---

1. See also David J.A. Clines, 'Ethics as Deconstruction, and, The Ethics of Deconstruction', in John W. Rogerson, Margaret Davies, and M. Daniel Carroll R. (eds.), *The Bible in Ethics: The Second Sheffield Colloquium* (JSOTSup, 207; Sheffield: Sheffield Academic Press, 1995), pp. 77-106.
2. Harrill, 'Slavery', in *NIDB*, V, p. 307.

Representativism

For my purposes, 'representativism' affirms that a particular biblical ethical view is 'representative' while others (usually bad ones, like slavery and genocide) are unrepresentative. In actuality, representativeness affects all areas of history. In his penetrating study of the historiography of ancient slavery, Niall McKeown acutely summarizes the problem:

> Historians have a double problem, as they are usually faced paradoxically with too much information about the past and too little. Having more information about the past than they can fit in to their narratives forces historians to edit, inevitably introducing a degree of subjectivity in deciding what to leave out. On the other hand, they never have the full facts about the past either, forcing them to use their imaginations to fill the gaps and provide a wider context for the material they do possess.[3]

The same applies when trying to reconstruct 'biblical ethics'. Biblical scholars pick-and-choose what counts as representative texts, and leave out or diminish those text that do not represent the 'core teachings' of the Bible. Walter Brueggemann provides an instance when he claims that Israel's God, 'full of sovereign power and committed in solidarity to the needy, and especially to Israel in need—dominates the narrative of Israel's liturgy and imagination (cf. Deut. 10.12-22)'.[4] He tells us that '[it] is important to accent that something like "God's preferential option for the poor" is deeply rooted in Israel's testimony, so deeply rooted as to be characteristic and definitional for Israel's speech about God'.[5] Accordingly, slavery would be against the representative or core teachings of the Bible.

However, Brueggemann, much like almost every other biblical theologian, never establishes criteria for what is 'characteristic and definitional'. Is it a statistical criterion? That is to say, is it the number of times a specific concept or term is repeated? Or is it qualitative? That is to say, is it something said to be the most important concept, regardless of how many times others are repeated?

If it is qualitative, then is a representative teaching one that the biblical authors say is representative, or is it something a modern scholar is retrojecting into the biblical text?

---

3. McKeown, *The Invention of Ancient Slavery?*, p. 8. For a general treatment of biblical hermeneutics, see Anthony C. Thiselton, *Hermeneutics: An Introduction* (Grand Rapids: Eerdmans, 2009). Thiselton shows little interest in critiquing philosophically the forms of trajectorialism, representativism, and reinterpretation I describe.

4. Walter Brueggemann, *Theology of the Old Testament: Testimony, Dispute, Advocacy* (Minneapolis: Fortress Press, 1997), p. 144.

5. Brueggemann, *Theology of the Old Testament*, p. 144.

If we appeal to statistics to find out what is 'characteristic', we soon encounter a very complex and confusing situation. Brueggemann quotes Deuteronomy 10 to support the idea that a characteristic of God is his concern for the poor. Deuteronomy 10.12-22 is part of a larger work, usually denominated as the Deuteronomistic History, stretching from Joshua to 2 Kings (except Ruth) in Protestant Bibles. Yet, Frank Frick's study of the terminology of poverty in Deuteronomistic History concludes that this work is the least concerned with poverty compared to other biblical corpora. For example, Job has twenty instances of poverty terminology, while the much larger Deuteronomistic History has only eleven.[6]

Using a 'qualitative' criterion is not much more helpful in determining what is 'characteristic and definitional'. Consider Deut. 10.12-22, the very text Brueggemann cites:

> And now, Israel, what does the LORD your God require of you, but to fear the LORD your God, to walk in all his ways, to love him, to serve the LORD your God with all your heart and with all your soul, and to keep the commandments and statutes of the LORD, which I command you this day for your good? Behold, to the LORD your God belong heaven and the heaven of heavens, the earth with all that is in it; yet the LORD set his heart in love upon your fathers and chose their descendants after them, you above all peoples, as at this day. Circumcise therefore the foreskin of your heart, and be no longer stubborn. For the LORD your God is God of gods and Lord of lords, the great, the mighty, and the terrible God, who is not partial and takes no bribe. He executes justice for the fatherless and the widow, and loves the sojourner, giving him food and clothing. Love the sojourner therefore; for you were sojourners in the land of Egypt. You shall fear the LORD your God; you shall serve him and cleave to him, and by his name you shall swear. He is your praise; he is your God, who has done for you these great and terrible things which your eyes have seen. Your fathers went down to Egypt seventy persons; and now the LORD your God has made you as the stars of heaven for multitude (Deut. 10.12-22).

True enough, the text speaks about how Yahweh cares about justice for the widow, and how he loves the stranger.

But the text also repeatedly emphasizes how Israelites should 'fear', 'serve', and 'love' Yahweh with all their soul. Verbs commanding obligation toward Yahweh outnumber any commandments to be kind to widows or strangers. Statistically, we could make the case that this passage makes slavery to Yahweh 'characteristic and definitional' of Israel's status. Verse 14 speaks of how the earth belongs to Yahweh, and so we could just as well

---

6. Frank S. Frick, 'Cui bono?—History in the Service of Political Nationalism: The Deuteronomistic History as Political Propaganda', in Knight (ed.), *Ethics and Politics in the Bible*, pp. 79-92 (84).

argue that Yahweh's imperialism is 'characteristic and definitional', not some preferential option for the poor.

And how does loving and taking care of the stranger coincide with the genocide of the Canaanites that is also mentioned in other parts of Deuteronomy? Why not argue that it is 'characteristic and definitional' of Yahweh to slaughter unfavored groups of people? To explain such genocide, Brueggemann lapses back into a technique well known among fundamentalists, who also pick-and-choose what to take literally and what to take figuratively.[7] Brueggemann tells us that such genocidal texts are really 'a theological construct without any historical base'.[8] This, of course, assumes that talk about 'justice' is also not 'a theological construct without any historical base'.

A similar problem obtains in the New Testament. Ben Witherington applauds the supposedly benign slavery described in Col. 3.18–4.1 because '[l]ove and fairness were not generally part of the picture in Paul's world'.[9] For Witherington, the absence of love and fairness is representative of non-Christian cultures at the time of Paul. Harrill rightly criticizes S. Scott Bartchy for these sorts of generalizations about non-Christian cultures. 'Too often he [Bartchy] speaks of "Greek", "Roman", and "Jewish" law as if they composed monolithic institutions.'[10] Witherington does the same with 'Paul's world'.

Consider Seneca (c. 4 BCE–65 CE), the Stoic philosopher, who tells his readers in his forty-seventh epistle. 'Treat your inferiors as you would be treated by your betters. And as often as you reflect how much power you have over a slave, remember that your master has just as much power over you.'[11] Qualitatively, nothing in the New Testament compares to the extensive and thoughtful advocacy of fairness for slaves in Seneca's forty-seventh epistle. If we use a statistical criterion for Witherington's 'generally', then we could argue that Seneca's statements advocating fairness must be measured against many other statement advocating unfairness in Greco-Roman literature.

---

7. For a critique of how 'figurative' or 'metaphorical' interpretations are used to mitigate violent ethics, see J. Cheryl Exum, 'The Ethics of Biblical Violence against Women', in Rogerson, Davies, and Carroll R. (eds.), *The Bible in Ethics*, pp. 248-71 (263-64).

8. Brueggemann, *Theology of the Old Testament*, p. 497.

9. Witherington, 'Was Paul a Pro-Slavery Chauvinist?', p. 8.

10. J. Albert Harrill, *The Manumission of Slaves in Early Christianity* (Tübingen: Mohr Siebeck, 1995), pp. 98-99.

11. Seneca, *Epistles* 47.11 (Gummere, LCL): 'sic cum inferiore vivas, quemadmodum tecum superiorem velis vivere. Quotiens in mentem venerit, quantum tibi in servum liceat veniat in mentem tantundem in te domino tuo licere'. Ben Witherington III (*The Letters to Philemon, the Colossians, and Ephesians: A Socio-Rhetorical Commentary on the Captivity Epistles* [Grand Rapids, MI: Eerdmans, 2007], p. 79) quotes this very epistle.

Yet, notice that the metrics are not symmetrical. Seneca's writings might be compared to all other Greco-Roman non-Christian writings which span some 500 years (e.g., from 200 BCE to 300 CE), while Witherington might be content to compare Paul with a smaller corpus of New Testament writers. But let us suppose we compare the Pauline corpus to the entire corpus of early Christian writers from the first 500 years of Christian history. Would Paul fare as well in terms of what Christians 'generally' advocated?

Trajectorialism

Trajectorialism grants that certain undesirable biblical practices may exist in the Bible but they are nonetheless a step in the right direction or represent advances. Moses I. Finley, the prominent scholar of classical slavery, calls it the 'teleological fallacy', and describes it as follows:

> It consists in assuming the existence from the beginning of time, so to speak, of the writer's values—in this instance, the moral rejection of slavery as an evil—and then examining all earlier thought and practice as if they were, or ought to have been, on the road to this realization; as if men in other periods were asking the same questions and facing the same problems as those of the historian and *his* world.[12]

Although Finley rejects this sort of trajectorialism, he also says: '[s]lavery is a great evil. There is no reason why a historian should not say that'.[13] What Finley objects to is focusing only on slavery in an ancient culture to make our own society look superior.

We certainly expect this sort of trajectorialism from a fundamentalist Christian scholar such as Gleason Archer, who says:

> Not until the more exalted concept of man and his innate dignity as a person created in the image of God had permeated the world as a product of Bible teaching did a strong sentiment arise in Christendom in criticism of slavery and a questioning of its right to exist. No equivalent movement toward abolition is discernible in any non-Christian civilization of which we have any knowledge.[14]

---

12. Finley, *Ancient Slavery and Modern Ideology*, p. 85 (Finley's italics). See also Harrill, *The Manumission of Slaves*, pp. 92-93.

13. Finley, *Ancient Slavery and Modern Ideology*, p. 132.

14. Gleason Archer, *Encyclopedia of Bible Difficulties* (Grand Rapids, MI: Zondervan, 1982), pp. 86-87. For an evangelical Christian who critiques a variant of trajectorialist hermeneutics, see Wayne A. Grudem, 'Is Evangelical Feminism the New Path to Liberalism? Some Disturbing Warning Signs', *Journal for Biblical Manhood and Womanhood* 9 (Spring 2004), pp. 35-84 (39-40).

28   *Slavery, Abolitionism, and the Ethics of Biblical Scholarship*

But we find it in critical biblical scholars, as well. Michael Coogan tells us that 'the Bible is the beginning of a trajectory leading toward full freedom and equality for all persons'.[15] A less obvious version is found in popular historical works on slavery, such as in Susanne Everett's *History of Slavery*, which says, concerning the epistle of Philemon, 'that same epistle...revealed an incipient anti-slavery message in early Christianity'.[16]

The bibliolatrous bias in these trajectorialist statements is apparent insofar as it is not clear why Coogan believes the Bible should be credited with 'the beginning' of any trajectory, especially if we find pre-biblical or non-biblical texts in antiquity advocating the practices valued by modern people. Similarly, we find manumission before Philemon in Roman, Greek, and Mesopotamian literature, and so it is unclear why Philemon's supposed anti-slavery message is designated as 'incipient' when it could have been described as 'continuing' earlier traditions.

Trajectorialist arguments can support the slavery side quite well because slavery waxed and waned in many periods. Thus, if one takes any particular period when slavery is waxing, one can argue that this represents the endpoint of the trajectory. If slavery is waning, one can argue God wanted that decrease. Fred Ross used this very type of trajectorialism when he referenced the arrest of emancipatory movements in America that were proven right by the chaos of British emancipation efforts in Jamaica:

> Twenty-five years ago, and previously, the whole slave-holding South and West had a strong tendency to emancipation in some form. But the abolition movement then began and arrested that Southern and Western leaning to emancipation... God has a great deal to do before he is ready for emancipation... He put it into the hearts of abolitionists *to make the arrest*. And He stopped the Southern movement all the more perfectly by permitting Great Britain to emancipate Jamaica, and letting that experiment prove, as it has, a perfect failure and a terrible warning. JAMAICA IS DESTROYED.[17]

Thus, it is always precarious to think that our current period represents some permanent telos in emancipatory trajectories because the world could revert to slavery in the future.

Other problems with trajectorialism should be readily apparent. First, it depends on the uncertain relative dating of biblical materials. For example, how did Coogan decide that texts requiring greater enslavement are earlier than texts obligating greater freedom or universal freedom? In fact, Isa. 14.1-2 envisions a future trajectory wherein the entire world will be enslaved to

---

15. Michael D. Coogan, 'The Great Gulf between Scholars and the Pew', in Susanne Scholz (ed.), *Biblical Studies Alternatively: An Introductory Reader* (Upper Saddle River, NJ: Prentice–Hall, 2003), pp. 5-12 (11).
16. Susanne Everett, *History of Slavery* (Edison, NJ: Chartwell Books, 1999), p. 6.
17. Ross, *Slavery Ordained*, p. 72 (Ross's emphasis).

Yahweh and his chosen people:

> The LORD will have compassion on Jacob and will again choose Israel, and will set them in their own land, and aliens will join them and will cleave to the house of Jacob. And the peoples will take them and bring them to their place, and the house of Israel will possess them in the LORD's land as male and female slaves; they will take captive those who were their captors, and rule over those who oppressed them.

Thus, even if slavery was abolished in the nineteenth century, slavery will return, if we follow this version of biblical eschatology. The 'biblical' trajectory might envision universal slavery to Yahweh and his minions.

Reinterpretation: Does Original Intent Matter?

By far the most common strategy to explain slavery in the Bible is reinterpretation. Reinterpretation allows the original meaning of the text to be erased or changed to fit a later or modern context. In general, we can divide reinterpretation into two types: (1) communitarian, which privileges the harmonization of scripture with the needs of a later community; (2) analogical, which emphasizes similarities between a situation or teaching found in scripture and one in a modern context. In truth, we see a mixture of both, even if they can stand independently.

In a much-cited article in *The Interpreter's Dictionary of the Bible*, Krister Stendahl argued that scholars should distinguish 'what it meant and what it means'.[18] The background of this claim was Stendahl's admission that the Bible is so alien to our culture that only reinterpretation could keep it alive. Note Stendahl's own remarks: 'This understanding leads to the puzzling insight that in the living religious traditions continuity is affirmed and achieved by discontinuity. Authority is affirmed and relevance asserted by reinterpretation.'[19]

Stendahl claimed that reinterpretation, even when it means disregarding the 'original' sense of a text, was an essential function of scriptures, as evidenced by this statement. 'From a historical point of view, Paul did not mean what Augustine heard him to say... For better or worse that is how Scriptures function, and if so, we had better take note thereof in our treatment of the

---

18. Krister Stendahl, 'Biblical Theology, Contemporary', in *IDB*, I, p. 420. Compare Stendahl's view with that of E.D. Hirsch, *Validity in Interpretation* (New Haven: Yale University Press, 1967), p. 8: '*Meaning* is that which is represented by a text; it is what the author meant by a particular his particular use of a sign or sequence... *Significance*, on the other hand, names a relationship between that meaning and a person...' (Hirsch's italics).
19. Krister Stendahl, 'Biblical Studies', in Paul Ramsey and John F. Wilson (eds.), *The Study of Religion in Colleges and Universities* (Princeton, NJ: Princeton University Press, 1970), pp. 23-39 (31).

history of ideas.'[20] For Stendahl, it is the nature of scripture to be reinterpreted. Stendahl echoed the ideas of Hans-Georg Gadamer, who asserted that readers always recreate meaning to the extent that it does not much matter what an author meant.[21] In essence, a text can and should mean whatever a faith community needs it to mean to keep the text or the community alive.

The philosophical and ethical problems with reinterpretation are usually never addressed very thoroughly by biblical scholars.[22] Such ethical and philosophical problems can be seen more clearly if we realize that two positions can be identified for those who believe there is even such a thing as authorial intent:[23]

   A.   Authorial intent is the only one that matters
   B.   Authorial intent is not the only one that matters

If one chooses A, then biblical studies has been highly unsuccessful. We often do not possess enough information to determine what an author meant, even if we believe that authorial intent matters and should be the primary goal of interpretation.

If one chooses B, then the only result is chaos and relativism that renders all scholarly biblical studies moot and superfluous. Faith communities do not need academic biblical scholars to inform them about any original context in order to keep the Bible alive for themselves. So what is the purpose of academic biblical studies in such a case?

Communitarian/Analogical Reinterpretations

Communitarian reinterpretation affirms that the collective understanding of a particular religious tradition is either the sole or a parallel mode of biblical interpretation. Consider the case of Jon Levenson, a professor at Harvard Divinity School, who rejects the idea that the original intent of an author is

---

20. Stendahl, 'Biblical Studies', p. 31. See also Thomas F. Martin, '*Vox Pauli*: Augustine and the Claims to Speak for Paul: An Exploration of Rhetoric in the Service of Exegesis', *JECS* 8 (2000), pp. 237-72.

21. Hans-Georg Gadamer, *Truth and Method* (trans. Joel Weinsheimer and Donald G. Marshall; New York: Crossroad, 2nd edn, 1989).

22. One of those who does address these issues is Ben Witherington III, *The Indelible Image: The Theological and Ethical Thought World of the New Testament* (2 vols.; Downers Grove, IL: IVP Academic Press, 2010), especially I, pp. 38-46.

23. For the history and philosophical issues surrounding the concept of 'authorship' and authorial intentionality, see Jed Wyrick, *The Ascension of Authorship: Attribution and Canon Formation in Jewish, Hellenistic, and Christian Traditions* (Cambridge, MA: Harvard University Department of Comparative Literature, 2004); Jeffrey A. Mitscherling, Tanya DiTommaso, and Aref Nayed, *The Author's Intention* (Lanham, MD: Lexington Books, 2004).

supreme in the application of the Bible. He views most critical scholars as fixated on the idea that the only meaning the Bible should have is what its original authors intended. Any effort to understand the composition and meaning of a biblical text in its original context must be balanced by 'the need to put the text back together in a way that makes it available in the present and in its entirety—not merely in the past and in the form of historically contextualized fragments'.[24]

In his indictment of the monopoly of historical-critical analysis in the academy, Levenson uses a variant of the famous distinctions made by Stendahl. One of Levenson's main claims is that '[r]oom must be made for other senses of the text, developed by other traditions'.[25] If so, we must remember to distinguish two different generators of these 'senses' to which Levenson and most scholars refer: (1) senses generated by the original author; (2) senses generated by readers. Levenson clearly wants to establish the legitimacy of the second option, wherein readers, especially in the form of faith communities, can generate a sense that was not intended by the original author. For Levenson, reinterpretation is legitimate even when it might contradict what an original author meant. And both Levenson and Stendahl argue that since faith communities do apply other meanings to the Bible, then it is legitimate for them to do so. This rationale may be expressed more schematically as: 'People do X' = 'People should do X'.

Upon closer inspection, Levenson's argument (and that of Stendahl) bears serious flaws. First, it relies on a relativism that Levenson denounces elsewhere. If senses other than the original are to be allowed, then why argue against any of those other senses at all? Similarly, Levenson's own grievance against the monopolism of the historical-critical method is self-refuting. If a monopolistic approach is illegitimate, then his own idea would form yet another monopolistic position. After all, pluralism of meaning becomes a monopolistic position if pluralism of meaning is the only position allowed. Indeed, all Levenson is arguing is that his monopolistic approach should be the only legitimate one.

Another flaw is that his allowance of senses other than the original one would render superfluous his own warnings not to misunderstand him. For example, he says: 'My point would be misunderstood if it were taken to be that only a religious affirmation can justify the presence of biblical studies in a curriculum...'[26] But what if two hundred years from now, someone made

---

24. Jon D. Levenson, *The Hebrew Bible, the Old Testament, and Historical Criticism: Jews and Christians in Biblical Studies* (Louisville, KY: Westminster/John Knox Press, 1993), p. 79.

25. Levenson, *The Hebrew Bible*, p. 123. For a similar approach to Exodus liberation analogies, see Michael Walzer, *Exodus and Revolution* (New York: Basic Books, 1985).

26. Levenson, *The Hebrew Bible*, p. 124.

Levenson's own book into some sort of scripture that reinterpreted him to mean exactly the opposite of what he says he wants readers to understand? Would he allow 'room for other senses' to his own work, especially if such senses were the complete opposite of what he intended? Would he argue that since people do engage in such reinterpretations all the time, then it is proper for them to treat his work that way? I suspect he would find that unethical, and so the same applies to any reinterpretation of the sort he allows to faith communities.

Levenson's position is particularly problematic because he equates fundamentalism with the denial of change and development in the biblical text.[27] But, what Levenson regards as reinterpretation is often not regarded as such by members of faith communities. Such communities might insist that a text has always been interpreted that way. It is not usually the case that a modern faith community acknowledges that Text X has original Meaning A, but Meaning A will be disregarded or contradicted so that Text X now will have reinterpreted Meaning B. Rather, most members of faith communities assert that Text X means B, but not because it is reinterpreted. For them, A = B.

Academic scholars might call that 'reinterpreted' because they have concluded, on empirico-rationalist grounds, that what faith communities today are practicing is not original, even when faith communities might be claiming not a reinterpretation but rather a continuity in interpretation. Thus, Levenson's very judgment that a text has undergone reinterpretation presumes the sort of outside empirico-rationalist observation that he denies is legitimate when applied to the interpretations or stories of faith communities he favors.

But once an equation is made between a modern sense and an original sense, then it is not a matter of scholars allowing 'another sense' but rather a case where simple empirico-rationalism comes into play. As such, a secular biblical scholar is perfectly right in concluding that a modern community is falsely claiming that 'the modern sense = the original author's sense'. Followers of the historical-critical method in this case would be no more monopolistic or fundamentalistic than correcting anyone who claimed that $1 + 1 = 3$.

But even if we suppose that all authorial intention is irrelevant or indeterminate, the consequences of Levenson's position differs not in the least from ejecting that ancient text from modern life altogether. For if Text X has original Meaning A, then reinterpretation means accepting a different interpretation that can be described as Not-A (i.e., not the original meaning). But accepting Not-A is tantamount to saying that Meaning A no longer exists or has any relevance. If so, any reinterpretation of the Bible's teaching on a

---

27. Levenson, *The Hebrew Bible*, p. 79: 'unlike fundamentalism, it would not seek to deny the process of change and development...'

particular issue is similarly a rejection and abandonment of the Bible's teaching on that issue.

On a more practical level, we see the problems Levenson's inconcinnities cause when we examine his comparison of the use of scripture by Anglo-Israelites with the use of scripture by Martin Luther King. Briefly, Anglo-Israelites believe that the true Israelites were Aryans. Therefore, the British, and/or their kin, are the descendants of the Israelites.[28] In contrast, what are known as 'Jews' today are often considered counterfeits or the result of some genealogical corruption. Levenson uses this quote as his illustration of Anglo-Israelism's claims:

> Originally the Jews had been a blond people very similar to the modern Anglo-Saxons. After the crucifixion of Christ, according to one exegete, the physiognomy of the Jews had greatly altered for the worse... But the Jews who were members of the ten tribes retained their blondness and their beauty. The Anglo-Saxons were the true Jews, God's chosen people.[29]

Levenson sees such an Anglo-Israelite 'reappropriation' as illegitimate because they 'rewrote history so as to project themselves into the paradigmatic past'.[30]

In contrast, Levenson approves of how Martin Luther King used scripture in his last speech on 3 April 1968, a portion of which Levenson quotes as follows:

> I just want to do God's will. And He's allowed me to go up to the mountain, and I have looked over, and I've seen the promised land. I may not get there with you. But I want you to know tonight, that we, as a people, will get to the promised land.[31]

Levenson claims that one difference rests on motive. Dr King 'identified with Israel in its suffering and not just in its triumph. His words do not seek to claim a superior status for his own people but rather greater understanding of their affliction.'[32]

But Levenson never explains why King's analogical identification with Israel 'in its suffering' should be privileged over identifying with Israel just

---

28. For an excellent history of Anglo-Israelism, see Michael Barkun, *Religion and the Racist Right: The Origins of the Christian Identity Movement* (Chapel Hill: University of North Carolina Press, 1994).

29. Levenson, *The Hebrew Bible*, pp. 156 and 182 n. 61. Levenson is quoting Thomas F. Gossett, *Race: The History of an Idea in America* (Dallas: Southern Methodist University Press, 1963), p. 190. Gossett, however, is not an Anglo-Israelite, but rather a scholar of race.

30. Levenson, *The Hebrew Bible*, p. 156.

31. Levenson, *The Hebrew Bible*, p. 156.

32. Levenson, *The Hebrew Bible*, p. 156.

in its triumph. Who made up the rule that only suffering and humble reinterpretations/reidentifications should be deemed legitimate? Why not argue that any identification that purports to be historically true is illegitimate when it cannot produce verifiable evidence? That is to say, the Anglo-Israelite claim is illegitimate precisely because it asserts that A = B (where A = Biblical Israelites and B = Modern British).

If so, then motive has little to do with the legitimacy of an identification. The Anglo-Israelites are simply making a historical claim, while Martin Luther King is simply making an analogical and metaphorical claim ('we are like Israelites' vs. 'we are Israelites'), as Levenson himself observes. The historical claim is subject to good-old-fashioned empirico-rationalist verification or falsification, while an analogy can be allowed some artistic license.

And Levenson's complaints about Anglo-Israelism's flawed historical identification contradicts Levenson's own claim that the original sense should not be privileged. If so, then why not let the Anglo-Israelites go on thinking that they are the true Israel just like many other Christians believe that they are the true Israel? This is a very Christian notion if one reads Romans:

> But it is not as though the word of God had failed. For not all who are descended from Israel belong to Israel, and not all are children of Abraham because they are his descendants; but 'Through Isaac shall your descendants be named'. This means that it is not the children of the flesh who are the children of God, but the children of the promise are reckoned as descendants (Rom. 9.6-8).

If so, then Anglo-Israelite claims do not seem anymore farfetched than those of the author of Romans.

Furthermore, the comparison is unfair because it seeks to represent the basis for Anglo-Israelism's identification with ancient Israel through a secondary source, which does not represent the argumentation, flawed as it may be.[33] If one looks at the argument of Edward Hine, a well-known Anglo-Israelite, he quotes Isa. 3.9, which says in the KJV: 'The show of their countenance doth witness against them'.[34] Hine combines this statement with a well-known biblical tradition of people's appearance changing instantaneously because of sin or a curse. He, therefore, concludes that the Jews must have experienced a similar change of appearance as punishment for Christ's crucifixion.

---

33. As noted by Michael Barkun (*Religion and the Racist Right*) the Anglo-Israelite movement had various phases and diverse positions, ranging from philo-Semitic adherents to virulently anti-Jewish ones.

34. See Edward Hine, *Identity of the Lost Tribes of Israel with the Anglo-Celto-Saxons* (Boring, OR: CPA Book Publisher, abridged edn, n.d.), p. 27.

In fact, one could argue that Hine's exegesis represents a variant of long-honored Jewish interpretive traditions involving instantaneous changes of physical appearance. There are many biblical characters, whose physical appearance, including color, suddenly changed in both the Bible and in postbiblical Jewish interpretation. For example, Miriam turned 'white as snow' as punishment for speaking against Moses in Num. 12.10.

According to numerous Jewish, Christian, and Islamic interpreters, the so-called curse of Ham, deriving from an interpretation of Gen. 9.22-27, involved Ham turning black.[35] We find reference to that curse in Jewish medical treatises produced contemporaneously with Anglo-Israelite works. Thus, Julius Preuss, one of the most distinguished historians of Jewish medicine, said 'Ham became black (negro)...'[36] There was a far longer tradition that involved turning idolaters into apes, and it is found in Islamic and Talmudic sources.[37]

Moreover, the whole tradition of Anglo-Israelism is long and deep enough that some historians of Handel's music argue that to understand this music one 'cannot fail to notice both that the preachers habitually identify modern Britain with ancient Israel and that they make recurrent specific parallels which bear on the subjects of the librettos'.[38] So why is that interpretive tradition, and its corresponding faith community, not viewed as expressing another allowable sense?

And, of course, we can just as easily find a quote of Martin Luther King that re-writes history. Martin Luther King, for example, interprets Jesus as having a 'love ethic' despite Lk. 14.26, where Jesus enjoins disciples to hate their parents.[39] If Jesus preached hate, then it is re-writing history to say he had a 'love ethic'. And Anglo-Israelites, after all, have not rewritten history anymore than the Christianity on which Martin Luther King ultimately says he depends.

---

35. See David M. Goldenberg, *The Curse of Ham: Race and Slavery in Early Judaism, Christianity, and Islam* (Princeton, NJ: Princeton University Press, 2003).

36. See Julius Preuss, *Biblical and Talmudic Medicine* (trans. Fred Rosner; repr., London: Jason Aronson, 1994 [1978]), p. 460.

37. Azad Hamoto, *Der Affe in der altorientalischen Kunst* (Münster: Ugarit-Verlag, 1995). On the 'ape' tradition in Islam, see Michael Cook, 'Ibn Qutayba and the Monkeys', *Studia islamica* 89 (1999), pp. 43-74; Ilse Lichtenstadter, '"And become ye accursed apes"', *Jerusalem Studies in Arabic and Islam* 14 (1991), pp. 162-75. For how these traditions were reinterpreted in Nazi literature, see Hector Avalos, *Fighting Words: The Origins of Religious Violence* (Amherst, NY: Prometheus, 2005), pp. 309-10.

38. See Ruth Smith, *Handel's Oratorios and Eighteenth-Century Thought* (Cambridge: Cambridge University Press, 1996), pp. 219-20.

39. Martin Luther King, Jr, 'Pilgrimage to Non-Violence', in Staughton Lynd and Alice Lynd (eds.), *Nonviolence in America: A Documentary History* (Maryknoll, NY: Orbis, rev. edn, 2002 [1966]), p. 214.

Christianity sees Christ as present throughout the Hebrew Bible. When Christians identify the New Testament Christ literally with the suffering servant of Isaiah 53 or with one of the entities mentioned in Gen. 1.26 ('let us make humankind'), why do those identifications not constitute a rewriting of history any less than the Anglo-Israelites saying that their ancestors are also present in the Hebrew Bible?

Another difference made by Levenson is just as facile. Levenson says that Dr King 'does not project his own group into the past; he brings the past, the story of Israel, to bear upon the present'.[40] Levenson praises King for using Moses as an analogy, while the Anglo-Saxon identification with ancient Jews 'has already been justly forgotten'.[41] Again, here is a very nebulous distinction between 'projecting a group into the past' vs. using an ancient story to 'bear upon the present'.

Anglo-Israelites also see themselves as using ancient stories to bear upon their present condition, which some believe is one of oppression and affliction. I am not sure how Anglo-Israelites are less entitled to project their group into the past than Christians who claim that their seed was in Abraham. In short, the legitimacy of reinterpretation seems to be applied in an arbitrary manner.

John J. Collins, the president of the Society of Biblical Literature in 2002, once remarked. 'The Bible was written long ago and in another culture, vastly different from our own'. In the end, Levenson's pleas for the legitimacy of reinterpretation only exposes the fact that the Bible is so foreign to modern life that it can only survive by pretending that it is something other than it is. The fact that people reinterpret scripture does not mean that they should do so.

Summary

My argument is not that modern communities do not reinterpret scripture in the manner that Stendahl and Levenson describe. The problem is that these scholars believe that reinterpretation is a legitimate method to retain biblical authority. However, reinterpretation deconstructs the idea that the Bible is responsible for the abolition of slavery. If reinterpretation means that the original Meaning A is disregarded, and modern meaning, Not-A, is to be substituted instead, then it is not really 'the Bible' that we are using or perpetuating anymore. What we are doing is equating a modern construct with 'the original Bible'. It is a 'let's-pretend-it says-something-else' that we are crediting for whatever benefit we think derives from that manufactured meaning.

40. Levenson, *The Hebrew Bible*, p. 157.
41. Levenson, *The Hebrew Bible*, p. 157.

Of course, my toughest challenge consists of scholars who insist that they are not reinterpreting, but rather uncovering, the 'real' or 'true' meaning of the text. My challenge will encompass those who think that they have determined 'the proper context' to explain away any pro-slavery sentiments on the part of Paul, Jesus, or the Pentateuch. I shall show that those who represent themselves as uncovering the true teachings of the Bible regarding slavery are engaging in reinterpretation that is no less arbitrary than anything found among pro-slavery advocates.

Chapter 3

NEAR EASTERN ETHICS AND SLAVERY

Superficial comparisons between biblical texts and those of Near Eastern cultures constitute the primary strategy when exalting the superiority of biblical ethics. These Near Eastern cultures include those of Mesopotamia, Egypt, the Hittites of Anatolia (modern Turkey), Greece, and Rome. So, in order to show the utter weakness of the claim for the revolutionary advances brought by the Bible, it is important to survey how far ancient Near Eastern cultures had advanced on the question of slavery. In addition, it is important to see how modern religionist scholars often distort, erase, or hide the accomplishments of other Near Eastern cultures in order to paint biblical ethics in a much more favorable light. Generalizing denigrations of ancient Near Eastern cultures are poorly documented or offer distorted interpretations of primary materials.

While many of the non-biblical sources (e.g., Plato's *Laws*) may represent ideal visions rather than legal codes that were actually applied, the same may be said for much of what counts as 'biblical law'.[1] Here, I am primarily interested in the existence of concepts in non-biblical sources that might be described as 'advances' depending on different points of view. Thus, the fact that some of these legal concepts are found in idealized or utopian legal codes is not always as important as the fact that such concepts were expressed. This survey is not meant to be comprehensive, but rather it provides a sample of the attitudes that biblical ethicists have toward the neighboring cultures of the Near East.

---

1. The distinction between idealized and applied law has been reiterated by many scholars, including Wright, *God's Law*, p. 96, *et passim*. See also F. Rachel Magdalene and Cornelia Wunsch, 'Slavery between Judah and Babylon: The Exilic Experience', in Laura Culbertson (ed.), *Slaves and Households in the Ancient Near East* (Oriental Institute Seminar Series, 6; Chicago: Oriental Institute, 2011), pp. 113-34.

Mesopotamian Beginnings

Writing first arose in Mesopotamia, where we find the first extensive law codes and discussions of slavery.[2] Such achievements indicate a high degree of organization and development, which also was manifested in sophisticated urban planning and trade relations. Mesopotamia bears the first warnings about oppressing the needy and weak. Yet, we still witness modern historians and biblical scholars diminishing the ethical accomplishments of Mesopotamia in order to make the Bible look superior.[3]

Consider Alan Dershowitz, the famed legal scholar at Harvard Law School. In speaking of the biblical achievements in law, he points to *Lex talionis*, the principle that a perpetrator should suffer an analogous injury to the victim. Dershowitz realizes that this principle already existed in the Code of Hammurabi (*CH*) in the eighteenth century BCE. Dershowitz tells us why that Code does not quite measure up to the Bible's articulation of that principle: 'The Code of Hammurapi adumbrated this concept but without regard to individual culpability. For example, Hammurapi ordered the killing of the daughter of a man who has killed another's daughter.'[4] Yet, it does not seem to bother Dershowitz that the Ten Commandments begins with the principle of collective punishment in Exod. 20.5: 'for I the LORD your God am a jealous God, visiting the iniquity of the fathers upon the children to the third and the fourth generation of those who hate me' (cf. Noah's Flood).

---

2. For general treatments of the cultural and legal achievements of Mesopotamia and the Near East, see Wolfram von Soden, *The Ancient Orient: An Introduction to the Study of the Ancient Near East* (trans. Donald G. Schley; Grand Rapids, MI: Eerdmans, 1994); Samuel Noah Kramer, *History Begins at Sumer: Thirty-Nine Firsts in Man's Recorded History* (repr., Philadelphia: University of Pennsylvania Press, 1988 [1956]).

3. For a general survey of the comparative ancient Near Eastern law, see Raymond Westbrook (ed.), *A History of Ancient Near Eastern Law* (2 vols.; Leiden: E.J. Brill, 2003). For the methodology of comparison, see Meir Malul, *The Comparative Method in Ancient Near Eastern and Biblical Legal Studies* (Neukirchen–Vluyn: Neukirchener Verlag, 1990); Samuel Jackson, *A Comparison of Ancient Near Eastern Law Collections Prior to the First Millennium BC* (Gorgias Dissertation Series, 35; Piscataway, NJ: Gorgias Press, 2008). For a survey of Mesopotamian slavery, see Muhammad A. Dandamaev, *Slavery in Babylonia from Nabopolassar to Alexander the Great (626–331 B.C.)* (DeKalb, IL: University of Northern Illinois Press, 1984). For slavery in Second Temple and mishnaic literature, see Flesher, *Oxen, Women, or Citizens?*, and Hezser, *Jewish Slavery in Antiquity*.

4. Alan Dershowitz, *The Genesis of Justice: Ten Stories of Biblical Injustice that Led to the Ten Commandments and Modern Law* (New York: Warner Books, 2000), pp. 253 and 259 n. 11. In contrast, the distinguished Sumerologist, Samuel N. Kramer (*History Begins at Sumer*, p. 110), says: 'The Sumerian sages believed and taught the doctrine that man's misfortunes are the result of his sins and misdeeds, and that no man is without guilt'.

If Dershowitz's statement can be relegated to an off-hand or gratuitous remark of a non-historian, then this is not so with the following statements by Rodney Stark:

> There is no record that any philosopher in Sumer Babylon, or Assyria ever protested against slavery, 'nor is there any expression of the mildest sympathy for the victims of this system. Slavery was simply taken for granted.' Indeed the Code of Hammurabi (c. 1750 B.C.) prescribed death for anyone who helped a slave escape.[5]

But what is the source for such a sweeping generalization? Stark's footnotes show very little acquaintance with the literature of Mesopotamia, and no specific edition of the *CH* is cited. Stark cites no specific law number in the *CH*. His quote actually incorporates another quote found in Isaac Mendelsohn's *Slavery in the Ancient Near East*. Both Epsztein and David B. Davis repeat the very same quote from Mendelsohn.[6]

Orlando Patterson not only quotes Mendelsohn, but completely misrepresents him in a chapter subtitled, 'Why Freedom Failed in the Non-Western World'.[7] In particular, Patterson appeals to Mendelsohn to characterize Mesopotamian attitudes toward freedom as follows:

> So the desire for freedom existed. However, the evidence is equally conclusive that personal freedom never became a value of any importance in any of these societies. It is remarkable that, although the laws made provision for manumission, there is 'a conspicuous absence of manumission documents' in the hundreds of business records which have survived from ancient and neo-Babylonian times.[8]

But Mendelsohn said no such thing. Mendelsohn was discussing Law 117 of the *CH*, which pertained to wives and children who were handed over to creditors as pledges. That law specified that they had to be freed after three years of service.[9] Mendelsohn then speculates about whether this specific law was applied in reality:

> Whether this law was ever enforced in life, however, is highly doubtful. We have numerous documents from Ancient and Neo-Babylonia attesting to the widespread practice of selling or handing over wives and children to creditors, but documents of their release after the three-year term of servitude are conspicuous by their absence.[10]

---

5. Stark, *For the Glory of God*, p. 325, citing Mendelsohn, *Slavery in the Ancient Near East*, p. 123.
6. Epsztein, *Social Justice*, p. 119; Davis, *Slavery in Western Culture*, p. 62.
7. Orlando Patterson, *Freedom in the Making of Western Culture* (New York: Basic Books, 1991), p. 35.
8. Patterson, *Freedom*, p. 35, citing Mendelsohn, *Slavery in the Ancient Near East*, p. 75.
9. Mendelsohn, *Slavery in the Ancient Near East*, p. 74.
10. Mendelsohn, *Slavery in the Ancient Near East*, p. 75.

So, Patterson transformed the absence of documents relating to 'the three-year term of servitude' into 'a conspicuous absence of manumission documents' of any type and in every period ('Ancient and neo-Babylonian times') of Babylonian history. Yet, any reading of that section of Mendelsohn's book finds many examples of other types of manumission documents in Mesopotamia.

This sort of dependence on secondary sources is part of an endemic problem in scholarship because few scholars are able to read all the languages required to check the primary sources, and time or expertise cannot be obtained in every area of history. Yet, the fact remains that not checking the primary sources yields some of these flawed comparisons. In the case of Patterson, this supposed absence of manumission documents in Mesopotamia allows him to erase Mesopotamia from making any contribution, and to give greater credit to the Bible and Christianity.

The *CH* was a very important accomplishment in terms of both law and ethics.[11] It not only showed how dependent biblical law was on Mesopotamian precedents but it had many features extolled by biblical scholars when they appear in the Bible. The Prologue of the *CH* tells us:

> When the supreme Anu, King of the Anunnaki, and Bel, the master of Heaven and Earth, who decrees the fate of the land, assigned to Marduk, the firstborn son of Ea, God of righteousness, dominion over earthly man, and exalted him among the Igigi, they called Babylon by his illustrious name, made it great on earth, and founded an everlasting kingdom in it…then Anu and Bel called by name me, Hammurabi, the exalted prince, who feared God, to make justice shine forth in the land, to destroy the wicked and the evil-doers; so that the strong should not harm the weak; so that I should rule over the black-headed people like Shamash, and illuminate the land, to further the well-being of mankind.[12]

Thus, the *CH* clearly enunciates these principles for the laws:
(1) to make justice shine forth in the land,
(2) to destroy the wicked and the evil-doers;
(3) so that the strong should not harm the weak;
(4) so that I should rule over the black-headed people like Shamash, and illuminate the land,
(5) to further the well-being of humankind
(6) 'to protect widows and orphans' (Epilogue)

Preventing the strong from harming the weak is certainly recognition that oppression should not be tolerated. Protecting widows and orphans certainly qualifies as an expression of sympathy for those who suffer misfortunes not of their own making.

---

11. See Wright, *God's Law*.
12. My adapted translation of the cuneiform text in Martha T. Roth, *Law Collections from Mesopotamia* (Atlanta: Scholars Press, 2nd edn, 1997), pp. 76 and 133.

Prior to Hammurabi, there existed a law code attributed to Lipit-Ishtar, a king who reigned at Isin (southern Mesopotamia) around 1930 BCE. In the Prologue to the law code, Lipit-Ishtar states:

> I liberated the sons and daughters of the city of Nippur, the sons and daughters of the city of Ur, the sons and daughters of the city of Isin, the sons and daughters of the lands of Sumer and Akkad who were subjugated [by the yoke(?)] and I restored order.[13]

These ideas of liberation are premised on sympathy for the enslaved. If one were to follow the 'liberatory trajectory' model, then one could just as well argue that modern abolitionism was simply the culmination of a trajectory that had started with Lipit-Ishtar.

The Code of Lipit-Ishtar also illustrates that historians of slavery are often not familiar with internal developments in the field of biblical and Near Eastern Studies. For example, Mendelsohn's work, though still useful, is outdated in many crucial respects. Important law codes and fragments of law codes have been discovered or published in more accessible editions since the time of Mendelsohn.[14] For example, the Laws of Eshnunna were discovered in 1948, and Mendelsohn was unable to incorporate them by the time his book was published in 1949. Likewise, the Hittite law codes now have much better editions. Thus, Stark and Davis continue to cite an outdated source because they are not reading the latest reviews or journals in biblical studies.

Stark certainly uncritically accepts the claim that no one raised a protest or expressed sympathy with the plight of those caught in slavery. The historical record shows Stark to be wrong. In a work titled *Advice to a Prince*, a Mesopotamian sage warns the king:

> If he mobilized the whole of Sippar, Nippur, and Babylon and imposed forced labour on the people exacting from them a corvée at the herald's proclamation Marduk, the sage of the gods, the prince, the counselor, will turn his land over to his enemy so that the troops of his land will do forced labour for his enemy, for Anu, Enlil, and Ea, the great gods who dwell in heaven and earth, in their assembly affirmed the freedom of those people from such obligations.[15]

So, we see that the king is not supposed to be some arbitrary ruler that is allowed to enslave his people. The gods have affirmed the freedom of the people, and they are there to enforce it with the harshest penalties for despotic rulers. This is no different than the curses imposed for bad behavior in Deuteronomy 28.

---

13. Roth, *Law Collections*, p. 25.
14. For other brief criticisms of Mendelsohn's work, see Flesher, *Oxen, Women, or Citizens?*, p. 174.
15. W.G. Lambert, *Babylonian Wisdom Literature* (Oxford: Clarendon Press, 1960), p. 113.

Wilfred G. Lambert, the editor of many of these advisory (wisdom) Mesopotamian texts, comments:

> The impression is sometimes gained that ancient Mesopotamian kings were typical oriental despots following their own whims and unchallenged within their domains. In contrast...the Hebrew prophets fearlessly denounced their kings for any abuse of power. The *Advice* serves as a salutary corrective to this exaggerated contrast.[16]

In other words, Stark falls into a very basic chauvinistic trap, which assumes that polytheistic societies are somehow less humane in not recognizing oppression, even if they did not outlaw it any more than the Bible did.

While Stark asserts that no protests are recorded in ancient Mesopotamia, the fact is that some Mesopotamian laws allowed slaves to protest about their condition through legal means. For example, in a series of directives about fugitive slaves being harbored by persons other than the owner, Law 14 of the Code of Lipit-Ishtar states: 'If a man's slave contests his slave status against his master, and it is proven that his master has been compensated for his slavery two-fold, that slave shall be freed'.[17] One could easily cite this law as both unique and 'advanced' because we had not witnessed such rights given to slaves anywhere else before.

Egypt and Divine Care for Humanity

Egypt provides one of the earliest instances of a developed civilization that lasted far longer than any single European civilization. But, judging by the works of Christian historians and apologists, this civilization's moral standards were inferior to those of the Bible. In *For the Glory of God*, Stark applauds the values of the Judeo-Christian tradition and attempts to combat any notion that non-biblical religions were nearly as ethical. In the case of Egypt, Stark tells us: 'The many Gods of Egypt were not thought to concern themselves with how humans treated one another'.[18]

Stark's claim is patently false if one studies Egyptian literature even at a most superficial level. Consider *The Book of the Dead*, which refers to a compilation of materials that took final form in the Twenty-Sixth Dynasty of Egypt (685–525 BCE). Its origins can, though, be traced to the beginning of the New Kingdom and before, thus making it older than any book of the Bible. As a guidebook for the journey into the afterlife, *The Book of the Dead* is one of the first texts in history to provide an extensive list of specific actions that were valued by the gods. As preparation for this journey, a person is supposed to list actions the gods would find acceptable:

16. Lambert, *Babylonian Wisdom Literature*, p. 110.
17. Roth, *Law Collections*, pp. 29-30.
18. Stark, *For the Glory of God*, p. 326, caption to illustration on Egyptian slaves.

> I have acted rightly in Egypt.
> I have not cursed a god...
> I have done what people speak of,
> What the gods are pleased with...
> I have given bread to the hungry,
> water to the thirsty,
> clothes to the naked,
> a ferryboat to the boatless.
> I have given divine offerings to the gods.[19]

How does this not show concern by Egyptian gods for how human beings treated one another? Indeed, many of these specific actions are very similar to those repeated by Jesus hundreds of years later in a similar judgment scene (Mt. 25.42-43).[20]

The fact that Egyptians also thought they were loved by the gods, and made in their image, is evidenced by the famous *Hymn to the Aten*, which says: 'Your rays are on your son, your beloved... You love him, you make him like Aten... You build him in your image like Aten.'[21] This hymn probably was written at the time of the king Akhenaten (c. 1375 BCE), perhaps the first to introduce any sort of monotheism into world history.[22]

Similarly, the Egyptian work titled *The Instructions of Amenemope* bears valued directives that long antedate similar or identical ones in the Bible:

> Beware of robbing a wretch
> Of attacking a cripple
> Don't stretch out your hand to touch an old man,
> nor [open your mouth] to an elder.
> Don't let yourself be sent on a mischievous errand.
> Nor be friends with him who does it.
> Don't raise an outcry against one who attacks you.
> Nor answer him yourself.[23]

Many biblical scholars realize that Prov. 22.20, which refers to the 'thirty sayings', is probably a reference to the thirty chapters that compose *Amenemope*. Indeed, some of these instructions are so similar to what we find in Proverbs that the New American Bible (a Catholic version) inserts 'Amenemope' into

---

19. Miriam Lichtheim, *Ancient Egyptian Literature* (3 vols.; Berkeley: University of California Press, 1976), II, p. 128.

20. For other aspects of Egyptian morality, see Pnina Galpaz-Feller, 'Private Lives and Public Censure: Adultery in Ancient Egypt and Biblical Israel', *Near Eastern Archaeology* 67 (2004), pp. 153-61.

21. Lichtheim, *Ancient Egyptian Literature*, II, p. 93.

22. See Donald B. Redford, *Akhenaten: The Heretic King* (Princeton, NJ: Princeton University Press, 1984), p. 158; Cyril Aldred, *Akhenaten: King of Egypt* (London: Thames & Hudson, 1988), pp. 113 and 240.

23. Lichtheim, *Ancient Egyptian Literature*, II, p. 150.

the biblical text in Prov. 22.19 ('I make known to you the words of Amen-em-ope').

The dependence of Proverbs on *Amenemope* is now recognized routinely in modern biblical studies. Indeed, by 1951, John A. Wilson, the distinguished Egyptologist, for example, remarked: '[W]e believe that there is a direct connection between these two pieces of wisdom literature, and that Amen-em-Opet was the ancestor text. The secondary nature of the Hebrew seems established. Both texts may be as late as the seventh or sixth century B.C.'[24]

However, it is important to realize that the actual manuscripts of Amenemope are dated hundreds of years before any existing biblical manuscripts. Miriam Lichtheim remarks that 'the composition of this work is now usually assigned to the Ramesside period' (c. fourteenth–eleventh centuries BCE).[25] In any case, hundreds of years before any actual manuscripts of the Bible were produced, manuscripts of *Amenemope* already presented many concepts extolled in the Bible. Some of them are similar to what is placed in the mouth of Jesus (e.g., not resisting an enemy in Mt. 5.39).

Hittites and Lex talionis

The Hittites were part of a civilization that flourished in the late half of the second millennium BCE. Although Hittite is an Indo-European language, the population consisted of a variety of ethnic elements. Their capital was at Hattusa in what is now modern Turkey.[26] At the height of their empire, they had very active relations with Egypt and other neighboring cultures. Their trading networks brought materials from as far away as Afghanistan.

Following a common procedure of comparing the Christian 'best' with the pagan 'worst', some biblical scholars use one example from Mesopotamia to characterize all non-biblical civilizations, and then ignore an item from the Hittites that would offer a counterexample. Consider the statement of Paul Copan, an ardent foe of the New Atheists: 'While Israel was commanded to offer safe harbor for foreign runaway slaves (Deut. 23.15-16), Hammurabi demanded the death penalty to those helping runaway slaves (sect. 16)'.[27]

24. John A. Wilson, *The Culture of Ancient Egypt* (Chicago: University of Chicago Press, 1951), p. 303 n. 45.
25. For the dating, see Lichtheim, *Ancient Egyptian Literature*, II, p. 147.
26. For general treatments of the Hittites, see Billie Jean Collins, *The Hittites and their World* (Atlanta: Society of Biblical Literature, 2007); Trevor Bryce, *Life and Society in the Hittite World* (New York: Oxford University Press, 2002) and *The Kingdom of the Hittites* (New York: Oxford University Press, 1998); J.G. Macqueen, *The Hittites and their Contemporaries in Asia Minor* (London: Thames & Hudson, 1986).
27. Paul Copan, 'Are Old Testament Laws Evil?', in W. L. Craig and Chad Meister (eds.), *God Is Good: Why Believing in God Is Reasonable and Responsible* (Downers Grove, IL: IVP Books, 2009), p. 140.

Yet, it is not clear whether the penalty in the *CH* was merely for 'helping' runaway slaves, or for stealing a slave.

But even if it were true that Hammurabi called for the death penalty for anyone 'helping' a slave to escape, we can find a non-lethal approach in Hittite Law 24, which says: 'If a male or female slave runs away, he/she at whose hearth his/her owner finds him/her shall pay one month's wages; 12 shekels of silver for a man, 6 shekels of silver for a woman'.[28] So, why aren't the Hittite laws characterized as a humanizing improvement? In Law 24, a slave runs away, and the person harboring the slave only pays a fine. The existence of such fines even led Copan to retreat from his earlier comparisons on this issue.[29]

In fact, Hittite law systematically replaced death penalties with fines for many offenses. Thus, Law 166 demanded the death penalty for appropriating another man's farmland. But Law 167 says, 'But now they shall substitute one sheep for the man'.[30] In other words, the very symbol of the Christian substitutionary atonement had a preceding parallel in Hittite law.

So, the imposition of *Lex talionis* (eye-for-an-eye principle) in Pentateuchal laws, which are usually dated after the Hittite laws, even by Copan, should be seen as a regression. Yet, Copan also says that these biblical laws 'are not taken literally. None of the examples illustrating "an eye for an eye" calls for bodily mutilation, but rather just (monetary) compensation.'[31] This is nothing more than mere assertion. No biblical text is offered to support this allegation. In fact, Jesus seems to interpret this law very literally in Mt. 5.38-39: 'You have heard that it was said, "An eye for an eye and a tooth for a tooth". But I say to you, Do not resist one who is evil. But if any one strikes you on the right cheek, turn to him the other also.' Or should we suppose that the clause, 'if anyone strikes you on the right cheek', was actually a reference to a monetary infraction here?

---

28. Harry A. Hoffner, *The Laws of the Hittites: A Critical Edition* (Leiden: E.J. Brill, 1997), p. 33.

29. Compare Copan's essay 'Is Yahweh a Moral Monster? The New Atheists and the Old Testament' (online: www.epsociety.org/library/ articles.asp?pid=45), in which he did not mention these fines, with his 'Are Old Testament Laws Evil?' (p. 140), which does mention such fines in cuneiform law. (Copan's website essay is ten pages long + footnotes, and so I provide the link for each page where relevant.)

30. Hoffner, *The Laws of the Hittites*, pp. 133-34. See also Samuel Greengus, 'Some Issues Relating to the Comparability of Laws and Coherence of the Legal Tradition', in Bernard M. Levinson (ed.), *Theory and Method in Biblical and Cuneiform Law: Revision, Interpolation, and Development* (Sheffield: Sheffield Academic Press, 1994; repr., Sheffield: Sheffield Phoenix Press, 2006), pp. 65-72.

31. Copan, 'Is Yahweh a Moral Monster?' (online: www.epsociety.org/library/ articles.asp?pid=45&ap=4). In a later essay ('Are Old Testament Laws Evil?', p. 144), Copan reasserts his earlier claim but leaves unexplained why the clause, 'if anyone strikes you on the right cheek', could not be taken literally by Jesus.

Clearly, Copan must engage in special pleading to convince us that the Bible represents an advancement in *Lex talionis*. If one says that *Lex talionis* is an advancement, then this already had a precedent in the *CH* (Law 196). If one says replacing *Lex talionis* with fines or sacrifices was an advancement, then the Hittites did this already. Pre-Hammurabi codes also can be found without the *Lex talionis* principle (e.g., Laws 18-19 of the *Laws of Ur Nammu*, c. 2100 BCE).

We also find a sympathy for slaves among the Hittites. When Murshili, king of the Hittites, confronted a plague that afflicted his country, that king prayed to the gods as follows: 'If anything becomes too burdensome for a slave, he makes a plea to his master. His master hears him and pities him. Whatever is too burdensome for him [the slave], he [the master] sets right for him again'.[32] This certainly refutes Stark's claim that in the ancient Near East there is not 'any expression of the mildest sympathy for the victims of this system'.

The concern for justice for slave men and women also is clearly expressed in this Hittite instruction:

> The good lawsuit should not be defeated, and the bad lawsuit should not win. Do what is just. When you return to any town, call to all the people of the town. Whoever has a lawsuit, decide it for him and satisfy him. If the slave of a man, or the slave-woman of a man, or a solitary woman has a suit, decide it for them and satisfy them.[33]

In other words, there should be justice for all regardless of their status as free or slave. Even if Hittite society should not be confused with any sort of modern democracy, slaves did have the right to bring lawsuits, and judges were not supposed to show favoritism.

---

32. My translation of the Hittite text in René Lebrun, *Hymnes and prières hittites* (Louvain-la-Neuve: Centre d'Histoire des Religions, 1980), p. 208, lines 23-25: 'na-aš-ma ma-a-an A-NA ÌR^{ti} ku-e-da-ni-ik-ki ku-it-ki na-ak-ki-ya-aḫ-ḫa-an/nu-za A-NA EN-ŠU ar-ku-wa-ar i-ya-az-zi na-an EN-ŠU iš-ta-ma-aš-zi nu-uš-ši/ku-it na-ak-ki-ya-aḫ-ḫa-an na-at-ši SIG$_5$-aḫ-zi na-aš-ma ma-a-an A-NA ÌR^{ti} ku-e-da-ni-ik-ki'. An English translation of the prayer by Albrecht Goetze (*ANET*, p. 395) uses 'servant' for ÌR and 'lord' for 'EN', where I used 'slave' and 'master', respectively.

33. My translation of the Hittite text in Einar von Schuler, *Hethitische Dienstanweisungen für höhere Hof- und Staatsbeamte: Ein Beitrag zum antiken Recht Kleinasiens* (Graz: Archiv für Orientforschung, 1957), p. 48, lines 27-32: 'DI-NAM ša-ra-az-zi kat-te-ra-aḫ-ḫi li-e kat-te-ir-ra/ša-ra-az-ya-ḫi lie-e ku-it ḫa-an-da-an a-pa-a-at i-iš-ša/ku-e-da-ni-ma-aš-ša-an URU-ri EGIR-pa a-ar-ti nu LU^{MEŠ} URU^{LIM}/ḫu-ma-an-du-uš pa-ra-a ḫal-za-a-i nu ku-e-da-ni DI-NAM e-eš-zi/na-at-ši ḫa-an-ni na-an-kań aš-nu-ut ÌR LÚ GEME LÚ wa-an-nu-mi-ya-aš/SAL-ni ma-a-an DI-NU-ŠU e-eš-zi nu-uš-ma-ša-at ḫa-an-ni na-aš-kán aš-nu-ut'. Bryce (*Life and Society*, pp. 38-39) also provides an English translation based on that of Oliver R. Gurney (*The Hittites* [London: Penguin Books, 1990], p. 76), but Gurney's English translation does not follow the order of the Hittite text. My slashes separate lines in the original Hittite text.

Greece and the Bonds of Freedom

There is virtually nothing in early Christian ethics that was not first discussed by Greek philosophers and writers. In fact, Hans Dieter Betz, a biblical scholar who exalts Paul's views on freedom, says: 'The social criticism of the institution of slavery seems to have begun with the Sophists'.[34] The Sophists, an early Greek philosophical school, flourished in the fifth and fourth centuries BCE. Indeed, many liberatory and egalitarian ideas credited to Christianity were first found among the Greeks.

As with many other items from the ancient world, some of the ideas served the cause of abolition and some did not. One problem is that most apologists of biblical ethics either forget or overlook all of the Greek ideas that they would extol when voiced by Christian writers. Another problem is that apologists engage in a sort of detrimental representativism insofar as they assume that certain Greek laws were representative or are the only ones that existed. Consider Solon, one of the earliest Greek legal reformers. Whereas, biblical scholars applaud the fact that biblical law set limits on debt slavery for Hebrews, Solon (638–558 BCE) had gone further. According to Plutarch, debt slavery was completely outlawed by Solon the Athenian: 'The first of his public measures was an enactment that existing debts should be remitted, and that in future no one should lend money on the person of a borrower'.[35] Others thought Solon had simply reduced the interest rates on debts. In either case, Solon's actions are explicitly called 'an act of humanity' (φιλανθρώπευμα).

Athenian law also had other provisions that were considered humanitarian advances when found in the Bible. For example, biblical scholars frequently speak of how integrating the sojourner was a great humanitarian advance in ancient Israel. The fact is that similar laws can be found in the Athenian Constitutions. Consider this passage from Xenophon's description:

> In Sparta my slave will fear you; but if your slave fears me, there will be the chance that he will give over his money so as to not have to worry anymore. For this reason we have set up equality between slaves and free men [διὰ τοῦτ' οὖν ἰσηγορίαν καὶ τοῖς δούλοις πρὸς τοὺς ἐλευθέρους], and between metics and citizens. The city needs metics in view of the many different trades and fleet. Accordingly, then, we have reasonably set up a similar equality also for the metics.[36]

---

34. Hans Dieter Betz, *Galatians* (Philadelphia: Fortress Press, 1979), p. 193.

35. *Plutarch's Lives, Solon* 15.4 (Perrin, LCL): τοῦτο γὰρ ἐποιήσατο πρῶτον πολίτευμα γράψας τὰ μὲν ὑπάρχοντα τῶν χρεῶν ἀνεῖσθαι πρὸς δὲ τὰ λοιπὸν ἐπὶ τοῖς σώμασι μηδένα δανείζειν.

36. Xenophon, *The Polity of the Athenians* 1.11-12 (Marchant and Bowersock, LCL). Classicists still use 'Xenophon' for convenience, even though it was probably written by

3. Near Eastern Ethics and Slavery

This passage shows that we cannot treat slavery in Greece as monolithic. Different areas could differ in their treatment of slaves. Metics (μέτοικοι), who are similar to sojourners in Israel, provided services, and inducements were a way to attract them. Unlike Hebrew laws, which expected sojourners to conform to Hebrew religion and so took away freedom of religion, no such conformity was required in the Athenian Constitutions.

One cannot do justice to the study of slave law unless considering the work of Plato. The importance of Plato in western thought is immense, and he had many concepts on slavery that could be called advances relative to biblical law. Yet, Plato's opposition to enslaving fellow Greeks is dismissed by Stark as follows:

> Plato did oppose enslavement of his fellow 'Hellenes' (Greeks) but assigned 'barbarian' (foreign) slaves a vital role in his ideal Republic—they would perform all of the productive labor. In fact, the rules Plato laid out concerning the proper treatment of slaves were unusually brutal—'No American slave code was so severe'... While Plato believed that slaves should be sternly disciplined, he believed that, to prevent needless unrest, they generally should not be subject to excessive cruelty.[37]

The first thing we note is that Plato's willingness to enslave foreigners, but not fellow Hellenes, is precisely parallel to what we find in Hebrew law (Lev. 25.39-46).[38]

Second, Stark gives no specific examples of how Plato's treatment of slaves was more severe than anything found in any 'American slave code'. In fact, Stark's statement depends solely on a quotation from Davis's *The Problem of Slavery in Western Culture*:

> Plato would even deny them friendly intimacy with the master class, and would give any free person the right to judge and punish a slave for certain crimes, or to take summary vengeance against insult. No American slave code was so severe.[39]

---

someone else sometimes called pseudo-Xenophon or 'the Old Oligarch', on which see *Xenophon* (Marchant and Bowersock, LCL), pp. 461-62.

  37. Stark, *For the Glory of God*, p. 326. Stark (*The Victory of Reason*, p. 26) cites only one source (Robert Schlaifer, 'Greek Theories of Slavery from Homer to Aristotle', *Harvard Studies in Classical Philology* 47 [1936], pp. 165-204) for his pronouncement that Plato's laws were 'unusually brutal'. But Schlaifer ('Greek Theories', p. 191) explicitly says that, for Plato, 'slaves are not to be treated cruelly or flippantly'. For an extensive discussion of the parallels between Plato's *Laws* and biblical laws, see Philippe Wajdenbaum, *Argonauts of the Desert: Structural Analysis of the Hebrew Bible* (Sheffield: Equinox, 2011).

  38. For Plato's discussion of the injustice of enslaving fellow Hellenes, see *Republic* 5.469b-c (Shorey, LCL).

  39. Davis, *Slavery in Western Culture*, p. 66.

Davis cites nine specific passages from Plato's *Laws* to support his statements.[40] Yet, none of those laws can be said to surpass anything we can find in American laws, and some laws are much better than those we find in American law codes.

Consider Davis's claims that Plato's *Laws* 'deny them [slaves] friendly intimacy with the master class'. This is not quite what Plato says: 'There should be no jesting [μὴ προσπαίζοντας] with servants, either male or female, for by a course of excessively foolish indulgence in their treatment of their slaves, masters often make life harder both for themselves, as rulers, and for their slaves as subject to rule'.[41]

Plato uses a form of the Greek word *prospaizō* (προσπαίζω), translated as 'jesting' in the passage above. Yet, the same Greek word is used in Sir. 8.4: 'Do not jest with an ill-bred person [μὴ πρόσπαιζε ἀπαδεύτῳ], lest your ancestors be disgraced'. This is quite parallel to Plato's prohibition, and the motives are much better in Plato than in Sirach, which is considered a fully canonical biblical book for Catholic Christians. Sirach issues the prohibition solely for the interests of the upper class, while Plato includes the well-being of the slaves as a motive. Plato's *Laws* (7.794B) actually do allow for some integration of slaves insofar as all children, free or slave, are to be educated together at least up to the age of six.[42] Insofar as participation of slaves in religious activities, Walter Burkert observes: 'Occasionally they are excluded from cults, but at *Choes* they are expressly invited to join the meal, and at *Kronia* they become the superiors'.[43] *Choes* and *Kronia* are names of festivals, and the latter, held in honor of the god Kronos (Saturn), involved trading places between the superior and inferior members of society.[44] Similarly,

---

40. Davis, *Slavery in Western Culture*, p. 66. These passages are Plato, *Laws*: 6.776e, 6.777d, 6.778a; 9.865, 9.868, 9.872, 9.882, 11.914 and 11.936 (Bury, LCL). Davis did not always provide the standard lettered subdivisions (a,b,c, d, or e) when quoting Plato's *Laws*.

41. Plato, *Laws* 6.778a (Bury, LCL): μὴ προσπαίζοντας μηδαμῇ μηδαμῶς οἰκέταις μήτ' οὖν δηλείαις μήτε ἄρρεσιν. ἃ δὴ πρὸς δούλους φιλοῦσι πολλοὶ σφόδρα ἀνοήτως θρύπτοντες χαλεπώτερον ἀπεργάζεσθαι τὸν βίον ἐκείνοις τε ἄρχεσθαι καὶ ἑαυτοῖς ἄρχειν.

42. See further Glenn R. Morrow, *Plato's Laws of Slavery in its Relation to Greek Law* (repr., New York: Arno Press, 1976 [1939]), p. 44.

43. Walter Burkert, *Greek Religion* (trans. John Raffan; Cambridge, MA: Harvard University Press, 1985), p. 259. See also Jon D. Mikalson, *Ancient Greek Religion* (Malden, MA: Blackwell, 2005), pp. 156-57. For a more general treatment of slaves and religion, see Franz Bömer, *Untersuchungen über die Religion der Sklaven in Griechenland und Rom* (4 vols.; Wiesbaden: Akademie der Wissenschaften und Literatur, 1958–63).

44. See Burkert, *Greek Religion*, p. 231.

Ramsay MacMullen specifically notes the relatively greater religious freedom enjoyed by pagan slaves compared to slaves under Christianity in late antiquity.[45] Moreover, any sort of friendliness between slaves and masters in America did not necessarily improve treatment of slaves. Records of Moravian brethren from the Chesapeake valley in the 1770s give us glimpse into how masters alternated friendship with abuse: 'The main fault with our Brethren is that they are always with the Negroes in jokes and fun, and the next day they beat them like dogs'.[46]

Consider also Davis's claim that Plato gives any free person the right to judge and punish a slave for certain crimes or to take summary vengeance for certain insults. The fact is that Plato does not quite do that:

> If it be a slave [δοῦλος] that strikes the free man [ἐλεύθερον]—stranger or citizen—the bystander shall help, failing which he shall pay the penalty fixed according to his assessment; and the bystanders together with the person assaulted shall bind the slave, and hand him over to the injured person and he shall take charge of him and bind him in fetters and give him as many stripes with the scourge as he pleases, provided that he does not spoil his value to his master, to whose ownership he shall hand him over according to law. The law stands thus: Whosoever, being a slave beats a free man without order of the magistrates,—him his owner shall take over in bonds from the person assaulted, and he shall not loose him until the slave have convinced the person assaulted that he deserves to live loosed from bonds.[47]

Thus, the punishment is not unlimited. Punishment cannot jeopardize the value of the slave to the master.

More importantly, the right of any free citizen to punish a slave is not representative of all Greek law. As Morrow notes, 'under the law of Alexandria and Athens such punishment is inflicted by and under the direction of the magistrates'.[48] Alexandrian law also allowed the master to pay a fine instead of having his slave beaten.[49] Similarly, the Sophist thinker, Antiphon (fifth century BCE), says that 'not even slaves who have murdered their masters are

---

45. Ramsay MacMullen, *Christianity and Paganism in the Fourth to Eighth Centuries* (New Haven: Yale University Press, 1997), p. 7.

46. Jon F. Sensbach, *A Separate Canaan: The Making of an Afro-Moravian World in North Carolina, 1763–1840* (Chapel Hill: University of North Carolina Press, 1998), pp. 94-95. See also Philip D. Morgan, *Slave Counterpoint: Black Culture in the Eighteenth Century Chesapeake and Lowcountry* (Chapel Hill: University of North Carolina Press, 1998), p. 432.

47. Plato, *Laws* 9.882a-b (Bury, LCL).

48. Morrow, *Plato's Law of Slavery*, p. 47.

49. A.S. Hunt and C.C. Edgar, *Select Papyri* (LCL; 5 vols.; Cambridge, MA: Harvard University Press, 1934), II, pp. 6-7, Document 202 (dated to the middle of the third century BCE).

allowed to be put to death by the dead man's relatives'.[50] Such slaves must be handed over to the authorities 'in accordance with your ancestral laws' (κατὰ νόμους ὑμετέρους πατρίους).[51]

Plato's *Laws* here related to physical assaults by slaves. American laws could be much worse for violations that did not involve any sort of physical assault by slaves. Many statutes in America severely punished slaves merely for any verbal or other types of 'insolence'. According to North Carolina law in 1852, insolence may be difficult to define, but it could include 'a look, the pointing of a finger, a refusal to step out of the way when a white person is seen to approach'.[52]

By 1819, Virginia prohibited 'abusive and provoking language' on the part of slaves. On the simple oath of the offended party, the slave could be given thirty lashes. In 1858 Tennessee adopted a similar law, but 'did not limit the number of lashes'.[53] According to Thomas Morris, 'Texas stipulated that a free white person could punish a slave by a "moderate whipping" if the slave used "insulting language or gestures toward a white person"'.[54] So, why does Stark not conclude that treatment of slaves was sometimes harsher in Christian countries than in Plato's non-Christian laws?

And if it was dehumanizing and cruel for Plato to allow summary vengeance on a slave, Judge John Belton O'Neall (1793–1863), of South Carolina, dehumanized a slave even more. O'Neall stated in the case known as State v. Maner (1834), that 'the criminal offense of assault and battery cannot at common law be committed on the person of a slave. For…generally, he is a mere chattel personal, and his right of personal protection belongs to his master, who can maintain an action of trespass for the battery of his slave.'[55] In fact, comparison with 'American law' was completely unfair because we do find even more extreme treatment of slaves in many Christian lands besides America.

Likewise, what Ben Witherington applauds about Col. 4.1 is similar to what we find in Plato:[56]

> And the right treatment of slaves [οἰκέτας] is to behave properly to them, and to do to them, if possible, even more justice than to those who are our equals; for he who naturally and genuinely reverences justice, and hates injustice, is discovered in his dealings with any class of men to whom he can easily be unjust. And he who in regard to the natures and actions of his slaves [δούλων]

---

50. Antiphon 5.48 as quoted in Morrow, *Plato's Law of Slavery*, p. 70.
51. Antiphon 5.48 as quoted in Morrow, *Plato's Law of Slavery*, p. 70.
52. Morris, *Southern Slavery*, p. 502 n. 27.
53. Morris, *Southern Slavery*, p. 297.
54. Morris, *Southern Slavery*, p. 297.
55. Morris, *Southern Slavery*, p. 198.
56. Witherington, 'Was Paul a Pro-Slavery Chauvinist?', p. 44.

is undefiled by impiety and injustice, will best sow the seeds of virtue in them; and this may be truly said of every master, and tyrant, and of every other having authority in relation to his inferiors.[57]

In another case, Plato treats the murder of a slave the same as the murder of a free citizen:

> And if a man kill a slave when he is doing no wrong, actuated by fear lest the slave should expose his own foul and evil deeds or for any other such reason, just as he would have been liable to a charge of murder for slaying a citizen [πολίτην], he shall be liable in the same way for the death of such a slave.[58]

Similarly, the involuntary manslaughter of a free man requires 'the same purifications as the man that has killed a slave'.[59]

Of course, biblical scholars usually pass over in silence any advances Plato made over earlier or other Greek laws. For example, there is evidence that Plato, in contrast to some earlier laws, allowed slaves to give testimony without torture.[60] While Athenian law allowed emancipation of slaves when they acted as informants concerning misappropriated treasure or the neglect of parents, Plato (*Laws* 9.881c) adds emancipation for assisting parents who are being attacked by their children. This is unparalleled in biblical law.[61]

While Plato had an enormous influence on Western philosophy, the Greek philosopher who is credited with the most influence on Western conceptions of slavery is Aristotle. Writers from Aquinas to Sepulveda cited him to support their arguments. In his book, *Aristotle and the American Indians* (1959), Lewis Hanke, in particular, has explored Aristotle's influence on the treatment of Indians in the Americas.[62] In truth, Aristotle was elaborating the ideas found in Plato. Aristotle is primarily known for teaching that nature has separated human beings into slave and master classes. As Aristotle phrased it in his *Politics* (1.2.7-8):

> The nature of the slave and his essential quality: one who is a human being belonging by nature not to himself but to another is by nature a slave [οὗτος φύσει δοῦλός ἐστιν], and a person is a human being belonging to another if

---

57. Plato, *Laws* 6.777d-e. Here, I prefer the translation found in Plato, *Laws* (trans. Benjamin Jowett; repr., Mineola, NY: Dover Publications, 2006 [1892]), p. 131. For the Greek, I depend on Plato, *Laws* (Bury, LCL).

58. Plato, *Laws* 9.872c (Bury, LCL).

59. Plato, *Laws* 9.865d (Bury, LCL): ἐὰν δέ τις ἐλεύθερον ἄκων ἀποκτείνῃ, τοὺς μὲν καθαρισμοὺς τοὺς αὐτοὺς καθαρθήτω τῷ τὸν δοῦλον ἀποκτείναντι.

60. Morrow, *Plato's Laws of Slavery*, p. 81.

61. See further Morrow, *Plato's Laws of Slavery*, pp. 95-96.

62. Lewis Hanke, *Aristotle and the American Indians: A Study in Race Prejudice in the Modern World* (Bloomington: Indiana University Press, 1959); see also Brian Tierney, *The Idea of Natural Rights: Studies on Natural Rights, Natural Law and Church Law 1150–1625* (Atlanta: Scholars Press, 1997), pp. 255-86.

being a man he is an article of property, and an article of property is an instrument for action separable from its owner... Authority and subordination are conditions not only inevitable but also expedient; in some cases things are marked out from the moment of birth to rule or to be ruled.[63]

Aristotle's rationale was that just like the body has a hierarchy of members, then so does society. Just as the soul governs the body, the wise should govern the less wise. Men should rule women because 'the male is by nature superior [κρεῖττον] and the female inferior [χεῖρον]'.[64]

As elitist and chauvinistic as these ideas might seem, they are no worse than what we find in the Bible. The idea of the wiser leading the less wise is also echoed in Prov. 11.29: 'He who troubles his household will inherit wind, and the fool will be servant to the wise'. The idea that women should be ruled by men and that they are weaker by nature is echoed in Gen. 3.16 and also 1 Pet. 3.7, which says: 'Likewise you husbands, live considerately with your wives, bestowing honor on the woman as the weaker sex'. Aristotle's analogy between the body and social hierarchies is echoed in 1 Cor. 12.12-31 and Eph. 5.23.

What is not usually publicized is that Aristotle also had ideas of equality that are applauded by scholars such as Richard Horsley and Ben Witherington when found in biblical texts. For example, in his *Eudemian Ethics*, Aristotle speaks of how friendship differs from other types of relationships.

> The friendship of man and wife is one of utility, a partnership; that of father and son is the same as that between god and man and between benefactor and beneficiary, and generally between natural ruler and natural subject. That between brothers is principally the friendship of comrades, as being on a footing of equality. 'For never did he make me out a bastard/But the same Zeus, my lord, was called the sire/Of both...' for these are the words of men seeking equality. Hence, in the household are first found the origins and springs of friendship, of political organization and of justice.[65]

The latter portion in quotes is part of a poem that Aristotle quotes from Sophocles for support, the ellipsis indicating that the original ending may be lost. However, Philo of Alexandria may preserve the lost ending in *Every Good Man Is Free*: 'God and no mortal is my sovereign' (θεὸς ἐμὸς ἄρχων, θνητὸς οὐδείς).[66] Philo understands that serving God can entail serving a human intermediary of God, something that, as we shall see, biblical scholars often overlook.

---

63. Aristotle, *Politics* 1.2.7-8 (Rackham, LCL).
64. Aristotle, *Politics* 1.2.12 (Rackham, LCL).
65. Aristotle, *Eudemian Ethics* 7.10.8-9 (Rackham, LCL).
66. Philo, *Every Good Man Is Free* 19 (Colson, LCL).

A final powerful Greek idea to consider is one associated with Stoicism, as represented by Epictetus and Seneca, among others.[67] According to the Stoics, there is an inward and outer person. While the outer person may be enslaved, the inner person (or soul) could remain free. This idea was given clear and succinct expression by Philo of Alexandria, who said 'slavery then is applied in one sense to bodies, in another to souls'.[68] This powerful distinction was disseminated by Paul and later Christian thinkers. As Finley observes, '[a]part from the injection of original sin into the concept of natural slavery...neither the New Testament nor the Church Fathers added anything significant to the rhetoric of the Roman Stoics'.[69]

Rome: Home of Slavery and Freedom

The historiography of biblical slavery bears similarities and differences with the study of classical slavery, and especially as it pertains to Rome. As Niall McKeown astutely observes, there have been major divisions between classical scholars who see the slavery of Greece and Rome as mostly benign (e.g., the so-called Mainz School) and those who see it as predominantly brutal and repressive (e.g., Keith Bradley).[70] The exasperation of the debate is summarized by William Harris, who says: 'there is a long and tiresome tradition among classicists of softening the realities of the Roman slave system'.[71]

And despite the stigma that the Roman empire has for Christian scholars, there were a few developments that were later assimilated into the legal traditions of Christian countries. As I shall show later, many of the advances that Rodney Stark credits to Catholic law in Louisiana actually originated in Roman law. Yet, we never hear Stark praising Roman law for planting the seeds of abolition or greater liberality in at least some parts of the Americas.

First, manumission was greatly facilitated compared to other previous cultures. It is true that Greece also allowed manumission, and there are indications that slaves could hold property. But Rome seems to have made manumission more common. Davis comments, 'in Greece and Rome, where slaves suffered from the harshest exploitation, and where their status as a

---

67. Brad Inwood, *Ethics and Human Action in Early Stoicism* (New York: Oxford University Press, 1985). See also Glancy, *Slavery in Early Christianity*, pp. 30-34.
68. Philo, *Every Good Man Is Free* 17 (Colson, LCL): δουλεία τοίνυν ἡ μὲν ψυχῶν, ἡ δὲ σωμάτων λέγεται.
69. Finley, *Ancient Slavery and Modern Ideology*, p. 189.
70. McKeown, *The Invention of Ancient Slavery?*, pp. 30-51, 77-96. See Keith R. Bradley, *Slavery and Society at Rome* (Cambridge: Cambridge University Press, 1994).
71. William V. Harris, 'Demography, Geography, and the Sources of Roman Slaves', *Journal of Roman Studies* 84 (1994), pp. 67-68. See also Glancy, *Early Christian Slavery*, p. 81.

separate class was more sharply defined, manumissions were remarkably common'.[72] Accordingly, Combes, a biblical scholar, concludes that '[e]ven if the Church approved or even encouraged the manumission of slaves, it would have been doing nothing humane or radical for its time'.[73]

Second, Rome saw a clear development of a *peculium* tradition, which allowed the slave to accumulate property and funds, which could be used to purchase freedom. The *peculium* figured quite prominently in places such as Latin America and Louisiana, where the Roman tradition was continued by the Catholic Church. The *peculium* tradition in Louisiana helps to explain the larger proportion of free black people relative to Protestant slave-holding states. Nonetheless, Stark and others persist in crediting Christianity for something originating with the Romans.

Third, the granting of citizenship to freed slaves was a Roman distinctive. Orlando Patterson remarks,

> I know of no other case in the history of slavery, ancient or modern, which comes anywhere close to this situation. Other slave societies existed which manumitted an even higher proportion of slaves—those of the Tuareg of the Sahara and, in all likelihood, of the early eighteenth-century Spanish Caribbean—but in all of them the ex-slave population, separated from the native freeborn by race and ethnicity, came to form a separate, dependent, class approaching almost the status of a semicaste group with absolutely no pretensions to citizenship in the political community.[74]

Indeed, in Greece, emancipation was usually not followed by citizenship.[75] Thus, Roman citizenship accorded to former slaves represented an 'advance' that really had no equal in Hebrew law.[76] Patterson also notes that this manumission practice could change the demographics to the point that the majority of Roman citizens were the actual descendants of freedmen.[77]

Recall that Seneca voiced a version of the Golden Rule ('treat your inferiors as you would be treated by your betters...'), and specifically applied it to slaves.[78] Seneca reminds people that someday they may become slaves themselves and so should treat slaves well for that reason (cf. Deut. 15.12-15).[79] Seneca praises the virtue of treating slaves as family members, who

72. Davis, *Slavery in Western Culture*, p. 55.
73. Combes, *The Metaphor of Slavery*, p. 62.
74. Patterson, *Freedom*, p. 235.
75. Morrow, *Plato's Laws of Slavery*, p. 99.
76. For the status accorded freed slaves in Hebrew and Mishnaic law, see Flesher, *Oxen, Women or Citizens?*, pp. 21-23, 139-56.
77. Patterson, *Freedom*, pp. 236-37.
78. Seneca, *Epistles* 47.11-12 (Gummere, LCL).
79. Seneca, *Epistles* 47.10-11 (Gummere, LCL): 'Despise, then, if you dare, those to whose estate you may at any time descend'; Latin: 'contemne nunc eius fortunae hominem, in quam transire, dum contemnis, potes'.

might eat together with the master. About two thousand years before Martin Luther King, Seneca said, 'I propose to value them [slaves] according to their character and not according to their duties'.[80]

In all fairness, Augustine cites Seneca's dislike of the Sabbath, which may have been appreciated by slaves. Yet, Seneca's criticisms of the Sabbath are not unlike those of Jesus. Seneca, in particular, says that 'by failing to act in times of urgency they [Jews] often suffer loss' on the Sabbath.[81] Similarly, Jesus challenges the Pharisees by asking them if they ever act urgently to rescue an animal on the Sabbath (Lk. 14.5) in order to expose how differently they value acting urgently in the case of sick people. In any case, the point is not so much that Seneca should be seen as a modern egalitarian, but rather that his pronouncements on egalitarianism can be considered to be just as much of an 'advance' if we judge him by the standards apologists apply to biblical materials.

Overall, I am not arguing that Rome's 'advances' were always done for purely humanitarian reasons. Manumission, for example, could have functioned as an incentive to enhance the efficiency of the slave system. The large number of peoples controlled by the Romans certainly meant more people enslaved relative to previous empires. However, the point remains that 'advances' always represent a point of view, and we can find 'advances' (e.g., increased manumissions) in Rome that are exalted when found in Christianity. And, after all, no one probably enslaved more people than Christian empires did in terms of absolute numbers.

The Imago Dei *and Universal Inequality*

By universal equality, I refer to the idea that all human beings are equal in terms of rights. Christian apologists argue that this universalism has a basis in the biblical notion of the *imago Dei* (image of God), which posited that human beings were all created in the image of God.[82] Similarly, it is argued

80. Seneca, *Epistles* 47.15 (Gummere, LCL): 'non ministeriis illos aestimabo, sed moribus'. For a sympathetic Christian view of Seneca's views on slavery, see William Watts, 'Seneca on Slavery', *Downside Review* 90 (1972), pp. 183-95.

81. Augustine, *City of God* 6.11: 'et multa in tempore urgentia non aegendo laedantur'.

82. See, for example, Richard W. Wills, *Martin Luther King, Jr and the Image of God* (New York: Oxford University Press, 2009); David Cairns, *The Image of God in Man* (London: Collins, rev. edn, 1973); J. Richard Middleton, 'A Liberating Image: Interpreting the Imago Dei in Context', *Christian Scholar's Review* 24 (1994), pp. 8-25. For philological treatments in the context of the ancient Near East, see W. Randall Garr, *In his Own Image and Likeness: Humanity, Divinity, and Monotheism* (Leiden: E.J. Brill, 2003); Annette Schellenberg, 'Humankind as the "Image of God"', *Theologische Zeitschrift* 65 (2009), pp. 97-115. For an older treatment, see David J.A. Clines, 'The Image of God in Man', *Tyndale Bulletin* 19 (1968), pp. 53-103. See also Annette Schellenberg, *Der*

that all human beings stem from 'one blood' (Acts 17.26), and so human beings were all equally worthy.

But the common origin of all humanity is already mentioned in the *Enuma elish*, the famous Mesopotamian creation story, where a god named Kingu is sacrificed and humanity is created from his blood.[83] Thus, long before Christ, we already have the idea of a god being sacrificed to give life to humanity. It is also in the *Enuma elish* (1.16) that we have the idea of deities conceiving lesser gods in the same image. Thus, the god Anim made Ea in 'his likeness' (Akkadian: *tamšilašu*).[84]

While it is true that the Mesopotamian gods made human beings to serve them, Gen. 2.15 says: 'The LORD God took the man and put him in the garden of Eden to till it and keep it'. Adam was meant to be no less a slave in Yahweh's orchard/garden than human beings in the *Enuma elish*. Other animals and, lastly, woman, were created to help Adam in the service of Yahweh's orchard. They were ejected from that orchard when Yahweh realized that the human beings were trying to be like him. This power to be god-like was conferred by eating of the tree of life (and tree of knowledge).

We have already mentioned the idea of common divine descent in Aristotle and Philo of Alexandria. In addition, Epictetus (55–135 CE) proclaims that slaves and masters are all 'kinsmen...brethren by nature...the offspring of Zeus'.[85] Diogenes of Sinope (c. 404–323 BCE), when asked where he was from, said 'I am a citizen of the world [κοσμοπολίτης]'.[86] Although Aristotle, among others, urged a strict dichotomy between Greek and barbarian, Zeno wanted to treat Greeks and foreigners equally. Thus, if we used the 'trajectory' approach we could say that Christianity was merely a station in a long march to freedom that the Mesopotamians began.

Some later Christians even credited the Romans with initiating some of these concepts. In his *Institutiones divinae*, the Church Father Lactantius (early fourth century) discusses the meaning of equity (*aequitas*) and explains

---

Mensch, das Bild Gottes? Zum Gedanken einer Sonderstellung des Menschen im Alten Testament und in weiteren altorientalischen Quellen (Göttingen: Vandenhoeck & Ruprecht, in press).

83. *Enuma elish* 6.33: *ina da-me-šu ib-na-a a-me-lu-tú*, 'from his blood they formed humankind'. My translation from the cuneiform text in W.G. Lambert and Simon Parker, *Enuma elish, the Babylonian Creation Epic: The Cuneiform Text* (Oxford: Clarendon Press, 1969), p. 35. For an accessible English translation, see Alexander Heidel, *The Babylonian Genesis* (Chicago: University of Chicago Press, 1951).

84. Lambert and Parker, *Enuma elish*, p. 1.

85. Epictetus, *The Discourses* 1.13.4-5 (Oldfather, LCL): ὅτι συγγενῶν, ὅτι ἀδελφῶν φύσει ὅτι τοῦ Διὸς ἀπογόνων.

86. Diogenes Laertius 6.63 (Hicks, LCL). See also Eun Chun Park, *Either Jew or Gentile: Paul's Unfolding Theology of Inclusivity* (Louisville, KY: Westminster/John Knox Press, 2003), pp. 11-12.

that he refers to 'equalilty of oneself with others, which Cicero calls equability (*aequabilitas*). God who creates and inspires men wished them all to be fair, that is equal'.[87] Thus, Lactantius sees no problem in crediting Cicero with what some modern scholars seem to withhold from Greco-Roman culture.[88]

It is true that these Greco-Roman philosophers did not always live up to the ideals that they preached. However, such inconsistency poses no problem to Christian apologists who also admit that some popes owned slaves. Rodney Stark, for example, explains that these popes did not always practice what they preached, but 'laxity must not be confused with doctrine'.[89] Bad papal practice does not invalidate papal teachings against slavery. So, why can't we say the same for these pagan philosophers or rulers such as Plato or Hammurabi, whose stated doctrine was to not oppress the weak?

Reversing Comparative Ethics

Ironically, many modern apologists, who denigrate Near Eastern ethics, seem to overlook how positively those cultures were used by critics of slavery of the last five hundred years. In general, we see at least two ways in which Near Eastern cultures were used to show: (1) that even non-Christians perceived injustices Christians did not; (2) how much better Near Eastern cultures treated slaves compared with Americans.

Consider Morgan Godwyn (d. 1685), the Anglican missionary who argued that Africans were human beings and should be evangelized. Godwyn cited Greco-Roman authors to show that they did not need Christianity to teach them the equality of human beings. Insofar as how the Greeks and Romans saw their slaves, Godwyn said that '[r]eason prevailed so far with them as to confess them to be Men'.[90] Godwyn also quotes the Greek poet Philemon (c. 360–265 BCE), who said that 'No one is the less of a man for Servitude'.[91] By using the Greek word *anthropos* (ἄνθρωπος), Philemon clearly meant 'man' in the sense of human being rather than in the sense of a male.

Around 1612 a memorandum about slavery was prepared by an unknown author for King Philip II (1598–1621) of Portugal. It says, in part:

---

87. Lactantius, *Institutiones divinae* 15.14.15-16 (CSEL 19.446): 'se cum ceteris coaequandi quam Cicero aequabilitatem vocat'.

88. On the importance of Cicero in the development of the natural law tradition, see Richard A. Horsley, 'The Law of Nature in Philo and Cicero', *HTR* 71 (1978), pp. 35-59.

89. Stark, *For the Glory of God*, p. 330.

90. Morgan Godwyn, *The Negro's and Indian's Advocate Suing for their Admission into the Church* (repr., Whitefish, MT: Kessinger, 2003 [1680]), p. 31.

91. Godwyn, *The Negro's and Indian's Advocate*, p. 31.

60   *Slavery, Abolitionism, and the Ethics of Biblical Scholarship*

> In regard to the justification of slavery through condemnation for the crime committed, the laws of China do not condemn people to slavery for any crime...there they do not have the practice of men selling themselves, nor does it appear that fathers sell their children during periods of great famine, as happens sometimes in Cambodia, since general famines do not occur in China, the laws of China not permitting them, everyone there being given what he needs to maintain himself, without working. So that on occasions the people of that nation are shocked by the way the Portuguese make slaves against the law of their land, who are not their legitimate masters.[92]

Similarly, Frederick Douglass referred to Confucius, the paradigmatic Chinese philosopher, and remarked: 'He had the Golden Rule in substance five hundred years before the coming of Christ and has notions of justice that are not to be confused with any of our own "Cursed be Canaan" religion'.[93] These comparisons with China also are interesting insofar as most of the scholars who compare biblical ethics to those of other cultures hardly ever think of anything east of 'the Near East'.

David Walker, the famous African-American abolitionist and freeborn son of a slave (his father), used the Bible to show that Egyptian culture offered its slaves benefits not available to most American slaves. Walker, for example, noted how Pharaoh appointed Joseph, a slave, to be second in command in Gen. 41.44. Walker challenges white Christians in remarking: 'show me a coloured President, a Governor, a Legislator, a Senator, a Mayor or an Attorney at Bar'.[94]

Walker also points to Gen. 41.45, where Pharaoh gave Joseph an Egyptian wife. Walker comments, 'Compare the above with American institutions. Do they not institute laws to prohibit us from marrying among the whites?'[95] Walker adds that Pharaoh gave the Hebrews the land of Goshen, 'the most fertile land in all Egypt'.[96] Yet, Walker noted that black Americans could not own even a small plot of land, at least not without the fear that a white man

---

92. The document titled 'Proposta a sua Magestade sobre a escravaria das terras de Conquista de Portugal', may be found in translation in Robert E. Conrad, *Children of God's Fire: A Documentary History of Black Slavery in Brazil* (Princeton, NJ: Princeton University Press, 1983), pp. 11-15. Our quoted portion is from pp. 14-15. Robin Blackburn (*The Making of New World Slavery: From the Baroque to the Modern, 1492–1800* [London: Verso, 1997], p. 178) claims this document ends 'on an almost utopian note', but he does not question the authenticity of the Chinese practices described.

93. Douglass, 'Our Composite Nationality...7 December 1869', in Blassingame, *The Frederick Douglass Papers*, IV, p. 249.

94. David Walker, *David Walker's Appeal to the Coloured Citizens of the World but in Particular and very Expressly, to Those in the United States of America* (repr., Baltimore: Black Classic Press, 1993 [1830]), p. 28.

95. Walker, *Appeal*, p. 28.

96. Walker, *Appeal*, p. 29.

could come and take it with little provocation. Thus, in many ways, Walker was ahead of modern biblical scholars, who can only think of how to paint biblical ethics in a better light.

The irony is that any study of early Christian literature shows that even some of the most prominent Christian theologians are willing to credit Greeks with developing some concepts of justice. St Augustine, for instance, credits Plato with outlining 'a sharp and vigorous argument against injustice and on behalf of justice'.[97] In particular, Augustine argues against the notion that it was 'unjust for some men to serve as masters...to all this argument the reply on the side of justice was that the rule over provincials is just [*iustum esse*] precisely because servitude is in the interest of such men'.[98]

Summary

Glorifying the superiority of biblical ethics, especially in regard to slavery, relies routinely on devaluing the legal and cultural accomplishments of the cultures of the ancient Near East that neighbored Israel. In addition, many of the claims about these cultures are based on a very superficial acquaintance with the actual sources from Mesopotamia, Egypt, and Anatolia. Stark, for example, depends on secondary sources for many of his sweeping indictments of non-Christian cultures. Orlando Patterson completely misrepresented a secondary source he did cite.

Once we examine those primary Near Eastern sources, we do not find much that is new in Christianity, and we find many Near Eastern advantages that the Bible did not offer slaves. The biblical idea that human beings were made in the image of God (*imago Dei*) did not really have much practical effect on the ethics of slavery compared to what we find in the Near East. If Christianity made any advances, it would not be because it was original, but because it reverted to 'pagan' practices that preceded it.

---

97. Augustine, *City of God* 19.21 (Greene, LCL): 'Disputatur certe acerrime atque fortissime in eisdem ipsis de re republica libris adversus iniustitiam pro iustitia'.
98. Augustine, *City of God* 19.21 (Greene, LCL).

Chapter 4

SLAVERY IN THE HEBREW BIBLE/OLD TESTAMENT

Whereas the previous chapter explored the socioreligious biases that scholars display in claims about the cultural inferiority of Near Eastern cultures, this chapter investigates slavery in what Christians call the Old Testament. In Judaism this set of books is called the Tanakh, while academic biblical scholars often refer to it as the Hebrew Bible. The discovery of the Dead Sea Scrolls has overturned the idea of a fixed Old Testament canon at the time of Christianity's inception.[1] Yet, most Protestants accept as fully canonical the books of the Tanakh, while Catholic Christians have seven more books (so-called apocrypha in Protestantism) that are deemed just as canonical. In any case, this chapter explores how modern biblical scholars mitigate the ethical implications of specific terms and passages in the Old Testament (both Protestant and Catholic canons) that relate to slavery.

Lexicographers as Apologists

Lexicography is the discipline devoted to establishing the meaning of words. In more colloquial terms, lexicographers are dictionary-writers. Lexicographers are important because all good exegesis begins with the meaning of the basic words we use to reconstruct ancient institutions, such as slavery. And it is among lexicographers that we find the first line of defense against those who criticize biblical attitudes toward slavery.

One of the most frequent places where scholars mitigate biblical slavery is in the very words used to describe 'slavery'. The primary word for 'slave' in the Hebrew Bible is *'ebed* (עבד).[2] According to the *Theological Lexicon of the Old Testament* (*TLOT*), a standard reference tool, *'ebed* occurs 800 times a noun, and 268 times in the specific construction of 'servant of God'.[3] The

---

1. For a general treatment of these text-critical developments, see Emanuel Tov, *Textual Criticism of the Hebrew Bible* (Minneapolis: Fortress Press; Assen: Royal Van Gorcum, 2001).
2. *DCH*, VI, *s.v.*, has 'slave' as one of the primary meanings of this word.
3. Claus Westermann, '*'ebed*, servant', in *TLOT*, II, pp. 820-21. For a very comprehensive treatment of this word, see Ingrid Riesener, *Der Stamm* עבד *im Alten Testament:*

qal form of the verb ('to serve', 'to serve as a slave', 'to work') is used 271 times in the Hebrew Bible, while the causative hiphil ('to enslave') is used eight times.

TLOT provides the expected descriptive linguistic treatment of the word. But there is also a clear attempt by Claus Westermann, the prominent Old Testament scholar, to explain why slavery in ancient Israel was more ethically acceptable:

> In the social sphere, *'ebed* commonly designates the slave in the Old Testament. It is not, however, a technical term in the sense of Eng[lish] 'slave', which necessarily involves a negative preconception. One may never forget either that the same word can describe the officer and the minister of the king or the nuance of the term in the self-designation 'your servant...' The institution of slavery...predated Israel and was adopted when Israel settled in Canaan. This adoption is indicated by Israel's adaptation of the slave law of its neighbors... Israel's slave law tended toward the most humane treatment of slaves possible. This tendency probably results from the fact that the slave was originally integrated into the family and was a member of the family, even cultically.[4]

Here, Westermann wants to have it both ways. On the one hand, he admits that Israel adopted/adapted slavery from its neighbors. Yet, Israel was more humanitarian despite copying some of the slave customs of its neighbors.

Westermann is clearly exaggerating when he claims that Israelite slavery law 'tended toward the most humane treatment of slaves possible'. What does 'tended toward' mean? What does 'possible' mean when we can easily imagine a more humanitarian law than the ones in the Bible? For example, I can easily imagine that if beating a slave is allowed, then it was 'possible' to not beat a slave at all. Westermann, in fact, provides no specific instances of a more humanitarian law, and the ones Westermann cites (Exod. 21.2-11) are actually much harsher than ones we can find in Mesopotamia.

Speculation forms part of the evidence when Westermann claims that Israelite laws were probably more humanitarian because slaves were originally part of the family. Yet, slaves could be part of the family in Mesopotamia as well. The *CH* made provisions for adopting slaves. Law 170 of the *CH* says:

Eine Wortuntersuchung unter Berücksichtigung neuerer sprachwissenschaftlicher Methoden (BZAW, 149; Berlin/New York: W. de Gruyter, 1979).

4. Westermann, '*'ebed*, servant', II, p. 822. For similar views on the more humanitarian nature of Hebrew slavery, see also Hans Walter Wolff, 'Masters and Slaves: On Overcoming Class-Struggle in the Old Testament' (trans. Gary Stansell), *Interpretation* 27 (1973), pp. 259-72; Philip J. King, 'Slavery in Antiquity', in J. David Schloen (ed.), *Exploring the Longue Durée: Essays in Honor of Lawrence E. Stager* (Winona Lake, IN: Eisenbrauns, 2009), pp. 243-49.

> If a man's first-ranking wife bears him children and his slave woman bears him children, and the father during his lifetime then declares to (or: concerning) the children whom the slave woman bore to him, 'My children', and he reckons them with the children of the first-ranking wife—after the father goes to his fate, the children of the first-ranking wife and the children of the slave woman shall equally divide the property of the paternal estate; the preferred heir is a son of the first-ranking wife, he shall select and take a share first.[5]

This contrasts with biblical precepts where the son of a slavewoman could not inherit the father's property at all (e.g., Ishmael in Gen. 21.10-12).

Westermann makes much of the fact that slaves were integrated cultically, as if that were a sign of humanitarianism. It is the opposite. Following Israel's cultic law was another indicator of submission and lack of freedom on the part of the slave. The person would no longer be free to practice his or her original religion, and death could result if slaves did not faithfully serve Yahweh (Deut. 29.10-13). If freedom to worship one's god is accorded a higher value, then clearly Israel was less humanitarian by this standard. Other cultures did not generally force a slave to leave his or her religion. Moreover, we have already seen examples where some Greek religious festivals encouraged or allowed the participation of slaves. In contrast to biblical law, slaves in most Near Eastern cultures were not necessarily required to practice a religion with which they did not agree.

Similarly, Joshua Berman's attempt to exalt the nature of biblical egalitarianism entails this claim: '*'Ebed* means servant, a subordinate, an official, but does not connote ownership of the person'.[6] Yet Berman is clearly contradicted by Lev. 25.44-46, which we study in more detail below. Briefly, that passage uses the word *'ebed* when describing how the Israelites are allowed to buy slaves (תקנו עבד). Verse 45 states that an *'ebed* 'may be your property' (היו לכם לאחזה), and may be inherited by the slavemaster's children (v. 46).[7] If buying and inheriting an *'ebed* does not 'connote ownership of a person', then what does?[8]

---

5. Roth, *Law Collections*, pp. 113-14.

6. Joshua A. Berman, *Created Equal: How the Bible Broke with Ancient Political Thought* (New York: Oxford University Press, 2008), p. 106. For a recent plea to translate all instances of עֶבֶד as 'servant' because it has less negative connotations, see Peter J. Williams, 'The Meaning of the Word *'ebed*' (unpublished paper delivered at the Annual Meeting of the Society of Biblical Literature, Atlanta, GA, 20 November 2010).

7. *DCH*, I, pp. 187-88, specifically applies the general meanings of 'possession, inheritance, property' to 'non-Israelite purchased as a slave' in Lev. 25.45, 46.

8. For another biblical scholar who denies that humans are ever treated as economic property in the Hebrew Bible, see Michael Fishbane, 'Image of the Human in Jewish Tradition', in Leroy S. Rouner (ed.), *Human Rights and the World's Religions* (Notre Dame: University of Notre Dame Press, 1988), p. 18.

Yes, it is true that the Hebrew word, *'ebed*, could sometimes designate an official. It is true that it could include the self-designation of 'your servant'. However, that itself is no justification for saying that Israelite slavery was better. The equivalent word, *wardu*, in Mesopotamia, encompasses involuntary servitude and officialdom.[9] Thus, in a letter from Bel-ušezib, a prophet and official of Esarhaddon, the former says: 'I am your servant [*aradka*], your d[o]g and the one who fears you'.[10] Being a dog and showing fear of the master is quite consistent with a slave status.

Being an 'official' does not necessarily mean you were less of a slave insofar as you might have been forced into that profession or had to do whatever your master said. According to Assyriologist Igor Diakonoff, everyone who had a lord in ancient Mesopotamia was automatically the slave of that lord, whether that person was an official or not.[11] In his complaint against kingship, Samuel suggests that many of the officers were taken from their families ('he will take your sons and appoint them to his chariots...'). In 2 Kgs 10.5, we find some officers saying this to King Jehu: 'We are your servants, and we will do all that you bid us'. How would that differ from what a 'slave' would say to a master?

But since the word *'ebed* may have a wide variety of meanings, ranging from a chattel slave to an official with status and liberties a chattel slave would not have, we must now turn to the examination of individual passages to see how modern scholars have addressed the problems they pose for a more humanitarian view of biblical slavery.

Genesis 1.26: Let Dominion Begin

The essential features of slavery are inequality and dominance. The fact is that the Bible presents these features as part of the created order and from the beginning of human existence.

> Then God said, 'Let us make man in our image, after our likeness; and let them have dominion over the fish of the sea, and over the birds of the air, and over the cattle, and over all the earth, and over every creeping thing that creeps upon the earth'. So God created man in his own image, in the image of God he

---

9. See Hayim ben Yosef Tawil, *An Akkadian Lexical Companion for Biblical Hebrew: Etymological and Idiomatic Equivalents with Supplement in Biblical Aramaic* (Jersey City, NJ: Ktav, 2009), p. 269.

10. Martti Nissinen, C.L. Seow, and Robert K. Ritner, *Prophets and Prophecy in the Ancient Near East* (Atlanta: Society of Biblical Literature, 2003), p. 153, l. 7: *aradka ka[lab]ka u pāliḫka*.

11. See Igor Diakonoff, 'Slave-Labour vs. Non-Slave Labour: The Problem of Definition', in Marvin A. Powell (ed.), *Labor in the Ancient Near East* (New Haven: American Oriental Society, 1987), pp. 1-3.

created him; male and female he created them. And God blessed them, and God said to them, 'Be fruitful and multiply, and fill the earth and subdue it; and have dominion over the fish of the sea and over the birds of the air and over every living thing that moves upon the earth' (Gen. 1.26-28).

Although representativists and trajectorialists speak often of how liberation is an essential and representative theme, the fact is that it is dominion and subjugation that is viewed as part of the created order already in Genesis 1. Notice here that the *imago Dei* is connected specifically with dominion, not egalitarianism. The 'Image of God' means dominion if it means anything.[12]

From the beginning of creation, humankind was also intended for servitude. Genesis 2.5 suggests that Yahweh wanted the earth to be fruitful, but there was no one to till it. Yahweh plants an orchard/garden, and then we see the purpose of the man in Gen. 2.15, which says: 'The LORD God took the man and put him in the garden of Eden to till it and keep it'. Adam was meant to be no less a slave in Yahweh's orchard/garden than human beings in the *Enuma elish*. Yahweh is presented as a divine master and Eden is a horticultural estate, which needs humans to maintain it.

But Yahweh, who uses trial-and-error, discovers that Adam cannot do this all alone, and so animals are then made to help Adam (2.19). The animals are inadequate as fellow slaves, and so the woman was created to help Adam. However, both were ejected from that orchard when Yahweh realized that the human beings could become god-like by eating of the tree of life (and tree of knowledge). Yahweh's explicit rationale in Gen. 3.22-23 is:

> Then the LORD God said, 'Behold, the man has become like one of us, knowing good and evil; and now, lest he put forth his hand and take also of the tree of life, and eat, and live for ever'—therefore the LORD God sent him forth from the garden of Eden, to till the ground from which he was taken.

In other words, the idea of human servitude was there from the very creation of humanity. It is just that the first humans were to be servants of Yahweh. Yet, Yahweh being alike in image to human beings did not stop Yahweh from enslaving human beings. Likewise, the fact that human beings share an image with each other need not be an obstacle to enslaving each other.

Fred Ross, the pro-slavery advocate, was keen on showing that the *imago Dei* did not mean equality. In fact, the very order of creation already showed inequality, especially in regard to the woman. Ross says:

> For the man is not of the woman, but the woman of the man. Neither was the man *created for the woman*, but the woman *for the man* (1 Cor. xi)...he made the woman to be the weaker vessel (1 Pet. iii. 7).[13]

---

12. See further Garr, *In his Own Image*, pp. 128-34.
13. Ross, *Slavery Ordained*, p. 125 (Ross's emphasis).

In other words, subservience and hierarchy were part of God's design.

Yet, some modern scholars have attempted to mitigate the implications of this hierarchy of the sexes. A case in point is the work of Phyllis Trible, author of a number of very influential works, including *Texts of Terror* (1978) and *God and the Rhetoric of Sexuality* (1984).[14] Trible spent much of her academic career at Union Theological Seminary in New York City, and she served as president of the Society of Biblical Literature in 1994.

One of Trible's main arguments is that male interpreters have suppressed readings more friendly towards women in the Bible. That is to say, the Bible is often more gender-inclusive than male interpreters have indicated. In particular, she proposes that Adam was viewed by the biblical author as an androgyne or sexless creature.[15] This has, indeed, drawn fire not only from male interpreters, but also from some female interpreters.[16] If, as Trible believes, 'Adam' becomes a 'man' (Hebrew: איש) after the creation of Eve, then it leaves unexplained why the biblical author says that the woman was taken 'from the man' (Hebrew: מאיש) in Gen. 2.23. The latter statement presupposes that the entity from which she was taken was male.[17]

Genesis 3.16 and Female Subjugation

If dominion of human beings over animals is an essential part of God's creation, this dominion is also extended to other human beings. More specifically, males are to be masters of females according to Gen. 3.16: 'To the woman he said, "I will greatly multiply your pain in childbearing; in pain you shall bring forth children, yet your desire shall be for your husband, and he shall rule over you"'. As Ross points out, consent really has little to do with one's status. When God said to the woman 'He shall rule over thee' there was no consent requested from, or given by, the woman.[18]

This subjugation is important to recognize because, even when many theologians were willing to concede that human beings were all made equal, they would still say that this only applied to the pre-lapsarian condition, and not after the fall. This became the view, for example, of Augustine. In the

---

14. Phyllis Trible, *God and the Rhetoric of Sexuality* (Philadelphia: Fortress Press, 1978) and *Texts of Terror: Literary-Feminist Readings of Biblical Narratives* (Philadelphia: Fortress Press, 1984).

15. Trible, *God and the Rhetoric of Sexuality*, pp. 79-82.

16. For example, Susan S. Lanser, '(Feminist) Criticism in the Garden: Inferring Genesis 2–3', *Semeia* 41 (1988), pp. 67-84; John W. Miller, 'Depatriarchalizing God in Biblical Interpretation: A Critique', *CBQ* 48 (1986), pp. 609-16.

17. For these and other criticisms, see Robert Kawashima, 'A Revisionist Reading Revisited: On the Creation of Adam and Eve', *VT* 56 (2006), pp. 46-57; and Lanser, '(Feminist) Criticism', p. 72.

18. Ross, *Slavery Ordained*, p. 131.

nineteenth century, many pro-slavery advocates noted that this obligation of woman to be subservient to man was reiterated in the New Testament. Thus in Eph. 5.24, it says that the woman is to obey the man 'in all things'.[19] This subservience remains, therefore, under the new covenant and is not viewed as incompatible with the Golden Rule or with the *imago Dei* by New Testament authors.

But Phyllis Trible tells us that, in regard to the woman, '[h]er subordination is neither divine decree nor the female destiny. God describes the consequence but does not prescribe it as punishment.'[20] This is a most curious statement, as any statement of the type 'You shall be/do X' is, by definition, a 'divine decree' when uttered by a god, such as Yahweh. And the whole idea that subordination is a 'consequence' flounders on the observation that it is Yahweh who can make and unmake 'consequences'. Thus, Trible's exegesis becomes a more sophisticated form of biblical apologetics.

Carol Meyers also minimizes the hierarchical nature of this passage by translating it as 'and he shall predominate over you'.[21] According to Meyers, '"predominate", conveys the "dominion" notion of the Hebrew word and yet preserves the relative nature of the verb, unlike words such as "rule" which tend to imply some sort of monarchic or legal control'.[22] In fact, Meyers shifts the discussion to labor expenditure and suggests that 'predominate' refers to the man having a greater share of the labor so that the woman 'will not be put into a position of doing more than her mate in the subsistence sphere'.[23]

Even by her own admission, Meyers relies on a very unconventional view of the Hebrew word *mashal* (מֹשֶׁל), which is usually translated as 'to rule'.[24] However, nowhere in her discussion is there reference to how ancient Jews who translated the Hebrew understood it. The translators of the Septuagint chose the Greek word κυριεύσει to translate the corresponding Hebrew clause (αὐτός σου κυριεύσει). But κυριεύω is precisely one of the main verbs used to denote rulership and kingship.

Indeed, some New Testament authors also understood κύριος to express a hierarchical male rulership in Genesis: 'So once the holy women who hoped in God used to adorn themselves and were submissive to their husbands, as Sarah obeyed Abraham, calling him lord [κύριος αὐτὸν καλοῦσα]. And you

19. So Ross, *Slavery Ordained*, p. 55.
20. Trible, *God and the Rhetoric of Sexuality*, p. 128.
21. Carol Meyers, 'Gender and Genesis 3.16', in Carol L. Meyers and M. O'Connor (eds.), *The Word of the Lord Shall Go Forth: Essays in Honor of David Noel Freedman in Celebration of his Sixtieth Birthday* (Winona Lake, IN: Eisenbrauns, 1983), pp. 337-54 (344).
22. Meyers, 'Gender and Genesis 3.16', p. 348.
23. Meyers, 'Gender and Genesis 3.16', p. 348.
24. See J.A. Soggin, 'מֹשֶׁל', in *TLOT*, II, pp. 689-91.

are now her children if you do right and let nothing terrify you' (1 Pet. 3.5-6). Thus, 'lording' over someone does imply obedience and submission that is indistinguishable from that demanded of a slave. In many ways, therefore, women were very much like slaves for some biblical authors, even if modern biblical scholars may not like to admit it.

Genesis 9.19-27 and Noah's Curse

Stephen R. Haynes argues in his book, *Noah's Curse*, that no passage in Genesis has been more persistently connected with the justification of American slavery than the so-called curse of Ham, which is first introduced in Genesis 9.[25] Eugene D. Genovese, however, doubts that the passage had such importance because scientific arguments for racism were supplanting biblical ones, which mainly relied on the mere sanctioning of slavery by God.[26] Genovese attempts to shift the blame to scientific polygenesis, and even denies that the divines cited race before the Civil War. Haynes, however, makes a compelling case for the use of this text long before the Civil War.

Noah's curse takes place right after the Flood, when Noah and his family exited the Ark. This curious episode is related as follows:

> The sons of Noah who went forth from the ark were Shem, Ham, and Japheth. Ham was the father of Canaan. These three were the sons of Noah; and from these the whole earth was peopled. Noah was the first tiller of the soil. He planted a vineyard; and he drank of the wine, and became drunk, and lay uncovered in his tent. And Ham, the father of Canaan, saw the nakedness of his father, and told his two brothers outside. Then Shem and Japheth took a garment, laid it upon both their shoulders, and walked backward and covered the nakedness of their father; their faces were turned away, and they did not see their father's nakedness. When Noah awoke from his wine and knew what his youngest son had done to him, he said, 'Cursed be Canaan; a slave of slaves shall he be to his brothers'. He also said, 'Blessed by the LORD my God be Shem; and let Canaan be his slave. God enlarge Japheth, and let him dwell in the tents of Shem; and let Canaan be his slave' (Gen. 9.18-27).

It is not my intention to rehearse the entire history of exegesis of this text.[27] My comments here do not so much pertain to whether post-Christian Jewish

---

25. Stephen R. Haynes, *Noah's Curse: The Biblical Justification of American Slavery* (New York: Oxford University Press, 2002).

26. See Eugene D. Genovese, *A Consuming Fire: The Fall of the Confederacy in the Mind of the White Christian South* (Mercer University Press Memorial Lecture, 41; Athens: University of Georgia Press, 1998), p. 81.

27. For excellent histories of interpretation, see Goldenberg, *The Curse of Ham*; Stacy Davis, *This Strange Story: Jewish and Christian Interpretation of the Curse of Canaan from Antiquity to 1865* (Lanham, MD: University Press of America, 2008); Sylvester A. Johnson, *The Myth of Ham in Nineteenth-Century American Christianity: Race, Heathens,*

or Christian sources did understand Ham to be associated with blackness. Later, I will, however, discuss how Origen and other early Church Fathers already show evidence of an incipient racism when referring to the curse of Canaan.

Nonetheless, abolitionists are mostly correct. Ham cannot be equated with blackness or slavery either linguistically or exegetically. True, there is definitely a biblical tradition that places Ham in what we now call Africa: 'Then Israel came to Egypt; Jacob sojourned in the land of Ham' (Ps. 105.23). It is also true that the etymological association of Ham and blackness is admitted by some scholars who otherwise attempt to mitigate biblical slavery.[28] However, David Goldenberg articulates a compelling linguistic case that the root of the name, Ham, is not related to the word for 'black'.[29]

Yet even without any original racial implications for Genesis 9, this text shows that slavery and punishment could be linked. So, while there is no association between Ham and blackness in the Bible, pro-slavery advocates might plausibly conclude that God could allow the enslavement of an entire group for the misdeeds of an ancestor. The idea of an *imago Dei* certainly did not prevent the enslavement of entire groups in the Bible.

Genesis 16: Rape of a Slave Woman?

Hagar was a slave woman who fled her mistress, Sarah, the wife of Abraham. Sarah could not bear children and so allowed Abraham to impregnate Hagar. Sarah's actions are similar to those of *naditu* women in Mesopotamia who allow husbands to impregnate lower-status women (*CH* 146).[30] Abraham's action might qualify as rape today because Hagar was in no position to reject Abraham's impregnation. Hagar also fled after her mistress treated her badly.

Yet, it is what God told Hagar to do that became a prooftext for those who endorsed the return of fugitives to their slavemasters. According to

and the People of God (New York: Palgrave Macmillan, 2004); David M. Whitford, *The Curse of Ham in the Early Modern Era: The Bible and the Justifications for Slavery* (St Andrews Studies in Reformation History; Burlington, VT: Ashgate, 2009); Jan Christian Gertz, 'Hams Sündenfall und Kanaans Erbfluch. Anmerkungen zur kompositiongeschichtlichen Stellung von Gen 9, 18-29', in Reinhard Achenbach and Martin Arneth (eds.), *'Gerechtigkeit und Recht zu üben' (Gen 18, 19): Studien zur altorientalischen und biblischen Rechtsgeschichte, zur Religionsgeschichte Israels und zur Religionssoziologie* (Festschrift Eckart Otto; Beihefte zur ZABR, 13; Wiesbaden: Harrassowitz, 2010), pp. 81-95.

28. See, for example, Ephraim Isaac, 'Ham', in *ABD*, III, p. 31.
29. Goldenberg, *The Curse of Ham*, pp. 145-49.
30. For the similarities and differences between Sarah and *naditu* women, see Tammi J. Schneider, *Sarah: Mother of Nations* (New York: Continuum International, 2004), pp. 51-52.

Gen. 16.9: The angel of the LORD said to her, 'Return to your mistress, and submit to her'. Fred Ross said that this story contains facts that 'stare you in the face...in Hagar running away under her mistress's hard dealing with her, and yet sent back, as a fugitive slave, by the angel'.[31] Furthermore, according to Jennifer Glancy, '[w]e can trace the impact of ancient Christian toleration of sexual exploitation of slaves through interpretations of the biblical figure of Sarah and Hagar by two Christian theologians', who are identified as Paul and St Ambrose, bishop of Milan.[32]

Genesis 17.12 and Genital Mutilation

One of the most oft-missed and brutal institutions connected with slavery is circumcision. Usually, circumcision is not linked to slavery and is interpreted as a benign institution that could be shared by those who became part of the Israelite community. But circumcision is part of a broader class of genital mutilation, affecting males and females, that we see in many cultures.[33] In the Bible, circumcision involves mutilation of the penis, and it is difficult to explain why anyone would invent such an institution that was so painful. I suggest the answer lies in its origins as a slave mark.

It should be noted first that circumcision was probably not originally a Hebrew custom because there is an apparent depiction of circumcision from as early as 2400 BCE (Fifth Dynasty) in a bas relief from Saqqara, Egypt.[34] But within Jewish tradition, circumcision is traced to the 'mark' of the covenant outlined in Gen. 17.9-14:[35]

> And God said to Abraham, 'As for you, you shall keep my covenant, you and your descendants after you throughout their generations. This is my covenant, which you shall keep, between me and you and your descendants after you: Every male among you shall be circumcised. You shall be circumcised in the

---

31. Ross, *Slavery Ordained*, p. 100.
32. Jennifer A. Glancy, 'Early Christianity, Slavery, and Women's Bodies', in Brooten (ed.), *Beyond Slavery*, pp. 143-58 (150).
33. See Rogaia Mustafa Abusharaf, *Female Circumcision: Multicultural Perspectives* (Philadelphia: University of Pennsylvania Press, 2006); Nick Wyatt, 'Circumcision and Circumstance: Genital Mutilation in Ancient Israel and Ugarit', *JSOT* 33 (2009), pp. 405-31. For the argument that circumcision should be viewed as an empowering feature rather than a mutilation, see Saul Olyan, *Disability in the Hebrew Bible: Interpreting Mental and Physical Differences* (Cambridge: Cambridge University Press, 2008), especially pp. 36-38.
34. David L. Gollaher, *Circumcision: A History of the World's Most Controversial Surgery* (New York: Basic Books, 2002), pp. 1-2.
35. For source criticism of texts dealing with circumcision, see William H. Propp, 'The Origins of Infant Circumcision in Israel', *Hebrew Annual Review* 11 (1987), pp. 355-70; David A. Bernat, *Sign of the Covenant: Circumcision in the Priestly Tradition* (Atlanta: Society of Biblical Literature, 2009).

flesh of your foreskins, and it shall be a sign of the covenant between me and you. He that is eight days old among you shall be circumcised; every male throughout your generations, whether born in your house, or bought with your money from any foreigner who is not of your offspring, both he that is born in your house and he that is bought with your money, shall be circumcised. So shall my covenant be in your flesh an everlasting covenant. Any uncircumcised male who is not circumcised in the flesh of his foreskin shall be cut off from his people; he has broken my covenant.'

At least two features emerge from this institution: (1) it is a practice commanded by Israel's lord, Yahweh; and (2) it is not voluntary insofar as it is imposed on children and on slaves.

The hypothesis that circumcision originated as a slave mark rests on the following arguments: (1) persons do not normally submit to such a procedure without some coercion; (2) modification of the anatomy is a known method of slave marking, as indicated in Exod. 21.6: 'his master shall pierce his ear with an awl; and he shall serve him for life'; (3) a test of loyalty by a slave for a master would most naturally require an action that would be otherwise undesirable for a slave. That is to say, if a master wanted to test whether a new slave would be obedient, then the master could require the slave to mutilate himself as a test (see Gen. 34.22); (4) no other explanations, including supposed health benefits, have withstood scientific scrutiny.[36]

Genesis 17.23: Abraham, the Blessed Slavemaster

A fundamental passage for pro-slavery advocates can be found scattered throughout antebellum pro-slavery literature. Genesis 17.23 says: 'Then Abraham took Ish'mael his son and all the slaves born in his house or bought

---

36. Critics of the supposed medical benefits of circumcision include Leonard B. Glick, *Marked in your Flesh: Circumcision from Ancient Judea to Modern America* (New York: Oxford University Press, 2005); Ronald Goldman, *Questioning Circumcision: A Jewish Perspective* (Boston: Vanguard Publications, 1998). See also essays in Elizabeth Wyner Mark (ed.), *The Covenant of Circumcision: New Perspectives on an Ancient Jewish Rite* (Hanover, NH: University Press of New England/Brandeis University Press, 2003); Howard Eilberg-Schwartz, *God's Phallus and Other Problems for Men and Monotheism* (Boston: Beacon Press, 1994), pp. 170-74. The recommendations of the American Academy of Pediatrics ('Circumcision Policy Statement', *Pediatrics* 103 [1999], pp. 686-93) specifically emphasize the lack of medical benefits for circumcision. Recent reports of the success of circumcision in preventing HIV infections in Africa cannot be used to explain the origin of the ritual as HIV is not likely to have been a problem in ancient Israel, nor is any sort of sexual disease given in the biblical texts as the reason for circumcision. See further 'WHO and UNAIDS Announce Recommendations from Expert Consultation on Male Circumcision for AIDS Prevention' (27 March 2007). Online: www.who.int/hiv/mediacentre/news68/en/index.html.

with his money, every male among the men of Abraham's house, and he circumcised the flesh of their foreskins that very day, as God had said to him'. Fred Ross, the pro-slavery writer, suggests that this shows that slave-holding did not prevent God from blessing Abraham 'in all things' (Gen. 24.1).[37]

Exodus 1–15: A Liberationist Paradigm?

These chapters contain what many modern scholars see as the paradigmatic abolitionist and liberatory narrative of the entire Bible. The Exodus of the Israelites from an oppressive Egyptian slavery is taken as the principal evidence of the liberatory orientation of biblical ideology. This is particularly the case among many modern African-American theologians and biblical scholars. As Eddie S. Glaude explains: 'No other story in the Bible has quite captured the imagination of African Americans like the Exodus'.[38] Similarly, Allen Dwight Callahan, remarks: 'African Americans heard, read, and retold the story of the Exodus more than any other biblical narrative'.[39]

One case in point is the work of James Cone, the primary exponent of modern black liberation theology. In his *A Black Theology of Liberation* (1970), Cone makes the Exodus the model of liberatory narratives in the ancient world.[40] For Cone, '[t]he exodus of Israel from Egypt was a revelation-liberation. In this revelatory event, Israel came to know God as the liberator of the oppressed, and also realized that its being as a people was inseparable from divine concomitance'.[41]

While it is true that the Exodus refers to the liberation of the Hebrews from Egyptian slavery, it is quite another matter to see this narrative as the paradigm of abolition or liberation for everyone. First, and as Jon D. Levenson observes, the wider scope of the exodus narrative shows that slavery is not only legitimate but divinely sanctioned.[42] Yahweh himself is viewed as the slavemaster of the Hebrews (Lev. 25.55: 'For to me the people of Israel are servants, they are my servants whom I brought forth out of the land of

---

37. Ross, *Slavery Ordained*, pp. 151-53.
38. Eddie S. Glaude, Jr, *Exodus: Religion, Race, and Nation in Early Nineteenth-Century Black America* (Chicago: University of Chicago Press, 2000), p. 3. See also David Fleer and Dave Bland (eds.), *Reclaiming the Imagination: The Exodus as Paradigmatic Narrative for Preaching* (St Louis, MO: Chalice Press, 2009).
39. Allen Dwight Callahan, *The Talking Book: African Americans and the Bible* (New Haven: Yale University Press, 2006), p. 83.
40. I depend on James H. Cone, *A Black Theology of Liberation* (Maryknoll, NY: Orbis Books, twentieth anniversary edn, 1990 [1970]).
41. Cone, *A Black Theology*, p. 47.
42. Jon D. Levenson, 'Exodus and Liberation', *Horizons in Biblical Theology* 13 (1991), pp. 134-74.

Egypt: I am the LORD your God'). Thus, the intent of the narrative cannot be seen as a manifesto for abolition in general.

Second, the use of the Exodus as a paradigm of liberation betrays the religiocentric nature of these modern biblical scholars and theologians. Seeing the exodus as a paradigm of liberation relies on a representativist hermeneutic that we already critiqued as arbitrary. Cone, for instance, does not seem interested in the subsequent enslavement of the Canaanites. He does not explain why that enslavement of the Canaanites ought not be seen as the 'paradigm' of biblical ideology.

The Hebrews are later to eradicate the Canaanites and/or enslave them. Thus, the Exodus story, in its larger scope, is more a story of group privileging, wherein a particular group is entitled to liberation but not others (e.g., Canaanites). The group-privileging rationale is analogous to the rationale used in New World slavery wherein one group (white Europeans) felt entitled to liberty, but this did not mean that they felt liberty was owed to others. Viewed in this light, modern scholars who see the Exodus as a paradigm of liberation only betray a Judeo-Christian bias because they do not seem to consider the consequences of Hebrew liberation for the Canaanites.

Indeed, if we followed Cone's logic, we should be crediting the Egyptians, not the Hebrews, as the liberators. After all, it was the Egyptians who did the liberating. Of course, the biblical narrative emphasizes that Pharaoh acted only under duress. Yet, it remains true to say that most modern biblical scholars do not see the Egyptians or their gods as liberators, even when the narrative itself indicates that Egyptians did the liberating.

More recent readings of Exodus by African-American biblical scholars do identify the Canaanites as oppressed people in need of liberation. For example, Michelle Ellis Taylor, one of the commentators for *The Africana Bible*, a biblical commentary by 'African and African-Diasporan biblical scholars', remarks:[43]

> An Africana reading of this book would be to identify not with the Israelites but with the oppressed and rejected, with those in whom the dominant power once trusted but then turned against—that is, with the Midianites and the Moabites…with Miriam and Moses' Cushite wife…and with the daughter of Zelophehad.[44]

Other African-American scholars, such as Anthony Pinn and William R. Jones, who speak from more frankly secular humanist orientations, also have

---

43. I consider 'African and African-Diasporan biblical scholars' a self-description by the editors on the basis of the book flap from which the quote is taken.

44. Michelle Ellis Taylor, 'Numbers', in Hugh R. Page (ed.), *The Africana Bible: Reading Israel's Scriptures from Africa and the African Diaspora* (Minneapolis: Fortress Press, 2010), pp. 94-99 (98).

rejected the type of reading that Cone advocates.[45] In sum, the very idea that the Exodus is a model of any liberatory programme is itself a product of ethnocentric and bibliolatrous scholarship.

Exodus 20.10/Deuteronomy 5.12-15 and the Sabbath

Usually numbered as the fourth commandment in the Decalogue, the Sabbath directive appears in the Covenant Code (Exod. 20.10), and in Deut. 5.12-15, as follows:

> Observe the sabbath day, to keep it holy, as the LORD your God commanded you. Six days you shall labor, and do all your work; but the seventh day is a sabbath to the LORD your God; in it you shall not do any work, you, or your son, or your daughter, or your manservant, or your maidservant, or your ox, or your ass, or any of your cattle, or the sojourner who is within your gates, that your manservant and your maidservant may rest as well as you. You shall remember that you were a servant in the land of Egypt, and the LORD your God brought you out thence with a mighty hand and an outstretched arm; therefore the LORD your God commanded you to keep the sabbath day.

Modern biblical ethicists have evinced at least two patterns when discussing this passage. One is to omit any discussion of the fact that slavery is presupposed. A second pattern, which may be combined with the first, is to focus on the advances brought by the Sabbath. In the latter case such scholars echo the apologetics for the Sabbath given already by Josephus (*Apion* 2.282-83).[46]

Consider Walter J. Harrelson, who wrote *The Ten Commandments and Human Rights*.[47] Much of his discussion focuses on the origin of the Sabbath institution, and none of the discussion even mentions that this commandment presupposes that slaves were a normal part of Israel's society. After all, the commandment does not say 'you shall not have servants', but only that slaves should be given a day of rest.

Nonetheless, Harrelson applauds how the day of rest 'brought about remarkable social changes'.[48] And what were these changes? Harrelson remarks:

---

45. See Anthony B. Pinn, *Why Lord? Suffering and Evil in Black Theology* (New York: Continuum, 2000), especially pp. 91-111; William R. Jones, *Is God a White Racist? A Preamble to Black Theology* (Garden City, NY: Anchor Press, 1973). See also the comments critical of biblical ethics in Sylvester A. Johnson, 'The Bible, Slavery, and the Problem of Authority', in Brooten (ed.), *Beyond Slavery*, pp. 231-48.

46. See also Heather A. McKay, *Sabbath and Synagogue: The Question of Sabbath Worship in Ancient Judaism* (Leiden: E.J. Brill, 1994), p. 101.

47. Walter Harrelson, *The Ten Commandments and Human Rights* (Macon, GA: Mercer University Press, 1997).

48. Harrelson, *The Ten Commandments*, p. 77.

The prophetic checks upon kingship in ancient Israel are unthinkable apart from time to reflect on the dangers of political power in the hands of one person. The development of hymns and laments that identify the actual course of life under God and are brutally frank in their portrayal of how life often gets out of control, or appears to do so, is also hard to imagine apart from the observance of the Sabbath Day.[49]

True enough, the Deuteronomist seems to raise the issue of parity between the experience of Israelites in Egypt and those of the slaves owned by Israel. But, why not go further and say that because the Israelites were slaves in Egypt, they should not hold someone else in slavery? That would be an advance.

Harrelson's other supposed advances credited to the Sabbath are quite speculative. The development of hymns or laments about how life gets out of control did not need a Sabbath day in Mesopotamia, Greece, or Rome, which also had these genres of writing. Harrelson, moreover, does not consider the slavery still embedded within this Sabbath commandment as meriting any sort of ethical criticism.

Exodus 21.1-6 and Term Limits

Setting a term limit on the service of slaves has been touted as an advance for human rights. The key passage (Exod. 21.1-6) for this term limit states:

> Now these are the ordinances which you shall set before them. When you buy a Hebrew slave, he shall serve six years, and in the seventh he shall go out free, for nothing. If he comes in single, he shall go out single; if he comes in married, then his wife shall go out with him. If his master gives him a wife and she bears him sons or daughters, the wife and her children shall be her master's and he shall go out alone. But if the slave plainly says, 'I love my master, my wife, and my children; I will not go out free', then his master shall bring him to God, and he shall bring him to the door or the doorpost; and his master shall bore his ear through with an awl; and he shall serve him for life.

However, Law 117 of the *CH* offers terms superior to those of Exodus:

> If an obligation is outstanding against a man, and he sells or gives into debt service his wife, his son, or his daughter, they shall perform service in the house of their buyer or of the one who holds them in debt service for three years; their release shall be secured in the fourth year.[50]

---

49. Harrelson, *The Ten Commandments*, p. 77.
50. Roth, *Law Collections*, p. 103. These sets of laws in *CH* and the Bible are also used by Mendelsohn (*Slavery in the Ancient Near East*, pp. 33, 74-75) for comparison.

Thus, in the *CH*, a person serves only half as long as in the Hebrew case. Notice also that the *CH* is more equal in its treatment of native and foreign slaves in this case, as opposed to Exodus, which specifies that this limited service applies only to Hebrew slaves. Moreover, non-Hebrew slaves, especially those captured in war, are owned forever, and may be inherited. Thus, we could claim that Hebrew law represents a regression compared to the *CH* insofar as limits of servitude are concerned.

Exodus 21.16 and 'Manstealing'

Nineteenth-century abolitionists saw this passage as a definitive indictment of all the slave trade. According to Exod. 21.16: 'Whoever steals a man, whether he sells him or is found in possession of him, shall be put to death'. Today, some biblical scholars still credit this verse with bringing a humanitarian advance. Joe Sprinkle adds a plaudit to biblical ethics when he remarks:

> Kidnapping is generally related to the slave trade... Because transcendent life value is involved in stealing a human being, that made it unlike a case merely involving animals. Thus kidnapping was subject to the maximum penalty regardless of whether the kidnapper disposed of the person stolen.[51]

Sprinkle concludes that 'biblical law values human life above property to a greater degree than cuneiform law' because cuneiform law assigns the death penalty for stealing non-human property, while the Bible assigns it only for stealing human beings.[52]

Of course, Sprinkle is engaging in 'representativism' by selecting a cuneiform law that he then generalizes to the entire Near East. But cuneiform law is not representative of all Near Eastern law. Plato's *Laws* also differentiate between animal and human property because they prescribe ritual purification for the killing of a slave, but not for the killing of an ox or a sheep.[53] Lycurgus (ninth–eighth centuries BCE), the legendary Spartan jurist, also says that ancient lawgivers 'did not permit even the killer of a slave to escape with a fine'.[54]

Similarly, in the Laws of Eshnunna, property crimes are not necessarily punished with death. Law 6 says: 'If a man under fraudulent circumstances, should seize a boat which does not belong to him, he shall weigh and deliver 10 shekels of silver'.[55] But Law 24 at Eshnunna says that if a man seizes the

---

51. Joe M. Sprinkle, *Biblical Law and its Relevance: A Christian Understanding and Ethical Application for Today of the Mosaic Regulations* (Lanham, MD: University Press of America, 2006), p. 94.
52. Sprinkle, *Biblical Law and its Relevance*, p. 98.
53. Morrow, *Plato's Law of Slavery*, p. 50.
54. Morrow, *Plato's Law of Slavery*, p. 51.
55. Roth, *Law Collections*, p. 60.

wife or child of a man as debt-slaves, and those seized persons die in the captor's custody, then the latter will die.[56] Yet, we do not find Sprinkle praising the Laws of Eshnunna for imposing monetary fines for theft of objects, but death in the case of debt-slaves who were killed.

A more significant problem for Sprinkle's conclusion is that we can find cuneiform laws that fare much better against the Bible. *CH* 14 states: 'If a man should kidnap the young child of another man, he shall be killed'.[57] Kidnapping children can also be related to the slave trade, in which case the Bible fares far worse. Consider what the biblical author allows Hebrews to do to Midianite virgins:

> Now therefore, kill every male among the little ones, and kill every woman who has known man by lying with him. But all the young girls who have not known man by lying with him, keep alive for yourselves... And Moses gave the tribute, which was the offering for the LORD, to Eleazar the priest, as the LORD commanded Moses (Num. 31.17-18, 41).

Basically, the biblical author is allowing the killing of the families of these young virgins, who are then taken for what can be described as sexual slavery, as consent cannot be presumed on the part of these girls. Numbers 31.41 specifies that this abduction of virgins is part of God's plan, and not some rogue human action.

We can also find a very different attitude toward human life, as compared to material objects, in Joshua, when Jericho was attacked:

> Then they utterly destroyed all in the city, both men and women, young and old, oxen, sheep, and asses, with the edge of the sword... And they burned the city with fire, and all within it; only the silver and gold, and the vessels of bronze and of iron, they put into the treasury of the house of the LORD (Josh. 6.21, 24).

Without entering into all the legal complexities of the so-called Hebrew 'ban' (*ḥerem*/חרם) institution, it is apparent that there are instances where objects were spared and treasured, while human and animal life were both destroyed.[58] Humans and animals were treated exactly alike here. But Sprinkle does not denounce taking virgins as sex slaves or killing entire groups of people, while keeping their material possessions, when it occurs in the Bible.

In fact, if we follow Sprinkle's logic, then Jesus values human life no more than property because he prescribes the same non-resistive response for the abduction of a person and for the taking of a coat. Note Jesus' remarks:

---

56. Roth, *Law Collections*, p. 62.
57. Roth, *Law Collections*, p. 84.
58. See Philip Stern, *The Biblical Ḥerem: A Window on Israel's Religious Experience* (Atlanta: Scholars Press, 1991); Avalos, *Fighting Words*, pp. 162-66.

You have heard that it was said, 'An eye for an eye and a tooth for a tooth'. But I say to you, Do not resist one who is evil. But if any one strikes you on the right cheek, turn to him the other also; and if any one would sue you and take your coat, let him have your cloak as well; and if any one forces you to go one mile, go with him two miles (Mt. 5.38-41).

Taking a coat or a human being, even if for a short distance, is not really differentiated by Jesus.

In addition to conventional biblical scholars, translators have been one of the main purveyors of an abolitionist bias in understanding the Bible. The translation of the RSV is similar to what is found in almost every modern translation. But, as Westbrook notes, this translation 'has been universally rejected' by legal scholars because of the numerous philological and logical problems it creates.[59] Westbrook substitutes a translation he thinks more true to the Hebrew וגנב איש ומכרו ונמצא בידו מות יומת: 'He that steals a man and sells him and he in whose possession he is found shall be put to death'.[60] Westbrook argues that there is a change in subject so that it is the buyer, and not initial kidnapper, who is punished with death.

The ambiguity of the original still remains insofar as it is not clear whether the law prohibits 'manstealing/kidnapping' anyone, or whether it restricts itself to prohibiting Hebrews from stealing or kidnapping other Hebrews. The Septuagint understood it as restricted to stealing Israelites because it translates this verse as 'Whoever steals one of the sons of Israel [Ὅς ἐὰν κλέψῃ τίς τινα τῶν υἱῶν Ἰσραήλ], and prevail over him and sell him, and he be found with him, let him certainly die'. It is unclear whether the Septuagint is inserting its own interpretation or following a different Vorlage. Perhaps it is just harmonizing Exod. 21.16 with Deut. 24.7, which says: 'If a man is found stealing one of his brethren, the people of Israel, and if he treats him as a slave or sells him, then that thief shall die; so you shall purge the evil from the midst of you'.

Fred Ross said: 'The crime, then, set forth in the Bible was not selling a man; but selling a stolen man'.[61] The fact that abducting people could be regarded as permissible was supported by the episode at Jabesh-Gilead, where four hundred virgins were abducted to provide wives for the Benjaminites (Judg. 21.17-24). However, it is not clear that the narrator approves of this action at all, especially as these are Israelite women being abducted. Abducting Midianite virgins, however, does have divine approval.

---

59. Raymond Westbrook, *Studies in Biblical and Cuneiform Law* (Paris: J. Gabalda, 1988), p. 119.
60. Westbrook, *Studies in Biblical and Cuneiform Law*, p. 119.
61. Ross, *Slavery Ordained*, p. 141.

Exodus 21.20 and Killing Slaves

According to Rodney Stark, '[d]eath was decreed for any Jewish master who killed a slave'.[62] The nearest biblical text Stark cites for any support is Exod. 21.26-27, which does not really speak to this issue. However, Stark may have been referring to Exod. 21.20: 'When a man strikes his slave, male or female, with a rod and the slave dies under his hand, he shall be punished'. In either case, Stark is uninformed about problems with the interpretation of the Hebrew.

The main problem is that the Hebrew root *nqm* (נקם), translated as 'punished', does not necessarily mean that the slavemaster is killed. Usually, death penalty cases use the Hebrew expression *môt yûmat* (מות יומת), 'he shall surely die'. Note that the NRSV, REB, and NAB have 'punished', not 'killed'. Similarly, the New Jerusalem Bible has 'pay the penalty', and not 'killed'.

Westbrook argues that the best analogy to Exod. 21.20 is found in cuneiform laws addressing the death of persons who were used as collateral or pledges for loans.[63] If a person sent his son as a pledge to a lender, and that son dies, then the 'revenge' or 'punishment' might be the death of the lender's son, not the lender. In any case, Stark again shows himself utterly uncritical in his use of sources and in his knowledge of the field of biblical law.

Exodus 21.26-27: Beating Manumission

Stark cites the Hebrew law wherein 'freedom was to be awarded any slave as compensation for suffering acts of violence'.[64] He refers to the laws in Exod. 21.26-27: 'When a man strikes the eye of his slave, male or female, and destroys it, he shall let the slave go free for the eye's sake. If he knocks out the tooth of his slave, male or female, he shall let the slave go free for the tooth's sake.' Stark's assertion is half-true, at best. Freedom was granted for loss of certain organs only, and these included eyes and teeth. However, freedom was not granted for suffering other acts of violence, as is clear just a few verses (20-21) earlier: 'When a man strikes his slave, male or female, with a rod and the slave dies under his hand, he shall be punished. But if the slave survives a day or two, he is not to be punished; for the slave is his money.' So, why does Stark not regard these as acts of violence that merit freedom? A Hebrew master can beat a slave nearly to death, and not fear any punishment. The reason given is because 'a slave is his money' (כי כספו הוא), and 'money' is a thing, not a human being.[65]

---

62. Stark, *For the Glory of God*, p. 328.
63. Westbrook, *Studies in Biblical and Cuneiform Law*, p. 91.
64. Stark, *For the Glory of God*, p. 328.
65. Riesener (*Der Stamm* עבד *im Alten Testament*, p. 1) regards this statement as one of the clearest indications of a chattel view of a slave. She remarks: 'Hier wird der עֶבֶד als

4. Slavery in the Hebrew Bible/Old Testament 81

Paul Copan attempts to mitigate the significance of this Hebrew expression by claiming that '[t]he debt slave is referred to as the master's money, suggesting that the master harms himself if he harms his servant'.[66] However, the expression, 'for the slave is his money', is introduced by the Hebrew explanatory particle, *kî* (כִּי), which explains the previous statement regarding the master: 'he is not to be punished'. So, syntactically, it is not the 'potential loss' that is being explained by the phrase introduced by *kî*, but rather why the master is not punished. Accordingly, we can render also it as: 'he [the master] is not to be punished because the slave is his property'. Note that the REB has 'because the slave is his property' and the NRSV has 'for the slave is the owner's property' in Exod. 21.21.

However, even if 'his money' referred only figuratively to the slavemaster hurting his own income, this still does not mean that the slave is viewed as better than chattel or an animal in this situation. Wasting your money could equally apply to destroying chattel. A master is also not punished for beating his own animals. Accordingly, the phrase 'because the slave is his money' does not preclude understanding the harm to a slave as any more offensive than harm to a master's animals or non-living property.

The inhumanity of this biblical law is even more apparent when one compares it to the laws of Athens. In regard to violence against slaves at Athens, Xenophon says: 'You can't hit them there' (οὔτε πατάξαι ἔξεστιν αὐτόθι).[67] According to Stark's logic, we should hail the law at Athens as a great advancement for slaves because we have gone from being allowed to impart near-death violence upon slaves to not hitting them at all.

As for better manumission criteria, Plato encourages freeing a slave who rescues a father or mother being attacked by their children ('And if a slave come to the rescue, let him be made free').[68] No beating is necessary to be freed. Consider also Laws 170-171 of the *CH*, which describes what happens to the estate of a man who has children by both his first-ranking wife and his slave woman:

> If a man's first-ranking wife bears him children and his slave woman bears him children, and the father during his lifetime then declares to (or: concerning) the children whom the slave woman bore to him, 'My children', and he

---

der völlig zum Eigentum Verfallene gesehen, nämlich nur unter dem materiellen Gesichtspunk, dass er zum "Besitz" desjenigen gehört, der ihn gekauft und getötet hat'. On not including the killing of a slave within the laws of homicide, see also Pamela Barmash, *Homicide in the Biblical World* (Cambridge: Cambridge University Press, 2005), p. 124.

66. Copan, 'Are Old Testament Laws Evil?', p. 141 n. 30. For an interpretation similar to that of Copan, see Walter C. Kaiser, *Toward Old Testament Ethics* (Grand Rapids, MI: Zondervan, 1991), p. 102.

67. Xenophon, *The Athenians* 1.10.

68. Plato, *Laws* 9.881c (Bury, LCL): δοῦλος δὲ βοηθήσας μὲν ἐλεύθερος γιγνέσθω.

reckons them with the children of the first-ranking wife—after the father goes to his fate, the children of the first-ranking wife and the children of the slave woman shall equally divide the property of the paternal estate; the preferred heir is a son of the first-ranking wife, he shall select and take a share first.[69]

However, if the patriarch does not adopt the children of his slavewoman, then:

> The release of the slave woman and her children shall be secured; the children of the first-ranking wife will not make claims of slavery against the children of the slave woman.[70]

So, freedom is granted to slave-women and their children who were not formally adopted by a master. No beating is necessary to release these slaves. These children of slaves are not treated as property, but as an actual part of the master's family.

In addition, the children of slave-women could be co-inheritors with the children of the formal wife. This contrasts to the cruel attitude expressed by Sarah concerning Ishmael, Abraham's biological son by Hagar, a slave-woman in Gen. 21.10: 'Cast out this slave woman with her son; for the son of this slave woman shall not be heir with my son Isaac'. God tells Abraham to follow this injunction (Gen. 21.12) regardless of Abraham's sympathy for Ishmael. So, where Abraham might represent a humanizing tendency, God demands the more inhumane option.

According to Hezser, '[i]t seems that in contrast to later Roman and Jewish society the patrilineal principle governed the determination of the children's slave or freeborn status here'.[71] Thus, Ishmael would be considered free because Abraham is free. However, Hezser does not deny that Abraham did as Sarah wished in terms of disinheriting Ishmael. The point remains that God is portrayed as treating Ishmael's inheritance quite differently from what some Babylonian law might instruct.

Paul repeats and endorses Sarah's cruel actions in Gal. 4.30, which should be counted as a regression relative to the rights of the children of slave-women in the *CH*. Even Mendelsohn, the main source that Stark cites for his pronouncements on ancient Near Eastern law, is forced to admit that:

> The recognition that the slave, though legally a chattel, was a human being and that as such he possessed certain inalienable rights found its expression also in the law codes. The Hammurabi Code recognized as legally binding a marriage contracted between a slave and a freeborn woman and although legally the slave with all his possessions was the property of his master, the children born of such a marriage were free.[72]

---

69. Citing Law 170 in Roth, *Law Collections*, pp. 113-14.
70. Citing Law 171 in Roth, *Law Collections*, p. 114.
71. Hezser, *Jewish Slavery in Antiquity*, p. 192.
72. Mendelsohn, *Slavery in the Ancient Near East*, p. 122.

In actuality, Mendelsohn had many other comments that showed Near Eastern law in a better light, but Stark and others seem to ignore them.[73]

Leviticus 25.42: Who's your Master?

Moshe Weinfeld, one of the most acute observers of the parallels between biblical and Mesopotamian ethics, trumpets the superiority of the biblical concept of slavery expressed in Lev. 25.42: 'for they are My servants, whom I brought forth out of the land of Egypt; they should not be sold as slaves...' As Weinfeld notes, this is very similar to ideas found in Mesopotamia, Greece, and Egypt insofar as the release of slaves is premised on the idea that a human being should be serving a god rather than another human being. Weinfeld, however, still directs readers to significant differences:

> But there is a decisive difference between the Israelite approach and that of Mesopotamia or Egypt. In Israel, servitude to God is expressed as submission to the Divine will and to His religious and ethical commandments, while in Mesopotamia and Egypt it is literally understood as service of the gods in their temple. Thus, in the inscription of Maništušu, king of Akkad (22nd century BCE), we read that 'he freed thirty-eight cities from corvee and from levy that they might serve on behalf of the temple of the god Shamash alone'.[74]

The document to which he appeals is the Cruciform Monument, which purports to come from one of Sargon's successors, but is probably a late Babylonian composition.[75]

Weinfeld's generalizations are unwarranted. First, the genres of the biblical texts cited by Weinfeld are not analogous to the Cruciform Monument, a fictional biography in which the king releases thirty-eight cities from their normal servitude in order to serve the temple of the god Shamash. That is to say, they are not being released but rather transferred from one task to another. A better comparison, therefore, would be acts of *misharum* in

---

73. For example, Mendelsohn (*Slavery in the Ancient Near East*, p. 33) also commends the *CH* for halving the period of indentured servitude compared to the Bible.

74. Moshe Weinfeld, *Social Justice in Ancient Israel and in the Ancient Near East* (Jerusalem: Magness Press, 1995), p. 16. For a similar view, but comparing Hebrew and Greco-Roman cultures, see Benjamin G. Wright III, "EBED/DOULOS—Terms and Social Status in the Meeting of Hebrew Biblical and Hellenistic-Roman Culture', in Callahan, Horsley, and Smith (eds.), *Slavery in Text and Interpretation*, pp. 83-111; also reprinted in Benjamin Wright III, *Praise Israel for Wisdom and Instruction: Essays on Ben Sira and Wisdom, the Letter of Aristeas and the Septuagint* (SJSJ, 131; Leiden: E.J. Brill, 2008), pp. 213-45.

75. Weinfeld, *Social Justice*, pp. 80, 102. See further E. Sollberger, 'The Cruciform Monument', *Jaarbericht van het Vooraziatisch-Egyptisch Genootschap 'Ex Oriente Lux'* 20 (1967–68), pp. 50-70.

Mesopotamia, where people are released without being transferred to another task.[76]

Second, Weinfeld does not mention that Israel may have had a whole class of temple slaves (1 Chron. 9.2; Neh. 5.7). As Ze'ev Falk observes, '[t]he temple slaves, called *nethinim* (dedicated), developed in the course of time into a cultic guild of religious functionaries and returned from Babylonian exile together with other strata of Hebrew society'.[77] So why is Maništušu's dedication of some people to temple service regarded as characteristic of Mesopotamian practice, when a similar variety of slave assignments can be observed in the Bible?

Third, the reason that release of Hebrew slaves was comparatively less onerous is because Deuteronomy, in particular, used outsiders to do labor that Israelites might not want to do. Josephus seems very cognizant of this when he speaks of the Israelite exemption from slavery:

> But of the Hebrews no one was a slave—or was it reasonable when God had made so many nations subject to them, from whom they ought to raise their force of serfs that they may themselves should be reduced to that condition—but they bore arms and served in the field on chariots rather than lead the lives of slaves.[78]

In addition, biblical injunctions tell us that serving God involves all sorts of labor that is no less onerous than what Weinfeld mentions. For example, 'submission to the Divine will' could involve dying in a battle or killing Canaanite infants whose parents did not submit to Yahweh.

Leviticus 25.35-43: Jubilee Manumission

Paul Copan sees the releasing of Hebrew slaves in the seventh year as a moral advancement: 'Hebrew (debt) slaves—which could be compared to

---

76. On these edicts, see Gregory C. Chirichigno, *Debt-Slavery in Israel and the Ancient Near East* (JSOTSup, 141; Sheffield: Sheffield Academic Press, 1993), pp. 85-86.

77. Ze'ev W. Falk, *Hebrew Law in Biblical Times* (Winona Lake, IN: Eisenbrauns, 2001), p. 115. See also Alejandro Botta, 'Nethinim', in *NIDB*, IV, pp. 260-61; S. Zawadizki, 'A Contribution to the Understanding of *širkûtu* in the Light of a Text from the Ebabbar Archive', *AoF* 24 (1997), pp. 226-30. Baruch Levine ('The Netînîm', *JBL* 82 [1963], pp. 207-12) argues that the Nethinim were a professional guild rather than slaves. However, a servile and a professional status need not be mutually exclusive. See further Kristin Kleber, 'Neither Slave nor Truly Free: The Status of the Dependents of Babylonian Temple Households', in Culbertson (ed.), *Slaves and Households*, pp. 101-11.

78. Josephus, *Ant.* 8.161-162 (Thackeray and Marcus, LCL): τῶν γὰρ Ἑβραίων οὐδεὶς ἐδούλευεν (οὐδ' ἦν εὔλογον ἔθνη πολλὰ τοῦ Θεοῦ δεδωκότος αὐτοῖς ὑποχείρια, δεόν ἐκ τούτων ποιεῖσθαι τὸ θητικόν, αὐτοὺς κατάγειν εἰς τοῦτο τὸ σχῆμα) ἀλλὰ πάντες ἐν ὅπλοις ἐφ' ἁρμάτων καὶ ἵππων στρατευόμενοι μᾶλλον ἢ δουλεύοντες διῆγον.

indentured servants during the founding of America—were to be granted release in the seventh year (Lev. 29[sic].35-43)—a notable improvement over other ANE law codes'.[79] Yet, this seems to contradict his own footnote 52: 'The Code of Hammurabi also makes provision for manumission'.[80] So why is the release of slaves ('manumission') in Leviticus an improvement over *CH*, which also had manumission?

In fact, Leviticus 25 can be seen as worse than the *CH* when it comes to manumission. That chapter (vv. 8-13) also advocates release of slaves in the year of 'Jubilee' which would be the 50th (or 49th) year. As Matitiahu Tsevat notes, 'in the extreme case a slave would have to work forty-nine years, in an average case twenty-four years, leaving out of consideration failing health or early death'.[81] In addition, the *CH* does not restrict manumission to 'Babylonians', whereas Leviticus restricts manumission to Hebrews. Hammurabi's Code seems more open and without regard to ethnicity here.

Moreover, long before Leviticus 25, Mesopotamian kings promulgated so-called *misharum* (equity) acts, which could include the release of whole classes of people. As Raymond Westbrook notes:

> The proclamation of a *misharum* was an institution of the utmost significance in Old Babylonian society. It was originally thought that each king proclaimed a *misharum* as a once-only measure upon his accession to the throne, but J. Finkelstein has shown that misharum enactments might occur several times at intervals throughout a king's reign. For RimSin of Larsa there is a record of three such enactments falling on about the 26th, 35th, and 41st years... Samsuiluna in his first and eighth year.[82]

These releases by RimSin and Samsuiluna (c. eighteenth century BCE) were in intervals of 9, 6, and 7 years, respectively, and so quite comparable to the seven years of Leviticus.

Therefore, there is really no advance on this issue in the Bible. In fact, we can argue that some biblical practices resulted from imitating ancient Near Eastern institutions rather than from biblical innovations. We can find imitations of the *misharum* idea in Isa. 61.1-2:

79. Copan, 'Are Old Testament Laws Evil?', p. 141.
80. Copan, 'Is Yahweh a Moral Monster?' (online: www.epsociety.org/ library/ articles. asp?pid=45&mode=footnotes#52).
81. Matitiahu Tsevat, 'The Hebrew Slave according to Deuteronomy 15.12-18: His Lot and Value of his Work, with Special Attention to the meaning of מִשְׁנֶה', *JBL* 113 (1994), pp. 587-95 (594). For a more thorough treatment of the Jubilee, see John Sietze Bergsma, *The Jubilee from Leviticus to Qumran: A History of Interpretation* (Supplements to Vetus Testamentum, 115; Leiden: E.J. Brill, 2007). See also Calum M. Carmichael, 'Three Laws on the Release of Slaves (Exodus 21.2-11; Deuteronomy 15.12-18; Leviticus 25.39-46)', *ZAW* 112 (2000), pp. 509-25.
82. Raymond Westbrook, *Property and the Family in Biblical Law* (Sheffield: Sheffield Academic Press, 1991), p. 45.

> The Spirit of the Lord GOD is upon me, because the LORD has anointed me to bring good tidings to the afflicted; he has sent me to bind up the brokenhearted, to proclaim liberty to the captives, and the opening of the prison to those who are bound; to proclaim the year of the LORD's favor, and the day of vengeance of our God; to comfort all who mourn.

Jesus himself is simply continuing the *misharum* idea when he quotes this passage in Lk. 4.18-21.

Leviticus 25.44-46: Enslaving Outsiders

This passage was certainly one of the most often quoted by pro-slavery advocates to demonstrate that God allowed slavery. In its fuller context, the passage reads:

> And if your brother becomes poor beside you, and sells himself to you, you shall not make him serve as a slave: he shall be with you as a hired servant and as a sojourner. He shall serve with you until the year of the jubilee; then he shall go out from you, he and his children with him, and go back to his own family, and return to the possession of his fathers. For they are my servants, whom I brought forth out of the land of Egypt; they shall not be sold as slaves. You shall not rule over him with harshness, but shall fear your God. As for your male and female slaves whom you may have: you may buy male and female slaves from among the nations that are round about you. You may also buy from among the strangers who sojourn with you and their families that are with you, who have been born in your land; and they may be your property. You may bequeath them to your sons after you, to inherit as a possession for ever; you may make slaves of them, but over your brethren the people of Israel you shall not rule, one over another, with harshness (Lev. 25.39-46).

According to Bernard Levinson, the RSV, among other modern versions, incorrectly connects the Hebrew phrase *le'olam* (לעלם), usually translated 'forever', with the preceding clause ('inherit as a possession forever') instead of with the following ('forever—them—may you make work as slaves') in v. 46.[83] In any case, the text clearly allows the enslavement of 'outsiders'.

Levinson also makes a compelling argument that this passage is meant to revise the law in Exod. 21.6, which allows the enslavement of Hebrews.[84] Leviticus 25.39-44, in contrast, specifically prohibits enslaving Hebrews, and shifts slavery completely to outsiders. If this is the case, then calling this an 'advance' would be most questionable. On the one hand, one could argue

---

83. For a redactional analysis, which views this passage as revising the Covenant Code, see Bernard M. Levinson, 'The Birth of the Lemma: The Restrictive Reinterpretation of the Covenant Code's Manumission Law by the Holiness Code (Leviticus 25.44-46)', *JBL* 124 (2005), pp. 617-39 (625).

84. Levinson, 'The Birth of the Lemma', pp. 617-39.

that the categories of slaves have become more restricted, and that means theoretically less people can be enslaved. On the other hand, one could argue that it bespeaks of a further differentiation between insiders and outsiders that later authorized the enslavement of non-Christians, including Muslims and Africans.

Deuteronomy 15 and Inner-Biblical Progress

A case of inner-biblical trajectorialism is illustrated by Deuteronomy 15. When comparing the Bible to Near Eastern cultures, Paul Copan assures us: 'On the other hand, Israel's laws reveal a dramatic, humanizing improvement over the practices of the other ANE peoples'.[85] Within the Bible, he says we also find improvement: 'What is more, the three main texts regarding slave legislation (Exod. 21; Lev. 25; Deut. 15) reveal a morally improved legislation as the text progresses'.[86] This progression, of course, presupposes a textual chronology that is still debated.[87]

In any case, what was so improved in Deuteronomy 15 compared with Exodus 21 or Leviticus 25? The relevant passage states:

> If your brother, a Hebrew man, or a Hebrew woman, is sold to you, he shall serve you six years, and in the seventh year you shall let him go free from you. And when you let him go free from you, you shall not let him go empty-handed; you shall furnish him liberally out of your flock, out of your threshing floor, and out of your wine press; as the LORD your God has blessed you, you shall give to him. You shall remember that you were a slave in the land of Egypt, and the LORD your God redeemed you; therefore I command you this today (Deut. 15.12-15).

It is difficult to see any trajectory towards improvement, given that Copan admits that:

> [T]he Pentateuch's legal code in places does differentiate between Israelite and non-Israelite slaves (for example, Exod. 12.43, where non-Israelites are not to partake in the Passover); it grants remitting loans to Israelites but not to foreigners (Deut. 15.3); it allows for exacting interest from a foreigner but not from a fellow Israelite (Deut. 23.20); Moabites and Ammonites are excluded from the sanctuary (Deut. 23.3).[88]

---

85. Copan, 'Is Yahweh a Moral Monster?'
86. Copan, 'Is Yahweh a Moral Monster?'
87. For the argument that Lev. 25 is postexilic, see Adrian Schenker, 'The Biblical Legislation on the Release of Slaves: The Road from Exodus to Leviticus', *JSOT* 78 (1998), pp. 23-41. For the argument that Deuteronomy cannot necessarily be seen as an 'advance' relative to Near Eastern cultures, see Paul E. Dion, 'Changements sociaux et changements législatifs dans le Deutéronome', *Eglise et théologie* 24 (1993), pp. 343-60.
88. Copan, 'Is Yahweh a Moral Monster?'

Nonetheless, Copan offers us this reassurance:

> To stop here, as the new atheists do, is to overlook the Pentateuch's narrative indicating God's concern for bringing blessing to all humanity (Gen. 12.1-3). Even more fundamentally, human beings have been created in God's image as co-rulers with God over creation (Gen. 1.26-7; Ps. 8).[89]

If we used the intention to bring blessing to all humanity, then it is clear that the *CH* would also satisfy this requirement. Recall that the Prologue to the *CH* includes this motive: 'to further the well-being of mankind'.

If we look at what the 'blessing' of humanity means in the Bible, then it is also not as benign as it appears. Copan quotes Gen. 12.1-3 for support. But Gen. 12.6 foreshadows the fact that the native population of Canaan eventually will be slaughtered to make way for the Israelites. Genesis 12.3 indicates that those who do not agree with the Abrahamic plan will be cursed. In fact, the ultimate goal is for Yahweh to be in full control of all humanity, and humanity will be his slaves, and slaves to his people (e.g., the aforementioned Isa. 14.1-2). In short, Copan is already working with a very biased view of 'blessing'.

Deuteronomy 23.15: Fugitive Slaves

According to Rodney Stark, Deut. 23.15 shows humanitarian advances, especially when compared to the *CH*, which 'prescribed death for anyone who helped a slave to escape'.[90] Deuteronomy 23.15-16 says: 'You shall not give up to his master a slave who has escaped from his master to you; he shall dwell with you, in your midst, in the place which he shall choose within one of your towns, where it pleases him best; you shall not oppress him'. However, it is not clear that Stark is comparing analogous laws because he overlooks why hiding a slave could be viewed as an act of re-appropriating someone else's property rather than helping slaves gain freedom.

In actuality, Stark does not specifically cite the law in the *CH* he is referencing. Stark depends on Mendelsohn, and the latter is referring to Laws 15-20 of the *CH*.[91] Unfortunately, Stark does not tell readers that Mendelsohn also says: 'The death penalty decreed by the Hammurabi Code for enticing a slave to flee or for harboring a fugitive slave, seems to have become obsolete by the Neo-Babylonian period'.[92] So why does that not count as a humanitarian 'advance'?

---

89. Copan, 'Is Yahweh a Moral Monster?'
90. Stark, *For the Glory of God*, pp. 325, 328.
91. Mendelsohn, *Slavery in the Ancient Near East*, pp. 58-59.
92. Mendelsohn, *Slavery in the Ancient Near East*, p. 62.

In any case, Mendelsohn alludes more specifically to Law 16, which Martha Roth translates as follows: 'If a man should harbor a fugitive slave or slave woman of either the palace or of a commoner in his house and not bring him out at the herald's public proclamation, that householder shall be killed'.[93] Yet, it is not clear that the *CH* viewed this as a simple case of a person sheltering a fugitive slave who wanted freedom. The Akkadian word that Roth translates a '[should] harbor' is *raqû*, which also means 'to hide'.[94] One could use it to describe the concealment of stolen property.

The Akkadian word, *ḥalāqu*, which Roth plausibly translated as 'fugitive', can also mean 'missing' or 'lost'. Therefore, it can apply to objects, as in *CH* 126:

> If a man whose property is not lost [*ḥaliqma*] should declare 'my property is lost [*ḥaliq*]', and accuse his city quarter, his city quarter shall establish against him before the god that no property of his is lost [*ḥalqu*], and he shall give to his city quarter twofold whatever he claimed.[95]

In this law, the form *ḥalqu* is stative or adjectival, and analogous to what we find in *CH* 16. Thus, *ḥalqu* does not necessarily describe an active act of fleeing or even the state after fleeing on the part of any object 'lost' or 'missing'. Silver could be 'missing' without silver objects fleeing. Law 16 also does not say that the householder will be automatically killed. The householder is killed only if he does not heed the summon of the herald (presumably to return the slave).

In any case, *CH* 16 may regard that missing slave, fugitive or not, as having been kidnapped or stolen. We find a similar idea in the Theodosian Code (4.7.6), which states: 'It is unlawful to harbor another person's slave, and anyone guilty of such an act will be condemned for the abduction of the slave of another'.[96] If so, then the *CH* is prescribing the same penalty against manstealing that Sprinkle said was more humanitarian when it occurred in Exod. 21.16.

The Theodosian Code also suggests why we cannot consider harboring fugitives as purely humanitarian in all cases. Slaves could be coveted by other slave owners because it costs money to buy new slaves. Similarly, keeping fugitive slaves could mitigate the cost of purchasing slaves in ancient Israel. Furthermore, any foreign slave who fled to Israel had to become a slave of Yahweh, and submit to Yahwistic religious laws. Thus, a slave lost his religious freedom.

93. Roth, *Law Collections*, p. 84.
94. See *raqû*, in *CAD*, XIV, p. 175.
95. Roth, *Law Collections*, p. 105.
96. Clyde Pharr (ed.), *The Theodosian Code and Novels and the Sirmondian Constitutions* (Princeton, NJ: Princeton University Press, 1952), pp. 88-89.

90   *Slavery, Abolitionism, and the Ethics of Biblical Scholarship*

Furthermore, not all Near Eastern cultures returned fugitives. Raymond Westbrook observes, 'Kings had a traditional discretion to grant or refuse asylum to fugitives. As between kings of equal status, they were under no legal obligation to return fugitives upon demand, unless it was specifically provided for by treaty'.[97] Temples served as asylums in the Hellenistic world. A law passed by the Messenians around 91 BCE stated that 'slaves are allowed to flee to the Temple for refuge'.[98] Slaves could flee to temples if the master was cruel. If the slave owner demanded the slave's return from the temple, '[t]he priest is to make a ruling about any runaways who come from our own city... If he does not hand him over, the slave may go free from the master who owns him.'[99]

1 Samuel 8: Exclusive Service to Yahweh?

Dexter Callender offers a well-known argument for the distinctiveness of Hebrew slavery when he refers to 1 Samuel 8 as part of the evidence for his larger thesis: 'Israelite exclusive servitude to God is then precisely the basis for its sharp rejection of all forms of human servitude, whether chattel slavery, the prolongation of debt-slavery, or "forced labor", as discussed above'.[100] According to the biblical passage:

> And the LORD said to Samuel, 'Hearken to the voice of the people in all that they say to you; for they have not rejected you, but they have rejected me from being king over them'... He said, 'These will be the ways of the king who will reign over you: he will take your sons and appoint them to his chariots and to be his horsemen, and to run before his chariots... He will take your menservants and maidservants, and the best of your cattle and your asses, and put them to his work. He will take the tenth of your flocks, and you shall be his slaves' (1 Sam. 8.7, 11, 16-17).

For Callender, recognizing Yahweh as the only king leads the Israelites to view 'monarchy as an unacceptable slavery'.[101] As did Weinfeld, Callender

---

97. Raymond Westbrook, 'International Law in the Amarna Age', in Raymond Cohen and Raymond Westbrook (eds.), *Amarna Diplomacy: The Beginnings of International Relations* (Baltimore: The Johns Hopkins University Press, 2000), pp. 28-41 (36).

98. Thomas Wiedemann, *Greek and Roman Slavery* (London: Croom Helm, 1981), pp. 195-96. For comments on the rights of slaves at sanctuaries, see also Philo, *Every Good Man Is Free* 148, and *On the Virtues* 124 (Colson, LCL).

99. Wiedemann, *Greek and Roman Slavery*, p. 196. See also Justus H. Lipsius, *Das attische Recht und Rechtsverfahren mit Benutzung des attischen Processes* (2 vols.; Leipzig; O.R. Reisland, 1905), II, pp. 642-43.

100. Dexter Callender, 'Servants of God(s) and Servants of Kings', in Callahan, Horsley, and Smith (eds.), *Slavery in Text and Interpretation*, pp. 67-82 (79).

101. Callender, 'Servants of God(s)', p. 77.

also appeals to Lev. 25.55: 'For to me the people of Israel are servants, they are my servants whom I brought forth out of the land of Egypt: I am the LORD your God'.

However, there are a number of problems with the thesis that exclusive servitude to Yahweh led to rejection of 'all forms of human servitude'. First, Callender's own statement contains a glaring inconsistency. If 'all forms of human servitude' are rejected because the Israelites see themselves as exclusive servants of Yahweh, then how can there even be 'debt-slavery' at all? How does not prolonging debt-slavery show that 'all forms of human servitude' are rejected? By that logic, all *misharum* acts in Mesopotamia can mean that Mesopotamians rejected 'all forms of human servitude'.

Second, Callender is engaging in 'representativism' insofar as he believes 1 Samuel 8 represents all 'Israelite' attitudes toward servitude to human beings or kingship. But an opposing tradent within Samuel apparently saw monarchy as necessary because when referring to Saul, the first king of Israel, God says:

> Tomorrow about this time I will send to you a man from the land of Benjamin, and you shall anoint him to be prince over my people Israel. He shall save my people from the hand of the Philistines; for I have seen the affliction of my people, because their cry has come to me (1 Sam. 9.16).

In fact, other tradents even enjoin Judeans to serve foreign kings as does Jeremiah:

> Now I have given all these lands into the hand of Nebuchadnezzar, the king of Babylon, my servant, and I have given him also the beasts of the field to serve him. All the nations shall serve him and his son and his grandson, until the time of his own land comes; then many nations and great kings shall make him their slave. But if any nation or kingdom will not serve this Nebuchadnezzar king of Babylon, and put its neck under the yoke of the king of Babylon, I will punish that nation with the sword, with famine, and with pestilence, says the LORD, until I have consumed it by his hand. So do not listen to your prophets, your diviners, your dreamers, your soothsayers, or your sorcerers, who are saying to you, 'You shall not serve the king of Babylon'. For it is a lie which they are prophesying to you, with the result that you will be removed far from your land, and I will drive you out, and you will perish. But any nation which will bring its neck under the yoke of the king of Babylon and serve him, I will leave on its own land, to till it and dwell there, says the LORD (Jer. 27.6-11).

So, why not deem this text as 'representative' of Yahweh's preferences for Israel's servitude?

The fact is that even the passages that Callender cites for support do not show that Yahweh's exclusive claim to rulership was incompatible 'with all forms of human servitude'. Serving Yahweh was always done through human intermediaries and institutions. Serving Yahweh could mean serving an

Israelite king or a foreign king, such as Nebuchadnezzar, who is also deemed God's servant. It could mean being a good slave to a temple priest (e.g., Samuel at the temple at Shiloh) or servant to an Israelite king. This idea was well known to Philo of Alexandria (*Every Good Man Is Free* 19-20):

> Let us hear the voice of Sophocles in words which are as true as any Delphic Oracle: 'God and no mortal is my Sovereign' [θεὸς ἐμὸς ἄρχων, θνητὸς οὐδείς]. For in very truth he who has God alone for his leader, he alone is free, though to my thinking he is also the leader of all others, having received the charge of earthly things from the great, the immortal King, whom he, the mortal, serves as viceroy.[102]

Philo credits the Greeks, and not his own Jewish tradition, with emphasizing this idea.

So, a more accurate way to view this ideal of an exclusive service to Yahweh is to see which human 'viceroy' of God receives the actual service. In the Deuteronomistic History, those tradents that rejected the king as Yahweh's intermediary, favored serving the prophets or priests. Thus, in Deut. 18.15 we have: 'The LORD your God will raise up for you a prophet like me from among you, from your brethren—him you shall heed'. In other words, monarchy was only one form of servitude to Yahweh, and rejecting monarchy did not mean rejecting 'all forms of human servitude'.

Indeed, a priest such as Ezra had the power of death over those who did not obey God's law because he was the intermediary for God's law. Note the following:

> And you, Ezra, according to the wisdom of your God which is in your hand, appoint magistrates and judges who may judge all the people in the province Beyond the River, all such as know the laws of your God; and those who do not know them, you shall teach. Whoever will not obey the law of your God and the law of the king, let judgment be strictly executed upon him, whether for death or for banishment or for confiscation of his goods or for imprisonment (Ezra 7.25-26).

It is clear that Ezra's authority was part of God's larger plan (see also Ezra 6.14). In short, unless one sees Yahweh as a real king or god, then any servitude to Yahweh meant servitude to a human intermediary of some sort, whether it be a priest, king, or prophet (cf. Rom. 13.1-4).

Ezra 2.64-65 and Slave Societies

Almost every attempt to mitigate biblical slavery mentions how few slaves there were in ancient Israel relative to other cultures. Callender tells us that 'the reigning consensus has been that slavery in the ancient Near East

---

102. Philo, *Every Good Man Is Free* 19-20 (Colson, LCL).

4. Slavery in the Hebrew Bible/Old Testament 93

differed from that found in classical Greek and Roman societies'.[103] Callender then quotes Roland de Vaux, as follows: 'in Israel and the neighboring countries there never existed those enormous gangs of chattel [sic] slaves which in Greece and Rome continually threatened the balance of social order'.[104] In other words, many Christian apologists claim that ancient Israel was not a slave society on a par with neighboring cultures or New World slavery.

Although it may be true that ancient Israel probably did not have sizable plantations that required large gangs of slaves, we do have evidence that such large slave gangs were acceptable, at least in theory. For example, in 1 Kgs 5.13, we read: 'King Solomon raised a levy of forced labor out of all Israel; and the levy numbered thirty thousand men... Solomon also had seventy thousand burden-bearers and eighty thousand hewers of stone in the hill country'. However, Solomon perhaps just illustrated the evils of kingship (cf. 1 Sam. 8.17), and not actions approved by God.

But we also have more precise figures given in Ezra for the extent of slavery that seemed to be approved by the author. Ezra 2.64-65 says: 'The whole assembly together was forty-two thousand three hundred and sixty, besides their menservants and maidservants, of whom there were seven thousand three hundred and thirty-seven; and they had two hundred male and female singers'. These figures show that the percentage of slaves, at least in this returning community of Jewish exiles, compares quite reasonably with what we find in a list of 'Large-Scale Slave Systems' compiled by Orlando Patterson, and even when we use figures accepted by Rodney Stark. We can tabulate these comparisons (not counting singers) as follows:

49,697	Total population of Jewish 'assembly'
42,360	Free Jewish population
7,337	Slaves
14%	Percentage of slaves among Jewish 'assembly'
10%	Percentage of slaves in Roman Italy, 225–200 BCE[105]
16-20%	Percentage of slaves in the Roman Empire, 1–150 CE[106]
16.8%	Percentage of slave population in Kentucky in 1790[107]
17.7%	Percentage of slaves in America in 1790[108]

America in 1790 was called a slave society, and so why does the same not apply to this ancient biblical community?

    103. Callender, 'Servants of God(s)', p. 68.
    104. Callender, 'Servants of God(s)', p. 68. My copy of Roland de Vaux (*Ancient Israel: Social Institutions* [New York: McGraw–Hill, 1965], p. 80) omits 'chattel', and says: '...enormous gangs of slaves...'
    105. Patterson, *Slavery and Social Death*, p. 354.
    106. Patterson, *Slavery and Social Death*, p. 354.
    107. Stark, *For the Glory of God*, p. 321.
    108. Stark, *For the Glory of God*, p. 321.

Job 31.13-15 and Justice for Slaves

Marvin H. Pope was one of the ablest Semitic philologists and biblical commentators of his generation. But, in his commentary on Job, we detect apologetics within his philological commentary.[109] The relevant biblical passage says:

> If I have rejected the cause of my manservant or my maidservant, when they brought a complaint against me; what then shall I do when God rises up? When he makes inquiry, what shall I answer him? Did not he who made me in the womb make him? And did not one fashion us in the womb? (Job 31.13-15).

In the midst of arcane comments on caesuras and Semitic roots, Pope offers a digression about slaves in Israel: 'The lot of slaves in the ancient world was hard. The Mosaic Law attempted to mitigate their harsh treatment, especially of Israelite slaves, appealing to the fact that they once were a nation of slaves.'[110]

Pope then cites the usual passages (Exod. 21.2-11; Lev. 25.39-55; Deut. 5.14) and the ubiquitous Isaac Mendelsohn for support. But, as mentioned, Epictetus already told us that slaves and masters are all 'kinsmen...brethren by nature...the offspring of Zeus'.[111] The Sumerian Laws of Lipit-Ishtar allowed slaves to bring suits against masters.[112] Thus, the passage in Job is not necessarily more humanitarian than what we can find in the ancient Near East.

Joel 2.28-29: Possessing Slaves

In discussing the citation of Joel 2.28-29 in Acts 2.16-18, the German biblical scholar, Henneke Güzlow, proclaims this text to be revolutionary ('revolutionär gewesen sein') at the time Joel was written.[113] Joel 2.28-29 says:

> And it shall come to pass afterward, that I will pour out my spirit on all flesh; your sons and your daughters shall prophesy, your old men shall dream dreams, and your young men shall see visions. Even upon the menservants and maidservants in those days, I will pour out my spirit.

---

109. Marvin H. Pope, *Job* (AB, 15; Garden City, NY: Doubleday, 1986), pp. 232-33.
110. Pope, *Job*, p. 233.
111. *Epictetus* 1.13.4-5 (Oldfather, LCL).
112. Roth, *Law Collections*, p. 29.
113. Henneke Güzlow, *Christentum und Sklaverei in den ersten drei Jahrhunderten* (Bonn: Rudolf Habelt Verlag, 1969), p. 173: 'Dieser Ausspruch mag schon zu Zeiten Joels revolutionär gewesen sein, und auch Lukas hat die Sklaven nicht nur zufällig in sein Zitat aufgenommen'.

A closer look at what Güzlow considers 'revolutionary' yields nothing very significant. Güzlow believes that pouring the Spirit on slaves indicates their full participation in God's community. However, slaves who prophesied through some sort of spirit possession were already known in antiquity. At Mari (eighteenth century BCE), for example, one document tells us: 'In the temple of Annunitum, in the city of Ahatum, a servant girl of Dagan-Malik went into a trance and spoke'.[114] Güzlow ignores the fact that nothing is said in Joel about emancipating the slaves. They may be slaves who are being possessed by a divine spirit, but their bodies remained possessed by earthly masters.

Summary

This brief survey of representative biblical passages shows a repeated attempt by modern biblical scholars to mitigate the ethical implications of slavery in the Hebrew Bible. Some scholars ignore the slavery theme (e.g., Harrelson), and others try to engage in comparative ethics in order to show the superiority of biblical directives (e.g., Sprinkle, Weinfeld, Stark, Callender, Pope). A repeated technique is to compare the 'biblical' best with the pagan 'worst'. In all cases, we can find misrepresentation of neighboring cultures and/or the omission of countervailing examples and evidence.

---

114. Nissinen, Seow, and Ritner, *Prophets and Prophecy*, p. 48 (Akkadian): ina bīt Annunītum ša libbi ālim Aḫātum ṣuharat Dagan-Malik immaḫḫima kīam iqbi.

Chapter 5

SLAVERY IN THE NEW TESTAMENT

Christians regard the New Testament as their primary code of ethics. As is the case with the Old Testament, many Christian ethicists have a difficult time evading the fact that slavery was accepted by many New Testament authors. Briefly, scholars who discuss New Testament ethics use the following basic arguments when addressing slavery:
   (1) There is a canon within a canon, particularly privileging the 'authentic' Pauline epistles, which favor freedom.
   (2) Roman slavery is generally benign, and so any commands to be obedient slaves were not an unjust burden.
   (3) Roman slavery is generally brutal, and so the New Testament is benign by comparison.
   (4) Some passages that apparently support slavery actually do not (e.g., 1 Cor. 7.21 and Philemon).

Since I discuss Jesus in a separate chapter, here I focus on key New Testament passages that have been problematic for biblical ethicists. We aim to present the most plausible historical-critical conclusions about whether those passages endorse, condone, or condemn slavery.

Matthew 7.12: The Golden Rule

The Golden Rule was cited consistently by abolitionists as representing the Bible's anti-slavery message. Briefly the Golden Rule, as found in Mt. 7.12, states: 'So whatever you wish that men would do to you, do so to them; for this is the law and the prophets'. Yet, there are problems with crediting this rule with any movement toward abolition. As Alan Kirk notes, there are at least three ways to read this rule.[1] The first represents the Golden Rule as a completely disinterested action, and so it is the true paradigm of love. This interpretation is the one favored by many modern Christian interpreters,

---

1. Alan Kirk, '"Love your Enemies": The Golden Rule, and Ancient Reciprocity (Luke 6.27-35)', *JBL* 122 (2003), pp. 667-86.

especially those with pacifist leanings. A second interpretation emphasizes a reciprocal or neutral stance, in which equality is more of an economic transaction. A third interpretation focuses on self-interest.[2] This interpretation has antecedents in Greek authors who see a more Machiavellian strategy to vanquish the enemy. Thus, Thucydides speaks of the wisdom of one who 'vanquishes his foe by generosity'.[3] Being good to an enemy may oblige the enemy to return the favor. This interpretation is hardly ever assumed to be the motive behind Jesus' words.

Yet, whatever the motives, the Golden Rule did little to encourage abolition. For example, even in the New Testament, no author explicitly saw the Golden Rule as incompatible with slavery. Slaves were still told to obey their slavemasters in Eph. 6.5 and 1 Pet. 2.18. Jesus never condemned any slave holder with whom he interacted, and he never condemned slavery in general by citing the Golden Rule.

Second, slave owners could interpret the Golden Rule quite plausibly as directing people to treat others as they would like to be treated if they were in the same situation. Thus, all it would mean is that a slave should treat his master as he would like to be treated if he were the master. A master should treat his slave as he would like to be treated if he were a slave.

Finally, Christianity cannot claim any credit for originating the Golden Rule. As mentioned, Frederick Douglass had already observed that Confucius issued something similar to the Golden Rule about five hundred years before Christ. Again, Seneca also tells readers: 'Treat your inferiors as you would be treated by your betters'.[4] The Golden Rule is neither unique nor revolutionary in Christianity.

Acts 17.26 and Human Unity

One of the most oft-cited texts among American abolitionists supposedly establishes that human beings were all created equal. Some abolitionists cited it in the KJV which reads: 'And hath made of one blood all nations of men for to dwell on all the face of the earth, and hath determined the times before appointed, and the bounds of their habitation' (Acts 17.26). However, as modern scholars argue, the earliest and best manuscripts do not have the word 'blood', a conclusion indicated by the RSV rendition.[5]

---

2. See Jeffrey Wattles, *The Golden Rule* (New York: Oxford University Press, 1996), especially pp. 64-66.
3. *Thucydides* 4.19.1-4 (Smith, LCL): καὶ ἀρετῇ αὐτὸν νικήσας.
4. Seneca, *Epistles* 47.11-12 (Gummere, LCL).
5. See Bruce M. Metzger, *A Textual Commentary on the Greek New Testament* (London: United Bible Societies, 1975), p. 456.

> And he made from one every nation of men to live on all the face of the earth, having determined allotted periods and the boundaries of their habitation, that they should seek God, in the hope that they might feel after him and find him. Yet he is not far from each one of us, for 'In him we live and move and have our being'; as even some of your poets have said, 'For we are indeed his offspring' (Acts 17.26-28).

Note that previous expressions of similar thoughts by Greek thinkers are acknowledged by Paul himself in v. 28 ('even some of your poets have said...').

Indeed, all of this was not really new to Athenians or famous classical writers. As mentioned, Epictetus said something very similar. Seneca admonished his readers to 'remember that he whom you call your slave sprang from the same stock, is smiled upon by the same skies, and on equal terms with yourself breathes, lives, and dies'.[6] Cicero says 'men are grouped with Gods on the basis of blood relationship and descent...there is a blood relationship between ourselves and the celestial beings; or we may call it a common ancestry or origin'.[7] So why do Christian apologists credit Christianity for initiating the idea of universal brotherhood when even the New Testament says that the idea already existed in non-Christian cultures?

1 Corinthians 7.21: Better to Remain in Slavery?

Even if some scholars admit that pro-slavery views may be found in the New Testament, they still insist that Paul, a founding father of Christianity, was certainly not endorsing or condoning slavery. Ground-zero for this debate is 1 Cor. 7.21, which in a fuller context (1 Cor. 7.20-25) is translated by the NRSV as follows:

> Let each of you remain in the condition in which you were called. Were you a slave when called? Do not be concerned about it. Even if you can gain your freedom, make use of your present condition now more than ever. For whoever was called in the Lord as a slave is a freed person belonging to the Lord, just as whoever was free when called is a slave of Christ. You were bought with a price; do not become slaves of human masters. In whatever condition you were called, brothers and sisters, there remain with God.

---

6. Seneca, *Epistles* 47.10 (Gummere, LCL): 'Vis tu cogitare istum quem servum tuum vocas ex isdem seminibus ortum eodem frui caelo, aeque spirare, aeque vivere, aeque mori!!'

7. Cicero, *Laws* 1.7.24 (Keyes, LCL): 'ut homines deorum agnatione et gente teneantur...ex quo vere vel agnatio nobis eum caelestibus vel genus vel stirps appellari potest'.

In the NRSV rendition of v. 21, Paul seemingly encourages remaining in slavery even if there arose an opportunity for freedom. The NJB is even more explicit: 'even if you have a chance of freedom you should prefer to make full use of your condition as a slave'.

Richard Horsley strongly disagrees.[8] Indeed, the efforts to redeem this passage from a pro-slavery stance seem so urgent that at least two books have been written that focus on this single verse: J. Albert Harrill's *The Manumission of Slaves in Early Christianity* and Scott Bartchy's *First-Century Slavery and 1 Corinthians 7.21*.[9] As Horsley notes, the issue is whether 7.21 should be translated in one of the two following manners:

(1) 'Were you called a slave? Do not worry about it. But even if you can become free, rather make use of your slavery'.[10]
(2) 'You were called as a slave. Do not worry about it. But if you can indeed become free, use instead [freedom]'.[11]

A third option, favored by S. Scott Bartchy, argues that it is 'the calling' that Paul is urging slaves to choose.[12] However, Bartchy's reading can be considered a variant of the 'choose freedom' option.[13]

Choosing between these options centers, in part, on the Greek phrase *mallon chrēsai* (μᾶλλον χρῆσαι), which is translated 'use instead' in Option #2. The Greek aorist infinitive, χρῆσαι, does not have an explicit grammatical object. Thus, an object, usually in the dative case, has to be supplied. And so the issue is whether the object is:[14]

(1) τῇ δουλείᾳ: slavery (i.e., 'use slavery')
(2) τῇ ἐλευθερίᾳ: freedom (i.e., 'use freedom')

---

8. Horsley, 'Paul and Slavery', pp. 182-87; Horsley, *1 Corinthians* (Nashville: Abingdon Press, 1998), pp. 100-104.

9. Harrill, *The Manumission of Slaves*; Bartchy, *First-Century Slavery*. See also Güzlow, *Christentum und Sklaverei*, pp. 177-81. Both Harrill and Bartchy record an extensive history of interpretation that I need not repeat here.

10. Horsley ('Paul and Slavery', p. 183) calls this the 'standard established interpretation'. See also Harrill, *The Manumission of Slaves*, p. 101; Bartchy, *First-Century Slavery*, p. 183.

11. Harrill, *The Manumission of Slaves*, p. 122.

12. Harrill (*The Manumission of Slaves*, p. 101) considers the position of Bartchy to be a third 'possibility' because Bartchy has 'God's calling' as the object instead of 'slavery' or 'freedom'. I see Bartchy's position as a variant of the 'freedom' option.

13. Bartchy (*First-Century Slavery*, p. 183) translates 1 Cor. 7.21 as 'Were you a slave when you were called? Don't worry about it. But if, indeed, you become manumitted, by all means [as a freedman] live according to [God's calling].'

14. See 'χράομαι', BDAG, p. 1087b.

If one inserts 'slavery' as the object, then Paul is arguing that slaves should stay slaves even if they had the opportunity to be free. If one inserts 'freedom' as the object, then Paul is an advocate of freedom. As Bartchy notes, the choices have been so frustrating that one finds the same reference work, *TDNT*, displaying contradictory positions in separate articles.[15] The choice between those translations also depends on whether the phrase *ei kai* (εἰ καί) should be translated as:

(1) 'if indeed' OR
(2) 'even if'

If we chose 'if indeed', then this intensive phrase more naturally can be construed with the 'use freedom' option (e.g., 'If indeed you can become free, then use freedom'). If we use 'even if', then it would appear that Paul is using what is called a concessive clause, wherein the following clause usually requires an opposite sense. Under this scenario, Paul would mean: 'even if you can become free...use [slavery] instead [or: even more]'.[16]

Horsley believes that the argument is now settled. For Horsley, 'Paul cannot be understood to be helping legitimate the Roman institutional order, intentionally or unintentionally'.[17] Insofar as 1 Cor. 7.21 is concerned, Horsley claims that '[l]exical and syntactical considerations require the "choose freedom" reading'.[18] He calls this interpretation 'a fairly clear case, once we read the Greek text appropriately and get a sense of the rhetorical pattern of 1 Corinthians 7 as a whole and 7.17-24 in particular'.[19]

Part of Horsley's argument depends on a collection of Greek parallels compiled by Harrill.[20] These parallels are considered so powerful that Horsley confidently tells us:

---

15. Bartchy (*First-Century Slavery*, p. 5 n. 11) comments: 'It seems ironic that H. Schlier, writing on ἐλεύθερος in *TDNT*, II, supplies τῇ δουλείᾳ, while K. Rengstorf, writing on δοῦλος in the same volume, adds τῇ ἐλευθερίᾳ'.

16. Philip B. Payne suggests that μᾶλλον should be understood as 'elative' ('by all means'), and so would favor 'freedom'. But there is no reason serving Christ in a disadvantaged state cannot be viewed as a greater virtue, and just as 'elative'. Observe what Jesus said in Lk. 21.3 about the widow, who gave all she had even though others had given more: 'they all contributed out of their abundance, but she out of her poverty put in all the living that she had'. In any case, an elative is not grammatically determinative for selecting either reading. See Philip B. Payne, 'Twelve Reasons to Understand 1 Corinthians 7.21-23 as a Call to Gain Freedom' (2009), p. 3. Online: www.pbpayne.com/wp-admin/1_Cor._7-21_escape_slavery.pdf.

17. Horsley, 'Paul and Slavery', p. 164.
18. Horsley, 'Paul and Slavery', p. 184.
19. Horsley, 'Paul and Slavery', p. 195.
20. Horsley, 'Paul and Slavery', p. 184; Harrill, *The Manumission of Slaves*, pp. 108-17.

Even more decisive, it has recently been shown that 'the force of the adverb *mallon*, when used with the deponent verb *chraomai*', while occasionally appearing intensive, 'is usually adversative', so that it has the sense of 'instead' or 'preferably' rather than of 'more'.[21]

When we examine the parallels adduced by Harrill, however, the case is not so clear. The so-called parallels have a glaring difference from 1 Cor. 7.21 insofar as all, except perhaps one, have an explicit object.[22] So we are still without an example that shows clearly what the object should be when the object is missing. And while the majority of the examples might be adversative, the problem is that the object is still not identified clearly in 1 Cor. 7.21.

More importantly, Harrill chooses to not count as a parallel one example actually closer in context to 1 Cor. 7.21 than he suggests. This parallel is found in Josephus's *Antiquities* (18.243). Louis Feldman translates the relevant sentence in Josephus as: 'Do not inform the world that his poverty can make better use [μᾶλλον χρῆσθαι] of manly qualities [ἀρετῇ] than our riches'.[23] Harrill translates as follows: 'Do not broadcast that his poverty *can make use of* [μᾶλλον χρῆσθαι] virtue [ἀρετῇ] *more than* our riches'.[24]

Harrill gives this reason for dismissing μᾶλλον χρῆσθαι in Josephus as a parallel to 1 Cor. 7.21: '[b]ecause it is being used merely as a comparative between two nouns, one case of μᾶλλον and χρῆσθαι appearing together does not fit my typology'.[25] It is not clear, though, why we should disqualify the parallel in Josephus because it involves a comparison between two nouns. In 1 Cor. 7.21, there is no explicit object, but it could be there. In fact, two nouns (freedom/slavery) are already being inserted in many translations ('use freedom rather than slavery'). So, once we supply the hypothetical objects (e.g., slavery or freedom), why does having two nouns (virtue/riches; or poverty/riches for Harrill?) in a comparison offer less of a parallel than the others Harrill offers?[26]

---

21. Horsley, 'Paul and Slavery', p. 184, quoting Harrill, *The Manumission of Slaves*, p. 109. Glancy (*Slavery in Early Christianity*, p. 68) is also convinced by Harrill's parallels.

22. Harrill, *The Manumission of Slaves*, p. 116, example 15, where the object of μᾶλλον χρησομένην is not quite as clear.

23. Josephus, *Ant.* 18.243 (Feldman, LCL): μηδὲ πενίαν ἀποφήνῃς τὴν ἐκείνου τῆς ἡμετέρας εὐπορίας ἀρετῇ μᾶλλον χρῆσθαι. The last verb is a present middle infinitive rather than an aorist infinitive, but that should not detract from the parallel, and Harrill does not give that as a reason for rejecting the parallel.

24. Harrill, *The Manumission of Slaves*, p. 110 n. 179 (Harrill's italics).

25. Harrill, *The Manumission of Slaves*, p. 110 n. 179.

26. Harrill (*The Manumission of Slaves*, p. 109), himself speaks of 'two different situations' as allowable in some of his comparative examples whenever μᾶλλον + χράμομαι is used to express 'use X rather/instead'. But the expression, 'use situation X

In addition, Harrill ignores that the context of Josephus's passage is much more relevant to that of 1 Cor. 7.21 than to the other parallels he offers. Josephus is reporting the complaints of Herodias, who was irate because Herod, her husband and Tetrarch of Galilee and Perea, was not keeping up with the good fortunes of her brother, Agrippa. The latter was in debt and had been condemned to death. But Agrippa went to Rome, and came back to Palestine as a king.

Herodias wanted her husband to make every effort to surpass Agrippa in status, especially as Herod was actually richer than Agrippa. She says that Herod 'should not rest content to live as a commoner to the end of his life'.[27] In other words, Herodias complains that Herod wants to remain in the lower status in which he finds himself despite the opportunity to be better than Agrippa. It is at this point that Herodias utters this exasperated exclamation to Herod: 'Do not broadcast that his [Agrippa's] poverty *can make use of* virtue *more than* our riches'. In other words, a lower status sometimes was viewed as a virtuous advantage, and Herodias did not like that idea.

So it is difficult to see why Paul would deem it inconceivable to direct slaves to retain a lower status when Herod, a king, was thinking of retaining a lower status in his own case, and when Agrippa was perceived, by Herodias, to have used a disadvantaged status as a virtue. While this example alone does not prove which translation we should prefer in 1 Cor. 7.21, the parallel in Josephus should at least be evidence that some persons in Paul's culture viewed a disadvantaged condition as an opportunity.

As mentioned, the translation of the Greek phrase *ei kai* is also important for understanding the text. Scholars who prefer the 'better free' interpretation, assert that *ei kai* usually means 'if indeed' rather than 'even if/even though'.[28] Nonetheless, these same scholars admit that *ei kai* can mean 'even though'. Interestingly, the parallel from Josephus also includes an instance of ἀλλ' εἰ καί used concessively ('"Even if, O Herod," she said, "you were not distressed in the past to be lower in rank than the father from whom you sprang, now at least I beg of you to move in quest of the high position that you were born to"').[29]

---

rather/instead' usually can be more fully expressed as 'use situation X rather/instead than/of situation Y', and both X and Y can be nouns.

27. Josephus, *Ant.* 18.243 (Feldman, LCL): καθέζοιτο ἀγαπῶν ἐν ἰδιωτείᾳ διαβιοῦν.

28. Gordon Fee, *The First Epistle to the Corinthians* (Grand Rapids: Eerdmans, 1987), p. 317; Horsley, 'Paul and Slavery', p. 184.

29. Josephus, *Ant.* 18.243 (Feldman, LCL). The Greek reads: ἀλλ' εἰ καὶ πρότερόν γε, Ἡρώδη, μηδὲν ἐλύπει σε τὸ ἐν ἐλάσσονι τιμῇ πατρὸς οὗ γέγονας εἶναι, νῦν γοῦν ὀρέχθητι συγγενοῦς ἀξιώματος.

Most scholars search Josephus and other books of the New Testament for parallels. But usually missing in such comparisons is the Gothic version of the New Testament. That version, translated by Ulfilas, the apostle to the Goths in the fourth century, is often underutilized because most biblical scholars do not know the language or think it a minor version. However, the Gothic version displays one very important attribute, namely its severe literalness. As Bruce Metzger observes, 'Ulfilas' translation is remarkably faithful to the original, frequently to the point of being literalistic'.[30]

And how did the Gothic version understand *all' ei kai (ἀλλ' εἰ καὶ)*? That version translates the phrase in 1 Cor. 7.21 as *akei thaujabai*. The word *akei* means 'but', and *thaujabai* only has a concessive meaning: 'if also, even though'.[31] In fact, in 2 Cor. 4.16, where even Harrill says that we can understand *ei kai* concessively 'to mean "although" or "even if",' the Gothic version has *akei thaujabai*.[32] Therefore, the Gothic is more consistent with a translation of 'Even if you can become free...use [slavery] instead'.[33]

The Syriac version, admittedly less valuable, also lends support to the concessive interpretation of *ei kai*.[34] That version uses a compound conjunction *aphen* (ܐܢ +ܐܦ) to translate the Greek phrase.[35] The Syriac compound word *aphen* is usually understood as 'although' or 'even though'.[36] The fact that both the Gothic and Syriac translations understood that phrase as a

---

30. Bruce Metzger and Bart D. Ehrman, *The Text of the New Testament: Its Transmission, Corruption and Restoration* (New York: Oxford University Press, 4th edn, 2005), p. 116.

31. Winfred Lehman, *A Gothic Etymological Dictionary* (Leiden: E.J. Brill, 1986), p. 356; Joseph Wright, *A Grammar of the Gothic Language* (Oxford: Clarendon Press, 1910), p. 169. For a recent Gothic grammar, see Thomas O. Lambdin, *An Introduction to the Gothic Language* (Eugene, OR: Wipf & Stock, 2006).

32. Harrill, *The Manumission of Slaves*, p. 119: 'Although there are instances where Paul combines εἰ and καί to mean "although" or "even if" (e.g., 2 Cor. 7.8a; 4.3, 16)...'; Similarly, Horsley, 'Paul and Slavery', p. 184.

33. The NIV renders *ei kai* in 2 Cor. 4.16 concessively, as well ('though outwardly...').

34. For the Syriac text, I used the edition of *The Triglot Bible Comprising the Holy Scriptures of the Old and New Testaments in the Original Tongues also the Septuagint, the Syriac (of the New Testament) and the Vulgate Versions* (London: Richard Dickinson, 1897). That edition is largely supposed to represent the Peshitta, but the textual history of *The Triglot* is not always clear. Bartchy (*First-Century Slavery*, p. 6) simply mentions that the Syriac Peshitta version supports 'use slavery' but does not discuss it further.

35. In Syriac ܐܢ is the conjunction meaning 'if' while ܐܦ is the conjunction meaning 'even' in this case. See J. Payne Smith (ed.), *A Compendious Syriac Dictionary Founded on the Thesaurus of R. Payne Smith* (repr., Winona Lake, IN: Eisenbrauns, 1998 [1903]), p. 25.

36. Smith (ed.), *A Compendious Syriac Dictionary*, p. 25; Takamitsu Muraoka, *Classical Syriac: A Basic Grammar with a Chrestomathy* (Wiesbaden: Harrassowitz, 1997), p. 63*.

concessive one means that some advocates of an intensive translation ('indeed') are not considering all the available data.

One final grammatical issue to consider revolves around the use of the aorist infinitive, χρῆσαι, translated as 'to make use of'.[37] Gordon Fee believes the aorist infinitive favors the 'use freedom' option. As Fee phrases it: 'the verb "to make use of" is an aorist infinitive, suggesting a single action, not the present, which would carry the sense needed for "keep on in slavery"'.[38] Fee is echoed by Philip B. Payne.[39]

However, the use of the aorist infinitive does not pose any insuperable problems for the 'use slavery' understanding. As it is, a punctiliar ('single action') understanding of the aorist infinitive could equally pose a problem for the 'use freedom' translation, as presumably the use of freedom continues just as much as the use of slavery. Moreover, the difference between a punctiliar and a durative understanding of the aorist infinitive is not clear in all cases. A.T. Robertson acknowledges the use of what he calls the 'constantive' aorist infinitive in a number of places in the New Testament.[40] In Jn 13.36, for example, Jesus says 'where I am going you cannot follow me now'. Jesus uses an aorist infinitive, and the sense of 'follow' should be more durative than a one-time event. Another infinitive aorist (of λαμβάνω) occurs in Acts 15.37, which says that Barnabas 'wanted to follow' (ἐβούλετο συμπαραλαβεῖν) Paul, and this clearly meant Barnabas wanted to follow Paul on a continuing basis.

As noted by John Thorley, we see the interchange of the aorist infinitive and present infinitive in some Gospel parallels:[41]

Mt. 12.12

ἔξεστιν τοῖς σάββασιν καλῶς ποιεῖν ('it is lawful to do good on the sabbath')

Mk 3.4

ἔξεστιν τοῖς σάββασιν ἀγαθὸν ποιῆσαι ἢ κακοποιῆσαι ('Is it lawful on the sabbath to do good or to do harm?')

---

37. This form has also been interpreted as an aorist middle imperative, but we will follow the consensus and treat it as an aorist infinitive. See further Bartchy, *First-Century Slavery*, p. 8

38. Fee, *The First Epistle to the Corinthians*, p. 317.

39. Payne, 'Twelve Reasons', p. 3.

40. A.T. Robertson, *A Grammar of the Greek New Testament in Light of Historical Research* (Nashville, TN: Broadman Press, 1934), p. 857. See also James Boyer, 'A Classification of Infinitives: A Statistical Study', *Grace Theological Journal* 6 (1985), pp. 3-27.

41. John Thorley, 'Aktionsart in New Testament Greek: Infinitive and Imperative', *Novum Testamentum* 31 (1989), pp. 290-315.

Lk. 6.9

ἔξεστιν τῷ σάββάτῳ ἀγαθοποιῆσαι ἢ κακοποιῆσαι ('is it lawful on the sabbath to do good or to do harm?')

We could suppose that Mark and Luke are speaking of one-time instances of violating the Sabbath by healing a sick person, but it is not clear why Matthew did not understand it that way.

In Mk 4.3, there is no reason to understand the aorist infinitive (σπεῖραι), translated 'to sow', as more punctiliar than Mt. 13.3, which uses the present infinitive (σπείρειν). Thorley admits that 'it is difficult to see why Matthew felt the need to switch to the present'.[42] But what the switch may show is that a durative and punctiliar sense were not always so distinguishable (the process of sowing may be durative, but the total sowing event could be seen as punctiliar).

On a socio-rhetorical or contextual level, the results also have not been decisive. Harrill emphasizes how often Paul uses exceptions to a general rule in 1 Corinthians 7.[43] Thus, in v. 10, Paul, on behalf of the Lord, instructs that 'the wife should not separate from her husband'. However, Paul also makes an exception: 'If she does separate...' But, all the exceptions cited by Harrill are introduced by the conjunctions *ei de* (v. 15) and *ean de* (vv. 11 and 28). While *all' ei kai* may be parallel in meaning, there is no explanation as to why Paul switches to *all' ei kai* in v. 21.

As with most arguments about biblical interpretation, the word 'context' is used to support one side or the other. However, 'context' is often an interpreter's construct that reflects arbitrary preferences. A case in point is the use of the wider array of 'Pauline' letters to help determine 'the context' of 1 Cor. 7.21. Horsley, for one, assures us: 'With regard to slaves and slavery, Paul was clearly not a "conservative" advocating acceptance of slavery. Nothing in the letters of Paul himself suggests this.'[44] By Horsley's logic, since nothing in 'the letters of Paul himself' can be interpreted to favor slavery, then we must interpret 1 Cor. 7.21 as not favoring remaining in slavery for the sake of Christ. This seems fair enough until one looks more closely at what Horsley means by 'the letters of Paul himself', and only if we ignore many other instructions in letters regarded to be from Paul where suffering is valued.

---

42. Thorley, 'Aktionsart in New Testament Greek', p. 302. Thorley also does not really explain what he refers to as 'particularity' when using an aorist infinitive. How is 'sowing' more particular in Mark, who uses the aorist infinitive, than in Matthew, who uses a present infinitive?

43. Harrill, *The Manumission of Slaves*, pp. 121-26.

44. Horsley, 'Paul and Slavery', p. 195.

There are, indeed, many instances where Paul boasts about his suffering and where he indicates that submission for the sake of Christ is good. This would be the case even if we used only the letters that Horsley regards as 'Pauline', including Romans, Corinthians, and Philippians.[45] The following passage serves as an example of Paul's attitude:

> Let every person be subject to the governing authorities. For there is no authority except from God, and those that exist have been instituted by God. Therefore he who resists the authorities resists what God has appointed, and those who resist will incur judgment. For rulers are not a terror to good conduct, but to bad. Would you have no fear of him who is in authority? Then do what is good, and you will receive his approval, for he is God's servant for your good. But if you do wrong, be afraid, for he does not bear the sword in vain; he is the servant of God to execute his wrath on the wrongdoer. Therefore one must be subject, not only to avoid God's wrath but also for the sake of conscience (Rom. 13.1-5).

Submission to authority is good for the sake of Christ. So how is this not a 'conservative' position that serves the interests of the empire?

According to Paul, even Christ chose to become a slave when he could have chosen freedom in the famous passage in Phil. 2.4-11:

> Let each of you look not only to his own interests, but also to the interests of others. Have this mind among yourselves, which is yours in Christ Jesus, who, though he was in the form of God, did not count equality with God a thing to be grasped, but emptied himself, taking the form of a servant, being born in the likeness of men. And being found in human form he humbled himself and became obedient unto death, even death on a cross. Therefore God has highly exalted him and bestowed on him the name which is above every name, that at the name of Jesus every knee should bow, in heaven and on earth and under the earth, and every tongue confess that Jesus Christ is Lord, to the glory of God the Father.

If Paul thought being a slave (servant) served a greater good for Christ, then it remains unexplained why Paul could not have thought the same applied to human beings.

When Paul discusses, in 1 Cor. 6.1-6, persons victimized within a church, he advises that victims should not go to outside authorities, and adds, in 1 Cor. 6.7, 'Why not rather [*mallon*] suffer wrong? Why not rather [*mallon*] be defrauded?' If Paul thought this way about victimization, then why would Horsley think that Paul wanted people to receive freedom even when they could do so? Clearly, there is no reason why Paul cannot be urging slaves to remain in an unjust servitude in 1 Cor. 7.21, given that he said just one chapter earlier that being victimized is better if it serves the Christian cause.[46]

---

45. See Horsley, 'Paul and Slavery', p. 169.
46. For an eschatological reading of the advice to stay in slavery, see Hans Conzelmann, *1 Corinthians* (trans. James W. Leitch; Philadelphia: Fortress Press, 1975), p. 127.

A legal issue that must be addressed is whether slaves could refuse manumission. Bartchy contends that 1 Cor. 7.21 cannot mean that a slave should remain a slave even if manumitted because Roman law did not allow such a choice to the slave.[47] Once a master decided to manumit a slave, the latter had no choice, except that the slave could plead with his master to stay. However, 1 Cor. 7.21 is not necessarily speaking of refusing an act of manumission after an offer by the master. Instead, Paul may be referring to any achievable opportunity to gain freedom that was available. Alan Watson, the Roman legal specialist, acutely summarizes such opportunities:

> Roman slavery, viewed as a legal institution, makes sense on the assumption that slaves could reasonably aspire to being freed and hence to becoming Roman citizens, or at least, that the main rules of the institution were framed with those slaves primarily in mind who could reasonably have such an aspiration.[48]

There were three main methods of manumission summarized by Gaius, the famed compiler of Roman Law: 'by vindicta, by the census, or by testament'.[49] Enrolling a slave in the census, with an owner's consent, was a method of freedom probably not used at the time of Paul. *Manumissio vindicta* involved a legal fiction wherein a master arranged to have a friend file a claim on behalf of a slave's freedom. The master would accede to the claim on behalf of the slave before magistrates. A slave also could be manumitted at the death of the master if the latter's will so declared.

We also know from some classical authors that slaves could expect manumission on the basis of some predictable events. In the *Philippics*, Cicero says: 'For, Conscript Fathers, seeing that after six years we have entered upon the hope of freedom [*spem libertatis*] and have endured slavery longer than good and diligent slaves taken in war are wont to endure it'.[50] In other words, diligent slaves who had incurred their status through imprisonment in war had an expectation that they could be enslaved for no longer than six years. Another expectation could be freedom after the age of thirty for those born in servitude.[51]

Since there were various methods of manumission, it is not inconceivable that slaves could yearn for freedom and even place themselves in a position favorable for manumission. Slaves might harbor expectations of freedom after they turned thirty, or after giving good service. Given this understanding,

---

47. Bartchy, *First-Century Slavery*, p. 104.
48. Alan Watson, *Roman Slave Law* (Baltimore: The Johns Hopkins University Press, 1987), p. 23.
49. Gaius, *The Institutes of Gaius* 1.138: 'qui in causa mancipii sunt, quia servorum loco habentur, vindicta, censu, testamento manumissi sui iuris fiunt'.
50. Cicero, *Philippics* 8.11.32 (Ker, LCL).
51. Watson, *Roman Slave Law*, p. 24.

Paul could be saying that slaves should not be concerned at all about seeking opportunities for manumission, but should make the best of their enslaved condition, just as he has advised others to make use of their present condition.

Galatians 3.28: A Magna Carta of Humanity?

The importance of this text for egalitarian viewpoints has been summarized by Rebecca Groothuis: 'Of all the texts that support biblical equality, Gal. 3.26-28 is probably the most important'.[52] Hans Dieter Betz says Paul's statements here have 'revolutionary dimensions'.[53] Philip B. Payne goes further: 'Galatians 3.28 has been called the "Magna Carta of Humanity" since it affirms equality in Christ that transcends the three major social barriers to privilege. The ancient world offers no parallel to the verse.'[54]

Even historians of American slavery view this text as paradigmatic of Christian thoughts about slavery. Consider the remarks of Stephen Haynes, who has made a significant contribution to understanding the role of Noah's curse in justifying American slavery. When he describes the pro-slavery sentiments of Benjamin Palmer (1818–1902), the founder of what is now Rhodes College, Haynes adds:

> Specifically his worldview lacked utterly the baptismal vision of Christian unity that has been the church's ideal since Paul proclaimed to the Galatians, 'There is no longer Jew or Greek, there is no longer slave or free, there is no longer male and female; for all of you are one in Christ Jesus' (Gal. 3.28). Even if the Apostle failed to keep his goal in sight, it marks the acme of his ascent toward Christ's kingdom.[55]

But why does Haynes see this text as related to abolitionism? Why does Haynes think that this text provided 'the church's ideal since Paul proclaimed' it?

The key to answering these questions is Haynes's statement that Paul 'failed to keep his goal in sight'. Presumably, this means that Paul accepted or condoned slavery and so he failed in that regard. But, if so, could it be that Haynes misconstrues what Paul's goal was in Gal. 3.28? Was it really to proclaim a sort of egalitarianism that entailed ending slavery? Or was it limited simply to the partaking of Christ's salvation?

---

52. Rebecca M. Groothuis, *Good News for Women: A Biblical Picture of Gender Equality* (Grand Rapids: Baker Books, 1997), p. 25. See also Denise K. Buell and Caroline Johnson Hodge, 'The Politics of Interpretation: The Rhetoric of Race and Ethnicity in Paul', *JBL* 123 (2004), pp. 235-51.

53. Betz, *Galatians*, p. 190.

54. Philip B. Payne, *Man and Woman, One in Christ* (Grand Rapids, MI: Zondervan, 2009), p. 79.

55. Haynes, *Noah's Curse*, p. vii.

Those espousing a non-egalitarian understanding of this text have the advantage. Indeed, many conservative Christian scholars, such as Richard Hove, argue forcefully and cogently that this passage does not endorse the abolition of slavery.[56] The crucial portion states:

> So that the law was our custodian until Christ came, that we might be justified by faith. But now that faith has come, we are no longer under a custodian; for in Christ Jesus you are all sons of God, through faith. For as many of you as were baptized into Christ have put on Christ. There is neither Jew nor Greek, there is neither slave nor free, there is neither male nor female; for you are all one in Christ Jesus. And if you are Christ's, then you are Abraham's offspring, heirs according to promise (Gal. 3.24-28).

Verse 28 is embedded in a larger argument about how and why believers can be considered Abraham's offspring.[57] The best understanding of v. 28 may be paraphrased as: 'You, as believers, are the offspring of Abraham, whether you are male or female, Greek or Jew, slave or free because you are part of Christ by virtue of Baptism'.

This paraphrase captures well the key qualification Paul makes by using the phrase 'in Jesus Christ' in v. 28. Note, for example, the parallel in 1 Cor. 12.3: 'For by one Spirit we were all baptized into one body—Jews or Greeks, slaves or free—and all were made to drink of one Spirit'. Similarly, Gal. 3.28 is not meant to erase differences in gender, ethnicity, or social status in absolute or literal terms, but rather only as specified by the explicatory phrase, 'for you are all one in Jesus Christ' (πάντες γὰρ ὑμεῖς εἷς ἐστε ἐν Χριστῷ ᾽Ιησοῦ).

Galatians 3.29 continues the explication by linking that oneness in Jesus Christ to being Abraham's offspring. Being considered the offspring of Abraham, through whose seed the promise of salvation was to be fulfilled, is a theme that Paul begins with his question to the Galatians in 3.2: 'Let me ask you only this: Did you receive the Spirit by works of the law, or by hearing with faith?' Galatians 3.3-6 then illustrates how Abraham was considered righteous without doing the works of the law. Faith was enough. Paul describes the consequences of Abraham's example in Gal. 3.7-9:

> So you see that it is men of faith who are the sons of Abraham. And the scripture, foreseeing that God would justify the Gentiles by faith, preached the gospel beforehand to Abraham, saying, 'In you shall all the nations be blessed'. So then, those who are men of faith are blessed with Abraham who had faith.

---

56. Richard Hove, *Equality in Christ? Galatians 3.28 and the Gender Dispute* (Wheaton, IL: Crossway Books, 1999).

57. For an analysis of the entire structure of Galatians using socio-rhetorical analysis, see Betz, *Galatians*, pp. 16-23. I differ in many details, but agree with Betz that v. 28 is part of an 'argument' section of Galatians. See also Mika Hietanen, *Paul's Argumentation in Galatians: A Pragma-Dialectical Analysis* (New York: T. & T. Clark, 2007).

Another part of Paul's argument, in Gal. 3.16-18, revolves around the use of the singular of the Hebrew word, זרע, translated literally as 'seed', in an allusion to Gen. 12.7 and 15.13.[58] Paul explains the significance of the singular of this noun in Gal. 3.16: 'Now the promises were made to Abraham and to his offspring. It does not say, "And to offsprings", referring to many; but, referring to one, "And to your offspring", which is Christ.'[59]

Having argued that the singular noun, 'seed', in Genesis refers prophetically to Christ, Paul proceeds to show that Christ is the fulfillment of the promise that was made to Abraham, namely to bless all the gentiles through him. What this means more specifically to the Galatians, and to all believers, is found in 3.26: '…for in Christ Jesus you are all sons of God, through faith'. By believing in, and being baptized into, Christ, who is the heir to Abraham's promise to bless the gentiles, believers also become Abraham's heirs of that promise, regardless of being male or female, Gentile or Jew, slave or free.

However, being considered the offspring of Abraham, regardless of gender, ethnicity, or slave-status, does not mean that differences have been erased *in any other sense*. That is to say, Paul does not mean that slaves do not exist literally anymore. Thus, 'there is no slave or free' cannot mean 'there exist no slaves or free people'. Otherwise, if slaves do not literally exist anymore, then nor do free people. Colossians 4.1 alone refutes the idea that Paul thought slavery had been abolished in Christianity: 'Masters, treat your slaves justly and fairly, knowing that you also have a Master in heaven'.

Similarly, Paul's recognition that subordinate or lesser roles still were retained under Christ is evident in his advice in 1 Cor. 14.34: 'the women should keep silence in the churches. For they are not permitted to speak, but should be subordinate, as even the law says.' Whether Paul wrote Ephesians or not, that book does not understand Christian slaves to be absolved of any responsibility to do whatever a master tells them because Eph. 6.5 tells slaves to obey their earthly masters.

One of the main objections to a hierarchical reading of Gal. 3.28 today, and passages such as 1 Cor. 14.34, appeals to cultural relativism. Rebecca Groothuis provides an example:

> [T]he strategy of the New Testament church was to tolerate the social subordination of slaves and women so as to not risk alienating non-Christians from the gospel, and yet to modulate and moderate these customs, and ultimately to point beyond them to God's original intention for human relations. Today,

---

58. Betz (*Galatians*, p. 19) labels vv. 16-17 as 'Application of the illustration to scripture: Abraham tradition and Sinai Tradition'.

59. Of course, this does not mean that Paul's argument is a good one. The fact is that the Hebrew word was understood as plural in Genesis. I restrict myself here to describing Paul's hermeneutics, and not whether they are sound.

however, when non-Christians are not likely to be offended by an equalitarian gospel, but are likely to find a hierarchical gospel offensive, we have no reason to perpetuate the cultural practices that were initially intended for Christians living in patriarchal societies.[60]

Yet, note the contradictory and trajectorialist nature of this explanation. On the one hand, Groothuis claims that the core of gospel is freedom and equality. On the other hand, early Christians tolerated slavery and inequality in order to not alienate non-Christians. But why isn't tolerating slavery and inequality itself alienating to a gospel based on equality and freedom?

Another problem with Groothuis's explanation is that, by her logic, we might never have abolished slavery. As long as the dominant culture is alienated by demanding abolition and equality, then the Church might be justified to tolerate slavery and inequality. The Gospel, therefore, becomes simply a lackey to dominant cultural mores. It becomes meaningless to say the core of 'The Gospel' is freedom and equality as long as the dominant culture says otherwise.

Here we would agree, in part, with Wayne Grudem, an Evangelical traditionalist, who says:

> If we take the entire New Testament as the very words of God for us in the new covenant today, then any claim that Gal. 3.28 should overrule other texts such as Ephesians 5 and 1 Timothy 2 is a claim that Paul the apostle contradicts himself, and therefore that the Word of God contradicts itself.[61]

I agree that New Testament authors did not understand Gal. 3.28 to abolish subordination or slavery, but this is not because the New Testament is God's word. Rather, it is because Gal. 3.28 was clearly meant solely to establish the reckoning of believers as Abraham's seed regardless of their gender, ethnicity, or slave status. Other New Testament authors certainly did not see this passage as incompatible with having Christian slaves or ordering Christian slaves to serve their slavemasters (Eph. 5.24 or 6.5).

Finally, the claim that Gal. 3.28 is 'revolutionary' or some Magna Carta remains unsupported hyperbole. Such defenses often rest on diminishing the accomplishments of earlier non-Christians. For example, Betz cites the teachings of the Acildamas, the Greek Sophist, who said 'God has set all men free, nature has made no man a slave'.[62] Betz also notes that Zeno advocated equality for slaves. Indeed, Aristotle, a consummate patriarchalist, already knew of these egalitarian ideas when he remarked:

---

60. Groothuis, *Good News for Women*, p. 25.
61. Grudem, 'Is Evangelical Feminism...?', p. 40.
62. Betz, *Galatians*, p. 194 n. 96.

[o]thers however maintain that for one man to be another man's master is contrary to nature, because it is only convention that makes the one a slave and the other a freeman and there is no difference between them by nature, and that therefore it is unjust, for it is based on force.[63]

For Betz, though, such proclamations 'did not carry much weight, since philosophers lacked the power to implement their ideas'.[64]

It is not true, however, that notions of equality were never implemented. In fact, we find at least one instance of claimed implementation in Xenophon's description of Athens in the fifth century BCE: 'For this reason we have set up equality between slaves and free men, and between metics and citizens'.[65] In any case, Paul also did not have the power to implement any abolitionist ideas, and so why should his ideas be deemed more revolutionary than those of Acildamas or Zeno? If we say that Paul's ideas germinated and were later implemented by Christians, we could also say Paul adapted such ideas from earlier Greeks, and it is the Greek ideas that were implemented by later Christians.

In any case, we know that, with a few exceptions, early Christians did not use Gal. 3.28 as any sort of Magna Carta. Christianity kept slavery alive for about the next two thousand years precisely because they saw that Gal. 3.28 really had no necessary implications for earthly slavery, or at least not more than Eph. 6.5, 1 Pet. 2.18, and other scriptures that told slaves to obey their earthly masters.

Galatians 4.7: No Longer Slaves?

Brad R. Braxton, author of *No Longer Slaves: Galatians and the African American Experience*, cites this text as crucial to his African-American experience.[66] The passage says:

And because you are sons, God has sent the Spirit of his Son into our hearts, crying, 'Abba! Father!' So through God you are no longer a slave but a son, and if a son then an heir. Formerly, when you did not know God, you were in bondage to beings that by nature are no gods (Gal. 4.6-8).

For Braxton, 'there is no pre-existent, essential meaning of Galatians (or any text) for African Americans that can be discovered apart from the experience

---

63. Aristotle, *Politics* 1.2.3 (LCL): τοῖς δὲ παρὰ φύσιν τὸ δεσπόζειν, νόμῳ γὰρ τὸν μὲν δοῦλον εἶναι τὸν δ' ἐλεύθερον, φύσει δ' οὐθὲν διαφέρειν.

64. Betz, *Galatians*, p. 194.

65. Xenophon, *The Polity of the Athenians* 1.11-12 (Bowersock, LCL): διὰ τοῦτ' οὖν ἰσηγορίαν καὶ τοῖς δούλοις πρὸς τοὺς ἐλευθέρους ἐποιήσαμεν καὶ τοῖς μετοίκοις πρὸς τοὺς ἀστούς.

66. Brad R. Braxton, *No Longer Slaves: Galatians and the African American Experience* (Collegeville, MN: Liturgical Press, 2002), pp. x-xiv *et passim*.

of African Americans'.[67] This, of course, is already problematic because Braxton generalizes 'the African-American experience' as though it were monolithic.[68]

At the same time, Braxton seems to contradict the view that there is no pre-existing meaning when he says, '[o]n a personal note, as a biblical scholar, I have extensive knowledge of Jewish and Greco-Roman culture, and this knowledge is indispensable for my critical engagement with the Bible'.[69] But why is such a knowledge needed if not to help ascertain the original intent of authors?

He confirms the purpose of this knowledge when he argues against a futuristic interpretation of Gal. 3.28 by pointing out that the verbs are in the present tense, not the future tense.[70] He also tells us that 'I think Paul considered the law still to be binding for Jews and even Jewish Christians'.[71] In other words, Braxton is presuming that he can determine that Paul meant X (= law is binding) rather than Y (= law is not binding) on the basis of an examination of the historico-grammatical information at his disposal.

To support his view, Braxton appeals to the 'new perspective' on Paul, which is mainly pioneered by Euroamerican, rather than African-American, scholars. Braxton tells us that, in fact, 'Paul is loosing Abraham from his traditional moorings and offering Abraham as a critique against an improper understanding of the law'.[72] Yet, 'an improper understanding' of the law, presumes the existence of 'a proper understanding of the law', and his support comes again by looking at the original grammar and cultural context in which Galatians was written. Thus, he must be presuming that there is a preexisting meaning and not just one that is provided by a modern community, whether African-American, Hispanic, or Euroamerican.

The other main component of Braxton's method is analogy, wherein he simply finds that biblical element X is analogical to modern experience Y. In actuality, it is a continuation of typological, or non-literal, hermeneutics found already as inner-biblical exegesis.[73] While it may be true that modern

67. Braxton, *No Longer Slaves*, p. 110.
68. See further Debra J. Dickerson, *The End of Blackness* (New York: Pantheon Books, 2004).
69. Braxton, *No Longer Slaves*, p. 68.
70. Braxton, *No Longer Slaves*, p. 94. For further discussions of African-American perspectives on Paul and slavery, see Brian K. Blount (ed.), *True to our Native Land: An African American New Testament Commentary* (Minneapolis: Fortress Press, 2007), especially pp. 16-17, 229-30.
71. Braxton, *No Longer Slaves*, p. 121.
72. Braxton, *No Longer Slaves*, p. 122 n. 97.
73. For the problems between distinguishing typological and allegorical hermeneutics, see Peter W. Martens, 'Revisiting the Allegory/Typology Distinction: The Case of Origen', *JECS* 16 (2008), pp. 283-317.

communities do operate this way, it is a different matter to say that they should operate this way. This mode of interpretation, of course, can be applied to any ancient text, and so Braxton still leaves unexplained why the Bible should be authoritative when drawing analogies.

In any case, Gal. 4.7 does not support abolitionism. This particular passage is fully consistent with the idea that outsiders can be enslaved, but not insiders. After all, Paul's argument in Galatians 4 centers on the advantage in benefits that accrued to Christians because they are descendants of a free woman (Sarah), instead of the slave-woman (Hagar). In 4.31, Paul concludes his argument with: 'So, brethren, we are not children of the slave but of the free woman'. Accordingly, I concur with the assessment of Galatians 4 by Jennifer A. Glancy, who refers to 'Paul's inability to sustain rhetorically the dissolution of the categories of slaves and free that he signals in 3.28'.[74]

Ephesians 6.5: Obedience through Terror

Christian slaves are undeniably commanded to obey their slavemasters in Eph. 6.5: 'Slaves, be obedient to those who are your earthly masters, with fear and trembling, in singleness of heart, as to Christ'. Even Horsley, an avowed promoter of the anti-imperialist view of Christianity, is forced to admit that this passage provides an example where '[e]arly Christian writers reflect the ethos of slave–master relations'.[75]

Indeed, it is difficult to avoid the fact that Paul is issuing a very direct and frank command. The Greek imperative ὑπακούετε is addressed to slaves, and translated properly as 'obey'. The object of obedience for the slave is 'masters according to the flesh', which clarifies that these are your normal everyday slavemasters of the Roman world. The mode in which slaves are to obey is 'with fear and trembling' and equivalent to how they serve Christ himself.

Ben Witherington attempts to mitigate the strength of these instructions by making a distinction between the Greek verbs *hypotassō* (ὑποτάσσω/'to submit') and *hypakouō* (ὑπακούω/'to obey') in Eph. 6.5 and in 1 Pet. 2.18.[76] In fact, he says that '[u]nconditional and unquestioned "obedience"' (*hypakoē*) is reserved for the Christian's relationship to God in Christ (1 Pet. 1.2, 14, 22)'.[77] Witherington adds that *hypotassō* really means 'to defer' or 'to respect' rather than 'to submit' when applied to non-Christian masters.[78]

---

74. Glancy, *Slavery in Early Christianity*, p. 38.
75. Horsley, 'The Slave Systems', p. 38.
76. Witherington, *The Indelible Image*, II, p. 683.
77. Witherington, *The Indelible Image*, II, p. 572.
78. Witherington, *The Indelible Image*, II, p. 572.

When speaking of Rom. 13.1, Witherington also claims that 'submitting to governing authorities...is not quite the same as obeying them'.[79] Thus, civil disobedience is not precluded.

Witherington offers nothing but theology to justify his linguistic conclusions. The fact is that *hypotassō* and *hypakouō* are both used for actions owed to human masters. There is no distinction made between actions owed to God and actions owed to men by using these verbs (cf. Acts 5.29). Parallels in Josephus indicate that both words are either synonymous or 'obedience' is entailed in 'subjection'. For example, in the *Jewish War* (2.367-69), Josephus speaks of 'barbarians' being 'in subjection (ὑποτάσσεται) to three thousand [Roman] soldiers' and he mockingly adds concerning others: 'do they not obey (ὑπακούουσιν) the orders of two thousand Roman guards?'[80]

Given the clarity of Eph. 6.5, some scholars have resorted to logically incoherent denials that this text endorses slavery in any manner. Philip B. Payne, for example, claims: 'Paul's practical advice to slaves should not be equated with the acceptance of slavery in the sense of its approval'.[81] In part, Payne presumes that Gal. 3.28 and 1 Cor. 7.21 are in favor of abolition, and so Eph. 6.5 must be interpreted in that light. Witherington offers a similar claim: 'Paul is not endorsing slavery or providing a Christian rationale to bolster and undergird the institution'.[82]

Deconstructing this defense should begin by observing that Payne apparently distinguishes between 'practical advice' and 'approval'. Since Eph. 6.5 issues advice in the form of an imperative, then his argument can be schematized as follows: 'The command to do X should not be equated with approval of X'. In regard to Eph. 6.5, Payne's claim can be expressed schematically as: 'Do X ≠ Approval of X'.

Payne does not recognize the inconsistencies such a claim generates in biblical ethics. Indeed, almost anywhere else in biblical ethics we do assume that 'Do X = Approval of X'. Notice these commands, which can be reduced to 'Do X':

Matthew 19.19

1. Τίμα τὸν πατέρα καὶ τὴν μητέρα ('Honor your father and mother')

2. Ἀγαπήσεις τὸν πλησίον σου ὡς σεαυτόν ('You shall love your neighbor as yourself')

---

79. Witherington, *The Indelible Image*, II, p. 683.
80. Josephus, *War* 2.367-69 (Thackeray, LCL). See also occurrences of both words in Josephus, *War* 4.175-79.
81. Payne, *Man and Woman*, p. 274.
82. Witherington, *The Letters to Philemon...*, p. 339.

116   *Slavery, Abolitionism, and the Ethics of Biblical Scholarship*

Using Payne's logic, the command to honor father and mother should not be equated with approval of honoring one's father and mother. The command to love your neighbor as yourself should not be equated with approval of loving your neighbor as yourself. Clearly, this rationale is absurd because it is self-contradictory, and even unethical, to command someone to do something of which one does not approve. After all, would Witherington and Payne not view a command to commit homosexual acts as an endorsement of homosexuality? For similar reasons, it is absurd to claim, as does Witherington, that telling slaves to obey their masters does not represent an endorsement of the institution of slavery. Slavery, if anything, is maintained by the obedience of slaves to masters. If slavemasters do not wish to abolish the slavery system, then Paul's command to obey the master would mean that slavery might never end.

In any case, Witherington and Payne need to show clear examples where a command to 'Do X' signals disapproval of X by the one doing the commanding.[83] Second, there is no reason to suppose that 'practical advice' is not also moral advice. After all, almost all 'advice' given in command form in the Bible can be classified as 'practical advice' insofar as it is meant for a believer to undertake those actions that results in a life pleasing to God, the ultimate master. This is especially the case in Eph. 6.5, which, if anything, equates serving earthly slavemasters with service to Christ himself.

Philippians 2.4-6: Slavery as Human Destiny

I.A.H. Combes is among those willing to criticize some of the more benign interpretations of New Testament slavery. However, he is not free of apologetic concerns when he tells us:

> Nowhere in the New Testament (with the possible exception of Jn 8.30-35) is there any trace of the use of 'slave' as a label for the naturally inferior, the stupid, or the vicious, as is so common in other forms of literature... Although the New Testament has been criticized for its lack of interest in the abolition of slavery, it must be remembered that this consistent lack of prejudice against slaves and slavery, and emphasis on the equality of all people, already represents a significant departure from the conceptions of the time.[84]

This is indeed surprising because Combes's own book is full of examples that show how pervasive the metaphor of slave–master relationships was in the New Testament.

---

83. One possible one is 2 Sam. 24, where God tells David to number the people of Israel, and then David is punished for it.
84. Combes, *The Metaphor of Slavery*, p. 93.

No precise comparative statistics are provided to support the claim that the absence of negative portrayals of slaves in the New Testament differs from what 'is so common in other forms of literature'. We have already cited a number of ancient authors encouraging the just treatment of slaves (e.g., Seneca, Plato). Given that one is comparing a New Testament corpus that spanned about a hundred years, how would it be fair to undertake any statistical comparison with 'other forms of literature' that might span hundreds or thousands of years? And the whole idea that slavery is considered something inferior is belied by the very exaltation of freedom as a central concept by many New Testament scholars. If free Christians saw themselves as equal to enslaved Christians, then why praise any emancipatory sentiments? Why does Paul want freedom from the Roman empire if slavery is not so bad?

Contrary to Combes's claims, Phil. 2.6-8 does preserve a 'trace of the use of "slave" for the naturally inferior'. Note how the passage speaks about the humanization of Jesus:

> who though he was in the form of God, did not count equality with God a thing to be grasped, but emptied himself, taking the form of a servant, being born in the likeness of men. And being found in human form he humbled himself and became obedient unto death, even death on a cross (Phil. 2.6-8).

Here, we see a clear dichotomy between being divine and being human. Being human is equated with servitude. Jesus is praised for his willingness to become lower in status. If being human is equated with being a slave, then servitude is just as natural to humanity in Philippians as it is in Aristotle's writings. Notice that the slave is also supposed to be obedient 'unto death'.

Combes addresses Phil. 2.4-6 mainly as a study in how Church Fathers dealt with some of its Christological implications.[85] Otherwise, Combes paradoxically uses the passage in Philippians to show that *doulos*, as used by Paul in 1 Cor. 4.21, where Paul appears to be a higher status majordomo, 'was specifically meant to convey such a high status idea'.[86] Jesus' willingness to become a slave is also not unique. Petronius, a Roman courtier of the time of Nero, provides evidence in his famous work, *The Satyricon*. In this work, we have the story of Trimalchio, a king's son, who, as Dale Martin notes, 'voluntarily became a slave for what it would later bring'.[87]

---

85. Combes, *The Metaphor of Slavery*, pp. 102, 131-32.
86. Combes, *The Metaphor of Slavery*, p. 91. For an earlier defense of an honorific sense of *doulos*, see Gerhard Sass, 'Zur Bedeutung von *doulos* bei Paulus', *Zeitschrift für die neutestamentliche Wissenschaft* 40 (1941), pp. 24-32.
87. Dale B. Martin, *Slavery as Salvation: The Metaphor of Slavery in Pauline Christianity* (New Haven: Yale University Press, 1990), p. 41.

Combes also asserts that 'slaves are not to be treated in any way as second-class Christians. With the proviso that they serve and obey their masters...'[88] Yet, the very admonitions to treat Christians slaves justly (Col. 4.1) means that Paul did not assume that Christians masters would do that. Christian slaves were told to obey their masters, while free Christians never had an equivalent instruction. That difference is sufficient to treat slaves as second-class Christians (cf. Jas 2.4).

The fact that slaves partook of certain aspects of Christian ritual in the New Testament is not necessarily more significant than the baptism of slaves in the New World. We have seen that the Romans and the Greeks also allowed slaves to partake of many religious rituals. Hebrew law allowed slaves to rest on the Sabbath, but that did not imply that slaves were equal to masters in all other areas of life. Non-Christians could also successfully convince slaves to say that 'slavery was never unkind to me' (*servitus mihi nunquam invida fuisti*).[89]

Treating slaves more like equals to the master also could be viewed as an incentive for a better work ethic. Varro, the Roman author, argued that slaves who functioned as foremen should be treated with more consideration than regular slaves. Varro says: 'When this is done they are less inclined to think that they are looked down upon, and rather think that they are held in some esteem by the master'.[90] Columella advises slave owners to seek advice from slaves because slaves 'are more willing to set about a piece of work on which they think that their opinions have been asked and their advice followed'.[91]

Combes also assumes that slaves always saw themselves as their masters saw them, but, as Martin notes: 'terms scorned among the authors of Greco-Roman literature were worn without embarrassment by persons lower down in the social scale'.[92] Accordingly, even if free Christians did not treat enslaved Christians as second-class citizens, there is a perfectly good explanation. If all Christians thought of themselves as slaves of God, then their status was equal in that regard. But that equality between slaves is not a humanitarian advance because the same could apply in other societies where slaves of equal rank would have no reason to treat each other differently.

---

88. Combes, *The Metaphor of Slavery*, p. 93.
89. CIL 13.7119 as quoted in Martin, *Slavery as Salvation*, p. 48. See also Pedro López Barja de Quiroga, 'Freedmen Social Mobility in Roman Italy', *Historia* 44 (1995), pp. 326-48.
90. Varro, *On Agriculture* 1.7.6 (Hooper and Ash, LCL): 'quae facienda sint opera, quod, ita cum fit, minus se putant despici atque aliquo numero haberi a domino'.
91. Columella, *On Agriculture* 1.8.15-16 (Ash, LCL): 'Tum etiam libentius eos id opus adgredi video, de quo secum deliberatum et consilio ipsorum susceptum putant'.
92. Martin, *Slavery as Salvation*, p. 46.

Colossians 3.18–4.1:
The Magic of Socio-Rhetorical Criticism

Fred Ross saw this passage as irrefutable evidence that 'God has really sanctioned the relation of master and slave as those of husband and wife, and parent and child'.[93] Indeed, the instructions given here are consistent with the fact that Christians were allowed to own, and did own, slaves in the New Testament (e.g., Mary in Acts 12.12-14). Christianity and slavery seemed perfectly compatible.

Ben Witherington, however, sees Col. 3.18–4.1 as a moral advance. To make his case, Witherington deploys 'socio-rhetorical' criticism to explain what others see as contradictory messages about freedom, equality, and slavery in Paul's letters.[94] Colossians 3.18–4.1 says:

> Wives, be subject to your husbands, as is fitting in the Lord. Husbands, love your wives, and do not be harsh with them. Children, obey your parents in everything, for this pleases the Lord. Fathers, do not provoke your children, lest they become discouraged. Slaves, obey in everything those who are your earthly masters, not with eyeservice, as men-pleasers, but in singleness of heart, fearing the Lord. Whatever your task, work heartily, as serving the Lord and not men, knowing that from the Lord you will receive the inheritance as your reward; you are serving the Lord Christ. For the wrongdoer will be paid back for the wrong he has done, and there is no partiality. Masters, treat your slaves justly and fairly, knowing that you also have a Master in heaven.

For the moment, we avoid the very formidable problems of assuming that Colossians is a Pauline letter.[95] For the sake of argument only, we assume that Colossians is from Paul. So why does Colossians represent an advance? According to Witherington, Paul uses three levels or 'orders' of moral discourse that are graduated to the familiarity between Paul and his audience. In Witherington's own words '[w]hat one says to an intimate friend is likely to be more involved, direct, and free than what one says to strangers'.[96] Accordingly, Witherington describes these three orders of moral discourse as follows:

(1) The level of discourse one feels free to use with an audience one is familiar with but has not personally addressed before—what can be called the opening gambit;

---

93. Ross, *Slavery Ordained*, p. 64.
94. See Witherington, 'Was Paul a Pro-Slavery Chauvinist?', pp. 8, 44.
95. For the debates on authorship, see Witherington, *The Letters to Philemon...*, pp. 100-103.
96. Witherington, 'Was Paul a Pro-Slavery Chauvinist?', p. 8.

(2) the level of discourse that builds on what has been heard and believed by the audience before, of which they must be reminded in a way that is generally applicable to all in the audience, with elaborations on these commonly held beliefs; and

(3) the level of discourse one offers as if to an intimate with whom one can fully and truly speak freely, directly, and personally, without great fear of alienating the audience.[97]

In other words, the less well you know someone, the less frank you might be about your true feelings on a subject. Presumably this also absolves Paul from frankly telling masters at Colossae and Ephesus that slavery is a sin.

Witherington places Col. 3.18–4.1 in the first order of moral discourse assigned to the audience with which Paul is least familiar. Ephesians 6.5 belongs to a second order, while Philemon belongs to the third order, which displays the most familiarity and frankness between Paul and his addressee(s). Witherington explains that: 'Colossians is written to an audience Paul has not personally converted and that he has never met face to face; it is thus an example of what I call moral discourse of the first order'.[98] Furthermore, Witherington claims Colossians exhibits an advance over the ethics of the Greco-Roman world because '[l]ove and fairness were not generally part of the picture in Paul's world'.[99]

There are a number of fundamental methodological problems with Witherington's entire idea of three 'orders' of discourse. First, Witherington offers no evidence that the Greco-Roman rhetorical conventions he identifies also applied to written epistles. In his survey of Hellenistic epistolography, Jeffrey T. Reed remarks that, while we can find some analogies between rhetorical practices and letter writing, 'the majority of letters discovered from the Hellenistic period do not lend themselves to rhetorical analysis'.[100] Similarly, Stanley K. Stowers concludes that 'the letter-writing tradition was essentially independent of rhetoric'.[101]

In fact, the very classical sources Witherington cites—including Aristotle and Cicero—for some of his general evidence of Paul's rhetorical practices do not categorize rhetoric in this way. Cicero himself says that 'a letter is one thing, a court of law or a public meeting quite another'.[102] Witherington

97. Witherington, *The Letters to Philemon...*, p. 11.
98. Witherington, 'Was Paul a Pro-Slavery Chauvinist?', p. 8.
99. Witherington, 'Was Paul a Pro-Slavery Chauvinist?', p. 8.
100. Jeffrey E. Reed, 'The Epistle', in Stanley E. Porter (ed.), *Handbook of Classical Rhetoric in the Hellenistic Period, 330 B.C.–A.D. 400* (Leiden: E.J. Brill, 2001), p. 190.
101. S.K. Stowers, *Letter Writing in Greco-Roman Antiquity* (Philadelphia: Westminster Press, 1986), p. 52.
102. Cicero, *Letters to Friends* 9.21.1 (Bailey, LCL): 'nec enim semper eodem modo, quid enim simile habet epistula aut iudicio aut concinioni?'

quotes Aristotle's *Rhetoric* (1.2.3) to show that Aristotle believes in the use of emotional appeals similar to what Witherington posits in the introduction of Philemon.[103] Yet, that very passage in Aristotle's *Rhetoric* categorizes rhetorical arguments very differently from Witherington:

> Now the proofs furnished by the speech are of three kinds. The first depends upon the moral character of the speaker, the second upon putting the hearer into a certain frame of mind, and the third upon the speech itself in so far as it proves or seems to prove.[104]

None of these techniques are based on the level of intimacy one has with the listener. Similarly, Cicero states:

> There are three methods of bringing people to hold our opinion, instruction or persuasion or appeal to their emotions, one of these three methods we must openly display, so as to appear to wish solely to impart instruction, whereas the two remaining methods should be interfused throughout the whole of the structure of our speeches like blood in our bodies.[105]

Cicero does not say here that you must use a more frank approach with intimates or a less frank approach with lesser intimates.

A better piece of evidence for Witherington could be this statement by Cicero in a letter to his friend, Trebonius: 'Now our way of writing when we think we shall be read only by our addressee is not the same as when we write for a multitude of eyes'.[106] But this does not mean that a private letter is necessarily more frank because of the level of intimacy.

Indeed, one of the problems with Witherington's dependence on sociorhetorical analysis is that he offers few comparisons between the theory of rhetoric espoused by any one Greco-Roman theoretician and the way in which that theoretician actually writes letters. For example, in a letter to his friend, Lucceius, Cicero says: 'Although I have more than once attempted to take up my present topic with you face to face, a sort of shyness, almost

---

103. Witherington, *The Letters to Philemon...*, p. 58.
104. Aristotle, *Rhetoric* 1.2.3 (Freese, LCL): τῶν δὲ διὰ τοῦ λόγου ποριζομένων πίστεων τρία εἴδη ἐστίν. αἱ μὲν γάρ εἰσιν ἐν τῷ ἤθει τοῦ λέγοντος, αἱ δὲ ἐν τῷ τὸν ἀκροατὴν διαθεῖναί πως, αἱ δὲ ἐν αὐτῷ τῷ λόγῳ διὰ τοῦ δεικνύναι ἢ φαίνεσθαι δεικνύναι.
105. Cicero, *De oratore* 2.77.310 (Sutton and Rackham, LCL): 'Et quoniam, quod saepe iam dixi, tribus rebus homines ad nostram sententiam perducimus, aut docendo aut conciliando aut permovendo, una ex tribus his rebus res prae nobis est ferenda, ut nihil aliud nise docere velle videamur, reliquae duae, sicuti sanguis in corporibus, sic illae in perpetuis orationibus fusae esse debebunt'.
106. Cicero, *Letters to Friends* 15.21.4 (Bailey, LCL): 'aliter enim scribimus quod eos solos quibus mittimus, aliter quod multos lecturos putamus'. See further Reed, 'The Epistle', p. 173.

awkwardness, has held me back. Away from your presence, I shall set out with less trepidation. A letter has no blushes.'[107]

So, for Cicero, all letters ('letters have no blushes') seem to be frank because the writer is not face to face with the addressee, and not because of the level of intimacy between sender and addressee. Yet, Seneca tells us that some people 'fear to confide in their closest intimates; and if it were possible, they would not trust even themselves, burying their secrets deep in their hearts'.[108]

Another of Cicero's works, *De amicitia*, does counsel friends to 'dare to give true advice with all frankness...not only with frankness, but, if the occasion demands, even with sternness'.[109] But it would be unclear why the Colossians would not qualify as friends, given what Paul says in Col. 3.6-8: 'On account of these the wrath of God is coming. In these you once walked, when you lived in them. But now put them all away: anger, wrath, malice, slander, and foul talk from your mouth.' How does mentioning the 'wrath of God coming' and scolding the Colossians to put away 'foul talk from your mouth' not qualify as stern advice? On the contrary, these instructions sound brazen and presumptive because the author has no direct knowledge that the Colossians are engaging in any of the activities he describes.

Other statements in Colossians do not cohere with what Witherington says we should expect when writing to an audience who does not know the author so well. For example, in Col. 1.29, the author says: 'You, who once were estranged and hostile in mind, doing evil deeds'. How would Paul phrase this if he were speaking less freely? Furthermore, 2 Cor. 10.9-11 suggests that Paul is generally known to be a frank or brazen letter writer, whether he is known to the audience personally or not: 'I would not seem to be frightening you with letters. For they say, "His letters are weighty and strong, but his bodily presence is weak, and his speech of no account". Let such people understand that what we say by letter when absent, we do when present.' In any case, Witherington fails to explain specifically why Paul's exhortations in Colossians constitute speaking 'truly less freely' than what we see in Philemon.

In fact, there is no evidence that Paul saw his own rhetoric in the way Witherintgon portrays it. George A. Kennedy, one of the most prominent

---

107. Cicero, *Letters to Friends* 5.12 (Bailey, LCL): 'Coram me tecum eadem haec agere saepe conantem deterruit pudor quidam paene subrusticus quae nunc expromam absens audacius; epistula enim non erubescit'.

108. Seneca, *Epistles* 3.4 (Gummere, LCL): 'Quidam rursus etiam carissimorum conscientiam reformidant, et si possent, ne sibi quidem credituri interius premunt secretum'.

109. Cicero, *De amicitia* 13.44 (Falconer, LCL): 'consilium verum dare audeamus libere...ad monendum non modo aperte sed etiam acriter, si res postulabit'.

scholars of classical rhetoric, notes how emphatic Paul was about not using the conventions of Greek persuasion.[110]

> When I came to you, brethren, I did not come proclaiming [καταγγέλλων] to you the testimony of God in lofty words or wisdom. For I decided to know nothing among you except Jesus Christ and him crucified. And I was with you in weakness and in much fear and trembling; and my speech and my message [κήρυγμα] were not in plausible words of wisdom, but in demonstration of the Spirit and of power, that your faith might not rest in the wisdom of men but in the power of God (1 Cor. 2.1-4).

Here, *katangellōn* (καταγγέλλων) and *kerygma* (κήρυγμα) seem to refer to something that is done out of the spirit rather than something that follows some rhetorical convention. In fact, Kennedy concludes that '[t]his passage may be said to reject the whole of classical philosophy and rhetoric'.[111]

On a more general level, Witherington offers no empirical evidence for the practice of speaking more frankly to intimates than to strangers. One could just as well posit that one is less frank or honest with those one loves for fear of hurting their feelings, and more frank with those whom one does not know at all. What is required here are some sociological or psychological empirical data that Witherington never provides to test his hypothesis. Witherington's assignment of Colossians to the lowest level of intimacy, and Ephesians to a second level, is also very unclear. In particular, Witherington uses asymmetrical descriptions to distinguish the first and second levels:

(1) '...an audience one is familiar with but has not personally addressed before'.
(2) 'discourse that builds on what has been heard and believed by the audience before, of which they must be reminded...'

Yet, a better symmetry for 'discourse that builds on what has been heard and believed by the audience before' would be 'discourse that does not build on what has been heard and believed by the audience before'. Instead, Witherington analogizes familiarity with the speaker with familiarity with the message of the speaker. Yet, unfamiliarity with the speaker does not mean unfamiliarity with his message, which can be relayed by other intermediaries.

---

110. George A. Kennedy, *Classical Rhetoric and its Christian and Secular Tradition from Ancient to Modern Times* (Chapel Hill: University of North Carolina Press, 1980), pp. 130-31. Yet, Kennedy (*New Testament Interpretation through Rhetorical Criticism* [Chapel Hill: University of North Carolina Press, 1984]), analyzes New Testament literature on the basis of three divisions of rhetoric proposed by Aristotle: judicial, deliberative, and epideictic. See also George A. Kennedy, *The Art of Rhetoric in the Roman World 300 B.C–A.D 300* (Princeton, NJ: Princeton University Press, 1972).

111. Kennedy, *Classical Rhetoric*, pp. 131-32.

Witherington's more specific evidence for assigning Colossians to the first order is that Paul has merely 'heard' of their faith (Col. 1.4). However, Paul also says the same thing in Eph. 1.15-16: 'For this reason, because I have heard of your faith in the Lord Jesus and your love toward all the saints, I do not cease to give thanks for you, remembering you in my prayers'. Paul seems even unsure that the Ephesians had heard of his activities because he says: 'assuming that you have heard of the stewardship of God's grace that was given to me for you' (Eph. 3.1). So why does Witherington think the Colossians had less familiarity with Paul than the Ephesians?

As mentioned above, Witherington engages in a species of reverse representativism by claiming that 'love and fairness were generally not part of Paul's world'. Yet, when we inquire as to how he determined that love and fairness were not generally a part of Paul's world any more than they are of the New Testament writings, we see no specifics. In fact, Witherington repeats the problems we observed with Brueggemann's statements about the place of the poor and the needy in Deuteronomy, where it was not clear whether he had determined representativeness on the basis of quantity or quality.

Fairness was very important, according to Cicero, a classical author cited by Witherington. In his treatise on friendship, Cicero said: 'it is of the utmost importance in friendship that superior and inferior should stand on equality... the superior should put himself on a level with his inferior'.[112] Cicero includes those who have lived a menial life under this advice, including nurses and tutors.[113]

In short, Witherington's appeal to socio-rhetorical analysis is permeated by speculation rather than empirical data. The very classical sources he cites for evidence do not always agree with him. He relies on a hodge-podge of sources whose theories of rhetoric cannot always be reconciled. We can always find a source to confirm almost any theory we put forth about the 'rhetorical' import of a feature. Thus, we are justified to conclude that socio-rhetorical analysis functions here as an apologetic tool rather than a historical and literary tool.

1 Timothy 1.10: 'Manstealing'

A favorite abolitionist argument insisted that the Bible was against 'manstealing', which was equated with slave trading. However, a close study of 1 Tim. 1.10 indicates that translations are a principal means to perpetuate

---

112. Cicero, *De amicitia* 19.69, 20.71 (Falconer, LCL): 'Sed maximum est in amicitia superiorem parem esse inferiori...superiores, exaequare se cum inferioribus debent'.

113. Cicero, *De amicitia* 20.74 (Falconer, LCL): 'Isto enim modo nutrices et paedagogi iure vetustatis plurimum benevolentiae postulabunt'.

distorted understandings of the Bible's stance on slavery. The main prooftext states:

> [T]he law is not laid down for the just but for the lawless and disobedient, for the ungodly and sinners, for the unholy and profane, for murderers of fathers and murderers of mothers, for manslayers, immoral persons, sodomites, kidnappers [ἀνδραποδιστής], liars, perjurers, and whatever else is contrary to sound doctrine (1 Tim. 1.9-10).

The NRSV and NIV have 'slave traders' while the NAB has 'kidnappers'. The standard lexicon of New Testament Greek suggests 'procurer' as the translation of the Greek word, ἀνδραποδιστής (*andrapodistēs*), in 1 Tim. 1.10.[114] However, studies of this word show that it does not refer to slave trading per se.

Since the word occurs only once in the New Testament, we have to appeal to contemporary Greek sources outside of the New Testament to see how it was used.[115] Part of the evidence comes from Chariton, who is credited with authorship of a Greek story known as Callirhoe, which is dated to the first century (and so the time of Paul) or sometimes nearer to 200.[116] This story features a character named Leonas, a steward who is being lectured by Dionysius about a recent bad slave purchase from a man named Theron. Dionysius tells Leonas the following: 'This experience will make you more careful in the future… [H]e [Theron] was a kidnapper [ἀνδραποδιστὴς ἄρα ἦν] and that is why he sold you someone else's slave in an isolated place'.[117] Thus, we can see that an *andrapodistēs*:

(1) sells someone else's slave;
(2) does it in an isolated place.

A second piece of evidence is a Greek dictionary compiled by a man named Julius Pollux, who worked during the time of the emperor Commodus in the second century. For Pollux, an *andrapodistēs* 'is one who enslaves a free man or who kidnaps another man's slave'.[118] In Rome and Greece, 'freeborn' persons were usually other Romans or Greeks who had 'citizenship' and could not be 'kidnapped' into slavery. However, barbarians were not

---

114. See 'ἀνδραποδιστής', BDAG, p. 76a.
115. See Harrill, 'The Vice of Slave Dealers in Greco-Roman Society: The Use of a Topos in 1 Timothy 1.10', *JBL* 118 (1999), pp. 97-122 (98).
116. Chariton, *Callirhoe* (Goold, LCL). See also Pieter W. van der Horst, 'Chariton and the New Testament', *Novum Testamentum* 25 (1983), pp. 348-55.
117. Chariton, *Callirhoe* 2.1.7-8 (Goold, LCL).
118. Pollux, *Onomasticon* 3.78: ἀνδραποδιστὴς δέ ἐστιν, ὁ τὸν ἐλεύθερον καταδουλωσάμενος, ἢ τὸν ἀλλότριον οἰκέτην ἀπαγόμενος. My text is from Karl Wilhelm Dindorf (ed.), *Julii Pollucis onomasticon cum annotationibus interpretum* (Leipzig: Kuehn, 1824), p. 155.

included in this protected class. So, anyone who kidnapped freeborn Greek/ Roman citizens or stole someone else's slaves was an *andrapodistēs*.

Plato's *Laws* furnish an even wider scope for the corresponding crime of ἀνδραποδισμός (*andrapodismos*). According to Plato's *Laws*:

> If any man forcibly prevent any person from appearing in an action at law...and in case the person so prevented be a free man...the offender be imprisoned for a year and shall be liable to a charge of kidnapping [ὑπόδικον δὲ ἀνδραποδισμοῦ] at the hands of anyone who chooses.[119]

The same charge would be incurred for 'anyone who forcibly prevents a rival competitor at a gymnastic, musical, or other contest from appearing'.[120]

In any case, an *andrapodistēs* is condemned in Greek and Roman culture, too. The fact that slave societies of Greece and Rome condemned an *andrapodistēs* indicates that pure slave trading cannot be meant. Therefore, 1 Tim. 1.10 gives no indication that slave trading itself is bad. But if apologists are going to applaud the Bible for condemning an *andrapodistēs* then they should applaud the Greeks and the Romans for their condemnations, as well.

1 Timothy 6: Honoring Christian Slavemasters

Any thought that slavery or owning slaves was a sin or incompatible with the teachings of Christ in the New Testament must reckon with the author's advice in 1 Timothy:

> Let all who are under the yoke of slavery regard their masters as worthy of all honor, so that the name of God and the teaching may not be defamed. Those who have believing masters must not be disrespectful on the ground that they are brethren; rather they must serve all the better since those who benefit by their service are believers and beloved. Teach and urge these duties. If any one teaches otherwise and does not agree with the sound words of our Lord Jesus Christ and the teaching which accords with godliness, he is puffed up with conceit, he knows nothing (1 Tim. 6.1-4).

The passage shows that one could be both a Christian and a slavemaster.

So how do biblical scholars address this clear endorsement of slaveholding? Horsley tells us: 'It has already been recognized in the field that the Pastoral epistles and other deutero-Pauline letters are not the only continuation of Paul's legacy and certainly not the primary or at the time dominant line of early Christianity...'[121] This allows Horsley to eradicate many of the pro-slavery statements found in places that are not 'Pauline'. In other words, Horsley is expressing another form of 'representativism' in arguing that only

---

119. Plato, *Laws* 12.955a (Bury, LCL).
120. Plato, *Laws* 12.955a (Bury, LCL).
121. Horsley, 'Paul and Slavery', p. 194.

certain parts of the New Testament corpus are 'primary'. Of course, Horsley assumes that Pauline letters should be normative without even offering an argument as to why they should be.

Philemon: What Are You Insinuating?

One of the shortest letters in the entire canon has caused some of the most vexing problems for biblical scholars who promote the superiority of biblical ethics. Joseph Fitzmyer deftly summarizes the main positions that scholars have taken on the occasion for the letter.[122] The traditional and most prevalent view is that Onesimus is a fugitive slave, who has taken refuge with Paul, who is in prison. In the traditional interpretation, Paul is, therefore, sending back a fugitive slave, and affirming the rights of slavemasters to their property. S. Scott Bartchy, among others, prefers another position, wherein Onesimus is not a fugitive, but rather a slave at odds with his master.[123] Onesimus looks to Paul to help mediate the dispute.

So, is Philemon a testimony to Paul's anti-slavery stance, or does Paul affirm the right of masters to have their slaves returned? The answer to that question centers on two issues: (1) the relationship of Onesimus to Philemon; and (2) Paul's instructions to Philemon. A pro-slavery reading cannot be sustained if Onesimus is not a slave. A pro-slavery reading also cannot be sustained easily if Paul is encouraging Philemon to release Onesimus.

For our purposes, we select, from a long history of interpretation, the most recent and strongest challenge to the pro-slavery interpretation of Philemon. This is embodied in the work of Allen D. Callahan, who denies that Onesimus was a slave at all. In fact, Callahan sees Onesimus as Philemon's biological brother. For Callahan, the main issue in the epistle is that Onesimus was not regarded as a *beloved* brother by Philemon. While Callahan's theory has not gained wide acceptance, Horsley thinks it has some merit.[124]

---

122. Joseph A. Fitzmyer, *The Letter to Philemon: A New Translation with Introduction and Commentary* (AB, 34C; New York: Doubleday, 2000), pp. 17-19. See also John Byron, *Recent Research on Paul and Slavery* (Sheffield: Sheffield Phoenix Press, 2008), pp. 116-37; D. Francois Tolmie, *Philemon in Perspective: Interpreting a Pauline Letter* (Berlin: W. de Gruyter, 2010); Günther Schwab, *Echtheitskritische Untersuchungen zu den vier kleineren Paulusbriefe. I/A: Der Philemonbrief, Beobachtungen zur Sprache des Philipper und des Galaterbriefs* (Norderstedt: Books on Demand, 2011); Peter Müller, *Der Brief an Philemon* (Meyers kritisch-exegetischer Kommentar über das Neue Testament; Göttingen: Vandenhoeck & Ruprecht, in press).
123. S. Scott Bartchy, 'Philemon, Epistle to', in *ABD*, V, p. 307.
124. Horsley ('Paul and Slavery', p. 178) says: 'Recent studies have made clear that the letter to Philemon is not about a runaway slave, perhaps does not concern a slave at all'.

As Callahan indirectly acknowledges, he is resurrecting a theory voiced by George Bourne (1780–1845), who published *A Condensed Anti-Slavery Bible Argument by a Citizen of Virginia* in 1845.[125] Bourne argued that there was no evidence that Philemon 'was a slaveholder... Nor is there any evidence that Onesimus was a slave.'[126] As does Callahan, Bourne believed that 'Onesimus was a natural brother of Philemon'.[127] Although Callahan has expended considerable and impressive scholarly effort to support his position, ultimately he is as unsuccessful as Bourne.

Let's begin with Callahan's effort to deny that Onesimus was a slave. According to Callahan, '[t]he weight of establishing Onesimus's servile identity thus falls on verse 16a, οὐκέτι ὡς δοῦλον ἀλλ' ὑπὲρ δοῦλον ("no longer as a slave, but as more than a slave")'.[128] In particular, Callahan argues that 'ὡς indicates a virtual, not an actual, state of affairs'.[129] That is to say, the conjunction, *hōs* (ὡς), is not indicating that Onesimus is a slave, but that he is being regarded 'as though he were a slave'. Therefore, Callahan translates v. 16a as 'no longer as if he were a slave'.[130] By translating v. 16a in this manner, Callahan renders impotent any idea that Paul sent back a slave to his master.

If Callahan means that the conjunction *hōs* 'indicates a virtual, not an actual state of affairs' in general or exclusively, then he is clearly wrong. What follows *hōs* acknowledges the factuality of the predicate. For example, in 1 Thess. 2.6, the clause, 'we might have made demands as apostles of Christ', does not mean 'we might have made demands as though we were virtual apostles of Christ'.[131] So, in Mt. 14.5, ὡς προφήτην αὐτὸν εἶχον is translated rightly 'they held him to be a prophet' (RSV), not 'they held him as though he were a virtual prophet'.

Callahan appeals to Phlm. 17 (παραλαβοῦ αὐτὸν ὡς ἐμέ) to support his case. The RSV translates this clause as 'receive him as you would receive me'. Callahan points out that the clause should be interpreted as saying 'Onesimus is to be received as Paul's virtual presence; he is not Paul'.[132] In other words, just like 'as me' in v. 17 does not mean that Onesimus is Paul, so 'as a slave' in v. 16 ought not mean that Onesimus is a slave.

125. George W. Bourne, *A Condensed Anti-Slavery Bible Argument; By a Citizen of Virginia* (New York: S.W. Benedict, 1845).
126. Bourne, *Anti-Slavery Bible Argument*, p. 82.
127. Bourne, *Anti-Slavery Bible Argument*, p. 83.
128. Allen D. Callahan, 'Paul's Epistle to Philemon: Toward an Alternative *Argumentum*', *HTR* 86 (1993), p. 362.
129. Callahan, 'Paul's Epistle', p. 362.
130. Callahan, 'Paul's Epistle', p. 373.
131. See also Fitzmyer, *Philemon*, p. 114.
132. Allen D. Callahan, *Embassy of Onesimus: The Letter of Paul to Philemon* (Valley Forge, PA: Trinity Press International, 1997), p. 10.

However, Callahan is not analyzing the predicates correctly. In v. 17 the predicates are applied to different persons, whereas in v. 16 they relate to the same person. More importantly, the proper equation expressed by *hōs* is in the *manner* of reception and *not the identity of the persons* being received.[133] A better analogy to v. 17, therefore, is Mt. 19.19 where two persons are being compared with *hōs*: 'love thy neighbor as yourself (ἀγαπᾶν τὸν πλησίον σου ὡς σεαυτόν)'. Here, the manner is being equated, not the identity of the person, in other words, 'you shall love your neighbor in the same way as you love yourself'. The last portion does not mean 'as you virtually love yourself'.

More importantly, Callahan's interpretation of *hōs* would also undermine receiving Onesimus 'as a beloved brother'. The Greek predicates are elliptical insofar as one could supply *hōs* before every predicate in v. 16.[134] As it is, Callahan does supply 'as' before 'beloved brother' in his English translation of the sentence that spans vv. 15 and 16.

> For on this account he has left for the moment, so that you might have him back forever, no longer as though he were a slave, but, more than a slave, as a beloved brother very much so to me, but how much more so to you, both in the flesh and in the Lord.[135]

So, a fuller expression might have *hōs* before 'more than a slave' and *hōs* before 'a beloved brother' so that the complete predicates read: 'as more than a slave, and as more than a beloved brother'.[136] By Callahan's logic, here *hōs* also might mean 'as though he were more than a virtual slave, and as though he were more than a virtual beloved brother'. But Callahan is clear that Paul wants Philemon to treat Onesimus as an actual beloved brother, and not a 'virtual beloved brother'.

2 Thessalonians 3.15 provides a better analogy to Phlm. 16 because it bears *hōs* in contrastive predicates ('not as X, but as Y') with *alla* that apply to the same person. That example also repeats *hōs*, as I have suggested could be the case in Phlm. 16. Briefly, 2 Thess. 3.14 advises church members what to do when someone in their group disobeys Paul's letter. In 2 Thess. 3.15, Paul advises: 'Do not look on him as an enemy, but warn him as a brother' (καὶ μὴ ὡς ἐχθρὸν ἡγεῖσθε, ἀλλὰ νουθετεῖτε ὡς ἀδελφόν). Here, the sense is not likely to be 'warn him as though he were a virtual brother' but 'warn him as a brother' (i.e., 'because he is a brother'). Likewise, Paul is not issuing a directive because he thinks the congregation will treat the offender

---

133. See Joseph Henry Thayer, *A Greek–English Lexicon of the New Testament* (repr., Grand Rapids: Zondervan, 1974 [1889]), p. 680: 'in the same manner as'.
134. On ellipses and the use of *hōs*, see Robertson, *A Greek Grammar*, p. 481.
135. Callahan, *Embassy of Onesimus*, p. 21.
136. In his entry on ὡς, Thayer (*Greek–English Lexicon*, p. 680) says: 'sometimes in the second member of a sentence the demonstrative word...is omitted and must be supplied by the mind'.

as a virtual enemy. Rather, he is afraid the congregation will treat the offender as an actual enemy.

Surprisingly, in all the debates about Philemon, few scholars ever notice how similar Paul's advice to Philemon is to that found in Sir. 33.30-31:[137]

> If you have a servant, let him be as yourself [ἔστω ὡς σύ], because you have bought him with blood. If you have a servant, treat him as a brother [ἄγε αὐτὸν ὡς ἀδελφόν], for as your own soul you will need him. If you ill-treat him, and he leaves and runs away, which way will you go to seek him?

Sirach sees no incompatibility between treating someone as a brother and still retaining a slave status for that person. Sirach effectively refutes Petersen's claim that '[i]t is logically and socially impossible to relate to one and the same person as both one's inferior and as one's equal'.[138] Petersen's appeal to 'symbolic universes' shows that he is not considering all the data, since he does not mention Sirach's view.

In any case, since there is good reason to see Onesimus as a slave, then the next problem is whether Paul is encouraging Philemon to emancipate Onesimus. Here, apologetics takes a paradoxical reversal. While Callahan tries to defuse the pro-slavery implications of Philemon by denying that Onesimus is a slave at all, Witherington sees Onesimus's enslavement as a reason to refute the pro-slavery interpretations. Witherington, who utterly rejects Callahan's theory, argues that Paul's call for emancipation is what renders Philemon such a strong anti-slavery testimonial.[139]

The problem with using Philemon as a testimonial against slavery is that there is no clear and explicit directive to Philemon to emancipate Onesimus. Nowhere in the letter do we see Paul saying 'slavery is a sin, and you must free Onesimus'. Nowhere in the letter do we have anything even akin to the strong directive issued by Paul on such things as drunkenness and adultery (1 Cor. 6.8-9), incest (1 Cor. 5), or just not working hard enough (2 Thess. 2.10). Witherington, however, argues that such a directive is there, but we just have to read in between the lines.

As was the case with Colossians, Witherington believes the key to Philemon's interpretation is the correct application of socio-rhetorical criticism.[140] In fact, he chides Callahan and others for the failure to recognize

---

137. This passage is lacking in the scripture citation indices of Witherington (*The Letters to Philemon...*, p. 371), Norman R. Petersen (*Rediscovering Paul: Philemon and the Sociology of Paul's Narrative World* [repr., Eugene, OR: Wipf & Stock, 2008 (1985)], p. 304), Byron (*Recent Research*, p. 156), and Callahan (*Embassy of Onesimus*, p. 91).

138. Petersen, *Rediscovering Paul*, p. 289.

139. Witherington, *The Letters to Philemon...*, pp. 62-63.

140. As such, Witherington is following the approach of Petersen (*Rediscovering Paul*), and Frank F. Church, 'Rhetorical Structure and Design in Paul's Letter to Philemon', *HTR* 71 (1978), pp. 17-33.

some of these rhetorical nuances.[141] Yet, the wide variety of results using 'socio-rhetorical criticism' also signals the inability of this supposed 'method' to solve many issues in New Testament exegesis.

Methodologically, Witherington's approach to Philemon attempts to cut and paste statements about rhetoric from disparate sources (Aristotle, Quintilian, Cicero) in order to create the impression of some unified and parallel socio-rhetorical strategy being applied by Paul. However, my own analysis of how the theory of rhetoric coincides with the way in which, for example, Cicero actually writes, shows a lot of latitude. Indeed, the gap between theory and practice can be so variegated that we can quote rhetoricians to support just about anything we want to prove. Witherington seems to realize this problem, but discounts it in the rest of his exegesis.[142]

In the case of Philemon, Witherington claims Paul is using a rhetorical technique called *insinuatio* to appeal for Onesimus's freedom. According to Witherington, '[t]he nature of *insinuatio* is to begin indirectly so as not to offend or anger the audience and then in the *peroratio* to pull all the emotional stops and make one's appeal boldly and directly'.[143] Using *insinuatio* means that Paul

> does not attack the problem head on, but rather builds rapport with Philemon, praises his character and previous behavior, appeals to the deeper emotions, and then shows how the requested action gives Philemon an opportunity to continue to behave in such gracious Christian ways.[144]

At the same time, Philemon represents Witherington's third moral order of discourse in which the level of frankness is highest.

Support for *insinuatio* in Philemon derives partly from Cicero's *De oratore*, which Witherington quotes as follows:

> [W]e shall derive our greatest supply of openings designed either to conciliate or to stimulate the judge from topics contained in the case that are calculated to produce emotions...though it will not be proper to develop these fully at the start, but only to give a slight preliminary nudge to the judge, from topics contained in the case that are calculated to produce emotion.[145]

---

141. Witherington, *The Letters to Philemon*..., p. 62: 'Failure to recognize some of these rhetorical nuances signaling *insinuatio* has misled several interpreters and has even led to arguments that Onesimus was not a runaway...'
142. Witherington (*The Letters to Philemon*..., p. 2) says 'ancient writers who were rhetorically adept, as Paul was, adopted different styles for different audiences'.
143. Witherington, *The Letters to Philemon*..., p. 63.
144. Witherington, *The Letters to Philemon*..., p. 61. See also Andrew Wilson, 'The Pragmatics of Politeness and Pauline Epistolography: A Case Study of the Letter to Philemon', *JSNT* 48 (1992), pp. 107-19.
145. Witherington, *The Letters to Philemon*..., p. 61, quoting Cicero, *De oratore* 2.79.324.

However, this quote from Cicero is a perfect example of Witherington's arbitrary and hodge-podge approach to rhetorical analysis.

First, this passage in Cicero is not analogous to much of anything in Philemon. Cicero is describing the use of rhetoric in a court situation, where a lawyer might be defending a client, and where there is an audience that may consist of strangers. But Witherington's premise is that Philemon is a letter sent to very specific addressees who are intimately known to Paul. These are very different situations for Cicero. Recall Cicero's own words: 'a letter is one thing, a court of law or a public meeting quite another'.[146]

Second, one can find quotes in Cicero that seem completely contraposed to the way in which Witherington says Paul is writing. A few paragraphs earlier in *De oratore*, Cicero says: 'I also censure the people who place their weakest points first...in arrangement of a speech the strongest point should come first'.[147] Yet, Cicero also says that one really has to attune style to each situation. So, it is difficult to argue that even Cicero follows a consistent practice because his theory permits ample relativism and expediency.

The fact that one cannot follow a consistent theory of rhetoric to explain Philemon becomes apparent when Witherington must switch to Quintilian to explain Phlm. 17-22. These verses are supposed to be analogous to the peroration (or conclusive portion) of a speech. It is in the peroration that Witherington thinks Paul makes his strongest case for emancipation. Witherington cites Quintilian, when the latter says: 'It is in the peroration...that we must let loose the whole torrent of our eloquence'.[148] But, again, Quintilian is speaking of court settings, and not letters written to friends.

Verse 21 is also crucial to Witherington's emancipatory reading: 'Confident of your obedience, I write to you, knowing that you will do even more than I say'. According to Witherington, '[T]he "even more" presumably is that Philemon will not only welcome Onesimus and not only treat him no longer as a slave, but that he will actually send Onesimus back to Paul as a freedman'.[149] Thus, Paul can now be counted as an abolitionist hero, instead of someone affirming the right of a master to have his slave returned.

However, one might equally posit that the 'even more' simply refers to anything Paul had not asked directly or previously. It could be granting Paul's previous wish to keep Onesimus (v. 12), since Paul's direct request is simply for Philemon to treat Onesimus as a brother (vv. 16-17). Or the 'even

---

146. Cicero, *Letters to Friends* 9.21.1.
147. Cicero, *De oratore* 2.77.313-314 (Sutton and Rackham, LCL): 'Atque etiam in illo reprehendo eos qui minimae firma sunt ea prima collocant...sic in oratione firmissimum quodque sit primum'.
148. Witherington (*The Letters to Philemon*..., p. 83) citing Quintilian, *Institutio oratoria* 6.1.52.
149. Witherington, *The Letters to Philemon*..., p. 86.

more' could be the request to prepare a room for Paul (v. 21), something he did not ask before. Or the 'even more' could simply be a gracious hyperbole that is not meant as a directive.[150] Socio-rhetorical analysis is unhelpful here in deciding which choice is best.

In addition, Witherington must appeal to psychoanalysis to achieve an emancipatory reading. Psychoanalysis is difficult enough without knowing Paul, but even more so because Witherington admits that:

> In fact, it may not be Paul himself that should be praised for the rhetorically impressive style of those documents. Perhaps not Paul but Timothy knew this style, having grown up near Asia, and Paul was content to have him compose these documents accordingly to make them more nearly words on target.[151]

So how do we know how much is Paul's thinking and how much is Timothy's thinking?

Socio-rhetorical analysis seems to be a deflective approach because Witherington focuses on what is not said directly, and underrates what is actually said. What is said certainly shows Paul to uphold the right of masters to their property. The central focus of Paul's ideology could just as well be expressed in this passage:

> Accordingly, though I am bold enough in Christ to command you to do what is required, yet for love's sake I prefer to appeal to you—I, Paul, an ambassador and now a prisoner also for Christ Jesus—I appeal to you for my child, Ones'imus, whose father I have become in my imprisonment. (Formerly he was useless to you, but now he is indeed useful to you and to me.) I am sending him back to you, sending my very heart. I would have been glad to keep him with me, in order that he might serve me on your behalf during my imprisonment for the gospel; but I preferred to do nothing without your consent in order that your goodness might not be by compulsion but of your own free will (Phlm. 8-14).

To begin with, Paul says to Philemon: 'I preferred to do nothing without your consent' (χωρὶς δὲ τῆς σῆς γνώμης οὐδὲν ἠθέλησα ποιῆσαι). This alone shows that Paul prefers to leave the decision up to the master.

Callahan denies that the Greek word *gnome* (γνώμη) means 'consent', and he translates v. 14 as 'without taking your opinion into consideration'.[152]

---

150. We can find such hyperbolic statements at the end of some of Cicero's *Letters to Friends* (Bailey, LCL). For example, Letter 7.11.3: 'You will doubtlessly achieve all your aims even so by your own energies and my wholehearted zeal for your welfare' ('omnia tamen quae vis et tua virtute profecto et nostro summo erga te studio consequere'). Letter 7.14.2: 'I am very fond of you, and not only want you to be fond of me but am confident you are' ('a te amari cum volumus tum etiam confidimus').
151. Witherington, *The Letters to Philemon...*, p. 25.
152. Callahan, *Embassy of Onesimus*, p. 44. Those who disagree with Callahan include Witherington (*Letters to Philemon...*, p. 76), Fitzmyer (*Philemon*, p. 111), and BDAG, p. 203a.

He offers no detailed analysis of the Greek lexicon for this conclusion. In Josephus (*Ant.* 18.336), we find a king warning a military leader named Asinaeus to go to another country because there were generals who wanted to kill Asinaeus 'without my [the king's] consent' (δίχα γνώμης τῆς ἐμῆς). This is quite parallel to Phlm. 14.[153]

Callahan does refer to the Vulgate's reading of *sine consilio [autem] tuo* in Phlm. 14.[154] True enough, the Latin word *consilium* could mean merely advice or opinion. But *consilium* in the Vulgate could also express something just as strong as or stronger than consent. Note Acts 2.23: 'this Jesus, delivered up according to the definite plan and foreknowledge of God, you crucified and killed by the hands of lawless men'. The Vulgate has *definito consilio* where the English has 'definite plan'. Thus, *consilio* does not likely mean 'opinion' of God here.

Given that it is likely that *gnome* means 'consent', Paul's actions are more ethically egregious than Witherington's benign analysis would have us believe. Paul admits that he could have commanded Philemon 'to do what is required', but chose to defer to the master's consent instead. Witherington emphasizes that Paul was pressuring Philemon through the use of *insinuatio* and indirect appeals, but this does not help Paul's ethics either. As mentioned, Paul had no problem commanding and telling adulterers and drunkards that they were not part of the Kingdom of God:

> Do you not know that the unrighteous will not inherit the kingdom of God? Do not be deceived; neither the immoral, nor idolaters, nor adulterers, nor sexual perverts, nor thieves, nor the greedy, nor drunkards, nor revilers, nor robbers will inherit the kingdom of God. And such were some of you. But you were washed, you were sanctified, you were justified in the name of the Lord Jesus Christ and in the Spirit of our God (1 Cor. 6.9-10).

Paul did not feel he needed some subtle *insinuatio* to tell the Corinthians how horrible such conduct is. He did not seem to care that they would not like him for saying those things. Yet, in Philemon, Witherington wants us to praise Paul for leaving the even more horrible crime of slavery up to Philemon, even when Paul admits he could have commanded Philemon to emancipate Onesimus.

In all fairness, I do not think we have enough information to settle the question of Philemon's status or Paul's request. Many plausible scenarios can be achieved that do not require the conclusions of Witheringon or Callahan. Jennifer Glancy acutely observes: 'this brief letter does not permit us to deliver a final verdict on that question of whether Onesimus had his owner's

---

153. Josephus, *Ant.* 18.336 (Feldman, LCL).
154. Callahan, *Embassy of Onesimus*, p. 42.

permission to be with Paul...'¹⁵⁵ She adds that using this letter to investigate early Christian attitudes toward slavery is 'a futile enterprise'.¹⁵⁶

But, whether Philemon is ambiguous about Paul's attitudes toward slavery, both Callahan and Witherington fail in their attempts to rescue Paul from accepting the right of masters to their property. If Callahan is correct, then there are no emancipatory ideas expressed in Philemon at all. If Witherington is correct, Philemon does not represent much of an advance anyway. Plato already directs that members of the in-group should not enslave one another. Seneca told us to be kind and merciful to slaves. That did not make them abolitionists any more than Paul.

Why Was the New Testament Not More Vocal?

Perhaps the most convoluted ethical discussions center on explaining why New Testament authors, and especially Paul or Jesus, were not more vocal about abolishing slavery. The common apologetic proposal is that these New Testament figures did not wish to appear overly radical in their social agendas. Witherington cites with approval the rationale R.P. Martin offers for Christianity's seeming apathy toward the abolition of slavery: 'That would have required revolution, which in turn would have been a violation of the teaching of Jesus regarding non-violence. In other words, it was not a legitimate moral option, never mind an effective or practical option for a tiny minority sect.'[157]

Richard Horsley goes much further in his explanation for why Christianity was not more vocal against slavery:

> Finally, over against apologists for Christianity working from liberal individualistic perspectives and assumptions, it must be recognized that taking a stand in favor of abolishing slavery in Greek and Roman antiquity would not have occurred to anyone. Slavery was part and parcel of the whole political-economic religious structure. The only way even of imagining a society without slavery would have been to imagine a different society.[158]

These rationales are not only incoherent with other statements about the revolutionary nature of Christianity, but also flounder when we consider other facts.

---

155. Glancy, *Slavery in Early Christianity*, p. 91.
156. Glancy, *Slavery in Early Christianity*, p. 92. For a similar conclusion, see Byron, *Recent Research*, p. 137.
157. Witherington, *The Letters to Philemon...*, p. 51 n. 2; R.P. Martin, *Ephesians, Colossians, and Philemon* (Atlanta: John Knox Press, 1991), p. 138.
158. Horsley, 'The Slave Systems', p. 59.

First, it is not necessarily true that requiring abolition, at least from Christians, would have necessitated some revolution or violence.[159] The Quakers required their members to give up slavery in America in the late eighteenth century. There was resistance, but not much revolution or violence within Quakerism. Christianity need not have required non-Christians to abolish slavery. It could have had an ethical impact even if it only prevented its own members from having slaves. After all, there was no Roman law that said Christians were *required* to have slaves.

Again, Paul had no trouble demanding that people stop being drunks and adulterers, which would require a social revolution, as we found out with prohibition in the United States. Lester Scherer acutely observed the relative importance that Christians placed on slavery when compared to the use of alcohol and sexual conduct in his study of antebellum American churches: 'Self-proclaimed and widely recognized as the nation's "conscience" the churches appeared to be saying that drinking whiskey or enjoying sex without marriage was more scandalous than holding slaves'.[160]

Second, at least some early Christian beliefs were known to be revolutionary, and that did not stop Christians from continuing to voice those beliefs. Consider Acts 17.7 where Christians are described as 'acting against the decrees of Caesar, saying that there is another king, Jesus'. What could be more revolutionary than proclaiming that there was another emperor besides Caesar? By definition, the overthrow or substitution of another emperor would be 'revolutionary'. Yet, we are supposed to believe that not allowing Christians to hold slaves was too revolutionary.

If Seyoon Kim is correct, and these passages in Acts simply represent false charges of sedition, we can still find other instances where Jesus and early Christians clearly knew their teachings would generate social conflict.[161] Acts does not portray Paul as stopping his mission because his message was upsetting Jewish communities. Jesus says (Mt. 10.34-37) that his teachings would split up families. Early Christians are portrayed as willing and able to upset the social order in many ways, and so slavery, one of the greatest of human tragedies, should have been challenged even more.

Third, Horsley's claim that abolition 'would not have occurred to anyone' is refuted by the existence of groups who were advanced ethically enough to eliminate slavery from their group. We have evidence that Locris and

---

159. For similar conclusions, see Margaret Davies, 'Work and Slavery in the New Testament: Impoverishment of Traditions', in Rogerson, Davies, and Carroll R. (eds.), *The Bible in Ethics*, pp. 315-47 (346).
160. Lester B. Scherer, *Slavery and the Churches in Early America* (Grand Rapids: Eerdmans, 1976), p. 158.
161. Seyoon Kim, *Christ and Caesar: The Gospel and the Roman Empire in the Writings of Paul and Luke* (Grand Rapids: Eerdmans, 2008), pp. 75-76.

Phocis in ancient Greece prohibited slavery.[162] Philo tells us that among the Essenes,

> not a single slave [δοῦλος] is to be found among them, but all are free, exchanging services with each other, and they denounce the owners of slaves, not merely for their injustice in outraging the law of equality, but also for their impiety in annulling the statute of Nature, who mother-like has born and reared all men alike, and created them genuine brothers, not in mere name, but in every reality, though this kinship has been put to confusion by the triumph of malignant covetousness, which has wrought estrangement instead of affinity and enmity instead of friendship.[163]

So, clearly the idea of abolition, or at least not having slaves, had occurred to a number of people. Before Christianity, there were already groups who were much more vocal in their denunciations of slavery. They already were appealing to a 'higher' law rather than expediency. The Essenes did not seem to have a fear of 'revolution' by requiring their own members to be slave-free or by denouncing non-members who were slaveholders.

Fourth, these apologists seem to think that Jesus demanded non-violence, when he did not. In Mt. 10.34, Jesus says: 'Do not think that I have come to bring peace on earth; I have not come to bring peace, but a sword'. Modern ethicists have dismissed this passage with very little evidence. Roland H. Bainton says that '[e]vidently here the word "sword" was used "metaphorically" because in the parallel passage in Luke we read instead the word "division"'.[164] Bainton exemplifies a very common technique among Christian apologists: interpret favored ideas literally, and unfavored ideas figuratively.

It is arbitrary to argue that Jesus could not have meant violent conflict when he used the word 'sword'. Using Luke to explain Matthew is not a very legitimate procedure because it assumes that those reading Matthew had recourse to Luke, which is probably not the case at a time when the canon was not yet formed. Likewise it is futile to argue that Jesus preached love, and so he could not have meant violence in Mt. 10.34-37. One can simply reverse that rationale, and say that Jesus could not have meant 'love' literally anywhere else because he spoke of literal violence in Mt. 10.34-37.

Moreover, despite common claims that Jesus was speaking about the consequences of following Jesus in Mt. 10.34-37, the fact is that, grammatically, the clause, 'I have not come to bring peace, but a sword' (οὐκ ἦλθον βαλεῖν εἰρήνην ἀλλὰ μάχαιραν), is a purpose clause not a result clause in Greek.[165]

---

162. Morrow, *Plato's Law of Slavery*, 130 n. 8.
163. Philo, *Every Good Man Is Free* 79 (Colson, LCL).
164. Roland Bainton, *Christian Attitudes toward War and Peace: A Historical Survey and Critical Re-evaluation* (repr., Nashville: Abingdon Press, 1989 [1960]), p. 56.
165. On the commonality of verbs of motion (e.g., 'came'/ ἦλθον) + infinitives in purpose clauses, see F. Blass, A. Debrunner, and Robert Funk, *A Greek Grammar of the*

Accordingly, Jesus is affirming that violence is the purpose, not the result, of his advent. That is one reason Mt. 10.34-37 provided plausible support for Christian violence and enslavement throughout history.

Fifth, and contrary to Horsley, imagining a different society was very much alive in the ancient Near East and in the Bible. Horsley himself says that Paul 'had been commissioned to organize communities as beachheads of the alternative society that would come fully into existence at the parousia of Christ'.[166] After all, apocalyptic biblical literature is all about imagining different, and often utopian, societies. What is the book of Revelation if not the imagining of a different society? Plato's *Republic* is the imagining of a different society. Indeed, the fact that biblical authors could not imagine a society free of slavery should be seen as an indictment of a corpus for which ethical superiority is claimed.

Finally, it seems that these apologists want to have it both ways. On the one hand, they want to credit Christianity for being a revolutionary new ethical system, and yet they want to deny that it even could be revolutionary when it came to slavery. Apologists want to credit Christianity with energizing abolition movements, some of which were quite violent, and yet shy away from saying that Christianity should have done the very same thing earlier.

Summary

Attitudes toward slavery are sometimes worse and more inhumane in the New Testament than in the Old Testament. In fact, I wholly concur with Margaret Davies, who concludes that 'a comparison with Deuteronomy and Leviticus shows the New Testament represents an impoverishment of traditions'.[167] While the Old Testament set term limits for some slaves, New Testament slavery can be indefinite. While the Old Testament railed against enslaving fellow Hebrews, the New Testament allows Christians to own fellow Christians. The Old Testament required the emancipation of some severely injured slaves, but the New Testament advised Christian slaves to be submissive even to cruel masters. So if there is a trajectory from the Old Testament to the New Testament, it is toward an increasing acceptance of slavery and its cruelties.

New Testament and Other Early Christian Literature (Chicago: University of Chicago Press, 1975), p. 197, paragraph 390. A parallel example is found in Mt. 5.17.

    166.   Horsley, 'Paul and Slavery', p. 190.

    167.   Davies, 'Work and Slavery in the New Testament', p. 347. For a more apologetic view, see Carolyn Osiek, 'Slavery in the Second Testament World', *Biblical Theology Bulletin* 22 (1992), pp. 174-79.

Chapter 6

CHRIST AS IMPERIAL SLAVEMASTER

I began this book by observing that Jesus is never portrayed as doing anything bad or evil in books on biblical ethics. It is usually the opposite—Jesus is a liberator. Richard Horsley, in particular, authored a series of books portraying Jesus as an anti-imperialist bent on freeing humanity from earthly oppression and slavery.[1] Similarly, Obery Hendricks claims: 'Jesus was a victim of empire, not its proponent... Jesus himself consistently stood against the empire by openly challenging the religious establishment.'[2]

In contrast, this chapter explores how the portrayal of Jesus as an imperialist and slavemaster is vital to understanding slavery and why it lasted as long as it did in Christianity. This chapter also demonstrates that the efforts represented by scholars such as Horsley and Hendricks are really more an exercise in Christian apologetics than they are a historical description of how Jesus was portrayed by the earliest documents we have for Christianity.

I am an agnostic as to the existence of the so-called historical Jesus. I have already argued that our sources are far too late and confused to ever compose a consistent portrait of any historical person behind what we find in the biblical texts.[3] Thus, almost any picture of Jesus one constructs is subjective because the data are varied and contradictory. Likewise, efforts to find the 'earliest' stratum or the right 'symbolic universe' of the Jesus traditions are no less subjective than any other method to find the historical Jesus.[4] I have

---

1. See Richard A. Horsley, *Jesus and Empire: The Kingdom of God and the New World Disorder* (Minneapolis: Fortress Press, 2003); Horsley (ed.), *Paul and Empire: Religion, Power and Society in Roman Imperial Society* (Harrisburg, PA: Trinity Press International, 1997). For some critiques of such anti-imperialist readings, see Kim, *Christ and Caesar*; Joel White, 'Anti-Imperial Subtexts in Paul: An Attempt at Building a Firmer Foundation', *Biblica* 90 (2009), pp. 305-33.

2. Obery Hendricks, Jr, *The Politics of Jesus: Rediscovering the True Revolutionary Nature of Jesus' Teachings and How They Have Been Corrupted* (New York: Doubleday, 2006), p. 223.

3. Avalos, *The End of Biblical Studies*, pp. 185-218.

4. For such an effort, see Gerd Theissen, *The Religion of the Earliest Churches: Creating a Symbolic World View* (Minneapolis: Fortress Press, 1999).

already illustrated this at length in *The End of Biblical Studies*, and so I will not do so here.

However, one certainly can find plenty of evidence that the New Testament saw Jesus or Christ as a slavemaster rather than as a liberator in the sense of advocating the conventional emancipation of slaves or the abolition of slavery itself. While I do not claim that the imperial Jesus is any more representative of the real historical Jesus, I argue that such a picture of Jesus as slavemaster is no more or less subjective than that of the 'liberatory' Jesus.

Imperial Political Rhetoric 101

Obery Hendricks claims that: '[t]he rhetoric of empire certainly is not consistent with the politics of Jesus'.[5] This claim emanates partly from a lack of familiarity with political science. In particular, Hans Morgenthau, the famed advocate of political realism, postulated that any entity that seeks a favorable change in power status is, in fact, pursuing an imperialist policy, defensive or not.[6] By extension, those who oppose any empire simply seek to substitute their own empire.

That is to say, everyone is pursuing a hegemony for their view and that often requires force. So, even those who say they want a pluralistic society seek to overthrow a non-pluralistic society. Extending a pluralistic society may require imperialistic actions when opponents do not want to yield peacefully. Similarly, Americans pursuing an abolitionist society eventually required force, as the US Civil War demonstrated.

Another mistake biblical ethicists commit is referencing the benign, liberative, and peaceful proclamations of Jesus as proof that Jesus is antiimperialistic. We find such claims in the work of Richard Horsley, Seyoon Kim, Ronald Sider, Walter Wink, and John Yoder.[7] Yet, all imperialists speak of how their hegemony will bring peace, prosperity, and social improvement. Empires usually frame their agendas in benign terms and peaceful terms, and claim that any violence is defensive or necessary.

If we read the accomplishments recorded in the *Res gestae* of Caesar Augustus (reigned 27 BCE–14 CE), we would find at least some of these benign actions of the emperor being extolled:

---

5. Hendricks, *The Politics of Jesus*, p. 222.
6. See Hans Morgenthau, *Politics among Nations: The Struggle for Power and Peace* (ed. Kenneth Thompson; New York: McGraw–Hill, 1993), pp. 50-51.
7. Horsley, *Jesus and the Spiral of Violence*; Kim, *Christ and Caesar*; Ronald Sider, *Christ and Violence* (repr., Eugene, OR: Wipf & Stock, 2001 [1979]); Walter Wink, *Jesus and Nonviolence: A Third Way* (Minneapolis: Fortress Press, 2003); John Howard Yoder, *The Politics of Jesus* (Grand Rapids: Eerdmans, 1972).

6. Christ as Imperial Slavemaster

> At the age of nineteen on my own responsibility and at my own expense I raised an army, with which I successfully championed the liberty of the republic when it was oppressed by the tyranny of a faction... I undertook many civil and foreign wars by land and sea throughout the world, and as victor I spared the lives of all citizens who asked for mercy. When foreign people could safely be pardoned I preferred to preserve rather than to exterminate them... [I]n my eleventh consulship I bought grain with my own money and distributed 12 rations a piece...These largesses of mine never reached fewer than 250,000 persons.[8]

Here, we find that some of the benign actions expected of the emperor include mercy, selflessness (taking monetary expenses upon himself), and equality, insofar as his distributions of rations were '12 apiece'. His largesse was massive, reaching no fewer than a quarter million people. Jesus also is supposed to be merciful, and he even feeds masses of people just as Caesar claims to do (Mk 6.34-42; 8.1-10).

Christ as Emperor

There is clear evidence that Christians were, at the very least, perceived as preaching that another king had come to rival the Roman emperor. Consider this example in Acts:

> But the Jews were jealous, and taking some wicked fellows of the rabble, they gathered a crowd, set the city in an uproar, and attacked the house of Jason, seeking to bring them out to the people. And when they could not find them, they dragged Jason and some of the brethren before the city authorities, crying, 'These men who have turned the world upside down have come here also, and Jason has received them; and they are all acting against the decrees of Caesar, saying that there is another king, Jesus'. And the people and the city authorities were disturbed when they heard this (Acts 17.5-9).

So, why are Christians perceived as preaching that Christ is a parallel to the Roman emperor? Perhaps because Christ *is* sometimes patterned very clearly on the Roman emperor or other kings of the ancient Near East.[9]

In early Christianity, Jesus is referred to as *kyrios* (κύριος), the Greek word for 'lord' or 'master', and *dominus* (in Latin), the very word related to 'domination'. Christ is called the 'king of kings and lord of lords' in Rev. 19.16, and that is as imperialistic as it gets in terms of rhetoric. Otherwise,

---

8. P.A. Brunt and J.M. Moore, *Res gestae Divi Augusti: The Achievements of the Divine Augustus* (London: Oxford University Press, 1967), pp. 19, 25.

9. See Manfred Clauss, *Kaiser und Gott: Herrscherkult im römischer Reich* (Stuttgart/Leipzig: Teubner, 1999); Justin K. Hardin, *Galatians and the Imperial Cult: A Critical Analysis of the First-Century Social Context of Paul's Letter* (Tübingen: Mohr Siebeck, 2008); S.R.F. Price, *Rituals of Power: The Roman Imperial Cult in Asia Minor* (Cambridge: Cambridge University Press, 1985).

Jesus comes to set up the Kingdom of God/Heaven, which is an empire. As previously noted, all divine kings have human agents, just like every other empire sponsored by a deity in the ancient world.

Jesus is called the son of God. The Roman emperor is called *divi filius*, the Latin term for the son of a god that is found on the coins of Augustus Caesar before Jesus began his ministry.[10] Jesus demands that followers transfer allegiance from their families to him (Lk. 14.26). This is a very common royal practice, and many new reigns began with the populace swearing an oath of allegiance to the new king.

The *familia Caesaris*, the family or household of Caesar, was a very well-developed concept in the Roman empire.[11] The household of Caesar consisted of slaves, freedmen, as well as officials. Those who had the closest or equal relationships to kings were called 'friends' or 'brothers'. Similarly, Jesus redefined his family as his followers (Mk 3.35; Mt. 10.37; Lk. 14.26). Being a 'follower' is no less a militaristic/imperialistic a term than what is found in the accounts of other leaders or emperors.

Other statements by early Christians see Christ as an emperor or view Christianity as a type of future or present empire. In Acts 2.30, David prophetically envisions Jesus as one who would inherit 'his throne'. The coming new empire is clearly described by Paul:

> But each in his own order: Christ the first fruits, then at his coming those who belong to Christ. Then comes the end, when he delivers the kingdom to God the Father after destroying every rule and every authority and power. For he must reign until he has put all his enemies under his feet. The last enemy to be destroyed is death. 'For God has put all things in subjection under his feet'. But when it says, 'All things are put in subjection under him', it is plain that he is excepted who put all things under him. When all things are subjected to him, then the Son himself will also be subjected to him who put all things under him, that God may be everything to every one (1 Cor. 15.23-28).

When Christian apologists are confronted with such imperialist passages, one recourse is 'representativism'. For example, Hendricks argues that the book of Revelation is not representative of Jesus' teachings.[12] I do not argue that Revelation is representative of all early Christians, but I do affirm that selecting Revelation as representative of Christ's teachings is no less arbitrary than selecting Matthew or Mark.

---

10. S.R.F. Price, 'Gods and Emperors: The Greek Language of the Roman Imperial Cult', *Journal of Hellenic Studies* 104 (1984), pp. 79-95.

11. See P.R.C. Weaver, *Familia Caesaris: A Social Study of the Emperor's Freedmen and Slaves* (Cambridge: Cambridge University Press, 1972).

12. For example, Hendricks (*The Politics of Jesus*, p. 3) says: 'I don't mean the scary, vengeful Book of Revelation Jesus who the fire-and-brimstone preachers claim will burn up everyone except the Elect…'

Seyoon Kim follows a representativist approach in his book, *Christ and Caesar* (2008). Kim is responding to Richard Horsley and other advocates of anti-imperialist views of Christianity. For Kim, Christ's kingship is purely soteriological and spiritual, and has no political or military connotations in the real world. However, Kim also confuses being against the Roman empire with being against imperialism. As we have argued the two are not the same. Early Christians simply yearned to replace the Roman empire with their empire.

Even Kim acknowledges, 'Luke makes it clear that the empire of Rome and the lordship of Caesar are to be replaced by the Kingdom of God and the Lordship of Jesus Christ'.[13] But, for Kim, this empire is realized by 'healing the sick, restoring sinners to God, and building a community of love and service'.[14] However, Kim is simply reproducing the rhetoric of all empires, which tend to see their mission as benign (e.g., *Res gestae*).

Kim does not appreciate the fact that even in Luke, which Kim sees as a paradigm of New Testament Christology, Jesus may be seen as an advocate of 'deferred violence'. Deferred violence means that Jesus can command pacificism for the moment on the premise that he will return to violently avenge his followers (cf. Mt. 25.41-45). In Luke, Christ is to return in 'power and glory' (Lk. 21.27), and he has no healing in mind for those who destroyed Jerusalem. Luke 21.21-24 describes real violence, not spiritual violence, and Luke suggests Jesus will return as a king, whose normal functions would involve military intervention on behalf of his followers.

Nor is Kim's appeal to Rom. 13.1-10 ('Let every person be subject to the governing authorities...') proof that Paul was not an anti-imperialist.[15] Similarly, Rom. 12.14 often is invoked as an example of Christian love toward enemies: 'Bless those who persecute you; bless and do not curse them'. But, Paul also advocates 'deferred violence'. Christians must do what is expedient while awaiting the final overthrow of the Roman empire or whatever non-Christian empire is in force as indicated in Rom. 12.19: 'Vengeance is mine, I will repay, says the Lord'.

Thus, the tactical and utilitarian aspect of this advice in Rom. 12.14 becomes clearer in v. 20: 'if your enemies are hungry, feed them; if they are thirsty, give them something to drink; for by doing this you will heap burning coals on their heads'. The latter clause about 'heaping burning coals on their heads' is an allusion to Prov. 25.21-22, where the vengeful nature of the metaphor is very apparent. Once read as a whole, the commandment to be generous becomes an instrument of deferred violence against the opponent.

---

13. Kim, *Christ and Caesar*, p. 191.
14. Kim, *Christ and Caesar*, p. 193.
15. Kim, *Christ and Caesar*, pp. 36-43.

The kinder one is to the opponent, the more violence will be deserved by the opponent when God repays them.[16]

Christ as Slavemaster

The persistence of slavery in the Western world is better understood once we see that the New Testament portrays the fundamental relationship between Christ and his followers as a slave–master relationship. Paul specifically refers to Christ as *kyrios*, which means 'Lord', and calls himself a *doulos* of Christ. Norman R. Petersen says: 'Christ is the Lord and Master of all believers, including Paul, and they are therefore all slaves of Christ'.[17] Petersen, however, still sees that language as metaphorical. Dale Martin argues that Paul identified so thoroughly with slaves that he saw that title as an honor, and not a badge of dishonor.[18]

But, according to Horsley, '[*k*]*yrios* is, at base, the title of Jesus, and that title has the primary sense of political ruler, not of slave-master'.[19] He adds: 'Although Paul refers himself in a semi-titular way as a "slave of Christ", it is simply not true that he refers to believers generally as "slaves of Christ" or conceives of God/Christ–human relationship in terms of master–slave relations'.[20] In order to make such sweeping claims, Horsley disregards a massive amount of evidence or he appeals to notions of 'symbolic universes' that yield speculation rather than sound history. Horsley also creates a canon within a canon to eject objectionable pro-slavery passages.

As Stanley K. Stowers rightly observes, Horsley is wrong to say that Paul does not portray all believers as slaves of Christ.[21] For example, in Rom. 6.22, Paul says to believers: 'But now that you have been set free from sin and have become slaves of God, the return you get is sanctification and its end, eternal life'. We find similar sentiment in Rom. 14.18: '[H]e who thus serves Christ is acceptable to God and approved by men'.

But Horsley specifically challenges the supposition that '*doulos* automatically referred to a chattel slave'.[22] Horsley argues that to understand how Paul uses *doulos*, one must understand the 'cultural background from which Paul appears to be coming'.[23] He elaborates:

---

16. See further Gordon M. Zerbe, *Non-Retaliation in Early Jewish and New Testament Texts: Ethical Themes and Social Contexts* (Sheffield: JSOT Press, 1993), pp. 251-54.
17. Petersen, *Rediscovering Paul*, p. 24.
18. Martin, *Slavery as Salvation*, p. 46.
19. Horsley, 'Paul and Slavery', p. 170.
20. Horsley, 'Paul and Slavery', p. 176.
21. Stowers, 'Paul and Slavery: A Response', p. 303.
22. Horsley, 'Paul and Slavery', p. 167.
23. Horsley, 'Paul and Slavery', p. 168.

> In the ancient Near Eastern societies from which ancient Israel emerged, the people generally were understood as the 'servants/slaves' of the gods and/or of the human regents of the gods (i.e., the 'great ones', 'kings', or 'high priests'). These 'servants' owed their lords goods and labor services, but they were not chattel slaves in the same sense as those of the Roman or the later American slave systems.[24]

But the cultural background of the ancient Near East is certainly one in which lord–vassal and slave–master relations also were pervasive. Indeed, Horsley seems to ignore that 'political rulers' in the ancient Near East could be viewed as slavemasters of an entire people. 1 Samuel 8.17 makes perfectly clear when Samuel tells the Israelite people that having a king will mean that 'you shall be his slaves'. Of course, Pharaoh, the ruler of Egypt, enslaved the Hebrews. Yahweh himself declares that rulership by the Egyptian king, Shishak, will entail slavery:

> When the LORD saw that they humbled themselves, the word of the LORD came to Shemaiah: 'They have humbled themselves; I will not destroy them, but I will grant them some deliverance, and my wrath shall not be poured out upon Jerusalem by the hand of Shishak. Nevertheless they shall be servants to him, that they may know my service and the service of the kingdoms of the countries' (2 Chron. 12.7-9).

Yahweh here might be saying that slavery to him is better, but it is still slavery comparable to that of earthly kings.

The Israelite people themselves were explicitly considered Yahweh's slaves no less than they were slaves of the Egyptian Pharaoh. Leviticus 25.55 makes the point: 'For to me the people of Israel are servants, they are my servants whom I brought forth out of the land of Egypt: I am the LORD your God'. Combes rightly sees that '[s]lavery to God is just as real as earthly slavery', though Combes erroneously thinks being God's slave disallows earthly slavemasters.[25]

Just as some earthly rulers do, Yahweh expects life-long service from his Hebrew slaves (Deut. 5.29) instead of limited service required when Hebrews enslave other Hebrews. Yahweh marks his slaves permanently with circumcision just as slavemasters might mark their slaves. Combes notes that the seals on the foreheads of followers in Rev. 7.3 may go back to Babylonian slave-marking traditions.[26]

Yahweh also punishes his Hebrew slaves physically for serving other gods just as a normal slavemaster might punish fugitive slaves or disloyal vassals. Like any Lord in the ancient Near East, Yahweh punishes the entire nation for rebellion (Deut. 28.15-68). According to the Greek orator, Demosthenes

---

24. Horsley, 'Paul and Slavery', p. 168
25. Combes, *The Metaphor of Slavery*, p. 43.
26. Combes, *The Metaphor of Slavery*, p. 76.

(384–322 BCE): 'If you wished to consider what the difference between a slave and a freeman was, this most of all you will find—that in the case of slaves, their body is answerable for all their wrongdoings, while the free even in the most unlucky circumstances can protect themselves'.[27] In fact, Paul himself acts like God's majordomo when he threatens to discipline the Corinthian congregation with a rod (1 Cor. 4.21).

We find 'servants' of Yahweh willing to give up their lives for their Lord, just as was expected in many lord–vassal treaties of the Near East. For example, Esarhaddon (681–669 BCE), king of Assyria, tells his vassals that after the king's death, the Assyrian prince, Ashurbanipal, will rule over them. Esarhaddon further says his vassals will 'fight and (even) will die for him'.[28]

Contrary to Horsley's claims that slaves of Yahweh are not considered chattel, the people of Israel are said to be a possession of Yahweh, as is indicated in Deut. 7.6: 'For you are a people holy to the LORD your God; the LORD your God has chosen you to be a people for his own possession [סגלה], out of all the peoples that are on the face of the earth'. The Hebrew word סגלה (*segullah*) translated as 'possession' is used precisely for valued material chattel such as gold and silver (1 Chron. 29.3; Eccl. 2.8).

Horsley attempts to equate Paul being a *doulos* of Christ with merely receiving a prophetic call. However, we have already seen that messengers of the king in the ancient Near East could be slaves.[29] In addition, and as Samuel A. Meier observed: 'when the king sent a messenger, there could be no bargaining. In the Neo-Assyrian empire some men were certainly conscripted to serve as messengers for the palace bureaucracy and military, though we know very few details.'[30]

In the Hebrew Bible we find evidence that being God's prophet was not always completely voluntary. God often chose the prophet long before a prophet could even volunteer (Jer. 1.5), and being a prophet could be considered a form of conscription, as Jonah discovered when he tried to avoid his duties. The death penalty was imposed for prophets who were falsely speaking for Yahweh (Deut. 18.20). Of course, Joel 2.29 prophesied that slaves would be prophets.

---

27. Demosthenes, *Against Androtion* 55, as quoted in Combes, *The Metaphor of Slavery*, p. 29 n. 21. For a historical review of the meaning of *doulos* in Greek, see Lewan Gordesian, *Zur mykenischen Gesellschaftsordnung* (Tbilisi: Logos-Verlag, 2nd edn, 2002), pp. 30-40.

28. D.J. Wiseman, *The Vassal-Treaties of Esarhaddon* (London: The British School of Archaeology in Iraq, 1958), p. 34, lines 50-51; Assyrian text on p. 33, lines 50-51: 'la ta-ma-ḫaṣ-a-ni la ta-mut-ta-a-ni'.

29. For example, Nissinen *et al.*, *Prophets and Prophecy*, p. 153.

30. Samuel A. Meier, *The Messenger in the Ancient Near East* (HSM, 45: Atlanta: Scholars Press, 1988), p. 28.

In Mt. 22.1-14, the slaves sent by the king to invite guests to a wedding seem to be viewed as representatives of the king. Defying those messengers was tantamount to defying the king. Commenting on this passage, Dale Martin remarks, '[i]t is certain that the slaves are to be taken as prophets who represent God'.[31] Paul himself experienced a very violent call to be a messenger in Acts 9.3-9, where he was struck on the Road to Damascus with blindness.

The other evidence provided by Horsley is even weaker. Horsley focuses on 'recently discovered rhetorical criticism' and appeals to 'symbolic universes' to show that Paul's symbolic universe does see a believer's relationship to Christ as a slave–master relationship.[32] Using these techniques, Horsley is able to draw these sweeping conclusions:

> Paul cannot be understood to be helping legitimate the Roman institutional order, intentionally or unintentionally. Even though he writes in standard Hellenistic Roman rhetorical conventions and uses numerous 'symbols' in the language of the dominant culture, his letters indicate an opposition to the dominant order. Indeed, if passages such as 1 Thess. 4.14-18 or 1 Cor. 7.29-31 and 15.20-28 or Rom. 8.18-25 and 11.25-26 are an indication, Paul himself expected the dominant order to be terminated soon, with the imminent *parousia* of his lord. Insofar as Paul knew the symbolic universe of Roman imperial society he appears to have been using it in order to subvert and replace the institutions it legitimated.[33]

At once, we see that all this appeal to 'symbolic universes' is simply another mechanism to divide interpretations into 'literal' and 'figurative'. By making some of Paul's statements into mere figurative expressions, Horsley can erase the more literally imperialistic nature of Paul's slavemaster views.

On a more semantic level, a fundamental problem is that Horsley seems to equate 'the dominant order' with imperialism in general in some cases, but in other cases 'the dominant order' refers specifically to the Roman empire. But speaking against the Roman empire cannot be equated necessarily with speaking against imperialism. As mentioned, Hans Morgenthau shows that anti-imperial rhetoric belies an attempt to replace one empire with another. Therefore, nothing Paul says in the passages cited by Horsley shows that Paul was against imperialism, it is just that he wanted 'his lord', or Christ, to be the head of the empire to be established at the *parousia*.

While it is true that 1 Cor. 7.31 may indicate that the dominant order would pass away soon ('For the form of this world is passing away'), that does not mean that imperialism would pass away—only that this particular

---

31. Martin, *Slavery as Salvation*, p. 52.
32. Horsley, 'Paul and Slavery', p. 157. For a brief history of this 'symbolic universe' and 'narrative world' approach, see Petersen, *Rediscovering Paul*, pp. 17-30.
33. Horsley, 'Paul and Slavery', p. 164.

Roman empire would pass away. As we have mentioned, Horsley offers barely a comment on Paul's clear instructions to obey the Roman institutional order until the eschaton arrived: 'Let every person be subject to the governing authorities. For there is no authority except from God, and those that exist have been instituted by God. Therefore he who resists the authorities resists what God has appointed, and those who resist will incur judgment' (Rom. 13.1-2).

Horsley points to Phil. 3.20 to show that '*soter* as well as *kyrios* has explicit political ruler connotations with believers' "citizenship"'.[34] But nothing in that verse precludes an understanding that Christians will be slaves of God in heaven. Note the passage: 'But our commonwealth is in heaven, and from it we await a Savior, the Lord Jesus Christ, who will change our lowly body to be like his glorious body, by the power which enables him even to subject all things to himself' (Phil. 3.20-21). Verse 21 expresses as imperialist a notion as we can find because Christ is said to 'subject all things to himself'. Subjection is the essence of imperialism.

Despite all of the evidence that Christ is portrayed as the mirror image of the Roman emperor, Horsley also claims: 'If *kyrios* should be understood primarily in the sense that Christ is exalted as the true (if temporary) ruler or regent of God, then it is difficult to find any evidence for "master–slave relations in Paul's symbolic universe", let alone that master–slave was an organizing metaphor therein'.[35]

Horsley's reasoning disregards a multitude of expressions clearly associated with slavery. For example, Paul in 1 Cor. 6.19-20 says, regarding believers: 'Do you not know that your body is a temple of the Holy Spirit within you, which you have from God? You are not your own; you were bought with a price. So glorify God in your body.' Here, believers are bought, just like other slaves, and their body does not belong to them.[36] The possession of a slave's body by a master is one of the essential features of slavery in the Greek 'symbolic universe'.

Horsley dismisses these expressions by saying that these 'metaphors such as "purchase" and "redemption" and "buying", do not constitute evidence for a symbolization of the believer–Christ relation as that of master–slave'.[37] However, Horsley still leaves unexplained why we cannot regard these expressions as evidence for a slave–master view of Christianity, while counting allusions to liberty and freedom as evidence for the true views of Paul. Indeed, Horsley is using another version of 'representativism'.

34. Horsley, 'Paul and Slavery', p. 170.
35. Horsley, 'Paul and Slavery', pp. 170-71.
36. On the slavery imagery of this passage, see Glancy, *Early Christian Slavery*, pp. 65-67.
37. Horsley, 'Paul and Slavery', p. 171 n. 3.

6. *Christ as Imperial Slavemaster* 149

Horsley makes much of 1 Thess. 3.13, which he interprets to mean that Jesus will return 'with all his *saints*, not his slaves'.[38] However, nothing about the word saint (ἅγιος) precludes them also being slaves of God. Daniel 7.18 says that saints (ἅγιοι) will receive the kingdom from God, and presumably can act as regents for the master they serve. The Greek translation of Ps. 34.9 (33.10 LXX) states: 'O fear [φοβήθητε] the LORD, you his saints [οἱ ἅγιοι], for those who fear him have no want!' 'Fearing' a master and a king is what a slave is supposed to do (Prov. 24.21). Therefore, 1 Thess. 3.13 does not disprove that a slave–master model did not apply to the saints, who served God.

Finally, Horsley treats as anti-imperialist the notion that Jesus and Paul also describe themselves as servants of the people. But Philo of Alexandria already knows of a topos in which statesmen are viewed as the *douloi* of the people they rule: 'the true statesman knows quite well that the people has the power of a master, yet he will not admit that he is a slave [οὐχ ὁμολογήσει δοῦλον]…'[39] Today, we still find the idea of serving the ruled or constituents among many politicians.

Jesus and God's Plantation

Obery Hendricks cites the parable of the vineyard workers in Mt. 20.1-16 to show that Jesus supports economic justice and equality, at least in wages for workers. As Hendricks phrases it: 'Jesus is likening the kingdom of God to a greater reality that will correct economic justice and economic exploitation'.[40] However, that parable actually shows how much Jesus endorses inequality and the right of property owners to treat workers as they see fit. Briefly, in the parable some workers, who arrived first, labored all day for the promised wages of one denarius. However, some workers were hired later, and ended up working only an hour. The crucial portions says:

> For the kingdom of heaven is like a householder who went out early in the morning to hire laborers for his vineyard… And when evening came, the owner of the vineyard said to his steward, 'Call the laborers and pay them their wages, beginning with the last, up to the first'. And when those hired about the eleventh hour came, each of them received a denarius. Now when the first came, they thought they would receive more; but each of them also received a denarius. And on receiving it they grumbled at the householder, saying, 'These last worked only one hour, and you have made them equal to us who have borne the burden of the day and the scorching heat'. But he replied to one of them, 'Friend, I am doing you no wrong; did you not agree with me for a denarius? Take what belongs to you, and go; I choose to give to this last

---

38. Horsley, 'Paul and Slavery', p. 170.
39. Philo, *Joseph* 67 (Colson, LCL).
40. Hendricks, *The Politics of Jesus*, p. 137.

as I give to you. Am I not allowed to do what I choose with what belongs to me? Or do you begrudge my generosity?' So the last will be first, and the first last (Mt. 20.1, 8-16).

Clearly, this parable views as just the payment of equal wages for an unequal amount of work as measured by time.

Hendricks understands the injustice, but insists that it is not meant to represent God's (or Jesus') view of wages. Hendricks begins his misinterpretation of the parable by overlooking that Matthew repeatedly uses a specific formula to introduce certain parables of the Kingdom of Heaven: 'the Kingdom of Heaven is like Person X' (Person X usually with a dative in Greek). Note this example from Mt. 13.45-46: 'Again, the kingdom of heaven is like a merchant in search of fine pearls' (ὁμοία ἐστὶν ἡ βασιλεία τῶν οὐρανῶν ἀνθρώπῳ ἐμπόρῳ ζητοῦντι καλοὺς μαργαρίτας). One can find the same pattern in Mt. 13.24, 18.23, 20.1, and 22.2.

In every parable where this introductory formula is found, the actions of the main character are parallel to the actions of God, and presumably endorsed just the same by the author.[41] Thus, in the parable of the great pearl in Mt. 13.45-46, the man treasures the great pearl just as God would treasure his chosen ones. In Mt. 18.23 and 35, the correspondence of the actions of the main character with God's actions is made very explicit insofar as the latter verse says: 'So also my heavenly Father will do to every one of you, if you do not forgive your brother from your heart' (Οὕτως καὶ ὁ πατήρ μου ὁ οὐράνιος ποιήσει ὑμῖν).

Similarly, the parable in Matthew 20 begins as follows: 'For the kingdom of heaven is like a householder [ὁμοία γάρ ἐστιν ἡ βασιλεία τῶν οὐρανῶν ἀνθρώπῳ οἰκοδεσπότῃ] who went out early in the morning to hire laborers for his vineyard'. Just as in all other parables of the kingdom we have cited, we find the same formula, 'the Kingdom of God is like Person X'. It uses the dative (ἀνθρώπῳ οἰκοδεσπότῃ) to identify the person to whom the Kingdom of God is compared.

So why does Hendricks still deny that the actions of the person to whom the Kingdom of God is compared are parallel to the actions of God? As Hendricks phrases it:

> Such a notion does bespeak a God complex, but its arrogance and callousness do not reflect the merciful, loving Father of Jesus. Biblical scholar Warren Carter puts it well: '[W]e should not assume that the householder is God... [C]lues such as his large accumulation of land and subsequent inconsistent behavior in not addressing the inequality of his own wealth suggest that that identification would be inappropriate'.[42]

---

41. For similar conclusions to mine, see Davies, 'Work and Slavery in the New Testament', pp. 330-31.

42. Hendricks, *The Politics of Jesus*, p. 137, citing Warren Carter, *Matthew and the Margins: A Socio-Political and Religious Reading* (New York: T. & T. Clark International,

However, Warren Carter is arbitrary because the main formal cue is the introductory formula, which in every other instance has identified the actions of God with the person to whom the Kingdom of God is likened.

Carter switches to 'moral' cues that are more compatible with what he deems to be just. We can reduce Carter's rationale to: 'Action X is unjust, therefore, the text cannot ascribe action X to God'. But this rationale is a theological judgment, and not one based on linguistic or philological evidence. It rests on the idea that God acts according to our definition of justice. Moreover, saying that we do not think that God would behave that way is not the same as demonstrating that the biblical author does not think God behaves that way.

In fact, the biblical author even offers a clear rationale as to why the actions of the vineyard owner are not unjust in v. 15: 'Am I not allowed to do what I choose with what belongs to me?' The owner is master of his own money, and can do as he will with it. This is parallel to the rationale given for other practices that we might judge unjust but which biblical authors did not. For example, in the law about beating a slave nearly to death (Exod. 21.21), the owner is not punished precisely because the slave 'is his money' (כי כספו הוא). A possession can be treated as the owner wills.

In the disquisition in Rom. 9.20-22 about why God shows preferences that seem unjust to us, Paul compares God to a potter who owns the pot, and the pot cannot complain about inequality. In Rom. 9.15, Paul quotes God (Exod. 33.19): 'I will have mercy on whom I have mercy, and I will have compassion on whom I have compassion'. Thus, God is the master of the world, and he can do what he pleases with his property. Whether we call it just or not is a different question.

Indeed, many early Christian interpreters had no trouble thinking that God's actions were those of the vineyard owner. One example is St Augustine, who saw a direct analogy between vineyard workers and Christians: 'For we are servants of his household, we are sent to hire labourers'.[43] Why should Augustine's sense of justice be any less privileged than Carter's when interpreting the parable in its ancient context?

So, in contrast to Hendricks's claims, Matthew says nothing about correcting what the vineyard owner did. The vineyard owner was considered right in what he did in the first place. If anything, the parable seems to reverse the just payment that workers seem to have expected in the existing economic structure. The Vineyard Master (= God) is the one introducing, rather than correcting, any disparity in the existing structure.

2004), p. 395. See further Warren Carter, *Matthew and Empire: Initial Explorations* (Harrisburg, PA: Trinity Press International, 2001).

43. Augustine, *Sermons on the New Testament* 37.9 (NPNF[1], VI, p. 375).

The parable of the vineyard workers illustrates well how some scholars use circular reasoning when judging what is 'biblical' or 'predominant'. For Hendricks, God cannot possibly be portrayed as acting in a way *we* would deem unjust, and so we can simply eliminate or reinterpret those texts that say God or Jesus acted unjustly. By skewing the data sample in this manner, we are left with benign texts that Hendricks believes represent the 'biblical sensibility of egalitarianism'.[44]

Otherwise, the actions of the master of the vineyard are not too dissimilar from the *modus operandi* described by Augustus Caesar in his *Res gestae*:

> In the eighteenth year of my tribunician power and my twelfth consulship I gave 240 sesterces apiece to 520,000 members of the urban plebs. In my fifth consulship I gave 1,000 sesterces out of booty to every one of the colonists drawn from my soldiers; about 120,000 men in the colonies...[45]

As in the case of parable of the vineyard workers, these moneys are distributed equally regardless of the amount of time or effort that might have been expended by different colonists, soldiers, or members of the plebs. So if Christ's parabolic actions are to be hailed as an advancement in social justice, surely the wages of Augustus Caesar, which are supposed to be real distributions (not parabolic), should be praised even more so.

Christ and the Least of my Brethren

According to Hendricks, among other interpreters, Jesus emphasizes his egalitarianism by referring to 'the least of these my brethren' (ἑνὶ τούτων τῶν ἀδελφῶν μου, τῶν ἐλαχίστων) in Mt. 25.40 (cf. v. 45).[46] But this egalitarianism overlooks the imperial imagery in Mt. 25.31-34: 'When the Son of man comes in his glory, and all the angels with him, then he will sit on his glorious throne. Before him will be gathered all the nations, and he will separate them one from another as a shepherd separates the sheep from the goats...' The sheep are rewarded, and the reason is given (v. 40): 'Truly, I say to you, as you did it to one of the least of these my brethren, you did it to me'.

In a discussion of Pope Gregory XVI's letter to American bishops, Stark goes much further and accepts the following retranslation of Mt. 25.40/45: 'just as Christ declared that whatever was done to the least of all humans it was done to Him, "it naturally follows", that Christians should treat slaves as their brothers'.[47] But the Greek does not say 'all humans'. On the contrary,

---

44. Hendricks, *The Politics of Jesus*, p. 116.
45. Brunt and Moore, *Res gestae*, pp. 25, 27.
46. Hendricks, *The Politics of Jesus*, pp. 9, 311.
47. Stark, *For the Glory of God*, p. 344. Stark is here discussing the argument of Pope Gregory XVI against slavery.

the Greek phrase (τῶν ἀδελφῶν μου, τῶν ἐλαχίστων), translated as 'the least of my brothers', consistently designates Jesus' followers.[48]

In fact, every instance in Matthew where Jesus uses 'my brother/ brethren' he clearly does not mean 'everybody'. In Mt. 12.46-50 Jesus redefines kinship terms explicitly, and reapplies them only to his followers:

> While he was still speaking to the people, behold, his mother and his brothers stood outside, asking to speak to him. But he replied to the man who told him, 'Who is my mother, and who are my brothers?' And stretching out his hand toward his disciples, he said, 'Here are my mother and my brothers! For whoever does the will of my Father in heaven is my brother [μου ἀδελφός], and sister, and mother' (Mt. 12.46-50).

This restrictive usage reappears in Mt. 28.10: 'Then Jesus said to them, "Do not be afraid; go and tell my brethren [τοῖς ἀδελφοῖς μου] to go to Galilee, and there they will see me"'. Clearly, Jesus did not mean that 'all humans' should go see him in Galilee. On the other hand, we never find any other indication that 'my brother(s)' should be interpreted to be everybody, and certainly we never see it applied to those who follow other gods. Matthew's usage of 'my brother(s)' is very consistent with how kings classify those whom they favor as their 'friends' and 'family'.[49] For example, in the Hellenistic period, Alexander Balas, the Greek Seleucid king (150–146 BCE), addresses Jonathan Apphus, the Hasmonean king (161–143 BCE), as a 'brother' (τῷ ἀδελφῷ χαίρειν).[50]

Any attack or slight on a member of the family of the king might be seen as an attack on him, just as Jesus does in Mt. 25.41-45. Jesus is following an idea found in Deut. 32.43: 'Praise his people, O you nations; for he avenges the blood of his servants'. Similarly, Jesus condemns those who did not serve his brethren as follows:

> Then he will say to those at his left hand, 'Depart from me, you cursed, into the eternal fire prepared for the devil and his angels…'…'Truly, I say to you, as you did it not to one of the least of these, you did it not to me' (Mt. 25.41, 45).

Throughout Matthew, Jesus is an advocate of 'deferred violence'. Any commandment to love one's enemy in Matthew (e.g., 5.44) is temporary and premised on the fact that Christ will return to punish the enemies of Christians at the judgment scene of Mt. 25.41-46. It is no different from Jesus

---

48. See David Cortés-Fuentes, 'The Least of These my Brothers: Matthew 25.31-46', *Apuntes* 23 (2003), pp. 100-109.

49. See Weaver, *Familia Caesaris*, pp. 299-300; Edward Champlin, *Final Judgment: Duty and Emotion in Roman Wills 200 B.C. to A.D. 250* (Berkeley: University of California Press, 1991), pp. 13 and 51.

50. Josephus, *Ant.* 13.45 (trans. Ralph Marcus; LCL; Cambridge, MA: Harvard University Press, 1933): τῷ ἀδελφῷ χαίρειν.

directing his disciples to not resist opponents because he will come back and beat up those opponents later.

Christ, the Torture Master

In *Early Christian Slavery*, Jennifer Glancy comments: 'New Testament scholars, however, have been reluctant to acknowledge the violence implicit in the parables' representations of slave bodies'.[51] Indeed, if the parables are analogous to God's kingdom, then God's kingdom can be a place of horrific torture. This passage provides an example:

> Therefore you also must be ready; for the Son of man is coming at an hour you do not expect. Who then is the faithful and wise servant, whom his master has set over his household, to give them their food at the proper time? Blessed is that servant whom his master when he comes will find so doing. Truly, I say to you, he will set him over all his possessions. But if that wicked servant says to himself, 'My master is delayed', and begins to beat his fellow servants, and eats and drinks with the drunken, the master of that servant will come on a day when he does not expect him and at an hour he does not know, and will punish him [διχοτομήσει], and put him with the hypocrites; there men will weep and gnash their teeth (Mt. 24.44-51).

The RSV, among other translations, obscures the violence that is contained here. First, observe that 'servant' translates the same Greek word (δοῦλος) elsewhere used for slave. There is no reason to translate it as other than 'slave'.

However, a more egregious whitewashing of this parable is in v. 51, where the RSV describes the consequences for the slave: '[the master] will punish him [διχοτομήσει], and put him with the hypocrites'. The NAB has 'punish him severely', while the NJB has 'cut him off', which is also recorded as a marginal reading in the NRSV. To say someone is 'cut off' could suggest merely social ostracism or exile. Otherwise, 'punish' or 'punish severely' can have a wide variety of meanings (e.g., anything from branding to whipping).

BDAG specifically notes these mitigating translations ('punish' and 'punish severely'), and comments that 'no exact linguistic parallels have been found to support this rendering or that of the NRSV'.[52] Indeed, the Greek word, διχοτομήσει, translated as 'will punish' means more literally and precisely

---

51. Glancy, *Early Christian Slavery*, p. 103. For more benign views of these parables as they relate to slavery, see Mary Ann Beavis, 'Ancient Slavery as an Interpretive Context for the New Testament Servant Parables with Special Reference to the Unjust Steward (Luke 16.1-8)', *JBL* 111 (1992), pp. 37-54.

52. See 'διχοτομέω', BDAG, p. 253a.

'will cut in half'. The word is etymologically related to our 'dichotomy', and so the bad slave is literally 'dichotomized'. Jennifer Glancy translates it as 'cut in pieces', a translation similar to the REB ('cut him in pieces').[53]

The point, of course, is not so much that Jesus was cutting people in half. The point is that he is portrayed as accepting, without any apparent moral objection, the practice of punishing a slave in such a brutal matter. Since God is analogous to the slavemaster in this parable, one must also presume that God is portrayed as considering the mutilation of a slave a just punishment. After all, we already have been told that burning people eternally was acceptable. Jesus has no problem telling disciples to cut off limbs or parts of themselves that might prevent them from entering the Kingdom of God (Mt. 18.6-9; 19.12). We are told that bodies are not as valuable as the soul in Mt. 10.28: 'And do not fear those who kill the body but cannot kill the soul; rather fear him who can destroy both soul and body in hell'.

Indeed, Matthew illustrates what I elsewhere have called a *pneumatocentric* orientation wherein the immaterial part of a human being is deemed more valuable than the bodily part.[54] Injury to the body for the sake of the soul/spirit, therefore, becomes very logical. In the opposing *somatocentric* orientation the value of the body is deemed paramount. Much of the New Testament's attitude toward slavery can be understood if we see the pneumatocentric orientation it has.

Are Believers Friends of Slaves?

John 15.12-18 has been used to argue that Jesus has transformed his followers into friends, rather than having them remain as his slaves:[55]

> This is my commandment, that you love one another as I have loved you. Greater love has no man than this, that a man lay down his life for his friends. You are my friends if you do what I command you. No longer do I call you servants, for the servant does not know what his master is doing; but I have called you friends, for all that I have heard from my Father I have made known to you (Jn 15.12-15).

There is nothing egalitarian or unique here. Seneca, the Stoic philosopher, tells us that slaves could become family:

> Associate with your slave on kindly, even on affable terms; let him talk with you; plan with you; live with you... Do you not see even this—how our ancestors removed from masters everything invidious and from slaves everything insulting? They called the master the 'father of the household', and

---

53. Glancy, *Early Christian Slavery*, p. 119.
54. Avalos, *Fighting Words*, p. 19.
55. See further Combes, *The Metaphor of Slavery*, p. 75.

slaves 'members of the household', a custom which still holds in the mime...
Yes, you are mistaken if you think I would bar from my table certain slaves
whose duties are more humble.[56]

So, Jesus is exercising a very well-known option of masters to adopt slaves or treat them as members of the household. These slaves can be like family to one another, but that does not mean slavery has ceased to exist. This privilege is extended only to those whom the master has 'chosen' (v. 19).

Summary

Jesus cannot be regarded as an abolitionist in any sense. He never required abolitionism from his followers; rather, the opposite is true. Jesus' parables portray the Kingdom of God as a slave colony, where God can do as he will with his slaves. In the Kingdom of God, bad workers are punished with horrific tortures. More importantly Jesus is patterned in some traditions as the parallel of the Roman emperor. Regardless of any other benign and loving portrayals of Jesus, that imperialistic portrayal has had detrimental consequences for non-Christians around the world for the last 2000 years.

---

56. Seneca, *Epistles* 47.13-15 (Gummere, LCL): 'Vive cum servo clementer, comiter quoque, et in sermonem illum admitte et in consilium e in convictum...Ne illud quidem videtis, quam omnem invidiam maiores nostri dominis, omnem contumeliam servis detraxerint? Dominum patrem familiae appellaverunt, servos, quod etiam in mimis adhuc durat, familiares...Erras si existimas me quosdam quasi sordidioris operae reiecturum.'

Part II

SLAVERY AND THE BIBLE IN CHRISTIAN HISTORY

Chapter 7

SLAVERY IN LATE ANTIQUITY

The phrase 'Late Antiquity' refers here to everything from the post-New Testament period to the Middle Ages, and so roughly between 150 to 1000 CE.[1] It is during this period that some of the basic attitudes toward slavery transitioned from having merely scriptural authority to having legal force.[2] Two basic developments were responsible for this transition. One was the establishing of Christianity as the imperial religion under Constantine.[3] The second development was the growth of an ecclesial legal tradition, adapted largely from Roman law, which could be enforced by Christian kings or by clerics.

Ramsay MacMullen aptly summarizes the experience of slaves in this period when he remarks: 'As to slaves, the disadvantages, which they had suffered for centuries...are well known; but nothing indicates that they were made easier by Christian masters or their congregations'.[4] Yet, some scholars still insist that slavery was ameliorated during this period because of biblical principles followed by Christianity. Accordingly, we provide in this chapter a brief survey of how slavery was accepted or encouraged by Christian theologians, popes, church councils, and rulers. We also focus on Gregory of Nyssa, St Anskar and St Bathilde, three key figures who supposedly favored the total abolition of slavery in this period.

1. For a general discussion of the nature and boundaries of this period, see G.W. Bowersock, Peter Brown, and Oleg Grabar (eds.), *Late Antiquity: A Guide to the Postclassical World* (Cambridge, MA: Harvard University Press, 1999). See also William E. Klingshirn and Mark Vessey (eds.), *The Limits of Ancient Christianity: Essays on Late Antique Thought and Culture in Honor of R.A. Markus* (Ann Arbor: University of Michigan Press, 1999). For a good discussion of the ethical transition from the New Testament to early Christianity, see Wayne A. Meeks, *The Origins of Christian Morality: The First Two Centuries* (New Haven: Yale University Press, 1993).

2. See further Ramsay MacMullen, 'Late Roman Slavery', *Historia* 36 (1987), pp. 359-82; Ross Sampson, 'Rural Slavery, Inscriptions, Archaeology and Marx: A Response to Ramsay MacMullen's "Late Roman Slavery"', *Historia* 38 (1989), pp. 99-110.

3. See Charles M. Odahl, *Constantine and Christian Empire* (New York: Routledge, 2004); David Frankfurter, 'Things Unbefitting Christians: Violence and Christianization in Fifth Century Panopolis', *JECS* 8 (2000), pp. 273-95.

4. MacMullen, *Christianity and Paganism*, p. 7.

Parabiblical Sanctions

Aside from the acceptability of slavery evidenced in the developing canon of New Testament writings, the acceptability of slavery during this period is enshrined in texts that had scriptural authority even if not present in our canon. The *Epistle of Barnabas*, for example, was part of the Codex Sinaiticus, which indicates a canonical or semi-canonical status.[5] The authors of the *Epistle of Barnabas* (19.7) and another important work, called the *Didache* (4.11), expressly equate service to earthly masters as service to God.[6] Note the *Didache*'s phraseology: 'As for you who are slaves, with humility and fear you shall be subject to your masters as replicas of God'.[7] So even if these books did not eventually have the authority of scripture in orthodox Christianity, their authors did not see slavery as incompatible with the teachings of Jesus.

Church Doctrine

Major statements of Church doctrine either assume slavery was acceptable or tried to regulate it further. Canon Five of the Council of Elvira (Spain) (c. 305 CE) punished the killing of a slavewoman in a fit of anger with seven years of excommunication if done deliberately by a mistress, but only five years if done accidentally.[8] The Apostolic Constitutions, which were a great source of general doctrine, also seem to see slavery as a normal part of society. It states, for example: 'the faithful may not go near a market, except in order to purchase a slave [*nisi ad mancipiolum emendum*]'.[9] In other

---

5. See further B.M. Metzger, *The Canon of the New Testament: Its Origin, Development and Significance* (Oxford: Oxford University Press, 1997), pp. 63-67; James Carleton Paget, *The Epistle of Barnabas: Outlook and Background* (Tübingen: J.C.B. Mohr, 1994).

6. De Ste Croix, 'Early Christian Attitudes', p. 20.

7. *Didache* 4.11. I depend on Aelred Cody, '*The Didache*: An English Translation', in Clayton N. Jefford (ed.), *The Didache in Context* (Leiden: E.J. Brill, 1995), p. 7; Greek text in Jefford (ed.), *The Didache in Context*, p. 26: ὑμεῖς δὲ οἱ δοῦλοι ὑποταγήσεσθε τοῖς κυρίοις ὑμῶν ὡς τύπῳ θεοῦ ἐν αἰσχύνῃ καί φόβῳ. See also Huub van de Sandt and David Flusser, *The Didache: Its Jewish Sources and its Place in Early Judaism and Christianity* (Assen: Van Gorcum, 2002).

8. Samuel Laeuchli, *Sexuality and Power: The Emergence of Canon Law at the Council of Elvira* (Philadelphia: Temple University Press, 1974), p. 127. On the issues and problems of reconstructing the canons of Elvira, see Hamilton Hess, *The Early Development of Canon Law and the Council of Serdica* (Oxford Early Christian Studies; New York: Oxford University Press, 2002), especially pp. 40-42.

9. *Constitutiones apostolorum* 2.62.4 (PG 1. 751a). See also Garnsey, *Ideas of Slavery*, p. 33 n. 8, where this citation is erroneously given as PG 1.725c. See J. Albert Harrill, 'Ignatius ad Polycarp, 4.3 and the Corporate Manumission of Christian Slaves', *JECS* 1 (1993), pp. 107-42.

words, buying a slave at a fair was no more transgressive than buying food there. Canon Four of the Council of Chalcedon (451), which helped to define orthodox Christianity, states that 'no slave shall be received into any monastery to become a monk against the will of his master'.[10]

Major Theologians

Some of the major theologians before the fifth century already had seminal ideas about race and slavery. By the time of Origen (c. 185–254), we already have some incipient racism linked with the slavery of Ham and his descendants. Origen said the following concerning Ham:

> For the Egyptians are prone to a degenerate life and quickly sink to every slavery of the vices. Look at the origin of the race and you will discover that their father Cham, who had laughed at his father's nakedness, deserved a judgement of this kind, that his son Chanaan should be a servant to his brothers, in which case the condition of bondage would prove the wickedness of his conduct. Not without merit, therefore, does the discolored posterity imitate the ignobility of the race.[11]

David M. Goldenberg argues that Origen's remark about imitating the 'ignobility of this race' referred to the imitation of bondage rather than to a linkage between bondage and color.[12] Yet even without any original racial implications for Genesis 9, Origen is correctly inferring that slavery and punishment could be linked.[13] Furthermore, Origen already links dark color with negative attributes.

St Chrysostom (347–407), although sometimes counted among those protesting slavery, accepted slavery. In his commentary on 1 Corinthians, Chrysostom alludes to Gal. 3.28, but interprets it to mean that it is not necessary to have a slave, though he adds, 'or if it be necessary at all, let it be about one only or at the most two'.[14] He does recommend training these slaves for an eventually independent life. According to Allen D. Callahan, it was Chrysostom who first clearly interpreted Onesimus as a runaway slave who was sent back to Philemon.[15]

---

10. Chalcedon, Canon 4 (NPNF² 14.270).

11. Origen, 'Homily XVI', in *Homilies on Genesis and Exodus* (trans. Ronald E. Heine; Washington: Catholic University of America Press, 1982), p. 215.

12. Goldenberg, *The Curse of Ham*, p. 169.

13. See also Denise K. Buell, 'Race and Universalism in Early Christianity', *JECS* 10 (2002), pp. 429-68.

14. Chrysostom, *Homilies on First Corinthians* 40.6 (NPNF¹ 12.248).

15. Callahan, *Embassy of Onesimus*, pp. 13-14. For a critique of Callahan's claim, see Margaret A. Mitchell, 'John Chrysostom on Philemon: A Second Look', *HTR* 88 (1995), pp. 135-48. See also Allen D. Callahan, 'Chrysostom on Philemon: A Response to Margaret Mitchell', *HTR* 88 (1995), pp. 149-56.

Arguably the most important theologian prior to St Thomas Aquinas was St Augustine, and he expressed ideas about slavery that helped to perpetuate the institution for about the next 1500 years. Born in Carthage in North Africa c. 354, Augustine initially lived a very dissolute life, even by his own reckoning. By the time he died in 430, he had served as the bishop of Hippo, and had become the preeminent theologian of the Church. A prolific writer, his main work is *The City of God*, which is one of the first systematic theologies of Christianity.[16]

The study of Augustine received new impetus in the 1980s because of the publication of previously unknown letters attributed to him. These letters were discovered by Johannes Divjak, who was in the employ of the Austrian Academy.[17] According to Brent D. Shaw, these letters 'reveal the considerable dimensions of the trade in humans in the late fourth and early fifth century western empire'.[18] Prior to this discovery, scholars had thought slavery was not very dominant in the North African provinces. In short, Augustine probably knew the horrors of the slave trade.

Insofar as slavery is concerned, Augustine believed that human rulers were the mediators of divine law. As he phrased it in his commentary on John:

> God has handed down to the race of men even the man-made laws through the medium of emperors and kings of the world... Take away the laws of emperors, and who will dare say: 'That villa is mine, that slave is mine or this house is mine'? People have accepted the laws of kings so that they can possess those very things.[19]

For Augustine, this right to property is ultimately derived from God's lordship over the entire earth. If Christians are God's favored slaves, then

---

16. For a recent biography, see James J. O'Donnell, *Augustine: A New Biography* (New York: HarperCollins, 2005). See also Peter Brown, *Augustine of Hippo: A Biography* (Berkeley: University of California Press, rev. edn, 2000). For Augustine's use of authorities, see Pamela Bright (ed.), *Augustine and the Bible* (Notre Dame: University of Notre Dame Press, 1999); Eric Rebillard, 'A New Style of Argument in Christian Polemic: Augustine and the Use of Patristic Citations', *JECS* 8 (2002), pp. 559-78.

17. Johannes Divjak (ed.), *Epistulae ex duobus codicibus nuper in lucem prolatae* (CSEL, 88; Vienna: Hoelder-Pichler-Tempsky, 1981). See also François Decret, 'Augustine d'Hippone et l'esclavage: problèmes posés par les positions d'un évêque de la Grande Eglise face à une réalité sociale dans l'Afrique de l'antiquité tardive', *Dialogues d'histoire ancienne* 11 (1985), pp. 675-85. For the discovery of new sermons of Augustine, see François Dolbeau (ed.), *Vingt-six sermons au peuple d'Afrique, retrouvé à Mayence* (Collection des Etudes Augustiniennes, Série Antiquité, 147; Paris: Institut d'Etudes Augustiniennes, 1996).

18. Brent D. Shaw, 'A Wolf by the Ears: M.I. Finley's *Ancient Slavery and Modern Ideology* in Historical Context', in Finley, *Ancient Slavery and Modern Ideology*, p. 23.

19. Augustine, *In Johannis Evangelium tractatus* 6.25 as quoted in Garnsey, *Ideas of Slavery*, pp. 207-208.

they also receive benefits not conferred to non-Christians. These benefits include the right to own non-Christian slaves, while non-Christians do not have the right to own Christian slaves. By the time Islam was expanding in the seventh and eighth centuries, it was clear that Muslims living in Christian territories were not to own Christian slaves.[20]

While Augustine saw equality as the original state of humanity, slavery could be seen as God's just punishment in the current era.[21] In *The City of God*, Augustine remarks:

> [T]he condition of slavery is justly imposed on the sinner. Wherefore, we do not read of a slave anywhere in the Scriptures until the just man Noah branded his son's sin with this word, so he earned this name by his fault, not by nature... The prime cause of slavery, then, is sin, so that man was put under man in a state of bondage; and this can only be by a judgment of God, in whom there is no unrighteousness, and who knows how to assign divers punishment according to the deserts of sinners.[22]

Augustine adds that, until the final paradise arrives, 'fathers are more obligated to maintain their positions as masters than the slaves are to keep their place as servants. So if anyone in the household by disobedience breaks the domestic peace, he is rebuked by a word or a blow or some other kind of just and legitimate punishment.'[23] In short, the most famous theologian of late Antiquity saw no incompatibility between slavery and being a Christian. Slavery was a normal and justified aspect of this postlapsarian phase of the world.

Clerical and Papal Acceptance

Some of the highest officials of the church were slaveowners or allowed slavery. For example, the last testament of Gregory of Nazianzus, bishop of Constantinople in the fourth century, releases his slaves at his death (Τοὺς οὖν οἰκέτας οὓς ἠλευθέρωσα...) and some of those slaves might become the property of the Church (τῇ αὐτῇ Ἐκκλησίᾳ).[24] Cyprian, the third-century bishop of Carthage, understood that enforcing obedience by Christian masters might include flagellation, starvation, or imprisonment of slaves.[25]

---

20. Davis, *The Problem of Slavery*, p. 103.
21. Davis, *The Problem of Slavery*, p. 113.
22. Augustine, *City of God* 19.15 (Greene, LCL).
23. Augustine, *City of God* 19.16 (Greene, LCL).
24. Gregory of Nazianzus, *Exemplum Testamenti* 202 (PG 37.392a). For a general biography, see John McGukin, *Gregory of Nazianzus: An Intellectual Biography* (Crestwood, NY: St Vladimir's Seminary Press, 2001).
25. Cyprian, *Ad Demetrianum* 8 (PG 4.550b): 'flagellas, verberas, fame, siti, nuditate, ferro etiam frequenter, et carcere affligis et crucias'.

At the highest level, Pope Gregory I (540–604) believed slavery to be the result of humanity's sinful state. In his *Pastoral Rule*, a manual of Church instruction, Gregory says that slaves should always view themselves humbly (*Servi, scilicet ut in se semper humilitatem conditionis aspiciant*).[26] Slaves are admonished not to despise the master (*Servi admonendi sunt ne dominos despiciant*).[27] Masters paradoxically are also admonished to treat slaves as equals. Aside from a reference to Eph. 6.9 (which warns masters to treat slaves well), Gregory supports this section with references to the Vulgate's translation of Col. 3.22 (*Servi obedite dominis carnalibus*) and 1 Tim. 6.1, which admonish slaves to obey masters.

Legal Sanction

Major law codes sponsored by Christian emperors also became the law of the Christian empire. In particular, Theodosius II (401–450) and Justinian the Great (483–565) issued 'Codes' that were revisions of Roman legal traditions, some of which exerted their influence even until modern times. The Justinian Code, for example, recognized 'war, birth, and self-sale as valid grounds for human bondage'.[28] Those justifications were used actively into the nineteenth century.

These codes also bore laws that were a regression or much worse when compared to non-biblical law codes of the ancient Near East. For instance, the Theodosian Code (9.9.1) prescribed death 'if any freeborn woman should join herself secretly to her own slave'.[29] Yet, the *Code of Hammurabi* 175 allows a slave to marry an upper-class woman, and any children born of that union cannot be claimed by the slave's master.[30]

Gregory of Nyssa

Of all the early Church Fathers, Gregory of Nyssa (c. 330–394) is often credited with the strongest abolitionist sentiments. John Francis Maxwell, who generally takes a critical stance on the Church's teachings on slavery, remarks that Gregory's *Fourth Homily on Ecclesiastes* 'provides the first

---

26. Gregory, *Regulae pastoralis liber* 3.5 (PL 77.56c). See further Adam Serfass, 'Slavery and Pope Gregory the Great', *JECS* 14 (2006), pp. 77-103.
27. Gregory, *Regulae pastoralis liber* 3.5 (PL 77.56c).
28. Davis, *The Problem of Slavery*, p. 102; Michele R. Salzman, 'The Evidence for Conversion of the Roman Empire to Christianity in Book 16 of the "Theodosian Code"', *Historia* 42 (1993), pp. 362-78.
29. Pharr, *The Theodosian Code*, p. 233.
30. Roth, *Law Collections*, p. 115.

truly "anti-slavery" text of the patristic age'.[31] The authoritative German reference work, *Theologische Realenzyklopädie*, goes further in saying that Gregory 'struggled against every form of human subjugation' ('wendet sich gegen jede Form menchlicher Untergebenheit') on the basis of his *Fourth Homily*.[32]

Indeed, even a brief look at Gregory's *Fourth Homily on Ecclesiastes*, written around 385, seems to confirm those conclusions.[33] When assessing the biblical author's statement that he 'owned slaves, both men and women', Gregory issues these criticisms:

> You condemn a person to slavery whose nature is free and independent, and you make laws opposed to God and His natural law. For you have subjected one who was made precisely to be lord of the earth, and whom the Creator intended to be a ruler, to the yoke of slavery... Tell me what price did you pay to acquire them? What is the equivalent in goods for the cost of human nature?... What price did you pay for the image of God?[34]

While it is true that these are the strongest sentiments against slavery found among the early Church Fathers, they are not as definitively abolitionist as Maxwell or the editors of the *Theologische Realenzyklopädie* may think.

Maxwell apparently is providing his own translation of Gregory's Fourth Homily from the standard edition in J.-P. Migne's *Patrologia graeca*. However, the translation by Stuart Hall indicates that Maxwell's rendition of the word 'independent' may be misleading. Note the differences between the translation provided by Maxwell and one provided by Hall in the first sentence we quoted above:

> PG 44.664: Δουλείᾳ καταδικάζεις τὸν ἄνθρωπον, οὗ ἐλευθέρα ἡ φύσις αὐτεξούσιος, καὶ ἀντινομοθετεῖς τῷ θεῷ, ἀνατρέπων αὐτοῦ τὸν ἐπὶ τῇ φύσει νόμον.[35]

---

31. John Francis Maxwell, *Slavery and the Catholic Church: The History of Catholic Teaching Concerning the Moral Legitimacy of the Institution of Slavery* (London: Barry Rose Publishers, 1975), p. 32.

32. Gerhard Müller *et al.* (eds.), *Theologische Realenzyklopädie* (36 vols.; Berlin: W. de Gruyter, 1977–2004), XXI, p. 380. See further Richard Klein, 'Gibt es eine Sklavenethik bei Gregor von Nyssa? Anmerkungen zur David R. Stains "Gregory of Nyssa and the Ethics of Slavery and Emancipation"', in Hubertus R. Drobner and Albert Viciano (eds.), *Gregory of Nyssa: Homilies on the Beatitudes* (Leiden: E.J. Brill, 2000), pp. 593-604.

33. For the chronology of Gregory's works, see Jean Daniélou, 'La chronologie des oeuvres de Grégoire de Nysse', *Studia patristica* 7 (1966), pp. 159-79. For the social and theological context of Nyssa's writings, see Anthony Meredith, *Gregory of Nyssa* (London: Routledge, 1999).

34. Gregory of Nyssa, *Homily IV on Ecclesiastes*, as quoted in Maxwell, *Slavery and the Catholic Church*, p. 33.

35. Gregory of Nyssa, *Homily IV on Ecclesiastes* (PG 44.665-67).

Maxwell: 'You condemn a person to slavery whose nature is free and independent, and you make laws opposed to God and His natural law'.[36]

Hall: 'You condemn man to slavery when his nature is free and possesses free will, and you legislate competition with God, overturning His law for the human species'.[37]

According to Hall, Gregory usually references inner free will by the term αὐτεξούσιος, but outer liberty with the term ἐλευθερία or ἐλεύθερος.[38] This difference between inner and outer liberty was a well-known Stoic tradition, and Gregory seems to be consistent with it.[39] According to Hall, the reference to 'free will' clarifies that Nyssa was objecting to a human being who infringed upon both the inner free will of a person and the outer civic status.

But, it is not clear here if Gregory objects to outer slavery if it did not involve inner slavery. Evidence that he did not object to all slavery comes from his *Homilies on the Song of Songs*. There, he says Abraham ordered 'his servant [not to get a bride for Isaac] from the people of Canaan, who were condemned to servitude'.[40] Clearly, Gregory not only believes that servitude of entire groups can be justified, but he is helping to perpetuate the idea of the curse of Canaan, something that no apologist or historian of the curse of Canaan ever mentions, as far as I have determined.[41]

---

36. Maxwell, *Slavery and the Catholic Church*, p. 33.

37. George Hall (ed.), *Gregory of Nyssa: Homilies on Ecclesiastes: An English Version with Supporting Studies, Proceedings of the Seventh International Colloquium of Gregory of Nyssa, St Andrews, 5–10 September 1990* (Berlin: W. de Gruyter, 1993), p. 73. See also T.J. Dennis, 'The Relationship between Gregory of Nyssa's Attack on Slavery in his Fourth Homily on Ecclesiastes and his Treatise *De Hominis Opificio*', *Studia patristica* 17 (1982), pp. 1065-72; Daniel F. Stramara, 'Gregory of Nyssa: An Ardent Abolitionist?', *St Vladimir's Theological Quarterly* 41 (1997), pp. 37-60.

38. Hall, *Gregory of Nyssa: Homilies on Ecclesiastes*, p. 196. For the usage of these words, see Friedhelm Mann (ed.), *Lexicon Gregorianum: Wörterbuch zu den Schriften Gregors von Nyssa* (8 vols.; Leiden: E.J. Brill, 1999–), I, p. 619 and III, pp. 155-56.

39. See Inwood, *Ethics and Human Action*; Glancy, *Slavery in Early Christianity*, pp. 30-34; David B. Hart, 'The "Whole Humanity": Gregory of Nyssa's Critique of Slavery in Light of his Eschatology', *Scottish Journal of Theology* 54 (2001), pp. 51-69; Gerhart B. Ladner, 'The Philosophical Anthropology of Saint Gregory of Nyssa', *Dumbarton Oaks Papers* 12 (1958), pp. 59-94.

40. Gregory of Nyssa, *Homily IV on the Song of Songs* (PG 44.853): τῷ ἰδίῳ οἰκέτῃ μή τινα τῶν τοῦ γένους Χανάαν τῶν τῇ δουλείᾳ καταδεδικασμένων. See also Saint Gregory of Nyssa, *Commentary on the Song of Songs* (trans. Casimir McCambley, OCSO; Brookline, MA: Hellenic College Press, 1987), pp. 43-56.

41. There are no indexed references to Gregory of Nyssa in Haynes, *Noah's Curse*, or in Davis, *This Strange Story*. Goldenberg (*The Curse of Ham*, pp. 49 and 246 n. 31) includes Gregory of Nyssa in a list of perpetuators of the curse of Ethiopian blackness, but does not elaborate upon or mention this passage about Canaan specifically.

Further evidence is found in *The Great Catechism*, another work credited to Gregory.[42] In that work, the author discusses the parallel between persons selling themselves voluntarily, and humanity selling itself to sin through its free will:

> For as they who have bartered away their freedom for money are the slaves of those who have purchased them (for they have constituted themselves their own sellers, and it is not allowable either for themselves or any one else in their behalf to call freedom to their aid, not even though those who have thus reduced themselves to this sad state are of noble birth; and, if any one out of regard for the person who has so sold himself should use violence against him who has bought him, he will clearly be acting unjustly in thus arbitrarily rescuing one who has been legally purchased as a slave, whereas, if he wishes to pay a price to get such a one away, there is no law to prevent that).[43]

Gregory, then, uses this analogy to illustrate how God can pay the ransom to Satan to rescue humanity from sin.[44] In any case, Gregory does recognize the legitimacy of selling oneself into slavery, and he even indicates it would be unjust for a slave to use violence against an owner who has bought him. As Richard Klein rightly notes, Gregory did not really differ that much from the prevailing view of other bishops.[45]

St Bathilde and St Anskar

Given that we can find little to indicate a Christian movement toward abolition anywhere in the first half of the first millennium, the next best thing that Christian apologists adduce is the existence of some isolated voices who supposedly did speak against slavery in the second half of the millennium. Two such examples are cited by Rodney Stark. One is St Bathilde (d. c. 680), the wife of Clovis II (637–655 or 658), and the other is St Anskar (c. 801–854), the apostle to the Scandinavians. Stark remarks:

42. For basic studies of Gregory's biblical interpretation, see Mariette Canévet, *Grégoire de Nysse et l'herméneutique biblique: Etude des rapports entre le langage et la connaissance de Dieu* (Paris: Etudes Augustiniennes, 1983); Sarah Coakley (ed.), *Rethinking Gregory of Nyssa* (Malden, MA: Blackwell, 2003); Harold Cherniss, *The Platonism of Gregory of Nyssa* (repr., Berkeley: B. Franklin, 1970 [1939]); Jean Daniélou, *Platonisme et théologie mystique: essai sur la doctrine spirituelle de Saint Grégoire de Nysse* (Paris: Aubier Editions Montaigne, 1944).
43. Gregory of Nyssa, *The Great Catechism* 22 (NPNF² V, pp. 492-93).
44. Gregory of Nyssa (*The Great Catechism* 23 [NPNF² V, p. 493 n. 4]), in opposition to orthodox Church traditions, sees the ransom paid to Satan instead of to God the Father. See further Gustaf Aulén, *Christus Victor: An Historical Study of the Three Main Types of the Idea of the Atonement* (trans. A.G. Hebert; New York: Macmillan, 1969), pp. 48-50.
45. See Klein, 'Gibt es eine Sklavenethik?', p. 604: '...Gregor sich in seinen Äusserungen nicht wesentlich unterscheidet von den übrigen Bischöfen...'

As early as the seventh century, St. Bathilde (wife of King Clovis II) became famous for her campaign to stop slave-trading and free all slaves; in 851 St. Anskar began his efforts to stop the Viking slave trade.[46]

For his documentation, Stark gives us two secondary sources, *The Penguin Dictionary of Saints* and Hugh Thomas's *On the Slave Trade*.[47] He gives us no page numbers for either of his sources.

Nonetheless, let us examine the *Penguin Dictionary of Saints*. The only source cited for the life of Anskar in the *Penguin Dictionary of Saints* is Charles H. Robinson's well-known English translation of the *Vita Anskarii* (*Life of Anskar*), which is the single most important source for Anskar's biography.[48] The Latin composition is attributed to St Rimbert, a colleague of Anskar in his mission to the Scandinavians. The whole work is a hagiography and propaganda for supporting missions in Scandinavia.

More problematic for Stark is that there are major reevaluations of the hagiographies of St Bathilde and St Anskar. It is recognized that hagiographies serve political as well as religious purposes.[49] It is particularly dangerous to use such hagiographies as accurate descriptions of pagans. Pagans are routinely accused of the worse atrocities and cruelties, just as Christians were accused of such atrocities and cruelties by their opponents. Anyone who reads polemic literature knows as much. Thus, the best sources about pagans are by pagans, but we really do not have many of those to confirm Christian descriptions.

The primary sources for the lives of St Bathilde and St Anskar reveal something less than the hyperbole Stark offers. Stark said that Bathilde campaigned to stop slave-trading and free 'all slaves'. However, the Latin source often used to document the life of the saint actually records that Bathilde 'prohibited the sale of Christian captives' (*Captivos homines christianos prohibuit*).[50] Even Catholic biographies of Bathilde admit that she did not work against slavery per se, but against the enslavement of

---

46. Stark, *For the Glory of God*, p. 329.

47. Hugh Thomas, *The Slave Trade: The Story of the Atlantic Slave Trade, 1440–1870* (New York: Simon & Schuster, 1997); Donald Attwater and Catherine Rachel John, *The Penguin Dictionary of Saints* (London: Penguin Books, 1995).

48. Attwater and John, *Penguin Dictionary of Saints*, p. 43. Charles H. Robinson, *Anskar, Apostle of the North, 801–865, Translated from the Vita Anskarii by Bishop Rimbert his Fellow Missionary and Successor* (London: Society for the Propagation of the Gospel in Foreign Parts, 1921). For the Latin text, we depend on G. Waitz, *Vita Anskarii auctore Rimberto* (Hanover: Hahn, 1884).

49. See James T. Palmer, 'Rimbert's *Vita Anskarii* and Scandinavian Mission in the Ninth Century', *Journal of Ecclesiastical History* 55 (2004), pp. 235-56.

50. See Charles Verlinden, *L'esclavage dans l'Europe médiévale* (2 vols.; Brugge: Rijksuniversiteit te Gent, 1955), I, p. 673 n. 113.

Christians.[51] Enslaving foreigners, and prohibiting the enslavement of people of your own privileged ethnic or religious group, was a routine practice in many cultures. There is no advance here relative to Plato or the Old Testament.

The case of St Anskar is similar. There are two principal passages where the *Vita Anskarii* refers to buying or redeeming slaves, and neither of those passages warrants Stark's conclusion that 'in 851 St. Anskar began his efforts to stop the Viking slave trade'.[52] As it is, Stark gives us no precise source for the statement, and we really do not know what event in 851 he speaks about. In any case, the *Vita Anskarii* states:

> They, themselves, being inspired by divine love, in order to spread their holy religion, made diligent search for boys whom they might endeavour to educate for the service of God. Harald also gave some of his own household to be educated by them; and so it came to be that in a short time they established a school for twelve or more boys. Others they took as servants or helpers, and their reputation and the religion which they preached in God's name were spread abroad.[53]

The Latin uses *servitores* for 'servants', which is the same word used for slaves.[54] One could make the case that *servitores* did not mean slaves here, but rather 'servants' or 'assistants'. One reason is that families are said to have willingly given their children up 'to be educated'. Nonetheless, notice that there is no record of asking the boys if they wished to do this. Rather than acting selflessly, St Anskar could be interpreted as undertaking a very selfish act because these boys would now provide virtually free labor for the monks.

In the more oft-cited episode, in Chapter 38 of the *Vita Anskarii*, Anskar scolded a group of Scandinavians called Northalbingians, who 'on one occasion committed a great crime, and one of terrible nature [*delictum nimis horribile*]'.[55] Barbarians had carried off some Christians, and, after escaping, these fugitives sought help from the Northalbingians. The latter, however,

---

51. Pierre A. Fournet, 'St Bathilde', in *The Catholic Encyclopedia* (New York: Robert Appleton, 1907). Online: www.newadvent.org/cathen/02348b.htm. Similar problems obtain when trying to credit Melania the Younger (fourth century) for abolitionist actions. The edition of Elizabeth A. Clark (*The Life of Melania the Younger: Introduction, Translation, and Commentary* [Lewiston, NY: Edwin Mellen Press, 1984], p. 33) shows that giving up possessions, not anti-slavery sentiments, were mainly behind Melania's emancipation of some 8,000 slaves. Besides, manumissions were not unknown in Greco-Roman culture, and so there was not much of an advance here.
52. Stark, *For the Glory of God*, p. 329.
53. Robinson, *Anskar*, p. 44.
54. Waitz, *Vita Anskarii*, p. 30.
55. Robinson, *Anskar*, p. 119; Waitz, *Vita Anskarii*, p. 72.

'showed no compassion, but seized them and bound them with chains. Some of them they sold to pagans, whilst others they enslaved, or sold to other Christians.'[56] When the bishop heard this he was greatly distressed that so great a crime had been perpetrated in his diocese.[57] Later Anskar lobbied for the release of these captives, and so these 'unhappy men were sought out wherever they had been sold and were given their liberty and allowed to go wherever they desired'.[58]

However, while Anskar deserves credit for freeing these slaves, this episode cannot qualify as an effort to fight 'the Viking slave trade'. Anskar was not against Viking slavery per se. Rather, Anskar reaffirms the long-standing policy against Christians enslaving Christians. Anskar's story is very reminiscent of one found in 2 Chron. 28.8-11, where a prophet named Oded scolds his people for enslaving fellow Hebrews. In any case, Anskar's actions cannot constitute a movement against slavery any more than Plato's prohibition against enslaving fellow Greeks can be called a movement against slavery.

Stark also overlooks that pagan Scandinavians already had a traditions of freeing slaves. As Philip Sawyer, the respected scholar of Viking culture, notes:

> The Church encouraged the liberation of slaves and forbade the enslavement or sale of Christians; but the liberation of slaves was not a Christian innovation. The Scandinavian term *leysingi*, which is used of a freedman in the twelfth-century, was in use as early as the ninth century in England, where it was used to refer to the freedmen of the Danes.[59]

In fact, according to the directives of the Sixteenth Council of Toledo (c. 693), churches were required to have a minimum number of slaves to have a priest: 'That the church which shall have as many as ten slaves shall have one priest over it, but that one which have less than ten slaves shall be united to other churches'.[60] Thus, slavery and church policy were not viewed as being incompatible at all. Anskar simply complains that Christian slave customs were not observed properly, and nothing more.

---

56. Robinson, *Anskar*, p. 119.
57. Robinson, *Anskar*, p. 119.
58. Robinson, *Anskar*, p. 120.
59. Philip H. Sawyer, *Kings and Vikings: Scandinavia and Europe AD 700–1100* (New York: Methuen, 1982), p. 40. See also Ruth Mazo Karras, *Slavery and Society in Medieval Scandinavia* (New Haven: Yale University Press, 1988).
60. For the Latin text of the Sixteenth Council of Toledo, I depend on John Fletcher, *Studies on Slavery in Easy Lessons, Compiled into Eight Studies, and Subdivided into Short Lessons for the Convenience of Readers* (Natchez, MS: Jackson Warner, 1852), p. 339: 'Ut ecclesia, quas usque ad decem habuerit mancipia, super se habeat sacerdotem, quae vero minus decem mancipia habuerit aliis conjugatur ecclesiis'.

Summary

The first millennium of Christianity saw an overwhelming acceptance of slavery by significant theologians, higher clerics, Church councils, and the Pope himself. That is why even Joel Panzer, a vigorous apologist for the Catholic attitude toward slavery, begins his defense of Catholic attitudes toward slavery in the fifteenth century, and speaks little of the first millennium.[61] His main defense is that very little real slavery existed before the fifteenth century, which is clearly false.

Gregory of Nyssa expressed the strongest anti-slavery sentiments we can find in the entire first millennium, but he was an isolated voice and cannot be said to be 'representative' of Christianity. Moreover, Gregory of Nyssa did not reject all slavery as some have claimed. He never demanded that Christians release slaves. The anti-slavery sentiments claimed for St Bathilde and Anskar are even less well documented and rest on clear misreadings of the primary sources.

---

61. Panzer, *The Popes and Slavery*, pp. 2-3: 'the popes have condemned what is commonly known as slavery from its beginnings in the 15th century'.

Chapter 8

ST THOMAS AQUINAS:
A MEDIEVAL ABOLITIONIST?

Apologists see the Middle Ages as a period where Christianity had brought new light to the oppressed. In fact, Rodney Stark, among others, touts the claim that slavery disappeared from most of Europe in the Middle Ages because influential theologians began to see slavery as a sin. In particular, Stark credits St Thomas Aquinas (1227–1274), the most important theologian of the Middle Ages, with great theological advances against slavery.[1] Accordingly, I focus this chapter on St Thomas Aquinas.

Does Aquinas See Slavery as a Sin?

Stark's discussion of St Thomas Aquinas is marred by his uncritical reading of Catholic apologetic sources. In particular, Stark relies on Stephen F. Brett's *Slavery and the Catholic Tradition* for many of his statements about Aquinas.[2] But, in contrast to what his footnotes might suggest, Stark is not really consulting the *Summa theologica* directly. Consequently, his claims evaporate once we read Aquinas's *Summa*, especially in the original Latin. To illustrate this point, we begin with Stark's principal passage about St Thomas Aquinas:

> Then, in the thirteenth century, Saint Thomas Aquinas deduced that slavery was a sin… It is significant that in Aquinas's day, slavery was a thing of the past or of distant lands. Consequently, he gave little attention to the subject per se, paying more attention to serfdom, which he held to be repugnant… Aquinas placed slavery in opposition to natural law, deducing that all 'rational creatures' are entitled to justice. Hence he found no natural basis for the enslavement of one person rather than another, 'thus removing any possible justification for slavery based on race or religion'. Right reason, not coercion,

---

1. For a recent assessment, see Nicholas M. Healy, *Thomas Aquinas: Theologian of the Christian Life* (Farnham, UK: Ashgate, 2003).
2. Stephen F. Brett, *Slavery and the Catholic Tradition: Rights in the Balance* (New York: Peter Lang, 1994).

is the moral basis of authority, for 'one man is not by nature ordained to another as an end'. Here Aquinas distinguishes two forms of 'subjection' or authority, just or unjust. The former exists when leaders work for the advantage and benefit of their subjects. The unjust form of subjection 'is that of slavery, in which the ruler manages the subject for his own [the ruler's] advantage'.[3]

None of these statements is an accurate representation of what either Brett or Aquinas himself says.

First, Stark is historically wrong and self-contradictory in regard to Aquinas's supposed lack of familiarity with slavery. Indeed, elsewhere Stark tells us that most of Medieval Europe was free from slavery 'except at the southern and eastern interfaces with Islam where both sides enslaved one another's prisoners'.[4] But those southern interfaces are exactly where Aquinas spent his formative years. Aquinas was born in the mainland portion of what was then the Kingdom of Sicily, and he lived in Italy into his 20s.[5]

The Kingdom of Sicily was thriving with the slave trade in the thirteenth century. Charles Verlinden, who has collected numerous documents relating to slave transactions in the Kingdom of Sicily, concludes that 'in Sicily, the notarial acts pertaining to the sales and manumissions of slaves multiply beginning in the thirteenth century'.[6] This historical fact obviously flies in the face of Stark's claim that 'in Aquinas's day slavery was a thing of the past or of distant lands'.

As mentioned, Stark betrays the fact that he is not checking the *Summa* directly because at least twice he miscopies citations from Brett's *Slavery and the Catholic Tradition*, which discusses Aquinas's view of slavery and dominion.[7] By not consulting the *Summa* directly, Stark grossly misrepresents Aquinas's views on slavery. Indeed, nowhere in the *Summa* does Aquinas state that slavery is a sin per se. And Aquinas did not really place slavery in

---

3. Stark, *For the Glory of God*, pp. 329-30 (Stark's brackets).
4. Stark, *For the Glory of God*, p. 329.
5. For a basic biography, see Healy, *Thomas Aquinas*.
6. Verlinden, *L'esclavage*, II, p. 138: 'En Sicile les actes notaries intéressant les ventes et affranchissements d'esclaves se multiplient à partir du milieu du xiiie siècle'.
7. For example, after citing Brett (*Slavery and the Catholic Tradition*, pp. 57, 78) in n. 172 (*For the Glory of God*, p. 412), Stark's n. 174 reads 'Ibid, q3 a3', following n. 173, which reads '*Summa* q3, a.3'. Using 'Ibid, q3 a3' presupposes that Brett is referencing the same work of Aquinas, when, in fact, Brett is referencing Aquinas's *Commentary* on Peter Lombard's *Sentences* in the first instance, and the *Summa* in the second. This is even clearer because the *Summa* is not usually cited in the manner that Stark does. Stark overlooked Brett's switch in sources, and so mistakenly assumed it was the same source. This error clearly suggests that Stark did not check the *Summa*, but simply misread Brett's discussion.

'opposition to the natural law'.[8] Stark certainly shows no interest in Aquinas's inconsistencies on the issue of slavery.

To understand Aquinas's more nuanced position on slavery's relation to natural law, one must consult the section of the *Summa* where Aquinas discusses whether natural law can be changed:

> A thing is said to belong to the natural law in two ways. First, because nature inclines thereto: e.g., that one should not do harm to another. Secondly, because nature did not bring in the contrary: thus we might say that for man to be naked is of the natural law, because nature did not give him clothes, but art invented them. In this sense, the possession of all things in common and universal freedom are said to be of the natural law, because, to wit, the distinction of possessions and slavery were not brought in by nature, but devised by human reason for the benefit of human life. Accordingly the law of nature was not changed in this respect, except by addition.[9]

Thus, slavery is no more sinful or against natural law than are clothes. Although we were born unclothed, clothing is not against natural law because the latter can be changed by adding provisions that are beneficial. Clothes are beneficial, and so not a sinful addition to natural law. Likewise, slavery, like clothes, is 'for the benefit of human life' and so a permissible addition to the natural law. Aquinas is even more explicit in the following passage of the *Summa*:

> Considered absolutely, the fact that this particular man should be a slave rather than another man is based, not on natural reason, but on some resultant utility, in that it is useful to this man to be ruled by a wiser man, and to the latter to be helped by the former as the Philosopher [= Aristotle] states... Wherefore slavery which belongs to the right of nations is natural in the second way but not the first.[10]

Indeed, Stark has misunderstood the distinction Aquinas makes between two types of 'natural law'. Thus, slavery is not against natural law per se, but rather fits a second type of natural law, which is based on utility and commensurability.

In addition, distinguishing between 'just' and 'unjust' servitude by whether it served the slave or the master was not really effective in promoting general

---

8. See also Oscar J. Brown, 'Aquinas' Doctrine of Slavery in Relation to Thomistic Teaching on Natural Law', *Proceedings of the American Catholic Philosophical Association* 53 (1979), pp. 173-81.

9. Aquinas, *Summa* I–II, q. 94, a. 5, ad 3/Benziger I, p. 1012. My citations of the *Summa theologica* are from the first complete American edition in three volumes translated by Fathers of the English Dominican Province (New York: Benziger Brothers, 1947). I will cite the divisions of the *Summa* itself, followed, after a slash, by the volume and pages from the Benziger Brothers edition. For the Latin text, I depend on Divi Thomae Aquinatis, *Summa Theologica...*a Leone XIII, P.M. (Rome: Forzani, 1823).

10. Aquinas, *Summa* II–II, q. 57, a. 3, ad 2/Benziger II, p. 1433.

abolitionism. The reason is that masters could conjure up all sorts of reasons why slavery was for the good of the slave. Aquinas himself states that an unwise man benefits by being a slave to a wiser man. New World slavemasters often spoke of how slavery kept people fed and away from cannibalism and other pagan practices that victimized people in Africa.[11]

It is also important to realize that Aquinas believed that any commandment of God automatically should be regarded as in accordance with natural law, even if it is considered sinful otherwise. For example, Aquinas cites the case of Hosea, who was ordered to commit adultery:

> Consequently, by the command of God, death can be inflicted on any man, guilty or innocent, without any injustice whatever. In like manner adultery is intercourse with another's wife; who is allotted to him by the law emanating from God. Consequently intercourse with any woman, by the command of God, is neither adultery nor fornication. The same applies to theft, which is the taking of another's property. For whatever is taken by the command of God, to Whom all things belong, is not taken against the will of its owner, whereas it is in this that theft consists. Nor is it only in human things, that whatever is commanded by God is right; but also in natural things, whatever is done by God, is, in some way, natural...[12]

So it is clearly an exaggeration to say that Aquinas removed 'any possible justification for slavery based on race or religion'. According to Aquinas's own logic, it is perfectly possible that God could ordain someone to enslave another person on the basis of race or religion. And since God said it, it would now be 'natural law'.

There are other indications that Aquinas did not see slavery as a sin per se. In his discussion of the extent of obedience we owe human beings, Aquinas states that slaves cannot be obligated to do something against human nature (e.g., slaves could not be prevented from giving birth). However, he voices no real objections to this idea of servitude:

> But in matters concerning the disposal of actions and human affairs, a subject is bound to obey his superior within the sphere of his authority; for instance a soldier must obey his general in matters relating to war, a servant his master in matters touching the execution of the duties of his service, a son his father in matters relating to the conduct of his life and the care of the household; and so forth.[13]

---

11. See, for example, Josiah Priest, *Bible Defence of Slavery and Origin, Fortunes, and History of the Negro Race* (repr., Whitefish, MT: Kessinger, 2007 [1852]), pp. 393-95, 415-25. For a more recent version of the argument, see William R. Fogel and Stanley L. Engerman, *Time on the Cross: The Economics of American Negro Slavery* (New York: W.W. Norton, 1974).

12. Aquinas, *Summa* I–II, q. 94, a. 6, ad 2/Benziger I, p. 1012.

13. Aquinas, *Summa* II–II, q. 104, a. 5, Objection 3/Benziger II, p. 1645. In his reply, Aquinas distinguishes three kinds of obedience, including 'lawful', but he clearly sees that slavery can be lawful.

So, how does Aquinas think slavery is a sin if he agrees slaves should perform duties masters expect from them?

Stark misses the fact that, much like the Greek Stoics, Aquinas believes that slavery of the soul is what is absolutely impermissible, whereas that of the body can be permissible. This is clearly expounded by Aquinas in his discussion of obedience:

> ...subjection whereby one man is bound to another regards the body; not the soul, which retains its liberty. Now, in this state of life we are freed by the grace of Christ from defects of the soul, but not from defects of the body, as the Apostle declares by saying of himself (Rom. vii. 23) that in his mind he served the law of God, but in his flesh the law of sin. Wherefore those that are made children of God by grace are free from the spiritual bondage of sin, but not from the bodily bondage, whereby they are held bound to earthly masters, as a gloss observes on 1 Tim. vi. 1, 'Whosoever are servants under the yoke', etc.[14]

In part, Aquinas comes to this conclusion by citing 1 Tim. 6.1, which, as we have seen, does relate to slavery ('Let all who are under the yoke of slavery regard their masters as worthy of all honor...'). Clearly, Aquinas aims to follow biblical teachings of slavery, and 1 Tim. 6 assumes that slavemasters can be Christians without the slightest hint that they are being sinful for having slaves.

Moreover, Stark only proves how inconsistent he is with himself. Note, in particular, how Stark approves of Aquinas's concept that 'Right reason, not coercion, is the moral basis of authority, for "one man is not by nature ordained to another as an end"'. Yet, when disparaging the God of the Greek Sophists, some of whom believed in abolitionism, Stark focuses on the fact that 'Sophists could not invoke One True God. Invoking a lesser God made no one tremble.'[15] So, Stark extols the biblical God because he can enforce morality through fear and force, but yet praises Aquinas for expounding a morality that is based on reason, and not on fear and force.

Serfdom or Slavery?

Stark's claim that Aquinas was speaking about 'serfdom' rather than actual slavery is apparently derived from Catholic apologists who insist that the Latin *servus* in Aquinas really refers to a 'bondservant' rather than a 'slave'.[16] Likewise, such apologists insist that the Latin term *servitus* often refers to

---

14. Aquinas, *Summa* II–II, q. 104, a. 6, ad. 1/Benziger II, p. 1646.
15. Stark, *For the Glory of God*, p. 327.
16. For a recent statement of such a position, see Hector Zagal Arreguin, 'Aquinas on Slavery: An Aristotelian Puzzle', *Atti del Congresso Internazionale su l'umanesimo cristiano nel III millennio: la prospettiva di Tommaso d'Aquino, 21–25 Settembre, 2003* 3 (2006), pp. 323-32.

'servitude' rather than 'slavery'. Stark adapts here the opinions of Stephen Brett and Joel Panzer, whom Stark quotes.[17]

This translation of *servus/servitus* as 'bondservant/servitude' is a clear sleight-of-hand because modern apologists are making an unjustified distinction, one that is not made by the contemporary sources. For example, note how Panzer phrases his translational preferences:

> We have been using above the words, 'servitude' and 'slavery'. Both words are possible translations of the Latin '*servitus*'. When speaking of the *servitus* which rested on one of the so-called 'just titles' we translate it as 'servitude'; when speaking of that form of *servitus* which did not rest on just title, we translate the Latin as 'slavery'.[18]

By 'just title', Panzer is referring to what he deems to be 'legitimate servitude', which often pertained to the mode of acquisition of the slave. *Las siete partidas* (The Seven Parts), the Spanish legal code of Alfonso el Sabio (1252–1284), known in English as Alfonso X 'The Wise' of Castile (now in Spain), specifies at least three ways to acquire slaves under a just title: (1) as prisoners of war who are enemies of the faith; (2) as children born of enslaved women; (3) by way of self-sale.[19] A Muslim prisoner of war, for example, could be considered a 'just title' slave. 'Just' enslavement could also be incurred as an ecclesiastical penalty for helping Muslims or other types of acts classified as crimes by the Church.[20]

Therefore, by restricting the English word 'slavery' to servitude that is not categorized as 'just title', these apologists are able to exclude forms of servitude that we otherwise would still call slavery and was so deemed by those Medieval sources. Alternatively phrased, these apologists call 'servitude' the form of forced servitude that they think is 'justified' and 'slavery' the form of forced servitude that they do not think is justified, even when both can result in all the violent, degrading treatment we associate with the so-called 'racialized' slavery of the more recent times.

The distinction between just and unjust slavery is itself irrelevant because both kinds of servitude are largely outlawed by international human rights conventions. Again, Article Four of the United Nations Universal Declaration

---

17. Brett, *Slavery and the Catholic Tradition*, p. 87 n. 75.
18. Panzer, *The Popes and Slavery*, p. 5.
19. *Las siete partidas* 4.21.1. I use the edition of [Alfonso El Sabio], *Las siete partidas del Rey Don Alfonso el Sabio cotejada con varios codices antiguos por la Real Academia de la Historia* (3 vols.; Madrid: Imprenta Real, 1807), III, p. 117. *Las Sietes Partidas* will be cited by its internal divisions: Part, Title, Law. Thus 4.21.1 = Fourth Part, Title 21, Law 1. The volume and page numbers are those of the Madrid edition, which retains many archaic spellings but is truer to the extant manuscripts than popular recent editions that modernize the orthography.
20. See Maxwell, *Slavery and the Catholic Church*, pp. 48-49.

of Human Rights states: 'No one shall be held in slavery or servitude; slavery and the slave trade shall be prohibited in all their forms'.[21] In short, both 'slavery' and 'servitude' are prohibited.

Panzer does point to the Geneva Conventions to show that prisoners of war could be compelled to work, but there are still vast differences between what was permitted by the Geneva Conventions and what was permitted by Church doctrine. For example, the Geneva Conventions specifically state that: 'If officers or persons of equivalent status ask for suitable work, it shall be found for them, so far as possible, but they may in no circumstances be compelled to work'.[22] But slavery entails, by definition, coerced labor, and so this cannot be applied to what is permitted by the Geneva Convention for captive officers.

In the case of general military personnel, the Geneva Conventions do permit captors to compel labor from prisoners, but 'conditions shall not be inferior to those enjoyed by nationals of the Detaining Power employed in similar work'.[23] In other words they must be treated equally to free citizens performing the same tasks. Finally, even if the Geneva Conventions permit something we could call slavery, this would not require Catholic doctrine to imitate something that it now considers to be wrong.

However, in terms of the final outcome, just title and unjust title slavery made no difference insofar as a slave was someone who was subjected to coerced labor and considered property in some sense. We have just such a statement in *Las siete partidas*, which is roughly contemporary with St Thomas Aquinas:

> Slavery [*servidumbre*] is the most vile and despicable thing that can exist among men, who is the noblest and freest creature among all the other creatures that God made. By it [slavery] is given to the power of others so that they can do with him what they please, alive or dead. And so despised a thing is such slavery that he not only loses his power to do what he wills, but he is not even in charge of his own person except to do what the master commands him.[24]

---

21. United Nations, *The Universal Declaration of Human Rights*, 1948.
22. Geneva Conventions, 12 August 1949, Part III, Section III, Article 49; Panzer, *The Popes and Slavery*, p. 3. For a convenient edition of the text of the Geneva Convention, see www.icrc.org/ihl.nsf/385ec082b509e76c4 1256739003 e636d/6756482d86146898c 125641e004aa3c5.
23. Geneva Conventions, Part III, Section IV, Article 95.
24. [Alfonso El Sabio], *Las siete partidas*, 4.5.1/Madrid edition, III, p. 30: 'Servidumbre es la más vil et la más despreciada cosa que entre los hombres puede ser; porque el hombre, que las mas noble et libre criatura entre todas las otras criaturas de Dios hizo, se torna por ella en poder de otri, de guisa que pueden hacer dél lo que quisieren como de otro su haber vivo o muerto; et tan despreciada cosa es esta servidumbre que el que en ella cae non tan solamiente pierde poder de no hacer de lo suyo lo que quisiere, mas aun de su personal mesma non es poderoso sinon quantol manda su señor' (my translation).

8. *St Thomas Aquinas*

Thus, there is no question that slavery was recognized for what it was in Medieval times—a vile institution for the enslaved, but yet permissible under some circumstances by the Church. Elsewhere, *Las siete partidas* (4.21.1) is explicit in using the term *siervo*, which it traces back to the Latin *servus/servare*, for someone subjected to this sort of institution.[25]

In any case, the claim that *servus* is best translated as 'servant' or 'bond-servant' in Aquinas's works is often arbitrary, and Panzer and Brett translate this and related terms (*servilis, servitus*) inconsistently. For example, despite accepting that '"*servus*" is best translated as "servant" and sometimes "bond-servant"', Brett translates these corresponding words in Aquinas's *Summa theologica* as follows:[26]

Summa	Aquinas	Brett
I, q. 92, a. 1, ad 2	*servilis*	slavery[27]
I, q. 96, a. 4	*servus*	slave[28]

When Panzer speaks of the prohibition of the 'enslavement of the Indians' by a papal document (*Pastorale officium*, 1537), he translates 'given into servitude' (*servitute delendos*) in one instance, and 'reduce...to slavery' (*in servitutem redigere*) in another instance, even when both are speaking of the same prohibited practice and use the same word, *servitus*.[29]

Indeed, Aquinas clearly defines *servus*, when he discusses how a *servus* differs from a 'free man':

> Mastership has a twofold meaning. First, as opposed to slavery [*servituti*], in which sense a master means one to whom another is subject as a slave [*servus*]. In another sense mastership is referred in a general sense to any kind of subject; and in this sense even he who has the office of governing and directing free men, can be called a master. In the state of innocence man could have been a master of men, not in the former but in the latter sense. This distinction is founded on the reason that a slave [*servus*] differs from a free man in that the latter has the disposal of himself...whereas a slave [*servus*] is ordered to another. So that one man is master of another as his slave when he refers the one whose master he is, to his own—namely the master's use. And since every man's proper good is desirable to himself, and consequently it is a grievous matter to anyone to yield to another what ought to be one's own,

---

25. My translation of [Alfonso el Sabio], *Las siete partidas* 4.21.1/Madrid edition, III, p. 117: 'Et siervo tomó este nombre de una palabra que es llamada en latin *servare*...' That etymology of *siervo/servus* is also that of Isidore of Seville's *Etymologies* 9.4.41. I use the edition of Stephen A. Barney, W.J. Lewis, J.A. Beach, and Oliver Berghof, *The Etymologies of Isidore of Seville* (Cambridge: Cambridge University Press, 2007), p. 205.
    26. Brett, *Slavery and the Catholic Tradition*, p. 82 n. 37.
    27. Brett, *Slavery and the Catholic Tradition*, p. 69.
    28. Brett, *Slavery and the Catholic Tradition*, p. 71.
    29. Panzer, *The Popes and Slavery*, p. 22.

therefore such dominion implies of necessity a pain inflicted [*poena subjectorum*] on the subject; and consequently in the state of innocence such a mastership could not have existed between man and man.[30]

This definition coincides with Orlando Patterson's concept of 'alienation' as the essence of slavery, and so it is disingenuous to claim that Aquinas was unfamiliar with the tragedy that this institution posed for the individual slave.[31] Nonetheless, Aquinas does not believe that this slavery is a sin per se because he allows that slavery is a consequence of sin, and so a permissible, and even beneficial, state in the current post-Fall condition of humanity. It would not have been permissible before the Fall (during the stage of 'innocence').

When Did Racism Begin?

In order to minimize the tragedy of Medieval slavery, Brett claims that 'the race-based slavery practiced in the New World after the arrival of Columbus and European colonialism is hardly what Aquinas meant when he wrote of *servitus*'.[32] Yet, this is not historically true either. European colonialism was already afoot during the Greco-Roman period, and Rome was a European imperial power with millions of slaves. It made slaves of foreigners, and many of its ideas about foreigners were racist. In terms of attitudes toward black persons, we now have much more evidence that black Africans were viewed as evil, in a theological sense, in the first millennium, and it was fueled in part by the myth of Ham. In her study of physical descriptions of non-Christians in the Middle Ages, Debra H. Strickland notes:

> I suggest that what the representations of Saracen/Ethiopian 'hybrids' actually reveal is the extent to which a common pejorative visual vocabulary is applied across different enemy types: This is why demons, Jews, Ethiopians, Saracens and other negative figures are all at various times portrayed with dark skin as well as with a number of other physiognomical features...[33]

30. Aquinas, *Summa* I, q. 96, a. 4, ad 3/Benziger I, p. 488.
31. For similar criticisms of Brett and others who attempt to mitigate Medieval slavery as compared to New World slavery, see Joseph E. Capizzi, 'The Children of God: Natural Slavery in the Thought of Aquinas and Vitoria', *Theological Studies* 63 (2002), pp. 44-45 n. 34. See further David Wyatt, *Slaves and Warriors in Medieval Britain and Ireland, 800–1200* (Leiden: E.J. Brill, 2009); Keith Bailey, 'Slavery in the London Area in 1086', *Transactions of the London and Middlesex Archaeological Society* 57 (2006), pp. 69-82.
32. Brett, *Slavery and the Catholic Tradition*, p. ix. Whitford (*The Curse of Ham in the Early Modern Era*, pp. 19-20) also dismisses the connection between race and servitude much too easily in his treatment of the Ham myth in the Middle Ages.
33. Debra H. Strickland, *Saracens, Demons, and Jews: Making Monsters in Medieval Art* (Princeton, NJ: Princeton University Press, 2003), p. 173. See also Jean Vercoutter *et*

Strickland gives copious examples of the link made by Christians, already in late Antiquity, between negritude and defective character. In turn, all of these supposed features later are used to justify the enslavement of black Africans.

Already, by the fourth century, Didymus the Blind, the Christian commentator, stated that 'Ethiopians...share in the devil's evil and sin, getting their name from his blackness'.[34] Pope Gregory the Great said that '"Ethiopia" signifies the present world whose blackness is a sign of a sinful people'.[35] Paulinus, the bishop of Nola (c. 354–431), remarked that 'The Dragon devours the people of Ethiopia, who are not burned by the sun but are black with vice [*uitilies nigris*], sin giving them the color of night [*crimine nocticolores*]'.[36] The latter explicitly rejects secular and natural explanations (e.g., exposure to the sun) of human physical features, pioneered by pagan Greco-Roman writers (e.g., the Hippocratic corpus, Pliny), and substitutes completely theological rationales pioneered by Jewish, Muslim, and Christian writers.[37] Once we see these historical antecedents of race-based slavery in Christian theology, we should not be surprised that black Africans were chosen to be the paradigmatic slave population by Christians.

Nor is it true that the color of slaves passed unnoticed in Aquinas's time. Documented sales of slaves collected by Charles Verlinden routinely record the color of the slave. Note these examples from the thirteenth century (c. 1287):[38]

1. 'a black Saracen named Fatimam'[39]
2. 'a white Saracen by the name of Aly'[40]
3. 'a black Saracen named Arrashte'[41]
4. 'his black Saracen slave named Museyd'.[42]

---

al., *The Image of the Black in Western Art* (2 vols.; Cambridge, MA: Harvard University Press, 1976–79).

34. Didymus the Blind, *Commentary on Zechariah* (trans. Robert C. Hill; The Fathers of the Church, 111; Washington, DC: Catholic University of America Press, 2006), p. 313.

35. As quoted in Strickland, *Demons, Saracens, and Jews*, p. 84. For a more general study of Didymus, see Richard A. Layton, *Didymus the Blind and his Circle in Late Antique Alexandria* (Urbana: University of Illinois Press, 2004).

36. Strickland, *Demons, Saracens, and Jews*, p. 84; Latin text on 270 n. 96.

37. For the Greco-Roman developments of the theory of environmental effects on human features, including color, see Benjamin Isaac, *The Invention of Racism in Classical Antiquity* (Princeton, NJ: Princeton University Press, 2004), pp. 55-102.

38. Verlinden, *L'esclavage*, II, pp. 141, 144.

39. Verlinden, *L'esclavage*, II, p. 141: 'quandam ancillam nigram saracenam, nomine Fatimam'.

40. Verlinden, *L'esclavage*, II, p. 144: 'une Sarrasine blanche du nom d'Aly'.

41. Verlinden, *L'esclavage*, II, p. 144: 'servum nigrum sarracenum nomine Arrashte'.

42. Verlinden, *L'esclavage*, II, p. 144: 'servum suum nigrum sarracenum nomine Museyd'.

We can argue that these are mere descriptors, but it certainly shows that color consciousness was there by the Middle Ages when evaluating slaves.

Summary

It is simply disingenuous to maintain that St Thomas Aquinas, perhaps the most pre-eminent theologian of Christianity, was unaware of the misery of slavery. Indeed, the brutality, alienation, humiliation, and the awareness of color were all there by the time of Aquinas. The difference in the New World was the scale, and the increasingly exclusive dependence on black slavery. There was no change in the principle that slavery itself could be acceptable, and not a sin, under some circumstances. Aquinas quoted 1 Timothy 6, among other texts, to support his view.

Chapter 9

Renaissance Popes and Slavery: A Whole Lot of Bulls

Vatican II (1962–65) generated a more honest and vigorous discussion about the role of the papacy in promoting or allowing slavery in the New World and beyond. On one side are historians, such as John F. Maxwell and John T. Noonan, who claim that the Catholic Church did not definitively repudiate slavery as inherently wrong until 1965.[1] Stephen F. Brett, among many other Christian apologists, claims that Catholic anti-slavery reaches at least as far back as the Middle Ages.[2] Such modern apologists follow Pope Leo XIII, who wrote a letter (*Catholicae ecclesiae*, 1890) defending previous popes from the charge of being pro-slavery.[3]

Rodney Stark, who depends heavily on the work of Joel Panzer and Stephen Brett, argues that abolitionism was a longstanding policy of Catholicism. However, as in previous cases, Stark reads the scholarly literature uncritically, and often does not independently check the original sources, written frequently in Latin and in Spanish, on which his secondary sources depend. Stark also lacks a clear grasp of the broader debates and context in which the original sources were written.

Particularly crucial is the attitude of the papacy during the Renaissance because this period included the discovery of the New World, which opened up vast new possibilities for enslavement. Although the Renaissance is difficult to define, I describe it as a period of Western history that spanned roughly from the mid-1400s to the late 1500s.[4] It is the first time that

---

1. Maxwell, *Slavery and the Catholic Church*, p. 13; John T. Noonan, *A Church That Can and Cannot Change: The Development of Catholic Moral Teaching* (Notre Dame: University of Notre Dame Press, 2005).
2. Brett, *Slavery and the Catholic Tradition*.
3. See Maxwell, *Slavery and the Catholic Church*, p. 117.
4. On the Renaissance, see Lisa Jardine, *Worldly Goods: A New History of the Renaissance* (New York: Doubleday, 1996). For a useful anthology on contemporary issues in Renaissance studies, see Keith Whitlock (ed.), *The Renaissance in Europe: A Reader* (New Haven: Yale University Press, 2000).

European empires achieved a truly global reach. It was a time of revolutions in religion (Protestant reformation) and communications (printing press).[5] Papal policies formulated in the Renaissance helped shape views toward the enslavement of both Indians and Africans for centuries afterward. Many of these papal policies were issued in the form of bulls, which are normally the highest form of papal communication. A bull may be defined more simply as 'an apostolic letter with a leaden seal'.[6] Other communications were issued in the form of a Brief, a shorter and less elaborate letter often treating a specific issue, and it could be sent to a king or a limited group. Therefore, it is useful to discuss crucial bulls individually in order to gain a sense of how apologists hyperbolize papal achievements, and suppress undesirable aspects. These papal communications show that appeal to biblical authority and ethics, especially in regard to the right of Christians to spread Christianity globally, supported rationales for slavery.

Sicut dudum *(1435)*

Sicut dudum is one of the first bulls to speak about the rights of newly encountered people—this time in the Canary Islands, which had endured both Portuguese and Castilian aggression.[7] Both Portugal and Castile (the latter only a kingdom in what is now Spain) contested ownership of the islands, and the bull *Sicut dudum*, issued by Pope Eugene IV (1383–1447) on 13 January 1435, was part of the effort to bring peace between those two powers. Stark describes the bull and its background as follows:

> During the 1430s, the Spanish colonized the Canary Islands and began to enslave the native population. This was not serfdom but true slavery of the sort that Christians and Moors had long practiced on one another's captives in Spain. When word of these actions reached Pope Eugene IV (1431 to 1447), he issued a bull, *Sicut Dudum*. The pope did not mince words. Under threat of excommunication he gave everyone involved fifteen days from the receipt of his bull 'to restore to their earlier liberty all and each person of either sex who were once residents of said Canary Islands…these people are to be totally and perpetually free and to be let go without exaction or reception of any money'.[8]

---

5. Elizabeth Eisenstein, *The Printing Press as an Agent of Change: Communications and Cultural Transformations in Early-Modern Europe* (2 vols.; New York: Cambridge University Press, 1979).

6. H. Thurston, 'Bulls and Briefs', in *The Catholic Encyclopedia* (New York: Robert Appleton Company, 1908). Online: www.newadvent.org/ cathen/03052b.htm.

7. See Frances G. Davenport (ed.), *European Treaties Bearing on the History of the United States and its Dependencies to 1648* (Washington, DC: Carnegie Institution of Washington, 1917), pp. 9-11.

8. Stark, *For the Glory of God*, p. 330.

9. *Renaissance Popes and Slavery*

Stark represents Pope Eugene as a champion of indigenous liberty regardless of religion. However, *Sicut dudum* is not a manifesto against slavery at all, but a continuation of the policy against enslaving fellow Christians. This fact is presented early in the bull, which describes the inhabitants initially as 'imitating the natural law alone and not having known any sect or apostates or heretics'.[9] However, these natives have 'been led to the Orthodox Catholic faith with the aid of God's mercy'.[10] The bull goes on to say that 'some of these people were already Baptized; others were even at times tricked and deceived by the hope and promise of Baptism'.[11]

The potential loss to the Church of these natives, who might resent such treatment by these Christians, and their potential return to their non-Christian religion, is the main concern of the bull. This context is better understood by reading *Sicut dudum* in light of a slew of papal and royal correspondence before and after that document was issued. This correspondence, of which Stark and Panzer seem completely unaware, was collected by Dominik Josef Wölfel of the Museum of Ethnology (Museum für Völkerkunde) in Austria.[12] It also shows that becoming Christian was a way for Canary Islanders to escape slavery.

In particular, a document, dated between 1474 and 1481 by Wölfel, was sent by Ferdinand and Isabella, the rulers of Spain, to the mayors of various towns concerning a petition by men named Pedro and Alonso, both Canary Islanders who had converted to Christianity. These men had petitioned the crown concerning the danger of being re-enslaved, and the royal couple responded as follows to those town officials:

> Please understand that the Canary Islanders, Pedro and Alonso, related to us that, at a time when they were non-Christian slaves, they went to the city of Malaga and were there for some time, and learning later how to they can be saved by being Christians, they came to the aforementioned city of Malaga and they were baptized and became Christians. Therefore, they are enfranchised and free according to the rights and laws of our kingdom by having come from Moorish lands and converted to our faith…[13]

---

9. For the Latin and English texts of *Sicut dudum*, I depend on Panzer, *The Popes and Slavery*, pp. 75-78 (passage quoted is on p. 75).

10. Panzer, *The Popes and Slavery*, p. 75.

11. Panzer, *The Popes and Slavery*, p. 76.

12. Dominik Josef Wölfel, 'La curia romana y la corona de España en la defensa de los aborígenes canarios', *Anthropos* 25 (1930), pp. 1011-83.

13. My translation of Wölfel, 'La curia Romana', p. 1051: 'Sepades que Pedro e Alonso canarios nos fisyeron rrelaçion por su su petiçion que ante nos en el nuestro consejo presentaron diziendo que ellos seyendo canarios e no cristianos e seyendo esclauos se fueron a la çibdad de Malaga estouieron en ella çierto tienpo e despues conosçiendo commo se saluauan en ser cristianos se vinieron de la dicha çibdad de Malaga e se baptizaron e tornaron cristianos e dis que como quier que segund derecho e leyes de nuestro

186   *Slavery, Abolitionism, and the Ethics of Biblical Scholarship*

In other words, the situation of Pedro and Alonso continued for decades after *Sicut dudum* insofar as it was difficult to tell Christian from non-Christians, and because unscrupulous slave traders would kidnap Christian Canary Islanders. In any case, *Sicut dudum* and related correspondence clearly recognize that non-Christians, especially Moors, can be enslaved. It is enslaving Christians that is the major problem.

Romanus Pontifex *(1454/55)*

Romanus Pontifex, a bull addressed to King Alfonso V (1438–1481) of Portugal, is one of the first to begin to divide up at least part of the known world between Castile and Portugal. This bull, which Panzer calls a 'brief', would later prove important in allowing Spain and Portugal to conquer and claim ownership of the New World. The bull explicitly authorizes enslavement of Muslims captured in war, and it also condones and authorizes the enslavement of black Africans who are not identified as initiating war at all. Note this passage:

> We [therefore] weighing all and singular the premises with due meditation, and noting that since we had formerly by other letters of ours granted among other things free and ample faculty to the aforesaid King Alfonso—to invade, search out, capture, vanquish, and subdue all Saracens and pagans whatsoever, and other enemies of Christ wheresoever placed, and the kingdoms, dukedoms, principalities, dominions, possessions, and all movable and immovable goods whatsoever held and possessed by them and to reduce their persons to perpetual slavery, and to apply and appropriate to himself and his successors the kingdoms, dukedoms, counties, principalities, dominions, possessions, and goods, and to convert them to his and their use and profit…[14]

Yet, Panzer, remarks: 'The 1454 brief of Pope Nicholas V to King Alfonso V…was concerned with the waging of just wars against the very real enemies of the Catholic Church, and should not be interpreted to apply to peoples and lands who were not at war with the Christian nations'.[15]

Yet, the bull does give permission to invade, capture, and subdue 'pagans and other enemies of Christ' and so it does seem to categorize pagans as enemies of Christ because they are unbelievers or because they might resist efforts to conquer them by Christians. Such resistance could be perfectly justified in modern international law. In any case, the bull does not say that all of these natives are at war with the Church, but rather that war was waged

rreynos ellos son horros e libres por ser aver venido de tierras de moros e tornarse a nuestra fe…'
    14. Davenport, *European Treaties*, p. 23.
    15. Panzer, *The Popes and Slavery*, p. 13 n. 18. Davenport (*European Treaties*, p. 12) dates this bull to 8 January 1455.

against these peoples on behalf of King Alfonso's commercial interests.[16] According to the following passage, the king of Portugal is justified to take them by force:

> [T]hey at length came to the province of Guinea, and having taken possession of some islands and harbors and the sea adjacent to that province, sailing farther they came to the mouth of a certain great river commonly supposed to be the Nile, and war was waged for some years against the peoples of those parts in the name of the said King Alfonso and of the infante, and in it very many islands in that neighborhood were subdued and peacefully possessed, as they are still possessed together with the adjacent sea. Thence also many Guineamen and other negroes, taken by force [*capti*], and some by barter of unprohibited articles, or by other lawful contract of purchase, have been sent to the said kingdoms. A large number of these have been converted to the Catholic faith, and it is hoped, by the help of divine mercy, that if such progress be continued with them, either those peoples will be converted to the faith or at least the souls of many of them will be gained for Christ.[17]

Such actions cannot involve anything we might call a 'just' war, as might be the case if Christian territory was being defended against a pagan invasion. Christians are the outsiders and invaders in these parts of Africa. The bull even admits that 'war was waged against these people' and there is no indication of it being defensive.[18]

In any case, I see no condemnation for taking these Africans by force or by sale. This clearly would be against their will, and so where is the emphasis on the will of the natives to accept or reject these encounters? Why are these natives not justified in defending their territory? So what if they are Muslims? Clearly, Panzer's claim that the Pope is speaking about a 'just war' is based on a failure to read the bull properly, and fails to confront the fact that his definition of a 'just war' would not be in accordance with the United Nations Declaration of Human Rights.

Inter caetera *and* Eximiae devotionis *(1493)*

These bulls attempt to prevent Portugal and Spain from infringing on each other's territories. Many historians interpret them to be another indication of how the Pope thought he had ownership rights to the earth, and was now allocating parts of the planet to Spain and Portugal. In *Inter caetera*, Alexander VI (Papal reign 1492–1503) tells Spain that it can possess lands nearly unconditionally in its allocation. Note this passage:

---

16. Davenport, *European Treaties*, pp. 22-23; see Davenport (*European Treaties*, pp. 16-17) for corresponding Latin text.
17. Davenport, *European Treaties*, p. 22.
18. Davenport (*European Treaties*, pp. 15-16): 'contra illarum partium populos nomine ipsorum Alfonsi Regis et infantis, per aliquos annos guerra habita extitit'.

...inasmuch as with eager zeal for the true faith you design to equip and despatch this expedition, you purpose also, as is your duty, to lead the peoples dwelling in those islands and countries to embrace the Christian religion...by the authority of Almighty God conferred upon us in blessed Peter and of the vicarship of Jesus Christ, which we hold on earth, do by tenor of these presents, should any of said islands have been found by your envoys and captains, give, grant, and assign to you and your heirs and successors, kings of Castile and Leon, forever, together with all their dominions, cities, camps, places, and villages, and all rights, jurisdictions, and appurtenances, all islands and mainlands found and to be found, discovered and to be discovered towards the west and south... With this proviso however that none of the islands and mainlands, found and to be found, discovered and to be discovered, beyond that said line towards the west and south, be in the actual possession of any Christian king or prince up to the birthday of our Lord Jesus Christ just past from which the present year one thousand four hundred and ninety-three begins.[19]

Despite the all-encompassing language of *Inter caetera* and *Eximiae devotionis*, Panzer claims that these bulls do not give away the newly discovered lands or authorize Spain or Portugal to enslave their inhabitants. Instead, argues Panzer, the Pope 'is giving to Spain and Portugal the rights to bring Christianity to these lands *on the presumption that the peoples of those lands freely choose the Kings of Spain and Portugal as their sovereigns*'.[20]

Panzer again misreads the plain sense and Latin grammar of the bulls. In *Inter Cetaera*, the direct objects of the verbs 'give, grant, and assign' (*donamus, concedimus et assignamus*) are 'all the islands and the mainlands' (*omnes insulas et terras*), and not 'the right to bring Christianity to the lands'.[21] In fact, within that complex Latin sentence, the Pope also does give all rights (*cum plena, libera, et omnimoda potestate, auctoritate, et juridisdictione*) to the king, but there is nothing mentioned about giving rights to the natives.[22]

The purpose of bringing Christianity to those lands is one of a number of purposes as indicated by the word 'also' in this statement 'you purpose, also, as is your duty, to lead the peoples dwelling in those islands and countries to embrace the Christian religion'.[23] The Pope is well aware, and explicitly mentions, the discovery of gold and other precious commodities as another of the purposes of such expeditions. So, *Inter caetera* does not just grant these kings the right to bring Christianity to these lands. The Pope allows the king of Castile to permit or forbid anyone 'to go there for the purpose of trade

---

19. Davenport, *European Treaties*, p. 77.
20. Panzer, *The Popes and Slavery*, p. 13 (Panzer's italics).
21. Davenport, *European Treaties*, p. 74.
22. Davenport, *European Treaties*, p. 74.
23. Davenport, *European Treaties*, p. 77.

or any other reason'.[24] There is no thought of the will or consent of those conquered. The grants are given 'forever' before any native necessarily has heard of these coming conquerors, and so how is their consent at all of any concern? In fact, the only significant condition outlined in *Inter caetera* is that such lands be not already in the possession of a Christian king (at least before 1493).

The fact that these bulls were understood as allowing conquest and subjugation as a precondition to evangelization is supported by many theologians and jurists of the time. Juan Ginés de Sepulveda, who advocated the enslavement of Indians, said that 'Alexander, in imitation of [Pope] Adrian, exhorted the rulers of Spain to attack barbarians, subject them to their dominion, and protect the way for proselytizing sermons'.[25] Sepulveda understood that subjection had to precede evangelization because otherwise the Indians would flee or resist before they could even hear the word. As Sepulveda phrases it: 'How can [apostles] be sent if the barbarians were not previously subjugated?'[26]

Ineffabilis et Summi Patris *(1497)*

In order to diminish further the imperialistic evangelizing agenda of *Inter caetera* and *Eximiae devotionis*, Panzer argues that the real intention of these bulls is clarified in a letter from Alexander VI to Emmanuel I, king of Portugal (1495–1521), and dated 1 June 1497. The letter, titled *Ineffabilis et Summi Patris* (henceforth, *Ineffabilis*), is found in a collection of papal documents edited by Francisco Javier Hernaez, the renowned editor of many Vatican documents.[27] In that letter, Alexander VI grants Emmanuel certain requests pertaining to territories that might submit 'voluntarily' to him.

However, the Latin text of *Ineffabilis* reveals that Panzer has misunderstood or misrepresented that document, as well. First, Panzer apparently believes that the Portuguese Cardinal mentioned in the letter is named Gregory, when the Latin text actually gives his name as *Georgium* (Jorge/George), who is none other than Jorge da Costa (1406–1508), the cardinal

---

24. Davenport, *European Treaties*, p. 77; Latin text (Davenport, *European Treaties*, p. 75): 'pro mercibus habendis vel quavis alia de causa'.
25. Juan Ginés de Sepulveda, *Democrates segundo o de las justas causas de la guerra contra los Indios* (ed. Angel Losada; Madrid: Consejo Superior de Investigaciones Cientificas, 1951), p. 67. That he was referring to these bulls is attested by the date (1493) that Sepulveda mentions (p. 80).
26. Sepulveda, *Democrates segundo*, p. 67.
27. Francisco Javier Hernaez, *Colección de bulas, breves y otros documentos relativos a la iglesia de América y Filipinas* (2 vols.; repr., Vaduz: Kraus, 1964 [1879]), II, pp. 836-37.

protector of Portugal. Second, nothing in this document indicates that this letter is meant to clarify *Inter caetera* or *Devotionis* per se, but rather it addresses, as shown in more detail below, a specific request made by Emmanuel.

The more important misunderstanding, though, comes in the passage that Panzer introduces and quotes from that document as follows: 'The Pope notes the value of the request and grants the privilege conditionally: "...if it has happened that certain cities, camps, lands places or dominions of the peoples without faith have wished to be subject to you, pay tribute to you and recognize you as their Sovereign"'.[28] Thus, according to Panzer, we should read what follows the conjunction, 'if', restrictively, as conditions imposed by Alexander upon Emmanuel. For Panzer, these conditions include principally that the natives submit willingly to Portugal's rule. However, Panzer has misunderstood the fact that the Pope is not granting anything conditionally at this point. The fuller passage is as follows:

> To be sure, the following matter was recently set before us on your behalf by our Venerable Brother George, Bishop of St Albans, who has the title of Cardinal of Lisbon of the Holy Roman Church, namely, that you, who in the manner of your ancestors intend to devote yourself to attacking the infidels, desire that, if by chance it should happen that certain cities, forts, lands and places, or dominions belonging to the infidels are subjected to your rule, or pay you tribute, and wish to acknowledge you as their master, you may lawfully be enabled to receive and retain such cities, forts, places, lands and dominions. For this reason we received a humble request on your behalf that we might deign to make timely provision for you in respect of the aforesaid by use of our Apostolic kindness.[29]

In contrast to Panzer's representation, at this point in *Ineffabilis* Alexander VI is not making a declaration of any grant, conditionally or unconditionally. Rather, the Pope here is actually quoting or paraphrasing Emanuel's desire ('that you [Emmanuel]...desire'/*quod tu...desideras*) to be granted newly discovered lands if those lands choose to be subjected to him. The Latin pronoun *tu* ('you') and corresponding verb ('desire'/*desideras*) are completely omitted by Panzer in his quotation.

---

28. Panzer, *The Popes and Slavery*, p. 13.
29. Hernaez, *Colección de Bulas*, II, p. 836: 'Sane pro parte tua nobis nuper per Venerabilem Fratrem nostrum Georgium, Episcopum Albanensem, Sanctae Romanae Ecclesiae Cardinalem Ulixbonensem nuncupatum, expositum fuit, quod tu, qui more tuorum progenitorum intendis Infidelium expugnationi vacare, desideras, si forsan contingeret aliquas Civitates, castra, terras, et loca seu Dominia Infidelium, ditione tuae subjici, seu tributum solvere, et te in eorum Dominum cognoscere velle, licite Civitates, castra, loca, terras et Dominia hujusmodi recipere et retinere posse. Quare pro parte tua nobis fuit humiliter supplicatum, ut tibi in praemissis opportune providere de benignitate Apostolica dignaremur' (my translation).

A second problem is that Panzer attempts to use *Ineffabilis* to explicate what the king of Spain should have (or would have) understood by the previous bulls. Panzer remarks: 'Thus it is quite clear that Alexander VI's intention was not simply to give other people's lands, but rather to give Spain and Portugal the authority of the church to bring the Catholic faith...*to those people who are freely willing to accept them*'.[30] But, even if true, this would not necessarily be understood by the king of Spain because *Ineffabilis* was addressed only to the king of Portugal. There is no mention of a similar letter to the king of Spain. Alexander is answering a more specific and new question posed by the Emmanuel.

But why would Emmanuel wonder if he can accept dominion over people who voluntarily submit to him in the first place? Should it not be understood that people who want to be subjected to him have such a right? To understand why Emmanuel is asking such a question, one has to understand that there are two modes of acquisition at issue: (1) possession by conquest; (2) possession by voluntary subjection, which parallel those of slave law, where a person can be enslaved by either (1) being captured in war, or (2) voluntary self-sale.

The fact that both modes of acquisition are allowed is already understood in *Romanus Pontifex* quoted above ('war was waged for some years...many islands in that neighborhood were subdued and peacefully possessed'). *Ineffabilis* certainly indicates that the Pope expects violence to be Emmanuel's standard mode of acquiring lands ('you...in the manner of your ancestors intend to devote yourself to attacking the infidels').

A more important reason why Emmanuel is wondering if he can accept dominion over people who 'voluntarily' submit to his rule is the bitter conflicts that have ensued when indigenous people became caught between the claims of Spain and Portugal. Some natives might have opted for Portuguese rule, and others for Castilian. A few decades earlier, Portugal had even helped the natives fight off the Castilians who also claimed the Canary Islands.[31] The Canary Islands conflict was adjudicated in the Treaty of Alcaçovas (1479), wherein Portugal ceded ownership to Castile, but nothing is said about the natives having determined that choice.[32]

Territorial disputes continued to be a problem in the 1480s and 1490s. By Panzer's own admission, Alexander is attempting to clarify *Inter caetera* (1493), among other bulls. Yet, *Inter caetera* is greatly concerned with Portugal and Spain not infringing on each other's territories. *Inter caetera* draws a line about one hundred leagues west of any of the Azores or Cape Verde

30. Panzer, *The Popes and Slavery*, p. 14 (Panzer's italics).
31. For some of the details of these conflicts, see Davenport, *European Treaties*, pp. 33-34.
32. Davenport, *European Treaties*, p. 34.

192   *Slavery, Abolitionism, and the Ethics of Biblical Scholarship*

Islands, and grants any territory found west of that line to Castile.[33] However, note again the exception issued by the Pope to Castile:

> With this proviso however that none of the islands and mainlands, found and to be found, discovered and to be discovered, beyond that said line towards the west and south, be in the actual possession of any Christian king or prince up to the birthday of our Lord Jesus Christ just past from which the present year one thousand four hundred and ninety-three begins.[34]

Indeed, the only significant condition outlined in *Inter caetera*, *Eximiae*, and *Ineffabilis* is that any new lands encountered be not already in the possession of a Christian king.

This sort of situation was particularly vexing because the world was round, and it was only a matter of time before Spanish sailors heading westward encountered lands that Portugal considered to be in 'the East'. *Dudum siquidem*, a bull issued by Pope Alexander VI on September 26, 1493, saw the problem: 'But since it may happen that your envoys and captains, or vassals, while voyaging toward the west or south, might bring their ships to land in eastern regions and there discover islands and mainlands that belonged or belong to India…'[35] Since it was in the 'east', India would have been Portugal's territory, but *Dudum siquidem* awards it to Spain.

So, in *Ineffabilis*, Emmanuel simply introduced a clever ploy for circumventing the line of demarcation that might award territories to Spain. Indeed, what Panzer leaves out is that 'voluntary' subjection is a euphemism. It was well known that 'voluntary subjection' constituted another legal 'title' for slavery. This title was discussed by Francisco de Vitoria (1492–1546), the influential Spanish moral theologian praised by Panzer himself for helping to bring more rights to the Indians.[36] Vitoria remarks:

> There is another title…'voluntary choice' [*electionem voluntariam*]. When the Spaniards arrive in the Indies, they tell the barbarians how they have been sent by the king of Spain for their own good, and they admonish them to receive them [the Spaniards] as king and lord. And they [the Indians] respond that they agree, because 'there is nothing more natural than to honor the will of an owner who wishes to transfer his dominion to another'…[37]

33. Davenport, *European Treaties*, p. 71.
34. Davenport, *European Treaties*, p. 77.
35. Davenport, *European Treaties*, p. 82.
36. For comments on Vitoria, see Panzer, *The Popes and Slavery*, pp. 25-27. See also Capizzi, 'The Children of God', pp. 31-52.
37. Francisco de Vitoria, *Relectio de Indis o Libertad de los Indios* (ed. L. Pereña and J.M. Perez Prendes; Madrid: Consejo Superior de Investigaciones Científicas, 1967), p. 73: 'Restat alius titulus…electionem voluntariam. Hispani enim cum ad barbaros perveniunt, significant eis quemadmodum rex Hispaniae mittit eo pro commodis eorum, et admonent eos ut illum pro domino et rege recipiant [et acceptent], et illi retulerunt placere sibi. Et

However, Vitoria saw through the pure subterfuge that such 'voluntary' submission entailed:

> This title is not legitimate. First, because it is evident that fear and ignorance should not interfere in diminishing choice. But this is precisely what interferes in those choices and acceptance, because the barbarians do not understand what they are doing, nor probably understand what the Spaniards are requesting of them. Moreover, such requests are made by armed people who surround a frightened and unarmed crowd.[38]

Vitoria's position is certainly not that of Alexander VI, who apparently decided to follow the tradition of allowing enslavement by using this sort of 'just title'.

At once, we see that Emmanuel is successful in his ploy. Lines of demarcation can now be disregarded if Emmanuel, 'by chance', finds lands that 'willingly subject' themselves to him. Alexander's answer certainly did not prohibit Emmanuel from attacking or obtaining cities that do not want to have him as their master when there is no territorial dispute with other Christian kings. In fact, Alexander clarifies that consent is not necessary at all in this phrase: 'Furthermore we bestow upon you free and full permission to conquer them…' (*assignamus, ac illa conquirendi plenam et liberam facultatem elargimur*).[39]

Given this permission, the Latin conditional construction (*si forsan…velle*) should not be understood restrictively (i.e., 'only if [they were] to wish'), but simply as 'if [they were] to wish' to be subjected. A good analogy is if someone asks: 'May I enslave person X if he sells himself voluntarily to me?' If the Pope says 'Yes', then the Pope should not be construed to mean that a person can be enslaved 'only if' the person sells himself because other titles of enslavement are still allowed (e.g., war prisoners). In fact, the Pope explicitly says Emmanuel also has permission to conquer them, which entails a lack of consent.

Thus, *Ineffabilis* is not a manifesto about the freedom of natives to resist Christian subjection, but rather a specific answer to Emmanuel, who wonders if he can disregard lines of demarcation if natives 'voluntarily' prefer his subjection over that of another Christian king. A choice exists only insofar as

---

'nihil tam naturale est quam voluntatem domini volentis rem suam in alium transferre ratam haberi' (my translation).

38. Vitoria, *Relectio de Indis*, p. 73: 'nec iste titulus est idoneus. Patet primo, quia deberet abesse metus et ignorantia quae vitiant omnem electionem. Sed haec interveniunt in illis electionibus [et acceptationibus]. Nesciunt enim barbari quid faciunt, immo forte non intelligunt quid petunt hispani. Item hoc petunt circumstantes armati ab imbelli turba [et meticulosa]' (my translation).

39. Hernaez, *Colección de Bulas*, II, p. 837.

the natives can choose to remain subjected to Emmanuel, and not to another Christian king. Otherwise, Emmanuel is free to conquer the natives, with their consent or not.

Sublimis Deus *(1537)*

According to Panzer, this bull, issued by Pope Paul III in 1537, is 'regarded as the most important pronouncement on the human condition of the Indians'.[40] Stark calls it a 'magnificent bull against New World Slavery'.[41] *Sublimis Deus* (henceforth, *Sublimis*) was particularly important because it was addressed to the entire Church, and so had a universal quality lacking in some of the previous letters addressed to specific kings. Some of the important portions bear repeating at length:

> Therefore, We, who though by no merit of ours, act on earth as the vicar of the same Lord for the sheep of His flock entrusted to us, and who seek with all our strength to bring into the same flock those outside the sheepfold, noting that the Indians themselves indeed are true men and are not only capable of the Christian faith, but, as has been made known to us, promptly hasten to the faith and wishing to provide suitable remedies for them, by our Apostolic Authority decree and declare by these present letters that the same Indians and all other peoples—even though they are outside the faith—who shall hereafter come to the knowledge of Christians have not been deprived or should not be deprived of their liberty or of their possessions... Rather they are to be able to use and enjoy this liberty and this ownership of property freely and licitly and are not be reduced to slavery and whatever happens to the contrary is to be considered null and void and as having no force of law.[42]

Despite positive signs of advancement, the fact is that this bull had limited efficacy, particularly because it was just one of a series of contradictory and half-hearted denunciations of Indian slavery and of slavery in general. Notice that the phrase Panzer translates as 'whatever happens to the contrary' can be translated as 'whatever may have been or may be said to the contrary' (*ac quidquid secu fieri contigerit*), a clearer allusion the contradictory nature of previous papal communications.[43]

What Panzer and Stark omit is that Paul III saw this bull as being extorted from him, and that he annulled it, or at least its companion piece, *Pastorale officium*, about a year later. Paul III's annulment shows more clearly how he functioned as a lackey of the Holy Roman Emperor Charles V (1519–1553),

---

40. Panzer, *The Popes and Slavery*, p. 16.
41. Stark, *For the Glory of God*, p. 331.
42. Panzer, *The Popes and Slavery*, pp. 80-81.
43. See also Noonan, *A Church That Can and Cannot Change*, p. 73. For an online translation of *Sublimis Deus*, see www.papalencyclicals.net/Paul03/p3subli.htm.

9. Renaissance Popes and Slavery

rather than as a protector of the indigenous people.[44] However, to understand Paul III's vacillations we must delve more in to the historical context of this bull.

The impetus for *Sublimis* was provided by Bartolomé de las Casas and Bernardino de Minaya (c. 1484–1566), a Dominican friar who evangelized parts of Mexico.[45] Eventually, Minaya's advocacy of Indian rights clashed with the views of Juan Garcia de Loaysa (1478–1546), the first president of the Royal and Supreme Council of the Indies, which supervised the entire New World for the king of Spain. Minaya had some allies, and these included Julian Garces, Archbishop of Tlaxcala (Mexico), who recommended Minaya to Pope Paul III. In 1537 Minaya went to the Vatican to persuade Paul III to help the Indian cause. In response, Paul III issued what became known as *Sublimis*.

At the same time, Charles V, the Holy Roman Emperor, who now had Spain and its possessions in the New World as part of his empire, had issued an edict in 1530 forbidding Indian slavery in the New World. But Charles revoked this edict in 1534, and allowed Indian slavery again. According to Panzer, Pope Paul III issued *Pastorale officium* (29 May 1537), a papal Brief, to enforce the 1530 edict of Charles V (in particular, excommunication for Christian violators).[46] Others see the *Pastorale* as a companion to the *Sublimis*, which lacked any mention of specific penalties for violations.[47]

In any case, the Pope seemed unaware that Charles had already revoked that 1530 edict in 1534. Eventually, according to Panzer, Charles V did convince Paul III to nullify the *Pastorale*. That nullification is contained in a Papal decree titled *Non indecens videtur* (19 June 1538). Panzer does not provide the text of this important document, which may be found in Latin (and with a Spanish translation) in the work of Helen-Rand Parish and Harold Weidman.[48] The crucial portions read as follows:

> It does not seem to us improper if the Roman Pontiff...revoke, correct, or change those [dispositions] in preference to one from whom they were extorted by stealth at a time when he was engaged in other matters...just recently he [Charles V] informed us that a certain letter in the form of a Brief was extorted from us and that it caused disruption to the peaceful state of the islands of the

---

44. Richard Maltby, *The Reign of Charles V* (New York: Palgrave, 2002), p. 63.
45. For a detailed study of Minaya's efforts, see Alberto de la Hera, 'El derecho de los indios a la libertad y a la fe', *Anuario de la historia del derecho español* 26 (1956), pp. 89-181, especially 141-67.
46. Panzer, *The Popes and Slavery*, p. 22.
47. See discussion in Helen-Rand Parish and Harold E. Weidman, *Las Casas en Mexico: Historia y obra desconocidas* (Mexico, DF: Fondo de cultura ecónomica, 1992), p. 379 n. 31, which also reports how the final draft of *Pastorale officium* omitted an order to free the slaves mentioned in an earlier draft.
48. Parish and Weidman, *Las Casas en Mexico*, pp. 313-14.

Indies to the west and south... Accordingly, by virtue of Apostolic authority, we revoke, invalidate, and annul the previous letter(s) and whatever is contained in it (or them) (whose tenor, content, and form should be expressed as though they were inserted word for word in the present [letter]).[49]

This is as thorough a revocation as one can issue because it encompasses 'whatever is contained in them' (*in eis contenta quaecumque*).

Many historians, including Panzer, agree that Charles V read *Non indecens* as abrogating both the *Pastorale* and *Sublimis*. However, Panzer and others allege that *Non indecens* was not meant to abrogate or retract *Sublimis*, but only the *Pastorale*. Yet, a closer look at *Non indecens* shows that Charles justifiably read it as an abrogation of both the *Pastorale* and the *Sublimis*.

All this may be moot, however, because *Non indecens* declared that 'whatever is contained' in the *Pastorale* be annulled, and the fact is that the *Pastorale* contained many of the same declarations we see in *Sublimis*. Thus, *Sublimis* is famous for containing the declaration that the Indians are 'truly human' (*veros homines*), and the *Pastorale* declares that Indians 'are men capable of faith and salvation'. *Sublimis* says that Indians should not be reduced to slavery, and so does the *Pastorale*. Therefore, if 'whatever is contained' in the *Pastorale* is annulled, then that would include those sentiments and instructions, as well.[50]

Furthermore, even if we assume only the *Pastorale* is referenced in *Non indecens*, Paul III describes this document as 'Letter(s) in the form of a Brief extorted from us' (*a nobis in forma Brevis litteras extortas fuisse*). This does not sound like the bold pronouncements of a Pope moved by the suffering of indigenous people, but rather describes his succumbing to some form of pressure.

In fact, we know Paul III was not entirely against slavery, because in 1548, in another document called *Motu propio*, he allowed slavery in Rome itself. The crucial sentence of *Motu propio* reads:

49. My translation of Parish and Weidman, *Las casas en Mexico*, p. 313: 'Non indecens videtur si Romanus Pontifex...quae aliquando ab eo variis negociis implicito in alicuius praeiudicium per circumventionem extorquentor, revocet, corrigat ac mutet... Carolus Romanorum Imperator...nobis nuper exponi fecit quasdam a nobis in forma Brevis litteras extortas fuisse—per quas Indiarum occidentalium ac meridionalium insularum prosper et felix status ac regimen interturbatur... Litteras praedictas (quarum tenores, continentias et formas ac si prasentibus de verbo ad verbum inserentur, pro expressis haberi volumus) et in eis contenta quaecumque, auctoritate apostolica per easdem praesentes cassamus, irritamus, et annulamus.'

50. It might be objected that 'whatever is contained' is too broad because *Pastorale* also contained praise for Charles V, and so it is not likely that Paul III is revoking that sentiment. However, even if we restrict it to the ideas to which Charles V is objecting, readers could plausibly include revocation of the idea that the Indians are human because that was the very basis on which enslavement was forbidden, even according to Panzer and other apologists.

> We enact and decree in perpetuity that slaves who flee to the Capitol and appeal for their liberty shall in no wise be freed from the bondage of their servitude, but that notwithstanding their flight and appeal of this sort they shall be returned to slavery to their owners, and if it seems proper they shall be punished as runaways.[51]

Concerning *Motu propio*, Panzer remarks: 'it becomes obvious that slavery in general was not sanctioned'.[52] Yet, when reading a document addressed only to King Emmanuel, Panzer wishes us to understand it as part of a 'general' anti-slavery record. While Panzer claims that *Motu propio* 'should be understood as applying only to those held in Italy under various legal titles to servitude', none of those 'legal titles' would be justified under the United Nations guidelines.[53]

Do as I Say, Not as I Do

Stark and other apologists admit, even if grudgingly, that many Popes practiced slavery. Popes held slaves and sold slaves. But the common defense is that these practices should not nullify the teaching of the Church. So, while Stark admits that Pope Innocent VIII accepted a gift of one hundred Moorish slaves from King Ferdinand of Aragon, Stark tells us that 'acceptance of a gift of slaves should not be confused with church teaching'.[54] What the Church teaches (e.g., the *magisterium*) is what justifies the claim that it was abolitionist, and not what its highest moral authorities were actually doing. Thus, we encounter a version of 'do as I say, not as I do'.

Yet, even if we were to accept Stark's premise, the problem is one of inconsistency. In fact, hypocrisy is used against other religions when their moral authorities practice something in opposition to what they teach. Thus, Hammurabi's Code said that it was based on the lofty and laudable principle that the strong should not oppress the weak, yet we don't see Stark excusing Mesopotamian kings for not living up to that principle.

The whole idea that papal actions did not invalidate papal teachings can be refuted easily. Biblical injunctions repeatedly indicate that faith without works is useless. James 2.17 says: 'So faith by itself, if it has no works, is dead'. Likewise, Jesus rejected the idea that teachings alone had any meaning in Mt. 7.16-17: 'You will know them by their fruits... So, every sound tree bears good fruit, but the bad tree bears evil fruit'.

---

51. Maxwell, *Slavery and the Catholic Church*, p. 75. *Motu propio* is also a general term for documents issued on Papal initiative rather than upon request. See also Felix Grat, *Etude sur le Motu Propio: des origins au debut du XVIe siècle* (Melun: Librairie d'Argences, 1945).
52. Panzer, *The Popes and Slavery*, p. 27.
53. Panzer, *The Popes and Slavery*, p. 27 n. 54.
54. Stark, *For the Glory of God*, p. 330.

Summary

The papacy of the sixteenth century was deeply involved in sustaining slavery. Not only did some popes own slaves, but they repeatedly enunciated policies that allowed Christian monarchs to enslave millions of people. The efforts to magnify certain liberatory bulls, such as *Sublimis*, are usually never countered by a thorough discussion of the background or how quickly it was rescinded. Neither Stark nor Panzer mention that, in contrast to being prompted by humanitarian impulses, the Pope felt *Pastorale* was 'extorted' from him.

The justifications given for slavery by those popes ultimately revolved around biblical sanctions for slavery. A second significant sanction was the fact that the Christian God owned the entire world, and his chosen people were entrusted with extending the Gospel throughout the world (Mt. 28.19-20). As the Vicar of Christ, the Pope had a duty to ensure that the world became subject to Christ, whether by peace or by force (Mt. 10.34).[55] Thus, the imperial nature of biblical principles had a logical trajectory in the global reach of Christianity first witnessed in the sixteenth century.

---

55. See further Lester I. Field, *Liberty, Dominion and the Two Swords: On the Origins of Western Political Ideology (180–398)* (Publications in Medieval Studies, 28; Notre Dame: University of Notre Dame Press, 1998).

Chapter 10

A BRAVE NEW WORLD:
LAS CASAS VS. SEPULVEDA

The enslavement of Africans through the Spanish Conquest of the Americas begins in earnest in the sixteenth century, and the rise of the sugar industry was the heart of the slave trade engine.[1] In 1493, Columbus reportedly had already brought sugar cane from the Canary Islands to the island of Hispaniola. By 1522, Hispaniola was exporting sugar, and by the 1530s some 34 mills were operating. Although capturing and moving slaves across the ocean had begun during Columbus's voyages, it is reasonable to say that 'the brief sugar boom from 1530 to 1570...saw the origins of the slave trade'.[2]

Although we can find African slaves mentioned in the Middle Ages and in Portuguese records of the 1400s, it was the decimation of Native American populations in the 1500s that was a major factor in encouraging the importation of African replacements. While the massive importations of slaves seen in Brazil was still about one hundred years away, some of the basic socio-economic structures that permeated the sugar growing areas can already be seen quite clearly during the initial Spanish Conquest. Thus, by 1548, Hispaniola had 35 plantations and sugar mills, and estimates showed that blacks outnumbered whites on Puerto Rico (12,000 to 5,000) already by 1546.[3]

1. See further Selwyn H.H. Carrington, *The Sugar Industry and the Abolition of the Slave Trade, 1775–1810* (Gainesville: University Press of Florida, 2002); Barbara L. Solow, 'Capitalism and Slavery in the Exceedingly Long Run', *Journal of Interdisciplinary History* 17 (1987), pp. 711-37; Steven D. Mintz, *Sweetness and Power: The Place of Sugar in Modern History* (New York: Penguin Books, 1985).

2. Jan Rogozinski, *A Brief History of the Caribbean: From the Arawak and the Carib to the Present* (New York: Penguin Putnam, 1999), p. 51. For a more general history of the slave trade, see also Thomas, *The Slave Trade*. For a standard collection of documents pertaining to the slave trade, see Elizabeth Donnan (ed.), *Documents Illustrative of the History of the Slave Trade to America* (4 vols.; Washington, DC: The Carnegie Institution of Washington, 1930–35). Some useful statistics developed through electronic databases on slavery have been summarized in David Eltis and David Richardson, *Atlas of the Transatlantic Slave Trade* (New Haven: Yale University Press, 2010).

3. Statistics for Hispaniola and Puerto Rico in Frank Moya Pons, *History of the Caribbean* (Princeton, NJ: Markus Wiener Publishers, 2007), p. 17.

Yet, some Christian apologists tell us that biblical principles favoring abolition can be seen clearly already in the Spanish Conquest. Indeed, Lewis Hanke, a foremost historian of this period, exclaims that the Spanish Conquest:

> ...was also one of the greatest attempts the world has seen to make Christian precepts prevail in the relations between peoples. This attempt became basically a spirited defense of the rights of Indians, which rested on two of the most fundamental assumptions a Christian can make: namely that all men are equal before God, and that a Christian has responsibility for the welfare of his brothers no matter how alien or lowly they may be.[4]

By Hanke's reckoning, therefore, the Spanish Conquest was a sort of blessing in disguise.

Accordingly, this chapter aims to test that assertion by examining the work of two sixteenth-century thinkers who became the paradigms of the struggle between slavery and abolition. One is Bartolomé de las Casas (1484–1566), perhaps the greatest advocate of Indian rights in history. The other is Juan Ginés de Sepulveda (1490–1573), who advocated enslaving Indians. As with previous examples, we shall show that, when it came to using biblical support, the abolitionist position stood on no more solid ground (and sometimes on even less solid ground) than the advocacy of slavery.

Bartolomé de las Casas

No figure stands taller than Bartolomé de las Casas in the history of Indian rights. Although his reputation has waxed and waned, depending on the era or biases of scholars evaluating his accomplishments, he is still widely regarded as the preeminent champion of Indian rights.[5] The well-known biographer of las Casas, Juan Friede, remarked that, during the age of revolutions, 'he was hailed as a precursor and prophet of the American, French, and Spanish-American struggles against foreign or domestic tyranny'.[6]

As is no surprise, many Christian scholars believe that las Casas is being true to biblical ethics. Thus, Paul Vickery, who produced a very laudatory biography, remarks that 'Las Casas spoke in the tradition of the Hebrew prophets'.[7] Helen-Rand Parish also compared him to an 'Old Testament

---

4. Lewis Hanke, *The Spanish Struggle for Justice in the Conquest of America* (Boston: Little, Brown & Co., 1965), p. 1.
5. For how las Casas's reputation has waxed and waned, see Juan Friede and Benjamin Keen (eds.), *Bartolomé de las Casas in History: Toward an Understanding of the Man and his Work* (DeKalb: Northern Illinois University Press, 1971), pp. 3-63.
6. Friede and Keen (eds.), *Bartolomé de las Casas in History*, p. 23.
7. Paul Vickery, *Bartolomé de las Casas: Great Prophet of the Americas* (New York: Paulist Press, 2006), p. 155.

prophet'.[8] Similarly, Lewis Hanke, one of the most preeminent scholars of las Casas, quotes with approval the words of Cardinal Josef Hoffner, who said, 'it was the noble Las Casas who most profoundly understood the spirit of the Christian gospel'.[9]

Las Casas lived a long and extremely active life. He was born in Seville, Spain in 1484, though some older biographies still have him born in 1474.[10] His mother apparently died while she was a young woman. His father, Pedro de las Casas, was a merchant who accompanied Columbus on his second voyage to the Americas. Las Casas's first encounter with Indians came in 1493, when he saw some of them exhibited in Seville by Columbus himself.

In 1502, las Casas made his first trip to the New World. He arrived in Santo Domingo, on the island of Hispaniola, which later became divided into the nations of Haiti and the Dominican Republic. He appears to have participated personally in the campaign against Higuey, a local indigenous chieftain. By 1513, he was working in Cuba as an *encomendero*, which meant that an allotment of Indians had been 'given' to him for the purposes of evangelization, though often those who were *encomendados* ('entrusted') were little more than slaves.

However, upon reading Ecclesiasticus/Sirach 34 and other biblical texts, las Casas resolved to renounce his life as an *encomendero* in 1514, and he began to advocate on behalf on Indian rights.[11] Las Casas went to Spain in 1516, where he was scolded for his pro-Indian activism by Juan Rodriguez Fonseca, the bishop of Burgos. However, las Casas found an ally in Fracisco Ximenes de Cisneros, the cardinal archbishop of Toledo, and also famous for printing the first edition of the New Testament in Greek. Ximenes appointed him officially as Protector of the Indians. Ximenes ordered some reforms, but he died in 1517. It was about this time that las Casas began to suggest that African slaves be substituted for Indians slaves.

Pleading his case before Charles V, the Holy Roman Emperor, was an important goal, and las Casas achieved this in 1519. However, little changed, and he returned to the New World by 1521. In that same year, Cumaná, a mission in Venezuela, was attacked and many Spaniards killed. Some managed to escape, and they blamed las Casas for thinking that peaceful means

---

8. Helen-Rand Parish and Harold E. Weidman, *Las Casas en Mexico: Historia y obra desconocidas* (Mexico, DF: Fondo de cultura ecónomica, 1992), p. 77: 'como un profeta del Antiguo Testamento'.

9. Lewis Hanke, *All Mankind Is One: A Study of the Disputation between Barthlomé de las Casas and Juan Ginés de Sepúlveda in 1550 on the Intellectual and Religious Capacity of American Indians* (DeKalb, IL: Northern Illinois University Press, 1974), p. 141.

10. On the date of his birth, see Parish and Weidman, *Las Casas en Mexico*, p. 9.

11. Hanke (*All Mankind Is One*, p. 7) notes that las Casas made the decision in 1514, but actually gave up his *encomienda* in 1515.

were going to convert the Indians. That brought new calls for forceful conquest rather than the peaceful missionizing that las Casas favored.

Undeterred by these setbacks, las Casas continued to advocate for peaceful missionary activities. *De unico vocationis modo* (*The Only Way*, 1534) one of his first expositions of his activism on behalf of Indians, argued that any missionary activity should be conducted by mostly peaceful means.[12] This work may have influenced the issuance of *Sublimis Deus* (1537) already discussed. Another experiment, using the peaceful principles of *The Only Way*, was trialed in 1537 in a region of Guatemala called Tuzutlán. The experiment succeeded spectacularly at first, but the Indians had revolted by 1556.[13]

In 1542, the so-called New Laws issued by the Spanish monarchy seemingly signaled a new stance that recognized the rights of Indians to be free. However, these laws were greatly resisted by Spanish colonists, and were widely ignored. The repeal of the New Laws in 1546 resulted in a great disappointment for las Casas. Such a royal repeal mirrored the issuance and retraction of communications regarding the legitimacy of slavery we had seen in the papacy.

Nonetheless, in 1544, las Casas managed to gain an appointment as the bishop of Chiapas (Mexico) despite opposition from local pro-slavery advocates, who rejected many of his directives and policies. He returned to Spain in 1547 and resigned his bishopric in 1550.[14] He devoted much of his time to studying theology, law, and the Bible at the monastery of San Gregorio in Valladolid, Spain. It was at that time that he became aware of *Democrates segundo*, the main work of Juan Ginés de Sepulveda, a theologian who advocated the enslavement of Indians. The high point of las Casas's dramatic life came in a debate at Valladolid, Spain in 1550 with Sepulveda.

Juan Ginés de Sepulveda

Sepulveda is widely acknowledged to be 'the bad guy' in the entire debate that surrounded the Spanish conquest and the enslavement of Indians.[15] However, not much is known about Sepulveda, and we depend heavily on the

---

12. For a standard English edition, see Helen-Rand Parish and Francis Patrick Sullivan (eds.), *Bartolomé de las Casas: The Only Way* (Mahwah, NJ: Paulist Press, 1992). They see a more complicated textual history consisting of at least three editions.

13. See Hanke, *The Spanish Struggle for Justice*, pp. 78-81. David M. Traboulay (*Columbus and Las Casas: The Conquest and Christianization of America, 1492–1566* [Lanham, MD: University Press of America, 1994], p. 171) speaks about the success of this experiment without noting its tragic end a few decades later.

14. Parish and Weidman, *Las Casas en México*, p. 77.

15. Sepulveda later insisted that he only wanted Indians to submit to Spanish rule rather than to enslave them. See Hanke, *All Mankind Is One*, p. 117.

biographical work of Luis Patiño Palafox.[16] As Palafox notes, Sepulveda was born in 1490 in Cordoba, Spain. In 1510 he entered the University of Alcala and studied philosophy for three years. Thereafter, he studied philosophy and theology in the College of San Antonio de Sigueña until 1515.

By 1523 he had received his doctorate at Bologna, one of the premier universities of the time. While in Bologna he was mentored by Julian de Medici, who became Pope Clement VII (1523–1534). After the latter's death, Sepulveda became the official chronicler for Emperor Charles V in 1534, and then the tutor of the latter's son, Philip II in 1542. Although his main debate was against las Casas, Sepulveda was an able polemicist who also confronted Protestants. He was widely read in law, philosophy, and in biblical studies. For our purpose Sepulveda's most important work was *Democrates segundo*, which summarized the main arguments las Casas tried to refute.

Basic Exegetical Principles

Both las Casas and Sepulveda used two basic sources of authority: (1) the Bible, with the plain literal sense being accorded priority; (2) Church tradition, which included papal pronouncements, the teachings of the Church Fathers, and contemporary doctors of the Church. Supplementary authorities included Aristotle, Cicero, and other Greco-Roman authors. Las Casas summarizes his principles while discussing the parable of the Wedding Feast (Lk. 14.22-23):

> Now parables may be explained in very many ways and receive very many interpretations, and the same parable can be applied to different things, according to the various points of similarity. Moreover, the literal sense, upon which other meanings are based and which cannot be false, is not that which anyone may want it to be… The determination of what or what sort of meaning may be, however, is not the function of just anybody but only of the sacred doctors, who have surpassed other men by their way of life and their teaching.[17]

Sepulveda is less explicit in outlining principles, but he does preface specific pieces of evidence by an appeal to both the Bible and Church leaders (e.g., 'Sed ut scriptura divina et sanctorum virorum piorumque testimoniis agamus…').[18]

The problem is that neither las Casas nor Sepulveda apply these principles consistently. Both lack some of the philological data needed to understand crucial biblical texts better in their original contexts. Both pick-and-choose

---

16. Luis Patiño Palafox, *Juan Ginés de Sepulveda y su pensamiento imperialista* (Mexico City: Los Libros de Homero, 2007), especially pp. 170-73.

17. Bartolomé Las Casas, *In Defense of the Indians* (trans. Stafford Poole; DeKalb, IL: Northern Illinois University Press, 1992), p. 269.

18. Sepulveda, *Democrates segundo*, p. 96.

the texts they think support them, and often ignore the ones that do not. Yet, las Casas's biblical support for anti-slavery is no better, and many times worse, than what Sepulveda can muster. The following are some illustrative examples.

Leviticus 19.18 and Neighborly Love

In arguing against any brutal treatment of Indians because of their 'idolatry', las Casas remarks: 'For we are commanded by divine law to love our neighbor as ourselves, and since we want our vices to be corrected gently, we should do the same with our brothers, even if they are barbarians'.[19] Las Casas is, of course, alluding to Lev. 19.18, which says: 'You shall not take vengeance or bear any grudge against the sons of your own people, but you shall love your neighbor as yourself: I am the LORD'.

This verse in Leviticus, in turn, was quoted by Jesus in Mt. 19.19 and by Paul in Rom. 13.9. Although Lev. 19.18 seems to enjoin us to love all human beings, the fact is that the original intent was the opposite. As Harry M. Orlinsky, the prominent scholar of Hebrew, has deftly noted, the Hebrew term (re'eka/רעך) translated as 'your neighbor' is best understood as 'your fellow Israelite'.[20] The verse's final instruction to love your fellow Israelite as yourself follows logically on the instruction not to hate anyone of your kin (benê 'ammeka/בני עמך) in the first half of the verse. Thus, the verse does not obligate universal love, but, in fact, is premised on privileging love for fellow Israelites over love for non-Israelites.

Jesus and Paul, therefore, are engaging in 'reinterpretation', which is unacceptable for the same reasons that we would not allow someone to change the meaning of our words into something opposite. Rather than being a universal law, Lev. 19.18 offers a very restricted injunction. In any case, Jesus and Paul saw this injunction as being clearly compatible with slavery.

So, it is not surprising that Sepulveda also cited Mt. 19.19 and Rom. 13.9, including the part about loving your neighbor (*diliges proximum tuum*), to prove his points.[21] Sepulveda did not understand Lev. 19.18 to prohibit slavery. Rather, Sepulveda saw the Golden Rule and love of neighbor as part of

---

19. Las Casas, *In Defense of the Indians*, p. 39.
20. Harry M. Orlinsky, 'Nationalism-Universalism and Internationalism in Ancient Israel', in Harry Thomas Frank and William L. Reed (eds.), *Translating and Understanding the Old Testament: Essays in Honor of Herbert Gordon May* (Nashville: Abingdon Press, 1970), pp. 206-36, especially 210-11. For a more expansive interpretation, see Bob Becking, 'Love Thy Neighbour... Exegetical Remarks on Leviticus 19.18, 34', in Achenbach and Arneth (eds.), *Gerechtigkeit und Recht zu üben*, pp. 183-87.
21. Sepulveda, *Democrates segundo*, p. 9.

natural law that functioned to 'ensure that humans fulfill their obligations'.[22] These obligations included living within the natural laws that God had prescribed for the world, and one of those natural laws is servitude.

Thus, neither Sepulveda nor las Casas is true to the more probable original meaning of Lev. 19.18. While las Casas may be following the more universal meaning given to it by Jesus and Paul, the latter two are not being true to the original meaning of the Hebrew Bible. Moreover, Sepulveda repeatedly and rightly observed how biblical authors endorsed slavery and conquest *despite* the existence of Lev. 19.18.

Leviticus 20.4-5: Criminalizing Indians

According to Sepulveda, the Spanish Conquest was necessary to stop crimes against nature being perpetuated by the Indians. These crimes included human sacrifice and idolatry. In order to support his case, Sepulveda appealed to Old Testament texts that allowed the Israelites to commit genocide on the Canaanites, especially when the reason given was idolatry or human sacrifice. Leviticus 20.4-5 states:

> And if the people of the land do at all hide their eyes from that man, when he gives one of his children to Molech, and do not put him to death, then I will set my face against that man and against his family, and will cut them off from among their people, him and all who follow him in playing the harlot after Molech.

Sepulveda, similarly quotes from Wis. 12.3-7:

> Those who dwelt of old in thy holy land thou didst hate for their detestable practices, their works of sorcery and unholy rites, their merciless slaughter of children, and their sacrificial feasting on human flesh and blood. These initiates from the midst of a heathen cult, these parents who murder helpless lives, thou didst will to destroy by the hands of our fathers, that the land most precious of all to thee might receive a worthy colony of the servants of God.

Las Casas admits that these texts allow the killing of the Canaanites, but he argues that they are not to be applied to people outside of Canaan. Indeed, las Casas mocks Sepulveda by remarking 'I am surprised that a Christian man does not prefer to admit those passages that speak about pagans outside the Promised Land'.[23]

However, las Casas misrepresents Sepulveda because the latter does explain why those genocidal texts apply outside of Canaan. Sepulveda grants

---

22. Sepulveda, *Democrates segundo*, p. 9: 'de rebus agendis pertinent ad homines in officio continendos'.
23. Las Casas, *In Defense of the Indians*, p. 107.

that these commandments were given to Israel, but he deduces that this must be part of natural law because the Canaanites were destroyed for these reasons before Christ came.[24] Natural law was in operation before Christ came (cf. Rom. 1.20-26).

Sepulveda similarly appeals to Lev. 18.29: 'For whoever shall do any of these abominations, the persons that do them shall be cut off from among their people'. For Sepulveda, the phrase 'whoever do any of these abominations' (*omnis iniquit almas*) has universal validity.[25] If idolatry and human sacrifice seemed abominable to God in Canaan, why would it be different in the New World? Eternal divine law is global, not local.

Las Casas also adduces the common argument that '[i]n this era of grace, however, we must think and act quite differently'.[26] However, Sepulveda observes that slavery is still accepted in the New Testament, and so the era of grace did not change that. More importantly, las Casas also cites the Old Testament to support the persecution of heretics. Yet, las Casas does not reject the persecution of heretics because 'in this era of grace, however, we must think and act quite differently' about heresy.

Deuteronomy 20.10-14 and Conquest

According to Sepulveda, this passage endorsed enslavement of some of the population and the taking of the wealth of any city that the Israelites besieged. The passage says:

> When you draw near to a city to fight against it, offer terms of peace to it. And if its answer to you is peace and it opens to you, then all the people who are found in it shall do forced labor for you and shall serve you. But if it makes no peace with you, but makes war against you, then you shall besiege it; and when the LORD your God gives it into your hand you shall put all its males to the sword, but the women and the little ones, the cattle, and everything else in the city, all its spoil, you shall take as booty for yourselves; and you shall enjoy the spoil of your enemies, which the LORD your God has given you. Thus you shall do to all the cities which are very far from you, which are not cities of the nations here (Deut. 20.10-14).

Verse 15, in particular, was interpreted by Sepulveda to authorize the conquest of nations very distant from Israel (*de procul remotis*), and this would fit the New World.[27] For Sepulveda, as long as the Spaniards provided 'terms for peace', then the city had a free choice to accept or reject these terms.

---

24. Sepulveda, *Democrates segundo*, p. 40.
25. Sepulveda, *Democrates segundo*, p. 41.
26. Las Casas, *In Defense of the Indians*, p. 107.
27. Sepulveda, *Democrates segundo*, p. 117.

Sepulveda reinforces the right to take Indian property by citing St Thomas Aquinas who stated: 'Unbelievers possess their goods unjustly in so far as they are ordered by the laws of earthly princes to forfeit those goods. Hence these may be taken violently from them, not by private but by public authority.'[28] For Sepulveda, this applied to both heretics and pagan idolaters (*paganos, idolorumque cultores*).[29] Indeed, for Sepulveda, idolatry was akin to a crime, and criminals should lose their property.[30]

In any case, the Spaniards attempted to follow this idea of offering terms for peace with a very notorious type of document called the *Requerimiento* introduced by the Laws of Burgos (1512).[31] The *Requerimiento* was to be read to Indians, and it offered them peace if they accepted the Christian Gospel, but war if they did not.[32] Of course, the Indians could not understand what was being read, and Spaniards often joked about the fact that they were reading aloud to empty villages just to comply with the technical letter of the law.[33]

Joshua 7.16-26 and Genocide

Sepulveda used this text to show that God could allow the killing of women and children who might otherwise have done nothing wrong. As long as a member of a particular family or clan was identified as committing some sin against God, then it was permissible to kill all the members of that family or clan. Briefly, a man named Achan had stolen some of the treasures meant for Yahweh. When these were found in Achan's tent, Joshua took the following actions with his entire clan:

> And Joshua and all Israel with him took Achan the son of Zerah, and the silver and the mantle and the bar of gold, and his sons and daughters, and his oxen and asses and sheep, and his tent, and all that he had; and they brought them up to the Valley of Achor. And Joshua said, 'Why did you bring trouble on us? The LORD brings trouble on you today.' And all Israel stoned him with stones; they burned them with fire, and stoned them with stones (Josh. 7.24-25).

---

28. Sepulveda, *Democrates segundo*, p. 89; Aquinas, *Summa*, II–II, q. 66. a. 8, ad 2/ Benziger II, p. 1481. Latin text of the *Summa* as cited in Sepulveda (*Democrates segundo*, p. 89): 'Ad secundum dicendum quod intantum aliqui infideles iniuste res suas possident, inquantum eas secundum leges terrenorum principum amittere iussi sunt. Et ideo ab eis possunt per violentiam subtrahi, non privata auctoritate, sed publica.'

29. Sepulveda, *Democrates segundo*, p. 89.

30. Sepulveda, *Democrates segundo*, p. 89.

31. Lewis Hanke, 'The Requerimiento and its Interpreters', *Revista de historia de América* 1 (1938), pp. 25-34.

32. For the text of the Laws of Burgos, see Rafael Altamira, 'El texto de las leyes de Burgos de 1512', *Revista de historia de América* 4 (1938), pp. 5-79.

33. See Hanke, *The Spanish Struggle for Justice*, pp. 33-35.

Las Casas had a very difficult time attempting to explain this passage. His first counterargument is as follows:

> [W]hen a city is justly condemned to be destroyed or given over to plunder, we are not obliged to investigate whether there are persons in it who are innocent and undeserving of such treatment, since all citizens are presumed to be enemies of the state or ruler who is waging a just war.[34]

In other words, Christians are allowed to kill innocent people as long as it is part of a 'just war'.

The second counterargument was even more contradictory to the idea that human beings are made in the image of God rather than possessions of God and more akin to slaves:

> God's judgements are inscrutable. Therefore just because God commanded something to be done, it does not follow that we can do it too. For men throughout the world belong to God. Therefore he can freely dispose of them inasmuch as men are his possession and, far more certainly, are the creator's very own.[35]

However, if God's judgments are inscrutable, then how can las Casas also know if the destruction of Indians is not part of God's judgment?

Las Casas offers a third counterargument centering on original sin. He states that everyone is 'guilty by reason of original sin'.[36] In other words, both Europeans and Indians are automatically deserving of God's punishment, even death, on the basis of original sin. Las Casas mitigates this only by arguing that this does not apply to crimes against secular rulers. That is to say, all people are not automatically held guilty of punishment for crimes against the state. For las Casas, '[a] man ought not to be punished for a crime he did not commit'.[37] But this contradicts his immediately previous claims that everyone in a 'justly' condemned city deserves punishment.

The fourth counterargument offered by las Casas explains that God knows things about people that we do not. For example, he might know that the people he commanded to be killed would commit some grave sin later, and so their killing was actually an act of mercy. Yet, later las Casas qualifies this stance by referring to the 'confused opinion of the doctors' concerning whether soldiers are obliged to divide the guilty from the innocent once a city has been condemned for just cause.[38]

---

34. Las Casas, *In Defense of the Indians*, p. 195.
35. Las Casas, *In Defense of the Indians*, p. 195.
36. Las Casas, *In Defense of the Indians*, p. 196.
37. Las Casas, *In Defense of the Indians*, p. 196.
38. Las Casas, *In Defense of the Indians*, p. 201.

Ecclesiasticus 34 and Sinful Gains

According to his own biography, las Casas was initially moved to his abolitionist stance by this chapter of Ecclesiasticus.[39] Its most important passage on this topic states:

> If one sacrifices from what has been wrongfully obtained, the offering is blemished; the gifts of the lawless are not acceptable. The Most High is not pleased with the offerings of the ungodly; and he is not propitiated for sins by a multitude of sacrifices. Like one who kills a son before his father's eyes is the man who offers a sacrifice from the property of the poor. The bread of the needy is the life of the poor; whoever deprives them of it is a man of blood. To take away a neighbor's living is to murder him; to deprive an employee of his wages is to shed blood (Sir. 34.18-22).

Las Casas interpreted this to mean that Spaniards were wrong to take away the property of the natives.

Yet, las Casas was very selective in how he used Ecclesiasticus, a book that also allows slavery, as evidenced by the following passage:

> Fodder and a stick and burdens for an ass; bread and discipline and work for a servant. Set your slave to work, and you will find rest; leave his hands idle, and he will seek liberty. Yoke and thong will bow the neck, and for a wicked servant there are racks and tortures. Put him to work, that he may not be idle, for idleness teaches much evil. Set him to work, as is fitting for him, and if he does not obey, make his fetters heavy. Do not act immoderately toward anybody, and do nothing without discretion. If you have a servant, let him be as yourself, because you have bought him with blood. If you have a servant, treat him as a brother, for as your own soul you will need him. If you ill-treat him, and he leaves and runs away, which way will you go to seek him? (Sir 33.24-31).

Despite some of the sentiments that seem to idealize equality (e.g., 'treat him as a brother'), the very idea of servitude contradicts the idea of brotherhood. The passage allows torture for 'wicked' and disobedient slaves ('if he does not obey, make his fetters heavy'). Furthermore, a utilitarian reason is given for any good treatment ('you will need him...runs away').

Curiously, Plato's *Republic* also indicates that taking weapons captured from other Greeks is forbidden because 'we shall fear that there is pollution [μίασμα] in bringing such offerings to the temple from our kind unless in a case where the god bids otherwise'.[40] Thus, the original context may have

---

39. See las Casas, *The Only Way*, p. 188. For a standard introduction and commentary to this book, see Patrick Skehan and Alexander A. Di Lella, *The Wisdom of Ben Sira* (AB, 39; New York: Doubleday, 1987).

40. Plato, *Republic* 5.16 (Shorey, LCL). See also comments in Robert Parker, *Miasma: Pollution and Purification in Early Greek Religion* (New York: Oxford University Press, 1983), p. 114.

involved some sort of ritual pollution. That ritual pollution was simply an idiom for what Greeks considered to be just and unjust offerings in the aftermath of a war.

Matthew 10.5-15 and Peaceful Missionaries

According to las Casas's *The Only Way*, the model of peaceful missionary activity is enshrined in some of the instructions given by Jesus himself in this passage:

> These twelve Jesus sent out, charging them, 'Go nowhere among the Gentiles, and enter no town of the Samaritans, but go rather to the lost sheep of the house of Israel. And preach as you go, saying, "The kingdom of heaven is at hand". Heal the sick, raise the dead, cleanse lepers, cast out demons. You received without paying, give without pay. Take no gold, nor silver, nor copper in your belts, no bag for your journey, nor two tunics, nor sandals, nor a staff; for the laborer deserves his food. And whatever town or village you enter, find out who is worthy in it, and stay with him until you depart. As you enter the house, salute it. And if the house is worthy, let your peace come upon it; but if it is not worthy, let your peace return to you. And if any one will not receive you or listen to your words, shake off the dust from your feet as you leave that house or town. Truly, I say to you, it shall be more tolerable on the day of judgment for the land of Sodom and Gomorrah than for that town' (Mt. 10.5-15).

This passage would definitely support las Casas's indictment of Spanish policy toward the Indians. Jesus enjoins completely peaceful means of proselytizing by his apostles, and adds that any rejection cannot be met with violence, but rather with a simple departure after shaking off the dust from their feet. Missionaries are to give their services for free, and take nothing from the prospective converts. This would certainly prohibit the Spanish from exploiting the gold and other resources of the Indians.

Sepulveda does not address this passage very directly. He mentions Mt. 10.12 only in an attempt to refute the idea that war is always unjustified.[41] For Sepulveda, there are many undesirable experiences, such as hunger and poverty, which may be acceptable when done for pious reasons or for a greater good. Yet, it remains the case that Sepulveda seems to be avoiding the problems that Mt. 10.5-15 would cause him.

Although this passage offers strong support for the position of las Casas, it is not completely without problems. First, in *The Only Way*, he does not quote the entire pericope, but only vv. 8-12, and then vv. 13-16 a few sentences later.[42] Given that las Casas elsewhere insists that passages must be

---

41. Sepulveda, *Democrates segundo*, p. 4.
42. Las Casas, *The Only Way*, pp. 70-71.

applied to the people and territories described in the passage (e.g., genocide in Deuteronomy applies to Canaanites, and not people outside of Canaan), he omits the very part of the passage in Matthew that restricts the instructions to missionaries going only to Israel: 'Go nowhere among the Gentiles' (Mt. 10.5). The gentiles would include the Indians, and so Sepulveda could argue that these instructions would not necessarily apply to them.

Las Casas also does not mention that Jesus had much more violent instructions later in the same chapter—Mt. 10.34: 'Do not think that I have come to bring peace on earth; I have not come to bring peace, but a sword'. Moreover, even in the part of Matthew 10 las Casas does cite, Christianity is not free of violence. Rather, Jesus can be interpreted to advocate 'deferred violence'. Those who reject the message will be punished even more harshly than Sodom (v. 15), a city whose population was burned (Gen. 19.24). Shaking the dust off the feet, therefore, becomes not a pacifistic gesture but a curse.

Luke 14.16-24 and Forced Conversions

Sepulveda cites this parable to show that Christ allowed force to be used to convert people. In the parable a man gave a banquet, but most of the people invited refused to come. When the master learns about the refusals, he orders his slaves to '[g]o out to the highways and hedges, and compel people to come in, that my house may be filled' (Lk. 14.23). This directive uses the word *compelle* in Latin (*obligalos* in Spanish), which Sepulveda interprets as referring to physical force.[43] Accordingly, Sepulveda views Lk. 14.23 as justifying the use of physical force to convert Indians.

Here, it is las Casas who has grave difficulty in explaining the seeming use of force:

> Now by the words of the parable, 'Force them to come in', Christ means that, immediately by himself, or through angels or men, he usually moves and attracts to himself in an intellectual fashion and, as it were, compels by a visible or invisible miracle those who do not know his truth, yet without exercising any force on their will... Christ wished to signify not external but persuasive violence... Now God either does this himself or through angels or men, by depicting the sufferings of hell, the eternal damnation of the soul, and other troubles of the present life and the life to come. The command 'Force them to come in' is carried out in these ways, that is: 'Persuade them increasingly and motivate them to be converted through threats of this type...'[44]

---

43. Sepulveda, *Democrates segundo*, p. 70; Sepulveda actually has *compellae*.
44. Las Casas, *In Defense of the Indians*, p. 271.

First, notice that even in las Casas's own explanation, 'force them', can mean threats of physical harm (in hell).

From a more modern academic viewpoint, it is still unclear what the crucial Greek word ἀναγκάζω (*anagkazō*), translated as 'force' or 'compel' meant in Lk. 14.23. Usage in the New Testament shows that it can refer to forcing, even through violent means, persons to perform certain actions against their will. Thus, Acts speaks of Paul's former persecution of the Church:

> And I did so in Jerusalem; I not only shut up many of the saints in prison, by authority from the chief priests, but when they were put to death I cast my vote against them. And I punished them often in all the synagogues and forced them to blaspheme; and in raging fury against them, I persecuted them even to foreign cities (Acts 26.10-11).

The phrase 'forced them to blaspheme' uses *anagkazō* in the context of other violent acts against Christians.

At the same time, there clearly are instances where the word does not have a more violent or strong connotation, as when Jesus urges the disciples to get into boats (Mk 6.45). Accordingly, we do have evidence of both a (1) strong meaning allowing even physical force and (2) a weak meaning that corresponds more to our 'urge', 'persuade', or even 'hurry along'.

However, the existence of a strong and weak sense does not really settle which of these is meant in Lk. 14.23, and modern commentators often do not give a good reason for choosing one or the other in this passage. BDAG just places the passage in the category of 'weakened' meanings.[45] Joseph Fitzmyer asserts that 'it means merely that the poor and others will understandably resist in their modesty such an invitation until they are gently taken and led into the house',[46] although he provides no explanation other than passages where it can be interpreted that way.

Since it can be interpreted either way, then citing passages with a weakened meaning is no better than citing passages with the strong meaning. This is especially the case because the parallel passage in Matthew has no trouble having the master of the feast use violence, though this time to throw guests out: 'He said to him, "Friend, how did you get in here without a wedding garment?" And he was speechless. Then the king said to the attendants, "Bind him hand and foot, and cast him into the outer darkness; there men will weep and gnash their teeth"' (Mt. 22.12-13; cf. Lk. 16.16).[47]

---

45. BDAG, p. 60b: 'weakened strongly *urge/invite, urge upon, press upon*' (emphasis in original).

46. Joseph A. Fitzmyer, *The Gospel according to Luke X–XXIV* (AB, 28A; Garden City, NY: Doubleday, 1985), p. 1057.

47. Illaria L.E. Ramelli, 'Luke 16.16: The Good News for God's Kingdom is Proclaimed and Everyone Is Forced into It', *JBL* 27 (2008), pp. 737-58.

In any case, both las Casas and Sepulveda could also find support in the interpretive history of the passage. Sepulveda, for instance, appealed to St Augustine's letter against the followers of Donatus, a bishop of Carthage eventually branded a heretic.[48] Augustine explicitly rejected the idea that Lk. 14.23 was speaking of persuasion through miracles, and he clearly saw it as allowing force because in his day 'the Church wields greater power, so that she might not only invite, but even compel men to embrace what is good'.[49] For support Augustine quotes Ps. 72.11 ('May all kings fall down before him, all nations serve him!'). In a letter to Vicentius, Augustine finds a parallel to Lk. 14.23 when Paul 'was compelled by the great violence with which Christ coerced him, to know the truth (Acts 9.3-7)'.[50]

Las Casas countered that those instances in Augustine, while allowing the use of force, are referring to heretics, and not to those who have never believed.[51] For las Casas, force is warranted when one reneges on a loyalty oath to Christ, which is what heretics are essentially doing. Indians, on the other hand, have never believed, and so they cannot be classed as heretics. Yet, Paul was not a believer when he was forced into Christianity. Moreover, las Casas contradicts this distinction by allowing the perpetual enslavement of Jews, who also have never believed. He reasons that 'because of the crime they [Jews] committed in killing our Lord Jesus Christ they are by law servants of the Church'.[52]

More importantly, las Casas contradicts his interpretation of the Wedding Feast when he tries to prove that heretics are subject to the use of force in order to punish them or to bring them back to the Church. Las Casas, in fact, cites the very same passage in Augustine cited by Sepulveda to show that the Church had now entered a second period in which Christian kings could enforce ecclesiastical directives against heretics.[53] Note these remarks by las Casas: 'After the kings of the world...were converted to Christ and thus the Church began to have believing rulers as sons and subjects it began to use their services for punishing and forcing heretics by laws and arms'.[54] However, las Casas does not seem to realize that he has just contradicted and

---

48. Sepulveda, *Democrates segundo*, p. 70.
49. Augustine, *Letters* 173.10 (NPNF[1], I, p. 547); Latin (PL 33.757): 'quod utique quanto magis impletur, tanto maiore utitur Ecclesia potestate, ut non solum invitet, sed etiam cogat ad bonum'.
50. Augustine, *Letters* 93.5 (NPNF[1], I, p. 383); Latin (PL 33.323): 'ad cognoscendam et tenendam veritatem, magna violentia Christi cogentis esse compulsum (Act. IX, 3-7)'.
51. Las Casas, *In Defense of the Indians*, p. 117.
52. Las Casas, *In Defense of the Indians*, p. 117.
53. Las Casas, *In Defense of the Indians*, p. 306. See further Daniel E. Doyle, *The Bishop as Disciplinarian in the Letters of St Augustine* (Patristic Studies, 4; New York: Peter Lang, 2002).
54. Las Casas, *In Defense of the Indians*, p. 307.

undermined his argument that the parable of the Wedding Feast did not refer to the use of physical force to accomplish its purposes.

In short, las Casas did not necessarily have an exegetical advantage over Sepulveda in Lk. 14.23. The Greek word *anagkazō* could literally mean to force someone to do something against their will, and there were doctors of the Church who saw it the same way.[55] Ironically, John Calvin, the Protestant reformer, would have agreed with Sepulveda's views, including the propriety of an appeal to Augustine's view of the Donatists to illuminate this passage.[56] Las Casas clearly contradicted himself because he accepts that the parable refers to the use of physical force in one instance, and denies that it refers to physical force in another instance.

1 Corinthians 5.12-13: Who's to Judge?

In this passage, Paul discusses the propriety of expelling a man who has had sexual relations with his father's wife (apparently the stepmother). 1 Corinthians 5.12-13 ends with these remarks by Paul: 'For what have I to do with judging outsiders? Is it not those inside the church whom you are to judge? God judges those outside. "Drive out the wicked person from among you"'. Las Casas remarks: 'All doctors, Greek or Latin, sacred or otherwise, interpret these words of Paul to mean that, as a rule, the Church cannot judge unbelievers who have never accepted the Christian faith'.[57] For Sepulveda, Paul's statements should be paraphrased as follows:

> What benefit is it to judge in vain the customs of infidels whom I cannot correct, when they don't obey, like Christians, of their own will nor against their will, as long as the Church does not possess the power to do so? Nonetheless, they will not escape the judgment of God.[58]

According to Sepulveda, Paul is simply alluding to cases where the Church is not yet able to correct outsiders. The Church cannot be expected to judge non-Christians when it does not have the police power to do so, as was the case in the Roman empire where Christians did not have such power.[59] However, once the Church gains the power of enforcement, then it becomes the instrument of God's judgment.

---

55. See las Casas, *The Only Way*, p. 231.
56. John Calvin, *Commentary on Matthew, Mark, and Luke*. Online: www.ccel.org/ccel/calvin/calcom32.ii.xxxii.html.
57. Las Casas, *In Defense of the Indians*, p. 63.
58. Sepulveda, *Democrates segundo*, p. 44: 'Nam quod Paulus ad se pertinere negat de ijs qui foris sunt iudicare hunc habet intellectum. Quid me oportet frustra de moribus infidelium iudicare? quos nec sua voluntate parentes, ut Christianos nec inuitos viribus Ecclesiae non suppetentibus corrigere possum, qui tamen dei iudicium non effugiunt.'
59. Sepulveda, *Democrates segundo*, p. 45.

To this end, Sepulveda appeals to St Augustine, who, in his letter to Vicentius, says that the Church should 'correct those it can correct, and tolerate those it cannot correct'.[60] As we have seen, las Casas also accepts the idea of two historical periods for the church, with the second one being marked by the appearance of kings who could enforce the will of the Church against heretics.

Although Sepulveda does not cite 1 Cor. 6.2-3, that passage indicates that Christians can judge not only 'the world', but also angels: 'Do you not know that the saints will judge the world? And if the world is to be judged by you, are you incompetent to try trivial cases? Do you not know that we are to judge angels?' If so, then we again have passages from Pauline letters that can be used in contradictory ways. Although Sepulveda may be stretching the meaning of 1 Cor. 5.12, other passages and interpretive traditions could be found to support his view.

Galatians 3.28 and Equality for All

Las Casas uses Gal. 3.28, not so much to prove that slavery is immoral or should no longer exist, but rather to show that all people have an equal opportunity to receive the Gospel.[61] For las Casas, Christians must preach to the free just as they do to the slave. Since Christians do not maltreat free persons when they preach the Gospel, Christians ought not do that with slaves. Sepulveda does not address this text directly. However, he argues elsewhere that pacification may be necessary before any preaching can even be done. Since pacification is applied equally to the slave and free members of Indian societies, then he may not see himself as violating Gal. 3.28. As we have seen, Gal. 3.28 is probably more about giving slave and free people the opportunity to be part of the Christian community than it is about their status in society. Being Christian will not erase a slave status.

Ephesians 6.5 and 1 Peter 2.18

Sepulveda appeals to 1 Pet. 2.18-20 and Eph. 6.5 to prove that God commands slaves to be obedient to masters.[62] 1 Peter 2.18-20 reads as follows:

> Servants, be submissive to your masters with all respect, not only to the kind and gentle but also to the overbearing. For one is approved if, mindful of God, he endures pain while suffering unjustly. For what credit is it, if when you do wrong and are beaten for it you take it patiently? But if when you do right and suffer for it you take it patiently, you have God's approval.

---

60. Sepulveda, *Democrates segundo*, p. 46: 'corrigit quos potest, tolerat quos corrigere non valet'.
61. Las Casas, *In Defense of the Indians*, p. 93.
62. Sepulveda, *Democrates segundo*, p. 98.

This passage is significant for a number of reasons. First, it not only endorses slavery, but it commands slaves to obey even cruel masters.

Second, a reason given for this command is that suffering is good if it enhances the name of Christ. Equally, and more importantly, Sepulveda notes that it is Peter, the prince of the Apostles (*princeps apostolorum*) and the first Pope in Catholic tradition, who is giving these instructions. Sepulveda also remarks that the Church itself and the popes hold slaves by pontifical right (*iure pontificio approbantibus*).[63] Sepulveda adds that these passages 'don't say to manumit slaves, liberate slaves, such as would be proper, if divine law condemned human slavery'.[64] And, indeed, even las Casas did not deny that slavery was condoned in the biblical texts. Las Casas accepted that the Jews could be condemned to servitude by the Church.

Las Casas vs. Sepulveda: An Innovation?

Commenting on the famous debate about slavery and just war between las Casas and Sepulveda, Lewis Hanke remarked that '[f]or the first time, and probably for the last, a colonizing nation organized a formal inquiry into the justice of the methods used to extend its empire'.[65] But pondering the justifiability of war did not need Christianity at all. As Ste Croix acutely observed: 'even the early Roman republic had a doctrine of *iustum bellum*, derived from the principle of fetial law; that no war was acceptable to the Roman gods unless it was a defensive war'.[66]

In fact, we can trace such discussions at least to the time of Plato's *Republic*:

> 'But again, how will our soldiers conduct themselves toward enemies?' 'In what respect?' 'First, in the matter of making slaves of the defeated, do you think it is right [δοκεῖ δίκαιον] for Greeks to reduce Greek cities to slavery, or rather that, so far as they are able, they should not suffer any other city to do so, but should accustom Greeks to spare Greeks, foreseeing the danger of enslavement by the barbarians?' 'Sparing them is wholly and altogether better', said he. 'They are not, then, themselves to own Greek slaves, either, and they should advise other Greeks not to?' 'By all means', he said; 'at any rate in that way they would be more likely to turn against the barbarians and keep their hands from one another'.[67]

---

63. Sepulveda, *Democrates segundo*, p. 98.
64. Sepulveda, *Democrates segundo*, p. 98: 'non dicit servos manu mittite, servos liberate, quod oportebat si lex divina servitutem humanam condemnaret'.
65. Hanke, *All Mankind Is One*, p. xi.
66. Ste Croix, 'Early Christian Attitudes', p. 36.
67. Plato, *Republic* 5.469e-470a (Shorey, LCL).

The discussion goes on to consider whether it is just to take possessions away from the vanquished dead soldiers. While Plato prohibited the enslavement of other Greeks, that custom is not really distinct from later Christian prohibitions against enslaving other Christians, though not Muslims, captured in war. Both of these issues discussed by Plato (enslavement and dispossession) became the same issues in the Spanish conquest.

Just as there was an assembly of scholars in Valladolid to debate the issue of the enslavement of the Indians, there was also an assembly in ancient Syracuse (Sicily) to discuss what to do with the Athenians whom they had just defeated. According to Diodorus Siculus (first century BCE), there was a three-way debate, with a man named Diocles arguing that the defeated Athenians should be tortured to death. Another man, named Hermocrates, argued for moderation. Finally, an elder named Nikolaus, who had lost two sons in the war with the Athenians, gave an extended speech outlining reasons for mercy. In part, Nikolaus says:

> Good it is indeed that the deity involves in unexpected disasters those who begin an unjust war [ἀδίκου πολέμου]... Do not, therefore, begrudge our country the opportunity of being acclaimed by all mankind, because it surpassed the Athenians not only in feats of arms but also in humanity [φιλανθρωπίᾳ]... [T]he spirits of civilized men are gripped, I believe, most perhaps by mercy, because of the sympathy [ὁμοπάθειαν] that nature has implanted in all.[68]

Nikolaus's arguments, though ultimately unsuccessful with the Syracusans, demonstrate a well-developed philosophical tradition that thought deeply about what practices in war should be deemed just.

While possessions and dispossessions figured largely in debates about slavery in the New World, there were at least some Greek groups who had already realized that possessions were at the root of a lot of human conflict. The Cyrenaics, a Greek school of philosophers, for instance, renounced 'all that for which men fight', meaning gold, silver, and other similar commodities.[69] Jesus, of course, would counsel something similar to the rich man (Mt. 19.21). However, we do not hear of scholars praising the Cyrenaics for introducing or promoting some enlightened view of possessions.

More importantly, the Valladolid debate ended indecisively. Many of the judges did not write their opinions for years. Las Casas thought the judges agreed with him, though he had to admit that official measures concerning the Indians were not well executed. Sepulveda reported that all the judges, except one, agreed with him.[70] The only preserved opinion is that of a man

---

68. Diodorus Siculus, *Historia* 13.20-27 (Oldfather, LCL).
69. Bainton, *Christian Attitudes*, p. 29. Bainton spells it as 'Cyreniacs'.
70. Hanke, *All Mankind Is One*, p. 113.

named Dr Anaya, who seemed to approve of the Conquest as a method of Christianization. Anaya also believed that stopping the Indians' sins against nature could be a worthy motive for the Conquest.[71]

This indecisive outcome is significant, because if one compares Sepulveda with las Casas, it is clear that las Casas had no better grounds for appealing to the Bible than did Sepulveda. Sepulveda was able to find very strong support for the notions that God could command or endorse enslavement and the wholesale destruction of entire peoples. While Sepulveda's book was not authorized for publication by the Church, his policies did hold sway for centuries.

Summary

Bartolomé de las Casas is rightfully known as a champion of indigenous rights. Yet, I concur with Davis's remarks: '[w]hile Las Casas challenged the legality of enslaving Indians, and eventually enslaving Africans, he never questioned the justice of slavery itself'.[72] Indeed, while las Casas is regarded as a hero in the area of Indian rights, he also endorsed what would qualify as war crimes, judging by the United Nations standards. More importantly, even if las Casas eventually rejected enslaving Africans, he did so by reinterpreting biblical texts in a manner that was no more faithful to the original sense than what Sepulveda was doing.

---

71. Hanke, *All Mankind Is One*, p. 114.
72. Davis, *Inhuman Bondage*, p. 355 n. 49.

Chapter 11

THE SIXTEENTH CENTURY: PROTESTANTS UNBOUND?

While Catholic clerics and theologians might garner the most attention in the debate about slavery in the sixteenth century, we cannot omit some of the major Protestant figures of this time. This is important because often their views are not even addressed by historians who credit Christianity with abolishing slavery. Comparing Protestant figures to the popes in the previous chapters is also important because the major Protestant figures did not live in societies that had much direct involvement in the New World slave trade. Yet, there were other types of slavery in their midst, and they also were aware of the historical events in the New World.

Martin Luther: To Hell with Equality

Martin Luther (1483–1546) is widely acknowledged to be the father of Protestantism. Briefly, the posting of Luther's Ninety-Five Theses on the door of the Castle Church at Wittenberg in 1517 marks the beginning of the Protestant movement, even though it was mainly a protest against indulgences, and had no intention of forming a new Church.[1] At the same time, some Christian apologists pass over Luther's views on slavery in silence, while extolling his views on religious 'liberty'.

One of the clearest expositions of Luther's views on slavery comes in his response to the Swabian peasants, who had written a manifesto in 1525 titled *The Twelve Articles*. These peasants complained about tax burdens and other oppressive practices by landowners that were impoverishing them. In particular, the third of the twelve articles issues this protest:

> Third, it has until now been the custom of the lords to own us as their property. This is deplorable for Christ redeemed and bought us all with his precious blood, the lowliest shepherd and the greatest lord, with no exceptions. Thus, the

---

1. For basic biographies of Luther, see Walther von Loewenisch, *Martin Luther: The Man and his Work* (trans. Lawrence W. Denef; Minneapolis: Augsburg, 1982); Heiko A. Oberman, *Luther: Man between God and the Devil* (trans. Eileen Walliser-Schwarzbart; New York: Image Books, 1992).

Bible proves that we are free and want to be free... Nor do we doubt that you, as true and just Christians, will gladly release us from bondage or prove to us from the gospel that we must be your property.[2]

Luther's response illuminates well his view of slavery and freedom, and bears repeating at length:

> You assert that no one is to be a serf [*Leibeigener*] of anyone else, because Christ made us all free. That is making Christian freedom a completely physical matter. Did not Abraham [Gen. 17.23] and other patriarchs and prophets have slaves [*Leibeigene*]? Read what St. Paul teaches about servants [*Knechte*], who, at that time, were all slaves. This article, therefore, absolutely contradicts the gospel. It proposes robbery, for it suggests that every man should take his body away from his lord, even though his body is the lord's property. A slave can be a Christian, and have Christian freedom, in the same way that a prisoner or a sick man is a Christian, and yet not free. This article would make all men equal, and turn the spiritual kingdom of Christ into a worldly, external kingdom; and that is impossible. A worldly kingdom cannot exist without an inequality [*Ungleichheit*] of persons, some being free, some being imprisoned, some lords, some subjects, etc.; and St. Paul says in Galatians that in Christ the lord and servant are equal.[3]

It is clear that both the Swabian articles and Luther's response are speaking about slavery in the sense of persons who are the property of others. In fact, Luther declares that freedom is robbery because the very body of the peasants is owned by their lords. Furthermore, Luther advocated the killing of some of these peasants who wanted their liberty. It is clear, therefore, that Luther was understanding slavery very much as most Christians (and Stoics) did before him. Equality was equality in spirit or in equal opportunity to be saved from sin rather than from physical servitude.

John Calvin: I Do Mean Slaves

John Calvin (1509–1564) is usually paired with Luther as one of the founders of Protestantism. Born into a Catholic family in France but later associated with Geneva, Calvin was probably more influential than Luther in attracting

---

2. I quote the text of *The Twelve Articles* in Peter Blickle, *The Revolution of 1525: The German Peasants' War from a New Perspective* (trans. Thomas A. Brady and H.C. Erik Midelfort; Baltimore: The Johns Hopkins University Press, 1985), p. 197.

3. Theodore G. Tappert, *Selected Writings of Martin Luther 1517–1546* (4 vols.; Philadelphia: Fortress Press, 1967), III, p. 339. For the German text, I depend on Martin Luther, *Ausgewählte Schriften* (ed. Karin Bornkamm and Gerhard Ebeling; 5 vols.; Frankfurt: Insel Verlag, 1982), IV, pp. 125-26. Luther's Bible translation uses 'Knechte' in Gen. 17.23, while Luther (*Ausgewählte Schriften*, IV, p. 125) uses 'Leibeigene' when referring to Abraham's slaves.

converts to Protestantism.[4] Stark, in fact, remarks that 'Calvinism really outdid Lutheranism' because its converts were attracted by persuasion rather than by royal edicts that might have declared Lutheranism the religion of a particular kingdom or state.[5]

Calvin's views of slavery are sprinkled throughout his writings. One instance is in his commentary on Eph. 6.5:

> His exhortation to servants is so much the more earnest, on account of the hardship and bitterness of their condition, which renders it more difficult to be endured. And he does not speak merely of outward obedience, but says more about fear willingly rendered; for it is a very rare occurrence to find one who willingly yields himself to the control of another. The servants (δοῦλοι) whom he immediately addresses were not hired servants, like those of the present day, but slaves, such as were in ancient times, whose slavery was perpetual, unless, through the favor of their masters, they obtained freedom,—whom their masters bought with money, that they might impose upon them the most degrading employments, and might, with the full protection of the law, exercise over them the power of life and death. To such he says, obey your masters, lest they should vainly imagine that carnal freedom had been procured for them by the gospel.[6]

Unlike some modern scholars who wish to mitigate the nature of slavery in the New Testament, Calvin does not shy away from describing it as a degrading and harsh condition.[7] Moreover, he faithfully follows at least some of the New Testament authors who state that slaves should obey their masters regardless of how harsh or cruel those masters are. Calvin leaves manumission entirely to the good will of masters. Accordingly, abolition of slavery might never have occurred unless masters agreed.

Jean Bodin, the Pragmatist

While Rodney Stark does not address the teachings of Luther and Calvin on slavery, he does credit at least one Protestant, Jean Bodin, with advancing the cause of abolitionism. Jean Bodin (1530–1596) is the famed political theorist who also influenced the American Plymouth separatist puritans. While the views of Luther and Calvin are easy to discern, it requires more effort to reveal the nuanced views of Bodin. Let us begin with Stark's remarks:

---

4. For basic biographies of Calvin, I depend on William J. Bouwsma, *John Calvin: A Sixteenth Century Portrait* (New York: Oxford University Press, 1988); François Wendel, *Calvin: The Origins and Development of his Religious Thought* (trans. Philip Mairet; repr., Grand Rapids: Baker Books, 1997 [1963]).

5. Stark, *For the Glory of God*, p. 95.

6. John Calvin, *Commentary on Ephesians*. Online: www.ccel.org/ccel/calvin/calcom41.iv.vii.ii.html.

7. See also comments in Bouwsma, *John Calvin*, pp. 194-96.

> A consensus quickly developed that slavery was both sinful and illegal—Jean Bodin, that mortal enemy of witches, thundered that slavery was 'A thing most pernicious and dangerous', and that having been cast off, it should not be revived.[8]

Stark implies that biblical teachings about slavery were responsible for seeing slavery as a sin.

Yet, a closer look at Stark's quotations of Bodin reveals that he has not read Bodin directly at all. Stark refers to Bodin's French work, *Le six livres de la République* (*The Six Books of the Commonwealth* or *The Six Books of the Republic*), as his source for Bodin's description of slavery as '[a] thing most pernicious and dangerous'.[9] But Stark's quotation of Bodin is in English, and so we expect him to provide the English edition used, unless the English translation is Stark's own.

Second, Stark gives no page numbers for the French edition he cites so that we can verify his quotation and view the context. He gives no year for the French edition he is citing, which is confusing because there were a number of editions of Bodin's work that had some changes. In any case, the phrase '[a] thing most pernicious and dangerous' is found in the standard English translation published by Harvard University Press, which Stark should have credited as a source.[10] Stark apparently is using an intermediate source, Blackburn's *The Making of New World Slavery* which he lists in his bibliography.[11] Blackburn offers this exact translation, and Blackburn explicitly references the Harvard edition of Bodin.

Scholars of Bodin's writings recognize that his thought underwent an evolution, and the Latin editions that Bodin himself wrote are not mere translations of the earlier French ones, but rather sometimes rework and change earlier concepts and emphases. For example, the 1586 Latin edition does not have the part about 'having been cast off, it should not be revived' in the corresponding French passage.[12] Instead, Bodin fully anticipates that slavery will return despite his wishes:

> [N]ot for that I should desire that slavery long since taken away out of our Commonweale, to be thereinto againe restored; but that forasmuch as the force and boldnesse of men is so farre broken out, as that we see servitude and slavery by little and little to creepe in and to return againe; it might be forseene

---

8. Stark, *For the Glory of God*, p. 305.
9. Stark, *For the Glory of God*, p. 409 n. 70.
10. Jean Bodin, *The Six Bookes of a Commonweale* (ed. Kenneth Douglas McRae; Cambridge, MA: Harvard University Press, 1962). Unless noted otherwise, my English translations are from this edition.
11. Bodin, *Commonweale*, p. 44.
12. For a comparison of these versions, see Bodin, *Commonweale*, p. A28-A38.

and provided for, that such slaves might not hereafter bee more hardly used than that the state and condition of man requireth, and might also have their certaine place an order in the citie.[13]

Bodin does say that slavery is 'pernicious' (French: *pernicieux*), but not for the reasons (because it is 'sinful and illegal') Stark attributes to Bodin.[14] Rather, Bodin has very practical reasons for saying slavery is pernicious and dangerous. Just prior to the statement quoted by Stark, Bodin enumerates many examples of how slavery can cause political instability. Here is the relevant section:

> ...seeing it is proved by the examples of so many worlds of years, so many inconveniences of rebellions, servile warres, conspiracies, eversions and chaunges to have happened unto Commonweals by slaves; so many murthers, cruelties, and destestable villanies to have been committed upon the persons of slaves by their lords and masters: who can doubt to affirm it to be a thing most pernitious and daungerous to have them brought into a Commonweale; or having cast them off to receive them again?[15]

Bodin may have wanted to be more humane to these slaves, but there is no reference here to abolishing slavery because it is a sin. The reason given is mainly practical and political—i.e., numerous mistreated and unhappy slaves in any society can lead to political instability.

Similarly, Bodin's account of why slavery was nearly eradicated from France supplies mainly economic reasons, not theological ones. For example, in explaining the diminution of slaves in Europe around 1300, Bodin does mention that 'by Christian lawes men might no more sell themselves', but he does not specify what was 'Christian' about those laws other than they were issued by 'Christian princes'.[16] As we have seen, Solon issued similar laws against selling oneself for a debt in ancient Greece. When elaborating on specific rationales, Bodin says:

> But it is more than 400 years agoe, since that Fraunce suffered in it any true slaves. For as for that which we read in our histories, that Lewes Hutin, who came to the crowne in the yeare 1313...set at libertie all slaves for money, to defray the charges of his warres.[17]

---

13. Bodin, *Commonweale*, pp. 387-88.
14. For the French text, I depend on Jean Bodin, *De la République ou traité du gouvernement* (repr., New York: Elibron Classics, 2005 [1756]), p. 93.
15. Bodin, *Commonweale*, p. 44. This passage should be familiar to Stark because it is also found in Blackburn (*The Making of New World Slavery*, p. 61), which is cited by Stark in his bibliography.
16. Bodin, *Commonweale*, p. 40.
17. Bodin, *Commonweale*, p. 41. Lewes Hutin is Louis the Stubborn, also known as Louis X. Similarly, in the case of England, Bailey ('Slavery in the London Area in 1086',

224 *Slavery, Abolitionism, and the Ethics of Biblical Scholarship*

Slaves could be used for public projects by a king when free men were at war, or liberty could be a price for military service when a king no longer could afford to pay a whole army. Bodin explains how many subsequent French kings followed this example. Bodin does not say that some great sense of guilt overcame these French kings at all. Instead, Bodin himself says that it was monetary motives that prompted Louis to act.

To be fair, Bodin does appeal to religious and biblical reasons to uphold some of his own seemingly anti-slavery statements. But even those are not quite what Stark would have us believe. For example, Stark emphasizes that Islam was inferior to Christianity in its attitudes toward slavery. Stark further states that '[t]he end of Islamic slaving (although it still continues on a minor scale) was the direct result of abolition in the west'.[18]

Yet, Bodin seemingly thinks that Islam should receive equal or more credit in any diminution in Medieval slavery. Note Bodin's statement:

> But after that Idolatrie began to decay, and the Christians religion to encrease, the multitude of slaves began also to diminish; and yet much more after the publishing of the law of Mahomet, who set at libertie all of them of his religion. To the imitation of whome, the Christians also so frankly set at libertie their slaves.[19]

Islam, in fact, has been credited with participating in some liberation movements in Latin America. In Brazil, for example, it was Muslims, called Malês, who led a slave revolt in 1835. In all fairness, the Malês were intent on enslaving mulattos they captured, but that would make them no less abolitionists than the Israelites who escaped Egyptian slavery only to enslave the Canaanites. The point remains that Islam could provide a liberatory motive for its adherents. Many Malês had been Muslims in the African lands of their birth. João José Reis, an historian who produced a detailed study of this rebellion, notes:

> Slaves and freedmen flocked to Islam in search of spiritual comfort and hope… The Koran's texts were especially appealing because of their sympathy for the discriminated, the exiled, the persecuted, and the enslaved.[20]

While the Muslims were not the majority of the population, they had tremendous influence in the revolt.[21] Amulets were found on the bodies of some of the rebels with Quranic references (e.g., 'In the name of God the

---

p. 79) argues '[t]he decline and ending of slavery in England seems more likely to have been for economic than ethical or religious reasons'.

18. Stark, *For the Glory of God*, p. 304.
19. Bodin, *Commonweale*, p. 40.
20. João José Reis, *Slave Rebellion in Brazil: The Muslim Uprising of 1835 in Bahia* (trans. Arthur Brakel; Baltimore: The Johns Hopkins University Press, 1993), p. 110.
21. Reis, *Slave Rebellion in Brazil*, especially pp. 93-111.

merciful...').[22] In other words, Reis, the modern historian, agrees with Bodin, who, though a Christian, saw this liberatory power in Islam in the sixteenth century.

Finally, while Bodin may have recognized the cruelty and inhumanity of many slave-holding practices, he does not advocate the abolition of all slavery. In fact, he uses the Bible to issue this directive: 'For as concerning debtors, if they be not able to pay, God his law commandeth them to be adiudged to their creditors for seven years, but yet not into perpetuall bondage'.[23] Yet, the *Code of Hammurabi* 117 required three years of service in some cases, and so there is really no advance represented by Bodin on this issue.[24] In short, Bodin accepts the type of temporary slavery described in Exodus 21, and it is perpetual slavery to which he objects.

Summary

The major Protestant figures of the 1500s, when New World slavery became firmly established, give little indication that they saw slavery as incompatible with the teachings of Christ. On the contrary, both Luther and Calvin thought that inequality was essential to good governance. Luther thought that slaves who wanted freedom were robbers because their bodies rightfully belonged to the master. Jean Bodin, whom Stark credits with the idea that slavery is a sin, reveals practical socio-economic reasons for any stance against slavery. Moreover, Bodin credits Islam equally, or more than, Christianity with advancing the cause of abolition.

22. Reis, *Slave Rebellion in Brazil*, p. 100. Photos of some of these Quranic texts appear on p. 101.
23. Bodin, *Commonweale*, p. 45.
24. For comparable terms in Roman slavery, see Wiedemann, *Greek and Roman Slavery*, p. 51.

Chapter 12

CATHOLICISM, PROTESTANTISM, AND LOUISIANA SLAVERY

If during the 1500s there was little difference between Protestant and Catholics concerning slavery, the situation did not change much in the 1600s. Hugh Thomas aptly notes that '[t]here is no record in the seventeenth century of any preacher who, in any sermon, whether in the cathedral of Saint-André in Bordeaux, or in a Presbyterian meeting house in Liverpool, condemned the trade in black slaves'.[1]

However, Rodney Stark believes that a sharp difference between Protestants and Catholics can be found in Louisiana in the late eighteenth and early nineteenth centuries. While Stark sees Christianity, in general, as the most important factor in abolitionism, he advances Louisiana as a case where a distinctively Catholic practice was more faithful to biblical ethics, and so resulted in the liberation of more slaves than in any other American slave state before the Civil War.

In particular, Stark notes that, according to the 1830 US census, 13.2% of the black population was free in Louisiana.[2] By comparison, in Alabama only 1.3% of the black population was free, and 0.8% in Mississippi. In New Orleans, 41.7% of the blacks were free compared to Richmond, Virginia, where only 21.1% were free, and Vicksburg, Mississippi (0.5%).[3] Stark attributes New Orleans's and Louisiana's larger numbers of free black persons to the implementation of Catholic law codes that were the basis of the French and Spanish legal traditions used in Louisiana. He asks: 'Can such immense differences stem from anything other than the effects of Catholic codes, and attitudes toward slavery?'[4]

Indeed, Stark seems to think that the Catholic version of Christianity was better than the Protestant version when it came to humanizing slavery. In so doing, Stark is repeating a well-known thesis bearing the name of Frank Tannenbaum, who posited that Catholic countries of Latin America were

1. Thomas, *The Slave Trade*, p. 451.
2. Stark, *For the Glory of God*, p. 322.
3. Stark, *For the Glory of God*, p. 323, Table 4.2.
4. Stark, *For the Glory of God*, p. 322.

much better in treating slaves than the Protestant countries, such as England. Tannenbaum expounded his thesis in his influential book, *Slave and Citizen* (1946).[5] It behooves us, therefore, to look more closely at these Codes.

The Catholic Codes

To understand Stark's biases, let us examine how he describes two of these 'Catholic' codes: The *Code noir* ([French] Black Code) and the *Codigo negro español* (Spanish Black Code). The *Code noir*, which was intended to regulate slavery in the New World, was promulgated in 1685 during the reign of Louis XIV.[6] Its main author was Jean-Baptiste Colbert (1619–1683), the French minister of finance. According to Stark, 'In drawing up the code... Colbert was assisted and greatly influenced by French Churchmen'.[7] A revised version of the *Code noir* was promulgated in Louisiana in 1724.[8]

For Stark, the *Code noir* marks an advance in the treatment of slaves—despite the fact that the *Code noir* denied slaves the right to marry, and prescribed punishments ranging from the branding of their bodies to execution. In particular, Stark largely ignores the fact that the *Code noir* denied freedom of religion in Article Three (only Roman Catholicism must be practiced). In fact, Stark attacks scholars who only note Article Three as part of 'an opportunity to rail against "Catholic intolerance"'.[9]

In regard to critics of the *Code noir*, Stark further insists that 'these historians ignored the many articles of the code that expanded on the premise that a slave is "a being of God"'.[10] Stark specifically scolds Peter Gay, a scholar who described the *Code noir* as 'extraordinarily severe—toward the slave of course'.[11] Stark responds that 'for this fraud to be perpetrated, it is

---

5. Frank Tannenbaum, *Slave and Citizen* (repr., Boston: Beacon Press, 1992 [1946]). See also Stanley M. Elkins, *Slavery: A Problem in American Institutional and Intellectual Life* (Chicago: University of Chicago Press, 1959).

6. For an edition of and commentary on both the original *Code noir* and the Louisiana version, see Louis Sala-Molins, *Le Code noir ou le calvaire de Canaan* (Paris: Presses universitaires de France, 2003). See also George Breathett, 'Catholicism and the Code Noir in Haiti', *Journal of Negro History* 73 (1988), pp. 1-11; Joseph Roach, 'Body of Law: The Sun King and the Code Noir', in Sara E. Meltzer and Kathryn Norberg (eds.), *From the Royal to the Republican Body: Incorporating the Political in Seventeenth- and Eighteenth-Century France* (Berkeley: University of California Press, 1998), pp. 113-30.

7. Stark, *For the Glory of God*, pp. 309-10.

8. See Judith Kelleher Schafer, *Slavery, the Civil Law and the Supreme Court of Louisiana* (Baton Rouge: Louisiana State University Press, 1994), p. 1.

9. Stark, *For the Glory of God*, p. 310.

10. Stark, *For the Glory of God*, p. 310.

11. Stark, *For the Glory of God*, p. 310, citing Peter Gay, *The Enlightenment: An Interpretation* (New York: W.W. Norton, 1969), p. 411.

necessary that there be no mention, not only of the many other articles already noted, but of Article 39, which ordered officers of justice "to proceed criminally against the masters and overseers who will have killed their slaves or mutilated them"'.[12] Ironically, Stark mentions that 'Article 38, which forbade masters to torture their slaves, allowed that they might be whipped'.[13]

Yet, it is Stark who is selective in his quotations of the *Code noir*. Consider Article Thirty-Eight in its entirety:

> We also prohibit all of our subjects of the aforesaid country, of whatever quality or status they may be, to administer, or by their private authority to have others administer, the rack or torture of their slaves, under whatever pretext it may be; nor to do them or to have others do them, any mutilation, under penalty of confiscation of the slaves and of being proceeded against extraordinarily. We only permit [masters], when they believe their slaves deserve it, to chain them and to beat them with rods and cords.[14]

If beating a chained person with rods or cords counts as torture, then Article Thirty-Eight certainly does allow the torture and mutilation of slaves. The *Code noir* simply defined 'torture' differently from Article Five of the United Nations Declaration of Human Rights: 'No one shall be subjected to torture or to cruel, inhuman or degrading treatment or punishment'.[15] Stark also neglects to mention that Article Twenty-Seven decrees death (*puni de mort*) for a slave who strikes a master. Thus, striking a master carries a disproportionate penalty compared to striking a slave. So, how does all of this make a slave more of a being of God?

What about Article Thirty-Nine, which Stark believes obligates the criminal prosecution of masters who killed or mutilated their slaves? Article Thirty-Nine is full of loopholes:

> We direct our officials to proceed criminally against the masters and overseers who have killed their slaves or mutilated their limbs while under their power or under their direction, and to punish murder according to the gravity of the circumstances. In case there is cause to absolve them [the masters], we permit the release of the masters as well as the overseers without the need to obtain letters of absolution from us.[16]

In other words, it depends on the circumstances for which a master kills or mutilates a slave. There is less oversight of such killings as letters of absolu-

    12. Stark, *For the Glory of God*, p. 310.
    13. Stark, *For the Glory of God*, p. 310.
    14. Sala-Molins, *Le Code Noir*, p. 175 (my translation).
    15. Article 5 of the United Nations' *Universal Declaration of Human Rights*. For a list of torture related laws and conventions, see also Karen L. Greenberg and Joshua L. Dratel, *The Torture Papers: The Road to Abu Ghraib* (Cambridge: Cambridge University Press, 2005), p. 1241.
    16. Sala-Molins, *Le Code Noir*, pp. 176-77 (my translation).

tion need not be obtained but can be issued at the local level. Moreover, the master can be released, which means that he is not really punished. The *Code of Hammurabi*, which did not require being abused to be manumitted (cf. Law 171), was much more humane by that standard.

Is Baptism a Sign of Humanity?

One of Stark's repeated evidences that Catholic slaves were regarded as children of God is that they were baptized. Article Two of the *Code noir* says: 'All the slaves in the aforesaid province [= Louisiana] shall be instructed in the Apostolic and Roman Catholic religion and baptized'.[17] But is this a sign of increased humanity? If one reads the *Code noir*, it becomes apparent that baptism did little to change the way slaves were treated. A baptized slave could be beaten (per Article Thirty-Eight), branded (per Article Thirteen), or killed (per Article Seventeen). So, for Stark, having water poured on a slave is a sign of increased humanity, but being beaten, branded, or killed is not a sign of increasing inhumanity.

Baptism actually was a denial of a slave's freedom of religion given what was said in Article Two of the *Code noir*. The act of pouring water on a slave signaled the religious submission of the slave to the Catholic Church. This was reinforced by Article Three, which prohibited slaves from attending any gatherings typical of their African religious traditions. The extinction of their native religion, and the often forced imposition of Christianity, only reaffirms that baptism is an imperialistic ritual just as much as or more than some symbol of equality.

The fact that baptism was viewed as an inviolable oath to a life-long submission to the Church is evidenced by the fact that one might be considered a heretic for leaving the Church after baptism. Even Bartolomé de las Casas, a vehement voice against the enslavement of Indians, endorsed the persecution of those who left the Church after baptism:

> [B]ecause a heretic has vowed himself to Christ in baptism, he can be compelled to return to the sheepfold...a heretic offends Christ, and commits the crime of *lèse majesté*. This offense is punished by the Church, of which the heretic is a subject, as he is also a subject of its head, the Roman Pontiff.[18]

So, Stark arguing for the beneficence of baptism is like a Muslim slave owner telling his slave he should be grateful for being regarded as human enough to participate in initiatory Muslim rituals, especially as not participating might result in execution. Releasing slaves would be a much better indicator of slaves' humanity than just pouring water on their head.

17. Sala-Molins, *Le Code Noir*, p. 95 (my translation).
18. Las Casas, *In Defense of the Indians*, pp. 304-305.

Was the Spanish Black Code Better?

Stark argues that the *Spanish Black Code* was even better than the *Code noir* in terms of facilitating the freedom of slaves. As mentioned, the French *Code noir* was first implemented in Louisiana in 1724, while the *Spanish Black Code* came into force after Spain took control of Louisiana from the French in the late 1760s. The *Spanish Black Code*, for one, allowed slaves to be freed without the approval of the Superior Council (*Conseil supérieur*), the highest judiciary body in Louisiana during the French period.[19] One less hoop theoretically meant increased numbers of emancipations.

To be fair, there is a spike in manumissions at 1770. This spike was due to the arrival of Alejandro O'Reilly, the Irish-born second governor of Louisiana, after that territory was acquired by Spain in 1763. In 1769, O'Reilly issued his *Ordinances and Instructions*, which were based on the French *Code noir*, but which, in practice, followed a version of the *Spanish Black Code*.[20]

However, O'Reilly did not say that this change was due to some increasing view of the humanity of slaves. Rather, he was trying to address insurrections that had resulted in the ouster of the previous governor, Antonio de Ulloa. O'Reilly himself refers to these insurrections ('to prevent hereafter evils of such magnitude') when issuing the following rationale for the change:

> The prosecutions which have been had in consequence of the insurrection which has taken place in this colony, having fully demonstrated the part and influence which the council have taken in those proceedings, countenancing, contrary to duty, the most criminal actions, when their whole care should have been directed to maintain the people in the fidelity and subordination due to their sovereign; for these reasons, and with a view to prevent hereafter evils of such magnitude, it is indispensable to abolish the said council, and to establish in their stead that form of political Government and administration of justice prescribed by our wise laws.[21]

---

19. On this provision concerning the permission of the Superior Council, see Hans W. Baade, 'The Bifurcated Romanist Tradition of Law in Louisiana', *Tulane Law Review* 70 (1996), pp. 1481-99 (1488). For the *Spanish Black Code* (= *Código negro español*), I rely on the text in Manuel Lucena Samoral, 'El Código negro español tambien llamado carolino: comentario y texto', *Estudios de historia social y económica de América* 12 (1995), pp. 267-324.

20. For the debates about whether the French or Spanish Code actually predominated in practice in Spanish Louisiana, see Jennifer M. Spear, *Race, Sex, and Social Order in New Orleans* (Baltimore: The Johns Hopkins University Press, 2009), pp. 103-109 and 265 n. 9.

21. B.F. French (ed.), *Historical Memoirs of Louisiana from the First Settlement of the Colony to the Departure of Governor O'Reilly in 1770* (New York: Lamport, Blakeman & Law, 1853), p. 254.

In other words, O'Reilly is abolishing the Superior Council because he saw members of that body as complicit or negligent in preventing the insurrections which ousted the previous governor. Nothing here is mentioned about increasing the humanity of the *Code noir*.

Another significant liberalizing aspect of the *Spanish Black Code* was the ability of a slave to purchase his or her own freedom. This practice is technically called by the Spanish term, *coartación*. But Stark is wrong to attribute this to some Catholic liberalizing tendency without noting that such a practice is actually Roman in origin.[22] A slave in Rome could accumulate property and savings (called a *peculium*), which, though technically still belonging to the master, could be used to buy a slave's own freedom.[23] Indeed, a number of scholars note how much these codes are indebted ultimately to Roman law rather than biblical law.[24]

The whole notion of 'advancement' is rather questionable because racialization also increased and neutralized many of the provisions of the first *Code noir* of 1685. So, by 1760s, things were generally worse for black slaves.[25] And the absolute number of freed slaves was never that large. According to the statistics compiled by Jennifer M. Spear, '[i]n the 1770s, an average of forty-four slaves were manumitted each year; by 1803 that number had doubled'.[26]

In fact, the *Digest of 1808*, imposed by the American legislature of Louisiana, began to supersede the *Spanish Black Code*. The Supreme Court of Louisiana issued a decision (Cottin v. Cottin, 1817) that permitted Spanish laws only when they did not conflict with, or were not repealed by, the *Digest of 1808*.[27] But, for the sake of argument, we grant that the *Spanish Black Code* was still in full force in 1830, when Stark makes his statistical comparisons.

22. Wiedemann, *Greek and Roman Slavery*, p. 51.
23. Wiedemann, *Greek and Roman Slavery*, p. 52.
24. For discussion of such Roman traditions, see Baade, 'The Bifurcated Romanist Tradition of Law in Louisiana'; Rodolfo Batiza, 'The Louisiana Civil Code of 1808: Its Actual Sources and Present Relevance', *Tulane Law Review* 46 (1971), pp. 4-165. For further discussion, see Robert Pascal, 'Sources of the Digest of 1808: A Reply to Professor Batiza', *Tulane Law Review* 47 (1972), pp. 603-27; Rodolfo Batiza, 'Sources of the Civil Code of 1808, Facts and Speculation: A Rejoinder', *Tulane Law Review* 47 (1972), pp. 628-52.
25. See the discussion in Alfred N. Hunt, *Haiti's Influence on Antebellum America: Slumbering Volcano in the Caribbean* (Baton Rouge: Louisiana State University Press, 1988), p. 14.
26. Spear, *Race, Sex, and Social Order*, p. 110.
27. See Schafer, *Slavery, the Civil Law*, pp. 17-18.

Sex, Race and Immigration as Factors

In order to explain the larger proportion of freed slaves in Louisiana and New Orleans, let us return to Stark's suggestive question: 'Can such immense differences stem from anything other than the effects of Catholic codes, and attitudes toward slavery?'[28] In fact, these differences stem from many other factors that are just as, or even more, important than those of any supposed philanthropic sentiments found in Catholic theology.

If one compares Louisiana with Cuba, which was theoretically also operating under a version of the *Spanish Black Code*, one discovers an immense diversity in the proportions of free colored people even under the same Spanish legal tradition. Statistics provided by Kenneth F. Kiple allow us to calculate that in 1841 in Cuba, the 152,838 free colored people formed 25% of the total colored population (589,333), of which 436,495 were slaves.[29] Thus, under the same Catholic Spanish legal tradition, the proportion of free blacks in 1841 could range from 13.2% (for the whole state of Louisiana) to 25% for all of Cuba to 41% for a city such as New Orleans.

Such disparities in the proportion of free colored persons under the same Spanish legal traditions suggests that other factors must be considered more important in explaining the differences between societies who were following 'Catholic' codes. Factors not considered by Stark can now easily be found in the vast databases of Louisiana slave records compiled by Gwendolyn Midlo Hall.[30] She has painstakingly assembled masses of records from the Spanish period and provided a wealth of data about the demography and manumission of slaves. This data has, in turn, been studied by scholars such as Kimberly Hanger and Jennifer Spear.[31]

In particular, Jennifer Spear's careful study of the motives listed for manumission in the New Orleans Notarial Archives, which recorded all such transactions during the Spanish period, allow us to test Stark's thesis quite directly and quantitatively. This is so because these Notarial Archives often listed the motives for the manumission. Some manumissions listed 'religious' and 'spiritual' motives, and some listed non-religious motives. Spear's study concludes that '[v]ery few manumitters claimed to have spiritual motives for

---

28. Stark, *For the Glory of God*, p. 322.
29. Kenneth F. Kiple, *Blacks in Colonial Cuba* (Gainesville: University of Florida Press, 1976), p. 90.
30. Gwendolyn M. Hall, *Databases for the Study of Afro-Louisiana History and Genealogy* (Compact Disk Publication; Baton Rouge: Louisiana State University Press, 2000).
31. Kimberly S. Hanger, *Bounded Lives, Bounded Places: Free Black Society in Colonial New Orleans, 1769–1803* (Durham, NC: Duke University Press, 1997); Spear, *Race, Sex, and Social Order*.

12. Catholicism, Protestantism, and Louisiana Slavery 233

unconditionally freeing their slaves, suggesting that religion played an insignificant role in their decision'.[32]

On the other hand, manumission records show that sex played a significant role. Black women, for example, were three times more likely to receive manumission than men.[33] This, despite the fact that women were not a greater proportion of the population than men. As Spear notes: 'in the last third of the eighteenth century, women comprised between 51 and 54 percent of the city's enslaved population, but they received over 60 percent of the manumissions'.[34] While boys and girls were manumitted in roughly equal proportions, adult women were two and half times more likely to be freed than men. That is because women often became the mistresses of masters, who then freed them in return for that relationship. In addition, it was cheaper to free women than men.

Similarly, race played a factor in terms of the cost of manumission. Calculations based on Hanger's statistics about the owner's phenotype (or racial profile) shows that 63.6% of slaves owned by free blacks were granted a release 'graciosa', meaning release without compensation to the owner, while only 39.0% of slaves belonging to whites were released in that manner.[35] Some 24% of white owners made slaves purchase their freedom, compared to 17% of slaves owned by free black persons.

Stark apparently also is not aware that immigration could be a significant factor that can account for the greater proportion of freed black persons in New Orleans in 1830 (as compared to cities in other slave states). If we use Stark's own numbers for our calculations, the number of freed black persons in 1830 in New Orleans was about 11,093 (41.7% of a total black population of 28,545).[36] Yet we can account for about a quarter of that number by immigration.

In 1791, when the Haitian revolution ignited, New Orleans had a population of 4,446. This population included 750 free black persons, and 1,800 slaves. By 1797, New Orleans had 8,056 inhabitants, and this included 1,335 free black persons and 2,773 slaves.[37] Clearly, even if we are not certain how many of these new inhabitants came from Haiti, we cannot ignore that event as a factor.

---

32. Spear, *Race, Sex, and Social Order*, p. 114.
33. Spear, *Race, Sex, and Social Order*, p. 112.
34. Spear, *Race, Sex, and Social Order*, p. 112.
35. Hanger, *Bounded Lives*, p. 33, Table 1.8. See also Laurence J. Kotlikoff and Anton J. Rupert, 'The Manumission of Slaves in New Orleans, 1827–1846', *Southern Studies* (1980), pp. 172-81.
36. Stark, *For the Glory of God*, p. 323, Table 4.2.
37. My population figures are from Hunt, *Haiti's Influence on Antebellum America*, p. 46.

The situation is clearer in 1809–1830, when about 9,000 refugees went to New Orleans from Haiti; about 3,102 of those were free people of African heritage.[38] To understand the significance of that number, one should recognize that in 1805 the total number of free blacks in New Orleans was 1,566. In other words, the immigrations of 1809–10 tripled (1,566 + 3,102 = 4,668) the number of freed black persons in New Orleans between 1805 and 1810. And 3,102 freed slaves is already about 27% of the 11,093 freed black persons Stark reckons in 1830 even if we assume no natural reproductive increases in that immigrant population.

Ursuline Nuns

If those devoted most to Catholic principles were not living by them, then this also ultimately undermines the whole notion that Catholic principles influenced manumissional practices. Moreover, if most slaveowners can be dismissed as ignoring the dictates of the supposedly benign Catholic Codes, the same cannot be said of the Ursuline nuns, who would presumably be extremely devoted to Catholic principles. Yet, the practices of the Ursuline nuns reveal the compatibility of slavery with Catholicism under the *Code noir* and the *Spanish Black Code*.

According to Emily Clark, a noted historian of the Ursulines, the group originated in Brescia, Italy in the 1530s 'under a middle-aged spinster named Angela Merici'.[39] Merici named the group after Ursula, a legendary fourth-century British martyr. Eventually recognized as an order by the 1570s, the Ursulines devoted themselves primarily to the education of young women from their communities. Since the group saw its greatest initial success in France, the Ursulines were largely seen as a French phenomenon for many of their early decades.

In 1727, twelve Ursulines arrived in New Orleans, then under French control, to found a convent devoted to educating that city's young women. By the late 1700s, the Ursulines were powerful players in New Orleans, with substantial plantations and other enterprises. They were also actively engaged in slaveowning. As Clark remarks:

> [T]he censuses reveal that the Ursulines were substantial slaveholders. The number of bondpeople they claimed put them in the top 30 percent of slaveowners among those with plantations on the Lower Mississippi River. In 1770 they were among the top 6 percent of slaveholders in this category.[40]

---

38. Emily Clark, *Masterless Mistresses: The New Orleans Ursulines and the Development of a New World Society, 1727–1834* (Chapel Hill: University of North Carolina Press, 2007), p. 247; Hanger, *Bounded Lives*, p. 165. See further Hunt, *Haiti's Influence on Antebellum America*.
39. Clark, *Masterless Mistresses*, p. 19.
40. Clark, *Masterless Mistresses*, p. 169.

This substantial engagement in slavery by the Ursulines is important because that same census of 1770 showed that 43% of the plantations in the lower Mississippi did not have any slaves.[41]

As noted, Stark attributes the increase in free black persons in New Orleans to Catholic principles, especially as imposed by the Spaniards. But an examination of the Ursuline manumission practices show that economics played just as much or more of a role than some increased notion of Christian charity. As Clark notes, 'the nuns did manumit a number of slaves but rarely on terms disadvantageous to the Ursulines'.[42] Indeed, manumission could be a lucrative business.

For example, in 1777 the Ursulines released three of their old female slaves, something that is not exactly charitable because those slaves were in their least productive years, both in terms of childbearing or in terms of labor. In the case of a slave named Marie Reine, her aunt gave the nuns 2,000 livres (French currency) and another slave from Guinea as compensation.[43] Since a slave was simply substituted, then there was no net gain in manumissions here.

While we do find some instances where people were released relatively cheaply, those were the exceptions even by the nuns' own reckoning. Thus, a granddaughter of a former slave named Joseph Leveillé was released without compensation, but the nuns recorded that this was 'only in her case, which will not serve as an example'.[44] In fact, we find clear instances where the nuns charged much more than the average price for a release. Peter Claver, a free man of color, paid the nuns 600 pesos for the manumission of Marie Angela, his goddaughter. Another slave named Ann had to offer 1,000 pesos for her freedom. Yet, the average price for manumission for females between 1771 and 1803 was 347 pesos in New Orleans.[45]

As did other slaveowners, Ursulines also practiced a sort of fictive freedom wherein the 'freed' slaves were required to continue their duties. In return, the 'freed' slave received food and lodging, which is not that different from what regular slaves received. The 'freed' slave may have been able to keep more of the usufruct than regular slaves, and may have owned slaves. One example is the aforementioned Joseph Leveillé, who was 55 years old when he was released in 1777.[46] However, the release was conditioned upon his continuing to perform his previous duties, which included conducting business dealings on behalf of the nuns.

41. Clark, *Masterless Mistresses*, p. 170.
42. Clark, *Masterless Mistresses*, p. 188.
43. Clark, *Masterless Mistresses*, p. 188.
44. Clark, *Masterless Mistresses*, p. 188.
45. Hanger, *Bounded Lives*, p. 31, Table 1.6.
46. For the details of the manumission of Joseph Leveillé, I depend on Clark, *Masterless Mistresses*, p. 189; Hanger, *Bounded Lives*, p. 41.

Summary

Stark's claim that Catholicism's dependence on authentic biblical/Christian ethics represented an advance for colored people in Louisiana is clearly an exaggeration. Stark did not consider new research revealing the many factors, most of them clearly more important than religion, that explain the greater proportion of freed colored people in Louisiana as compared to other states. Stark is unfamiliar with all of the primary documents that provide reasons and factors contrary to what he gives.[47] Stark also omits or mitigates counter-examples, such as that provided by the Ursuline nuns, who show that those most devoted to Catholic principles were actually some of the most significant slaveowners at a time when 43% of the plantations did not have slaves.

---

47. For a discussion about how the death rates of slaves in French Catholic colonies was just as high as in Protestant ones, see also Rogozinski, *A Brief History of the Caribbean*, p. 141.

Chapter 13

BRITISH ABOLITIONISTS

It is in Britain that the first successful abolitionist movement took root in Europe. According to Seymour Drescher, the prominent scholar of British abolitionism, we can begin the history of the abolitionist movement in 1772, when Chief Justice Mansfield ruled, in the famous Somerset case, that slavery within England was not supported by English law.[1] In 1807, the British Parliament abolished the slave trade, but not slavery itself. By 1833, the Abolition Act was passed, though agricultural workers were supposed to continue working as 'apprentices' until 1840, while domestic workers were to do the same until 1838.[2] Finally, all slaves became free in British colonies on 1 August 1838.[3]

The heroes of the religious side of British abolitionism are usually said to include James Ramsay, Granville Sharp, Thomas Clarkson, and William Wilberforce. Recent historiography, however, has shifted away from this 'great man' version of history because, in part, this version was promoted by the actors themselves.[4] Thomas Clarkson, for instance, wrote a history of abolitionism that even other abolitionists thought was too self-serving.[5] More

---

1. For a detailed account of this case and the contradictory interpretations and versions of Mansfield's verdict, see Steven M. Wise, *Though the Heavens May Fail: The Landmark Trial That Led to the End of Slavery* (Cambridge, MA: Da Capo Press, 2005), pp. 179-91.

2. Seymour Drescher, *Capitalism and Antislavery: British Mobilization in Comparative Perspective* (New York: Oxford University Press, 1987), pp. xiii-xiv.

3. I depend on Rogozinski, *A Brief History of the Caribbean*, pp. 185-87.

4. On this shift, see most recently David B. Davis, 'Foreword', in Seymour Drescher, *Econocide: British Slavery in the Era of Abolition* (Chapel Hill: University of North Carolina Press, 2nd edn, 2010), pp. xiii-xv. For older histories that lionize British heroism, see Frank J. Klingberg, *The Anti-Slavery Movement in England: A Study in English Humanitarianism* (New Haven: Yale University Press, 1926); Reginald Coupland, *Wilberforce: A Narrative* (Oxford: Clarendon Press, 1923).

5. I depend on this edition, Thomas Clarkson, *The History of the Rise, Progress, and Accomplishment of the Abolition of the African Slave Trade in the British Parliament* (2 vols.; London: John W. Parker, 1839). For the influence of Clarkson's history, see Christopher Leslie Brown, *Moral Capital: The Foundations of British Abolitionism*

recent histories pay much more attention to economic and geo-political factors.[6] The agency of slaves themselves has also gained prominence.

I will not delve into these debates in this chapter. Rather, this chapter examines the work of Ramsay, Sharp, Clarkson, and Wilberforce. I also discuss Ottobah Cugoano as an example of an Afro-British abolitionist. I demonstrate that, regardless of the validity of any other explanations, British abolitionism shows a definitive shift away from using the Bible in its abolitionist arguments. I also demonstrate that British abolitionist arguments based on the Bible were generally weak and incoherent.

James Ramsay

James Ramsay (1733–1789), a Scottish-born naval surgeon and Anglican priest, was the first to publish a significant anti-slavery tract in Britain. While he was the Vicar of Teston (Kent), Ramsay published *An Essay on the Treatment and Conversion of African Slaves in the British Sugar Colonies* (1784).[7] However, this tract was principally concerned with ameliorating the conditions of slavery and allowing the evangelization of slaves, and not with the abolition of slavery. Ramsay even admits that Moses allowed slavery, but he insists it was benign. Nonetheless, Ramsay's essay is credited with encouraging later abolitionists in their activities.

Unlike many modern Christian scholars, Ramsay believed that other cultures treated their slaves much better than Christian countries of his time. Concerning the Athenians, he remarks: 'Among those nations that had not the light of revelation to direct their conduct, the Athenians deserve the first place: they were indulgent, easy, and kind to their slaves when compared to their neighbours'.[8] Concerning 1 Cor. 7.21, Ramsay says that Paul 'gives positive preference to slavery'.[9] Otherwise, Ramsay merely alludes to how Jesus and Paul have been misinterpreted elsewhere, but provides no specific

---

(Chapel Hill: University of North Carolina Press, 2006), pp. 4-20. For a more general retrospective anthology of British abolitionism, see Brycchan Carey and Peter J. Kitson (eds.), *Slavery and the Cultures of Abolition: Essays Marking the Bicentennial of the British Abolition Act of 1807* (Woodbridge, UK: D.S. Brewer, 2007).

6. Examples include Brown, *Moral Capital*; Drescher, *Capitalism and Antislavery*; Selwyn H.H. Carrington, 'The American Revolution and the British West Indies' Economy', *Journal of Interdisciplinary History* 17 (1987), pp. 823-50.

7. James Ramsay, *An Essay on the Treatment and Conversion of African Slaves in the British Sugar Colonies* (London: James Phillips, 1784). For a biographical treatment, see Folarin Shyllon, *James Ramsay: The Unknown Abolitionist* (Edinburgh: Canongate, 1977).

8. Ramsay, *Treatment and Conversion of Slaves*, p. 21.

9. Ramsay, *Treatment and Conversion of Slaves*, p. 39.

textual examples.[10] In any case, there is not much biblical exegesis, as compared to practical and humanitarian arguments, for advocating the Christianization and good treatment of slaves.

Granville Sharp

Granville Sharp (1735–1813) is credited with being the first significant British abolitionist.[11] Sharp's fame rests principally on the successful humanitarian and legal aid he rendered in the cases of Jonathan Strong and James Somerset, former slaves who sought freedom on British soil.[12] Although Sharp is sometimes classed as part of the group of abolitionist British evangelicals called the Clapham Sect, the truth is that the origin of his religious views are still unclear.[13]

Sharp wrote a significant tract in 1769 called *A Representation of the Injustice and Dangerous Tendency of Tolerating Slavery*.[14] As Christopher Brown notes, this work 'lacks a single religious argument against slavery'.[15] Brown, in fact, thinks that Sharp religionized his argument after 1772. For our purposes, the tract that addresses the Bible most directly is Granville's *The Law of Passive Obedience* (1776), where he did attempt to refute pro-slavery interpretations in the New Testament in the form of a letter to an anonymous friend.[16]

Sharp begins *The Law of Passive Obedience* by conceding the following:

> There are…some particular texts in the New Testament, which, in the opinion of several well meaning and disinterested persons, seem to afford some proof of the toleration of slavery among the primitive Christians; and from thence, they are induced to conceive, that Christianity doth not oblige its professors to denounce the practice of slaveholding.[17]

---

10. Ramsay, *Treatment and Conversion of Slaves*, p. 46.

11. When naming important foes of colonial slavery, Thomas Clarkson (*An Essay on the Slavery and Commerce of the Human Species particularly the African* [London: J. Philips, 1776], p. xii) said: 'The first is Mr. Granville Sharp. This Gentleman has particularly distinguished himself in the cause of freedom.' (Note that here and throughout I use the facsimile edition of Clarkson's work available online at: files.libertyfund.org/files/1070/0590_Bk.pdf.) See also Edward C.P. Lascelles, *Granville Sharp and the Freedom of Slaves in England* (London: Humphrey Milford, 1928).

12. For a detailed account of these cases, see Wise, *Though the Heavens May Fail*.

13. See Brown, *Moral Capital*, pp. 169-70.

14. See Brown, *Moral Capital*, pp. 174-75.

15. Brown, *Moral Capital*, p. 174 n. 24.

16. I use the edition in Charles Stuart, *A Memoir of Granville Sharp, to Which is Added The Law of Passive Obedience or Christian Submission to Personal Injuries* (New York: American Anti-Slavery Society, 1836).

17. Sharp, *The Law of Passive Obedience*, p. 97.

240   *Slavery, Abolitionism, and the Ethics of Biblical Scholarship*

In contrast, Sharp aims to show the 'absolute illegality of slavery among Christians'.[18] However, to demonstrate this illegality, he first addresses the texts used by pro-slavery advocates, and these include Eph. 6.5, Col. 3.22-23, and 1 Tim. 6.1-8.

Despite his knowledge of Greek and Hebrew, Sharp does not focus on a close reading of these texts. Rather, he uses a more legalistic rationale:

> These texts are amply sufficient to prove the truth of my learned friend's assertion, so far as it relates to the duty of slaves themselves, but this absolute submission required of Christian servants, by no means implies the legality of slaveholding on the part of their masters... The slave violates no precepts of the gospel by his abject condition, provided that the same is involuntary (for if he can be made free, he is expressly commanded by the apostle to use it rather). But how the master who enforces involuntary servitude, can be said to act consistently with the Christian profession, is a question of a very different nature.[19]

Sharp's rationale assumes that 1 Cor. 7.21 commands a slave to use freedom if he can gain it. Yet, Sharp also says: 'I have already admitted that Christianity does not release slaves from the obligation they were under according to the custom and law of the countries where it was propagated'.[20]

So how can slaves ever be freed if they are not released from those obligations by a master? According to Sharp, Christian masters should just release slaves. Basing himself on 1 Tim. 6.1 and Titus 2.10, Sharp says that one principle is foundational: 'a zeal for the glory of God, and of his religion (the principles of the first great commandment) is the apparent ground and sole purpose of the Christian slave's submission, which was therefore to be "with singleness of heart as unto Christ"'.[21] Since the slave is commanded to serve 'heartily as unto the Lord, and not to men' (and cites Col. 3.2 and Lev. 25.52), Sharp reasons that God is the true master, and so even Christian masters lack slaveholding rights.[22]

When Sharp comes to 1 Pet. 2.18, his reasoning becomes quite forced. First, he acknowledges that Peter enforces the necessity of the servants' submission to their masters, in the strongest manner, commanding them to be subject "not only to the good and gentle, but also to the froward"'.[23] But Sharp argues that:

---

18. Sharp, *The Law of Passive Obedience*, p. 98.
19. Sharp, *The Law of Passive Obedience*, p. 100.
20. Sharp, *The Law of Passive Obedience*, p. 100.
21. Sharp, *The Law of Passive Obedience*, p. 101.
22. Sharp, *The Law of Passive Obedience*, p. 101.
23. Sharp, *The Law of Passive Obedience*, p. 101.

> [T]he apostle did not mean to justify the claim of the master because he enjoined the same submission to the servants that suffered wrongfully, as to those who had good and gentle masters; and it would be highly injurious to the gospel of peace, to suppose it capable of authorizing wrongful sufferings, or of establishing a right or power in any rank of men whatever, to oppress others unjustly[.][24]

However, the fact that a servant owes equal obedience to gentle and harsh masters proves only that obedience does not depend at all on how cruel a master might be.

Second, Sharp is redefining 'injurious to the Gospel of peace' very differently from Peter because the latter says that it is a slave's disobedience that is injurious to the Christian mission, and not slaveholding. Sharp simply cannot admit that Christianity is not as peaceful as he deems it, and so his reasoning becomes circular: 'Action X cannot be interpreted to be injurious to the Gospel because Action X is not supposed to be injurious to the Gospel'.

Sharp's argumentation becomes even more convoluted when faced with 1 Tim. 6.2, which says (RSV): 'Those who have believing masters must not be disrespectful on the ground that they are brethren; rather they must serve all the better since those who benefit by their service are believers and beloved'. This text seemingly undermines Sharp's idea that the New Testament regards slaveholding by Christians as absolutely sinful. After all, the text does not say that the slavemasters are sinning, but that they are believers and 'beloved'. Nonetheless, Sharp reasons:

> But these expressions are included in that part of the apostle's charge to Timothy, which relates merely to the instruction of servants, so that there is no room to suppose that any reference was intended to the practice of the masters by way of justification.—The meaning therefore can amount to no more than this, viz: That as it is the duty of servants to 'count their own masters'—even those that are unbelievers—'worthy of all honor, that the name of God and his doctrine be not blasphemed', so the same reason obliges them, more especially, to count their believing masters 'worthy of all lawful honor' because of their Christian profession, which renders them accepted of God.[25]

So, these Christian masters are worthy of honor because of their belief in Christ only and not because of their master status. But Sharp provides no other example where someone committing a grave offense against God is still called 'worthy of honor'. Thus, Sharp's notion of what is honorable is certainly not supported by any biblical text. Sharp ignores the many other times the New Testament has outrightly condemned any other action thought to be sinful.

---

24. Sharp, *The Law of Passive Obedience*, p. 102.
25. Sharp, *The Law of Passive Obedience*, p. 104.

Thomas Clarkson

Stark lists Thomas Clarkson (1760–1846) among the religious heroes of British abolitionism.[26] Ralph Waldo Emerson goes further, and anoints Clarkson as the founder of abolitionism.[27] Clarkson helped to found the Committee for the Abolition of the Slave Trade, and he is credited with helping to pass the Slave Trade Act, which abolished the British slave trade in 1807. An Anglican deacon, Clarkson had close ties with the Quakers, and was an ally of William Wilberforce, the evangelical abolitionist Minister of Parliament.

Clarkson was a paradigmatic combination of researcher and activist. As part of his assignments for the Committee for the Abolition of the Slave Trade, Clarkson reportedly interviewed some 20,000 sailors and collected equipment related to the slave trade. That indefatigable research aimed to provide verbal and visual testimonials to the horrors of the life of African slaves. He was sometimes attacked by his detractors, and he was ill for much of the time he was engaged in his abolitionist efforts.

For our purposes, the most significant work contributed by Clarkson is *An Essay on the Slavery and Commerce of the Human Species* (1786).[28] When we examine that work, it becomes apparent that biblical ethics are not the main focus of Clarkson's call for abolition. That essay is more of a history of slavery, and meant to highlight the inhumanity of the entire slave system. When Clarkson considers slavery in antiquity he credits non-Christians with being champions of abolition. Note this statement:

> Thus then, to the eternal honour of Ægypt and Athens, they were the only places that we can find, where slaves were considered with any humanity at all. The rest of the world seemed to vie with each other, in the debasement and oppression of these unfortunate people.[29]

Indeed, Clarkson's entire argument centers on showing that human sentiment against slavery was part of human nature, and so he adduced examples from many cultures. Clarkson also shows that many slaves in antiquity were able and capable individuals (e.g., Aesop), rather than the brutes portrayed by British slavemasters.[30]

Clarkson's *Essay* does attempt to refute the claim that Medieval slavery diminished merely because of shift to feudalism: Christianity was the only cause; for the greatest part of the charters that were granted for the freedom

---

26. Stark, *For the Glory of God*, pp. 350, 354.
27. Adam Hochschild, *Bury the Chains: Prophets and Rebels in the Fight to Free an Empire's Slaves* (Boston: Houghton Mifflin, 2005), p. 90.
28. See n. 11, above.
29. Clarkson, *Slavery and Commerce*, p. 20.
30. Clarkson, *Slavery and Commerce*, pp. 27-28.

of slaves in those times (many of which are still extant) were granted 'pro amore Dei, pro mercede animæ'. They were founded, in short, on religious considerations, 'that they might procure the favour of the Deity, which they conceived themselves to have forfeited, by the subjugation of those, whom they found to be the objects of the divine benevolence and attention equally with themselves'.[31] However, Clarkson makes an argument that is not really sustainable because we have evidence that other types of unfree labor continued in England and in the southern portions of Europe (e.g., in parish workhouses).[32] Nonetheless, Clarkson adds:

> But with respect to Christianity, many and great are the arguments, that it occasioned so desirable an event. It taught, 'that all men were originally equal; that the Deity was no respecter of persons, and that, as all men were to give an account of their actions hereafter, it was necessary that they should be free'.[33]

Clarkson appeals to 'representativism' to refute arguments that Christians are slavemasters. In an imaginary conversation with an African who wonders how Christians can be so cruel, Clarkson replies: 'But the people against whom you so justly declaim, are not Christians. They are infidels. They are monsters.'[34]

A sustained argument about scripture is found only in the latter parts of the *Essay*. First, Clarkson addresses the curse of Canaan. He makes sound historical arguments about why Africans cannot be considered part of the cursed progeny of Canaan, and challenges slavery advocates to find where the curse of Canaan involved their blackness. He concludes:

> If the scriptures are true, it is evident that the posterity of Cain are no more; that the curse of Ham has been accomplished; and that, as all men were derived from the same stock, so this variety of appearance in men must either have proceeded from some interposition of the Deity.[35]

---

31. Clarkson, *Slavery and Commerce*, p. 39.
32. See Ruth Paley, Christina Malcomson, and Michael Hunter, 'Parliament and Slavery 1660 to c. 1710', *Slavery and Abolition* 31 (2010), pp. 257-81; Nicholas S. Rogers, 'Vagrancy, Impressment, and the Regulation of Labour in Eighteenth Century Britain', *Slavery and Abolition* 15 (1994), pp. 207-26; C.S.L. Davies, 'Slavery and Protector Somerset: The Vagrancy Act of 1547', *Economic History Review* 19 (1966), pp. 533-49; J.H. Baker, 'Personal Liberty under the Common Law of England, 1200-1600', in R.W. Davies (ed.), *The Origins of Modern Freedom in the West* (Palo Alto, CA: Stanford University Press, 1995), pp. 178-202; Daniel James Ennis, *Enter the Press-Gang: Naval Impressment in Eighteenth Century British Literature* (Newark: University of Delaware Press, 2002); Michal J. Rozbicki, 'To Save them from Themselves: Proposals to Enslave the British Poor, 1698–1755', *Slavery and Abolition* 22 (2001), pp. 29-50.
33. Clarkson, *Slavery and Commerce*, p. 38.
34. Clarkson, *Slavery and Commerce*, p. 126.
35. Clarkson, *Slavery and Commerce*, p. 184.

Clarkson also adduced anatomical arguments from the Italian physician, Marcello Malphigi (1628–1694), to show that even the blackest people had white 'true skin' beneath the outermost layer of skin.[36] Thus, all people are really the same color beneath the outermost layer.

Finally, in Part III, Chapter 11 of the *Essay* Clarkson addresses a few of the pro-slavery arguments from the New Testament. As to Philemon, Clarkson accepts that Onesimus is a fugitive slave, but he returns a freedman. Clarkson remarks, '[i]t appears that the same Onesimus, when he was sent back, was no longer a slave, that he was a minister of the gospel'.[37] Clarkson offers no detailed exegesis or examination of the Greek text for these conclusions, and spends no time on any other text used by the pro-slavery side (e.g., Eph. 6.5; 1 Tim. 6.1ff.; 1 Pet. 2.18). Indeed, Clarkson is forced to explain the lack of any overt abolitionist statements in the New Testament.

> It is said again, that Christianity, among the many important precepts which it contains, does not furnish us with one for the abolition of slavery. But the reason is obvious. Slavery at the time of the introduction of the gospel was universally prevalent, and if Christianity had abruptly declared, that the millions of slaves should have been made free, who were then in the world, it would have been universally rejected, as containing doctrines that were dangerous, if not destructive, to society.[38]

As mentioned, this argument is very weak, and it could be used against abolitionism in Clarkson's day because slaveowners argued precisely that abolition was destructive to society. Of course, this meant 'white society' because African societies were routinely destroyed by slavery.

Although Clarkson concedes that there is no direct command against owning slaves in the New Testament, he still insists that 'it is evident that, in its general tenor, it sufficiently militates against the custom'.[39] He appeals to the rule to love neighbor as yourself and to the Golden Rule. But, unlike many previous abolitionists, Clarkson says that eschatology provides a key rationale for abolitionism.

> But the most important doctrine is that, by which we are assured that mankind are to exist in a future state, and to give an account of those actions, which they have severally done in the flesh. This strikes at the very root of slavery. For how can any man be justly called to an account for his actions, whose actions are not at his own disposal? This is the case with the proper slave. His liberty is absolutely bought and appropriated; and if the purchase is just

---

36. Clarkson, *Slavery and Commerce*, p. 194.
37. Clarkson, *Slavery and Commerce*, p. 246.
38. Clarkson, *Slavery and Commerce*, pp. 246-47.
39. Clarkson, *Slavery and Commerce*, p. 247.

and equitable, he is under the necessity of perpetrating any crime, which the purchaser may order him to commit, or, in other words, of ceasing to be accountable for his actions.[40]

This argument is rare, but it suffers a number of deficiencies. It does not address the possibility that inward disposition was supposed to be the measure of freedom in early Christianity. This idea goes back to the Stoics and was reinforced by Augustine. As long as you wanted to do otherwise, the bodily actions are not the final measure of any human freedom.

The main arguments against slavery are nicely summarized by the *Essay*'s last sentence: 'no custom established among men was ever more impious; since it is contrary to reason, justice, nature, the principles of law and government, the whole doctrine, in short, of natural religion, and the revealed voice of God'.[41] The bulk of **Clarkson's** essay is actually about gaining sympathy for the slaves by appealing to our humanity. The Bible, though cited, is not really the bulk or substance of Clarkson's classic abolitionist tract.

Quobnah Ottobah Cugoano

Decades before David Walker and Frederick Douglass had become the lights of African-American abolitionism, Ottobah Cugoano had performed a similar role in British abolitionism. Born in Ghana around 1757, and kidnapped and enslaved at around thirteen years old, Cugoano was brought to England in 1772, via Grenada, where he worked as a slave.[42] Although the circumstances of his emancipation are unclear, Cugoano was free by 1787, when he wrote *Thoughts and Sentiments on the Evil and Wicked Traffic of the Slavery and Commerce of the Human Species*. The date of his death is a mystery.

Cugoano does make repeated allusions to the Bible. However, except for the refutation of the curse of Canaan, there is no substantive interaction with biblical texts. Cugoano, in general, does not cite biblical texts very precisely, and he often seems to confuse biblical texts. For example, he speaks of slaves who 'refused to go out free when the year of jubilee came'.[43] But such a refusal is more consistent with the laws in Exod. 21.5 than those of the Jubilee (Lev. 25.8-17, 29-31).

40. Clarkson, *Slavery and Commerce,* p. 248.
41. Clarkson, *Slavery and Commerce*, p. 256.
42. For Cugoano's biography, we rely on Quobna Ottobah Cugoano, *Thoughts and Sentiments on the Evil of Slavery* (ed. Vincent Carretta; repr., New York: Penguin Books, 1999 [1787]), pp. ix-xxviii. Carretta's edition also contains Cugoano's abridged edition published in 1791. For a more general treatment of Afro-British literature, see Keith A. Sandiford, *Measuring the Moment: Strategies of Protest in Eighteenth-Century Afro-English Writing* (Selingrove, PA: Susquehanna University Press, 1988).
43. Cugoano, *Thoughts and Sentiments*, p. 36.

Cugoano's main challenge is explaining the laws of servitude in the Pentateuch. His principal argument is that Mosaic servitude was benign. Cugoano says: 'a bond-servant was generally the steward in a man's house, and sometimes his heir'.[44] He completely ignores that non-Israelites may be treated like inheritable chattel in Lev. 25.44-46, and instead focuses on the Gibeonites, who serve as hewers of wood and drawers of water.[45] Cugoano adds that the Gibeonites 'were paid for it in such a manner as their service required'.[46] However, Josh. 9.23-27 indicates that the Gibeonites are cursed into slavery, and nothing indicates that they are to be treated like voluntary laborers.

Cugoano achieves mixed success in refuting the curse of Canaan. He does effectively note that Cushites, the people usually associated with Africans, are not descendants of Canaan, but rather of Ham (Gen. 10.6-8).[47] However, he leaves unnoticed that many Canaanites still existed even at the time of Jesus (Mt. 15.22) and so were subject to the curse. So while Cugoano shows that the Africans are not Canaanites, he affirms the justice of enslaving the Canaanites, referring even to 'the subjection of the Canaanites for their crimes'.[48]

Cugoano ignores virtually all the New Testament passages that speak of servants obeying masters (Eph. 6.5; 1 Tim. 6; 1 Pet. 2.18). Representativism is his main tactic in the New Testament, and he chooses as paradigmatic Jesus' statements about the Golden Rule and loving one's neighbor.[49] Cugoano also alludes to the common origin of humanity.[50] Although Cugoano believes laws of servitude were abrogated by Jesus, the law against man-stealing (Deut. 24.7) remains intact.[51] Moreover, Cugoano uses Jesus' injunctions against retaliation to argue that deliverance, rather than revenge, should be the goal of mistreated slaves.

More importantly, Cugoano recognizes that biblical arguments may have lost some of their force:

> I am aware that some of these arguments will weigh nothing against such men as do not believe in the scriptures themselves nor care to understand; but let him be aware not to make use of these things against us which they do not believe.[52]

---

44. Cugoano, *Thoughts and Sentiments*, p. 36.
45. Cugoano, *Thoughts and Sentiments*, p. 37.
46. Cugoano, *Thoughts and Sentiments*, p. 37.
47. Cugoano, *Thoughts and Sentiments*, p. 33.
48. Cugoano, *Thoughts and Sentiments*, p. 48.
49. Cugoano, *Thoughts and Sentiments*, pp. 50, 52.
50. Cugoano, *Thoughts and Sentiments*, p. 29.
51. Cugoano, *Thoughts and Sentiments*, p. 53.
52. Cugoano, *Thoughts and Sentiments*, p. 135.

Indeed, the bulk of his book relies on eliciting humanitarian feelings and legal arguments in favor of abolition. Cugoano, it seems, refrained from centering his appeal on biblical passages, and relied more on his own story, emotional appeals, and general humanitarian principles.

William Wilberforce

A native of Yorkshire, William Wilberforce (1759–1833) became the most important member of Parliament in the fight against slavery.[53] He spearheaded the abolitionist campaign that culminated in the Slave Trade Act of 1807. Wilberforce led the way to the passage of the Slavery Abolition Act of 1833, which abolished slavery in the British empire. Autobiographical writings certainly indicate that Wilberforce was motivated by religious convictions. For that reason he is often lionized as the paradigm of the evangelical Christian abolitionist.

Yet more recent biographical research show how much his complicity in slavery has been overlooked by previous biographies. The most detailed case for such complicity comes from the work of Stephen Tomkins who authored a biography of Wilberforce, as well as a book on the so-called Clapham Sect with which Wilberforce was associated.[54] Tomkins notes that Wilberforce supported a system of apprenticeships, which differed not much from slavery, in Sierra Leone, a colony founded by Wilberforce and the Clapham Sect. Lieutenant Thomas Perronet Thompson, the first crown governor of Sierra Leone and one of Wilberforce's own protégées, realized that apprenticeship was simply slavery by another name, and moved to stop it. However, Wilberforce supported efforts to remove Thompson, and to maintain the apprenticeships. For Tomkins, Wilberforce was choosing the lesser of two evils, but many slaveowners used similar rationales to maintain slavery.

However, even if we assume that Wilberforce was led by sincere, though misguided motives in the Sierra Leone affair, that still does not mean that his abolitionist biblical exegesis was any better than that of the pro-slavery parties. Moreover, his main writings show little weight he gave to the role of the Bible in abolitionist arguments. In fact, in an unpublished letter (dated

---

53. Our general biographical information depends on Stephen Tomkins, *William Wilberforce: A Biography* (Grand Rapids: Eerdmans, 2007); Robin Furneaux, *William Wilberforce* (London: Hamish Hamilton, 1974).

54. See Stephen Tomkins, *The Clapham Sect: How Wilberforce's Circle Transformed Britain* (Oxford: Lion Hudson, 2010), pp. 200-11. For a more popular summary, see Stephen Tomkins, 'Wilberforce Was Complicit in Slavery', *The Guardian* (3 August 2010). Online: www.guardian.co.uk/commentisfree/belief/2010/aug/03/wilberforce-slavery-sierra-leone. See also Ted Olsen, 'The Abolitionist Scandal: William Wilberforce and the Clapham Sect Founded Sierra Leone Then Tolerated a Form of Slavery There, a New Book Reveals', *Christianity Today* 54 (October 2010), pp. 46-49.

248   *Slavery, Abolitionism, and the Ethics of Biblical Scholarship*

17 June 1806), Wilberforce frankly states that he discourages the use of the Bible in discussions about slavery in Parliament. This letter, written to an unknown addressee, is preserved in the archives of The Historical Society of Pennsylvania. The relevant portion states:

> ...there certainly cannot be a doubt as to the principle of the Holy Scriptures especially of the New Testament on the subject of the Slave Trade or even that of slavery; tho' on the latter point Explanations would be required. But I believe it was better not to enter into any such discussion in the House of Commons for many reasons.[55]

This advice is applied by Wilberforce in his own *An Appeal to the Religion, Justice, and Humanity of the Inhabitants of the British Empire, in Behalf of the Negro Slaves in the West Indies* (1823).[56]

As was the case with Clarkson's *Abstract*, Wilberforce begins his treatise with a humanitarian motive: 'to all who have any respect for justice or any feelings of humanity'.[57] Wilberforce also summarizes briefly and sharply the lengthy history of the slave trade: 'The long continuance of this system, like that of its parent the Slave Trade, can only be accounted for by the generally prevailing ignorance of its real nature and of its great numerous evils'.[58] That reason explains why so much time was spent cataloguing the numerous instances of inhumanity and suffering endured by the slaves.

One finds no biblical passages cited, and no direct references to Jesus or Paul in Wilberforce's *Appeal*. Wilberforce alludes to slavery's lack of Christian institutions, such as marriage, which 'the Almighty himself established as a fundamental law'.[59] Wilberforce notes that Sabbath (Sunday) rest is routinely violated, and even the law tacitly accepts work on Sundays.[60] Christianity had practical effects for Wilberforce because it would prevent slaves from revolting. As he phrased it, 'taught by Christianity, they will sustain with patience the sufferings of their actual lot'.[61] Wilberforce sees

---

55. William Wilberforce's letter is preserved in the Howard Edwards Collection of Letters of Anglican Clergymen and other British Public Figures (p. 102), Historical Society of Pennsylvania. My thanks to Mr David Haugaard, Director of Research Services for the Historical Society of Pennsylvania, for providing a copy. Davis (*Slavery in the Age of Revolution*, p. 525 n. 5) cites and paraphrases Wilberforce's letter but does not quote it directly.

56. William Wilberforce, *An Appeal to the Religion, Justice, and Humanity of the Inhabitants of the British Empire in Behalf of the Negro Slaves in the West Indies* (London: J. Hatchard & Son, 1823).

57. Wilberforce, *An Appeal*, p. 1.
58. Wilberforce, *An Appeal*, p. 2.
59. Wilberforce, *An Appeal*, p. 17.
60. Wilberforce, *An Appeal*, p. 27.
61. Wilberforce, *An Appeal*, p. 75.

Christianization as an intermediate step toward complete abolition rather than a way to keep blacks in their enslaved condition.

However, the danger of having large numbers of blacks in the West Indies is also part Wilberforce's argument. He asks rhetorically:

> Is this a time, are these the circumstances, in which it can be wise and safe, if it were honest and humane, to keep down in their present states of heathenish and almost brutish degradation, the 800,000 Negroes of our West Indian Colonies? Here, indeed, is danger, if we observe the signs of the times, whether we take our lesson from the history of men, or form our opinion from natural reason or from the revealed word of God.[62]

By this time, the world knew of the Haitian revolution, and some of the other uprisings in North and South America. Wilberforce's concurrent goal is to eliminate the slaves' African religion, which was usually maintained by 'Obeah Men'. Wilberforce encourages peaceful Christian education, not harsh measures, to achieve that goal.[63]

An Appeal concludes with an argument based mostly on humanitarian grounds, though he does mention God:

> Justice, humanity, and sound policy prescribe our course, and will animate our efforts. Stimulated by a consciousness of what we owe to the law of God and the rights and happiness of man, our exertions will be ardent, and our perseverance invincible.[64]

Wilberforce saw himself as a Christian, and he saw his efforts as part of his Christian mission. However, he was also willing to support slavery when he thought it politically advantageous to the broader abolitionist movement. More importantly, his arguments against slavery were definitely not centered on the Bible, and he explicitly stated that he avoided using biblical texts to support his argument in Parliament.

Summary

Contrary to those who think that the greatest British abolitionists were basing themselves on biblical ethics, the actual works written by these abolitionists show otherwise. We concur with John Barclay, whose study of British abolitionist exegesis concluded, 'when it came to detailed exegesis and a commitment to take the Bible at face value, the pro-slavery arguments often had the better case'.[65] Barclay thinks any exegetical shift had more to do with

---

62. Wilberforce, *An Appeal*, p. 75.
63. Wilberforce, *An Appeal*, pp. 28-30.
64. Wilberforce, *An Appeal*, p. 77.
65. John M.G. Barclay, '"Am I not a man and a brother?" The Bible and the British Anti-Slavery Campaign', *Expository Times* 119 (2007), pp. 3-14.

redefining slaves and integrating them in scriptures compatible with that redefinition. British abolitionists had to move beyond biblical ethics to be successful.

Indeed, James Ramsay did not focus as much on abolitionism as on amelioration of slavery. Granville Sharp did not use religious arguments before 1772 in his main tracts. Otherwise, he used convoluted explanations to diminish the force of pro-slavery passages. His greatest triumphs came when he used legal (e.g., the Somerset case) and humanistic arguments, some of which depended on Montesquieu.[66] Clarkson focused mainly on humanitarian arguments. Cugoano did not even attempt to address the pro-slavery texts in the New Testament. And, despite its title (*An Appeal to the Religion, Justice...*), Wilberforce's main tract did not even have direct references to Jesus or Paul. In short, the argumentation of British abolitionists shows how little they appealed to the Bible to support their cause.

---

66. See F.T.H. Fletcher, 'Montesquieu's Influence on Anti-Slavery Opinion in England', *Journal of Negro History* 18 (1933), pp. 414-25.

Chapter 14

AMERICAN WHITE ABOLITIONISTS

Although American opponents of slavery had a few voices in the 1600s and early 1700s, I adopt 1775, the year the first anti-slavery society was formed in Philadelphia by the Quakers, as the inception of the American abolitionist era. As James Tackach observed, 'No antislavery society formed before 1775, and no abolitionist newspaper circulated during the colonial era'.[1] However, it is not within our scope to rehearse the entire history of American abolitionism between 1775 and 1863, the year of the Emancipation Proclamation.

Nor do I attempt to address the so-called Great Awakening evangelicals because their historiography is highly artificial and because their abolitionist arguments did not differ much from those of the figures we study here. Jon Butler, among other historians, sees the importance of the Great Awakening as constructed by sectarian interests.[2] Lester Scherer makes a cogent case that Methodists largely abandoned the earlier anti-slavery sentiments of John Wesley in the early 1800s.[3] Mark A. Noll, an evangelical scholar himself, even admits that 'in the slave states the success of evangelicalism was

1. James Tackach, *The Abolitionist Movement* (Detroit: Thompson/Gale, 2005), p. 15.
2. Jon Butler, *Awash in a Sea of Faith* (Cambridge, MA: Harvard University Press, 1990), pp. 164-93. See William A. Sloat, 'George Whitefield, African-Americans and Slavery', *Methodist History* 20–23 (1994), pp. 3-13; Allan Gallay, 'The Great Sellout: George Whitefield on Slavery', in Winifred B. Moore, Jr, and Joseph F. Tripp (eds.), *Looking South: Chapters in the History of American Religion* (Westport, CT: Greenwood Press, 1989), pp. 21-23; Stephen J. Stein, 'George Whitefield on Slavery: Some New Evidence', *Church History* 42 (1973), pp. 243-56.
3. Scherer, *Slavery and the Churches*, pp. 137-41; David Hempton, *The Religion of the People: Methodism and Popular Religion, c. 1750–1900* (London: Routledge, 1996). For the view that Wesley was not more active in the abolition movement because of his age, among other things, see Leon O. Hyson, 'Wesley's Thoughts upon Slavery: A Declaration of Human Rights', *Methodist History* 33 (1994), pp. 46-57. For the view that individuals, rather than Wesleyan and allied churches, were mainly responsible for organizing abolition in England, see Elliott Kendall, 'The End of the British Slave Trade', *Epworth Review* 18 (1991), pp. 33-35.

marked also by a muting of the evangelical complaint against slavery'.[4] Accordingly, this chapter demonstrates that American abolitionist biblical interpretation relied on no better rationales or exegesis than what is found among slavery advocates.

John Woolman: A Quaker Hero

Quakers are usually credited with being the first Christian group to make a sustained plea for abolitionism.[5] Stark sums up the importance of the Quakers in the entire abolitionist movement thus: 'organized opposition to slavery arose (1) as a matter of conscience among Quakers having (2) personal contact with slavery, but (3) who were not slaveholders, although moral suasion did cause some Quakers to give up their slaves'.[6] Stark further asserts that 'very few people in the North profited directly from slaves'.[7] For Stark, therefore, Christian moral indignation, not economics, best explains the stronghold of abolitionism in the North.

Although Quakers did mark some significant departures from other Christian sects insofar as abolitionism is concerned, the role of Quakers and the ambivalent attitude of the Quakers toward slavery has not been well recognized by Stark and other scholars. John Nash, in particular, demonstrated how Quaker attitudes toward abolitionism correlated with labor availability and other economic forces in Philadelphia.[8] More careful study of Quakers shows that they were abusing scripture no less than the pro-slavery advocates in the South.

Consider John Woolman, one of the architects of the Quaker abolitionist movement in America. He fought tirelessly to convince fellow Quakers to enforce rules against slavetrading within his own Society.[9] Thus, it behooves

---

4. Mark A. Noll, *The Rise of Evangelicalism: The Age of Edwards, Whitefield and the Wesleys* (Downers Grove, IL: InterVarsity Press, 2003), p. 255.

5. For general treatment of the role of Quakers and slavery, see Jean R. Soderlund, *Quakers and Slavery: A Divided Spirit* (Princeton, NJ: Princeton University Press, 1988); Jack D. Marrietta, *The Reformation of American Quakerism 1748–1783* (Philadelphia: University of Pennsylvania Press, 1984); James Walvin, *The Quakers: Money and Morals* (London: John Murray, 1999); Sydney V. James, *A People among Peoples: Quaker Benevolence in Eighteenth Century America* (Cambridge, MA: Harvard University Press, 1963).

6. Stark, *For the Glory of God*, pp. 346-47.

7. Stark, *For the Glory of God*, p. 347.

8. Gary Nash, 'Slaves and Slaveowners in Colonial Philadelphia', *William and Mary Quarterly* 30 (1973), pp. 223-56.

9. For a recent study of Woolman, see Geoffrey Plank, 'The First Person in Antislavery Literature: John Woolman, his Clothes, and his Journal', *Slavery and Abolition* 30 (2009), pp. 67-91.

us to examine how Woolman's seminal tract, *Considerations on the Keeping of Negroes*, uses the Bible to make a case against slavery. According to Stark, this tract 'was a model of gentle Quaker persuasion'.[10] Yet, Stark, as many others, overestimates the persuasiveness of Woolman's biblical arguments.

The first thing we note about *Considerations* is that the biblical references are sparse and terse. The first biblical reference is from Mt. 25.40: 'Forasmuch as ye did it to the least of these my brethren, ye did it unto me'.[11] As previously shown, Woolman misunderstands 'my brethren' to include non-Christians or everyone. On the contrary, Jesus uses this phrase to refer exclusively to his own followers.

Within the main text, Woolman remarks that 'all nations are of one blood'.[12] This reference to Acts 17.26 (Woolman actually cites 'Gen. lii') establishes that Africans are human beings and deserve the same rights (cf. Epictetus, Seneca). Woolman further claims that even those of a higher station in life can be deceived into treating others as inferior:

> Thus Israel, according to the description of the prophet, Isa. lxv. 5, when exceedingly corrupted and degenerated, yet remembered they were the chosen people of God; and could say, 'Stand by thyself, come not near me, for I am holier than thou'.[13]

Similarly, but without citing the specific biblical passage (Acts 11), Woolman alludes to the example of Peter, who had to be disabused by God from his prejudice against Gentiles.[14] The Holy Spirit was poured on all people of the world, and so ethnicity did not matter.

Woolman's next move is to put his readers in the shoes of the slaves. He describes the oppression that readers might have to suffer if they were slaves. He cites Eccl. 7.7 to show that even Solomon, a wise king, was driven mad by oppressing others, and we should not expect any less madness to result from the oppression of Africans.[15] The Golden Rule comes near the center of his tract—though he never cites the biblical passage explicitly—to reinforce the point that we cannot treat others the way we would not want to be treated.

---

10. Stark, *For the Glory of God*, p. 340.
11. John Woolman, *Considerations on the Keeping of Negroes Recommended to the Professors of Christianity of Every Denomination* (Philadelphia: The Tract Association of Friends, 1754), title page. I use the online version: www.archive.org/stream/considerationson00wool/considerationson00wool_djvu.txt. The page numbers appear in parentheses in that version.
12. Woolman, *Considerations*, p. 2.
13. Woolman, *Considerations*, p. 4.
14. Woolman, *Considerations*, p. 4.
15. Woolman, *Considerations*, p. 5.

Woolman does believe this rule existed in the Old Testament, and he quotes Lev. 19.33-34 as follows: 'If a stranger sojourn with thee in your land, ye shall not vex him; but the stranger that dwelleth with you shall be as one born amongst you, and thou shalt love him as thyself'.[16]

Some biblical allusions involve figures from the Old Testament who suffered and experienced hunger before they found greater fortune. These include Abraham, Jacob, Joseph, and David. But his main example is Israel, who was a slave first. The lesson, for Woolman, is as follows:

> Though, for ends agreeable to infinite wisdom, they were chosen as a peculiar people for a time; yet the Most High acquaints them, that his love is not confined, but extends to the stranger; and to excite their compassion, reminds them of times past, 'Ye were strangers in the land of Egypt'. Again, 'Thou shalt not oppress a stranger, for ye know the heart of a stranger, seeing ye were strangers in the land of Egypt'.[17]

Woolman quotes Deut. 10.9 and 24.14 without giving the specific biblical references.

For Woolman, true Christian practice required not subjecting other people to labor, especially when educating Africans in the ways of Christianity is even more important. Christians who do engage in enslaving fellow human beings, 'not only deprive his fellow-creatures of the sweetness of freedom, which, rightly used, is one of the greatest temporal blessings, but therewith neglect using proper means for their acquaintance with the Holy Scriptures'.[18]

Woolman makes his most explicit appeal to biblical authority near the end of his discourse:

> In Holy Writ the Divine Being saith of himself, 'I am the Lord, which exercise loving-kindness, judgment and righteousness in the earth; for in these things I delight, saith the Lord'. Again, speaking in the way of man, to show his compassion to Israel, whose wickedness had occasioned a calamity, and then being humbled under it, it is said, 'His soul was grieved for their miseries'. If we consider the life of our blessed Saviour, when on earth, as it is recorded by his followers, we shall find that one uniform desire for the eternal and temporal good of mankind, discovered itself in all his actions.[19]

Woolman concludes:

> It is a truth most certain, that a life guided by wisdom from above, agreeably with justice, equity and mercy, is throughout consistent and amiable, and truly

---

16. Woolman, *Considerations*, p. 6. Woolman may be adapting the wording of the KJV or other versions, and he often does not give very specific biblical citations.
17. Woolman, *Considerations*, p. 9.
18. Woolman, *Considerations*, p. 11.
19. Woolman, *Considerations*, p. 11.

beneficial to society; the serenity and calmness of mind in it, affords an unparalleled comfort in this life, and the end of it is blessed.[20]

His final sentence consists of a biblical quote without a specific citation: 'O that they were wise, that they understood this, that they would consider their latter end!' (cf. Deut. 32.29).[21]

So, how effective was Woolman's tract? Nash's study of Philadelphia Quakers shows that slavery increased among Quakers after Woolman published his treatise. Indeed, Woolman completely fails to address the passages that slaveowners used to justify their slavery. Nowhere is Eph. 6.5 or 1 Pet. 2.18 addressed, for example. If Quakers already believe in abolition, then he is not making any new converts. If Quakers are slaveowners, then they also would be familiar with passages that justify slavery.

George Bourne: A Singular Scholar

Born in England, but active in America, George Bourne (1780–1845) was a Presbyterian minister who focused heavily on the Bible to fight slavery. While living in Virginia, Bourne published *A Condensed Anti-Slavery Bible Argument; By A Citizen of Virginia* (1845).[22] This work allows us to see at once the main texts used against slavery, and the responses to texts being used to support slavery.

The first main argument against slavery is based on the prohibition of 'man-stealing' found in Exod. 21.16 (KJV): 'he that stealeth a man, and selleth him, or if he be found in his hand, he shall be put to death'.[23] Since most of slave trading was assumed to involve involuntary abductions in Africa, Bourne thought man-stealing covered most of the slavery in the Americas. Bourne illustrated that this was a 'sin' even before the Mosaic law because the narrative about Joseph being sold by his brothers includes Reuben's recollection of his warning to his brothers when they were deliberating about selling Joseph ('do not sin against the child', Gen. 42.22).[24]

Bourne makes distinctions among *man-stealing* (kidnapping), *man-selling* (slave-trading), and *man-holding* (slaveholding). Within that context, Bourne appeals to Deut. 15.12: 'And if thy brother, a Hebrew man, or a Hebrew

---

20. Woolman, *Considerations*, p. 13.
21. Woolman, *Considerations*, p. 13.
22. Bourne reiterates a previous argument by Samuel Sewall, *The Selling of Joseph: A Memorial* (Boston: Bartholomew Green & John Allen, 1700).
23. Bourne, *Anti-Slavery Argument*, p. 9.
24. Bourne, *Anti-Slavery Argument*, p. 9.

woman, be sold unto thee, and serve thee six years; then in the seventh year thou shalt let him go free from thee'.[25] Therefore, he tells us:

> By force of this one short Levitical statute, the act of *man-stealing* (kidnapping), *man-selling* (slave-trading), and *man-holding* (slaveholding), are, like several other crimes, condemned by the Levitical law; declared by the statute to be punishable with *sure death*—it being very remarkable that the sentence of punishment is expressed in the strongest terms, see Lev. xxiv. 17: 'And he that killeth any man shall surely be put to death'.[26]

Of course, the problem is that Lev. 24.17 says nothing about slavery, and it refers solely to a case where someone murders another person. Nowhere in Lev. 24.17 does it say that slavery or exceeding a term of service described in Deut. 15.12 constitutes murder. The only apparent connection between the text in Deuteronomy and Leviticus is that they are both 'levitical' for Bourne.

Moses Stuart, the famed Andover Hebraist, denied that Exod. 21.16 prohibited all man-stealing, and he said that this law 'applied only to the stealing of Hebrews'.[27] He based this on Deut. 24.7. In addition, Stuart would have in his favor the most ancient understanding of Exod. 21.16, which existed in the Septuagint ('if someone steals one of the sons of Israel…', v. 17 LXX).

Leviticus 25.44 posed an even more serious problem for Bourne, and his main defense was to claim that translations were flawed. In particular, he argued, the Hebrew words *'ebed* and *'amah* should be rendered man-servant or maid-servant, respectively, and not as bond-servant (= slave). In an interesting passage, Bourne gives a very modern view of how translation, in this case the KJV, can be used to preserve oppression:

> King James' translators, in imitation of the Catholic priests who first forged these perversions, falsely dressed up their English version of this statute, so as to resemble the modern Christian practice of negro slavery as nearly as possible—that species of slavery having at the period of their translation, under the sanction of these and similar perversions of the Scriptures, become very extensive, respectable, and popular, in several Christian countries, especially in their tropical territories.[28]

In opposition to the KJV, Bourne translates v. 44 as follows: 'And thy man servant, and thy maiden, which shall be to thee (shall be) from the nations which surround you. From them shall ye procure (the) man servant and the

---

25. Bourne, *Anti-Slavery Argument*, p. 10.
26. Bourne, *Anti-Slavery Argument*, p. 10.
27. Moses Stuart, *Conscience and the Constitution: With Remarks on the Recent Speech of the Hon[orable] Daniel Webster in the Senate of the United States on the Subject of Slavery* (Boston: Crocker & Brewster, 1850), p. 28.
28. Bourne, *Anti-Slavery Argument*, p. 47; cf. 52.

maiden.'[29] Bourne further alleges that the Hebrew word, *qanah*, does not mean to 'buy' but rather to 'procure, acquire, obtain'. Thus, the passage is not dealing with slaves at all, but rather with servants, or hired personnel.

The fact that *'ebed* does mean slave can be demonstrated from the same chapter (Lev. 25.39): 'And if your brother becomes poor beside you, and sells himself to you, you shall not make him serve as a slave'. If *'ebed* means a contracted laborer, then it leaves unexplained why it is so bad for an Israelite to have this status. In fact, the biblical author indicates that it would be oppressive to do this to an Israelite. As mentioned, Bernard Levinson argues that Lev. 25.44-46 actually restricts slavery to outsiders in contrast to Exod. 21.6.

However, Bourne deploys an even more sophisticated grammatical argument in his arsenal. Bourne claims that directives phrased in the singular are meant for individuals, while those phrased with plural verbs or pronouns are meant for the collective Israel. Since Lev. 25.44 uses plural verbs (e.g., *tiknū* [תִּקְנוּ] = 'you [plural] shall buy, acquire'), then this refers collectively to Israel having care of immigrant laborers, and cannot refer to individual ownership of slaves. Bourne concludes:

> This change of the address is a circumstance which indicates, more than any other the principal object of the statute which was to encourage the settlement of foreigners in the Jewish nation, and provide for their support, for the more effectual promotion of the true religion—for which purpose it was the most equitable and excellent naturalization act that ever existed in this world. For the same righteous purpose each native Israelite was allowed by the statute, to procure as many of these foreign servants as he chose, by contracts made with the servants themselves, or with their parents or guardians, in which sense, and by which means alone, the native Jews and their posterity, were to 'inherit' or 'possess' these adopted foreigners and their posterity, by circumcision and incorporation into the body of the nation.[30]

Thus, these are really contracted servants, who would be managed by Israel as a nation.

Bourne is correct to note that the addressee does frequently change from you (singular) to you (plural). This phenomenon has been denominated *Numeruswechsel* (German for 'number switching'), and explanations are still highly contested.[31] However, Bourne clearly errs in his claim that the plural refers only to collective directives, while a singular addressee refers to obligations incumbent on individual Hebrews.

---

29. Bourne, *Anti-Slavery Argument*, p. 46.
30. Bourne, *Anti-Slavery Argument*, p. 48.
31. C.T. Begg, 'The Significance of the *Numeruswechsel* in Deuteronomy', *ETL* 55 (1979), pp. 116-24.

Bourne's claim, in fact, is contradicted by other statements in the same chapter, including Lev. 25.14: 'And if you [plural] sell to your neighbor [singular] or buy from your neighbor [singular], you [plural] shall not wrong one another [singular]'. By Bourne's logic, the first plural 'you' is the entire nation of Israel. If so, then 'your neighbor' would be Israel's neighbor, and an outside nation. Yet 'one another' is grammatically singular in the last part of the verse, and so it must mean that the directive is meant to prohibit individual Hebrews from oppressing other individual Hebrews.[32] In any case, Bourne's defense typically relies on these sort of linguistically dubious and easily refutable arguments.

Summary

Euroamerican abolitionists we studied rely on weak interpretive rationales. Woolman, who is credited with very effective arguments by Stark, actually pays very little attention to biblical arguments in his main tract, *Considerations*. George Bourne deploys philological analysis of specific passages in his *A Condensed Anti-Slavery Bible Argument*, but he ultimately relies on very questionable and dubious arguments that biblical linguists of the time (e.g., Moses Stuart) could easily overturn. At least in the examples we have studied, historical-critical exegesis favored the pro-slavery position.

---

32. The RSV obscures the identity of the neighbor. The Hebrew word *'amîteka* (עמיתך) is best rendered 'your people'. The RSV's phrase 'one another' (אחיו) more literally means 'one's brother'. Those are all indicators of insiders, fellow Hebrews.

Chapter 15

AFRICAN-AMERICAN ABOLITIONISTS

None of the American white abolitionists we have discussed ever experienced slavery themselves. So, how did biblical argumentation work when the abolitionist was a slave? In Antebellum America, the response was quite diverse. The Bible could be used to promote opposing views of liberation. Thus, we have Edward Blyden, a Presbyterian minister, who used the Exodus narrative to promote the idea that African Americans should migrate to Liberia.[1] But we also have another Presbyterian minister, Henry Highland Garnet, who thought the Exodus model was not an appropriate analogy because African Americans were native-born American citizens, and so it was their country they would flee.[2]

Without claiming to do justice to the diversity seen in nineteenth-century African-American abolitionist thought, this chapter concentrates here on David Walker and Frederick Douglass, two of the main nineteenth-century African-American abolitionists. As we shall see, the appeal to the Bible made a difference sometimes, but not in the manner that modern Christian apologists may envision. Douglass is particularly deserving of extended attention because most modern biblical scholars still have not appreciated the depth of his secular humanism. Yet Douglass illustrates that one did not need religious motives to promote abolitionism even if the large number of African-American thinkers of the time did think religion mattered.

David Walker: Egypt Was Better

David Walker (1785–1830) is widely regarded as the first African American to write a significant indictment of American slavery. Born in Wilmington, North Carolina, David Walker was the son of a free woman, through whom he had a freeborn status. However, he travelled widely and witnessed first-hand the suffering being endured by enslaved African Americans. He eventually settled in Boston, Massachusetts where he began to network with

---

1. On Blyden, see Callahan, *The Talking Book*, pp. 125-26.
2. See Henry Highland Garnet, 'An Address to the Slaves of the United States, Buffalo, NY, 1843' (Lincoln, NE: Electronic Texts in American Studies, 2007), p. 7. Online: digitalcommons.unl.edu/cgi/viewcontent.cgi?article=1007&context=etas.

other abolitionists. He was able to marshal his wide reading, especially in history, in a short but powerful critique of American slavery that also attacked Christianity.

In the late 1820s Walker published *An Appeal to the Coloured People of the World*, which originated as a series of tracts. The standard edition that we shall study is from 1830. One of the most salient aspects of Walker's *Appeal* is that it effectively refutes those apologists (e.g., Stark) who argue that Christianity resulted in an improvement for slaves. In fact, Walker utilized his knowledge of biblical history to argue that Egyptian slavery was nowhere near as racist as American slavery:

> I call upon professing Christians…to show me a page of history, either sacred or profane, on which a verse can be found, which maintains that the Egyptians heaped the insupportable insult upon the children of Israel, by telling them that they were not of the human family.[3]

Walker also knew enough about Roman slave law to see that slaves could purchase their own freedom, and could even become prominent citizens. American Christians, on the other hand, blocked any sort of advancement for Blacks even if they were freed.[4]

In terms of the usage of the Bible to support abolitionism, Walker cited Acts 10.34-35, and paraphrased it as 'his Apostle Peter declared before Cornelius and others that he is no respecter of persons, but in every nation he that feareth God and worketh righteousness is accepted with him'.[5] As with other abolitionists who cited such texts, they did not address the argument that God being the respecter of persons was restricted to the opportunity for salvation. Walker did not even attempt to explain the texts in the New Testament that commanded slaves to be obedient. Such texts would at least show that New Testament authors did not see a contradiction between God not being a respecter of persons, and God allowing slavery.

Indeed, this very same Cornelius is portrayed as a slave owner earlier in the same chapter (Acts 10.7) when it says: 'When the angel who spoke to him had departed, he called two of his servants and a devout soldier from among those that waited on him'. The Greek word, οἰκέτης, is used more specifically for a domestic slave. However, 1 Pet. 2.18 uses the same Greek term, and shows that such domestic slaves could be subject to cruel abuse.

Walker also cited the idea that humans are made in the image of God.[6] However, as with other appeals to the *imago Dei* argument, Walker leaves unexplained how the *imago Dei* idea still allowed slavery, genocide, and the

3. Walker, *Appeal*, p. 30.
4. Walker, *Appeal*, p. 30.
5. Walker, *Appeal*, p. 57. For Walker, 'he is no respect to persons = he is no respector of persons'.
6. Walker, *Appeal*, p. 80.

subordination of women in scripture. Canaanite children can be killed despite their being made in the image of God just as much as the Hebrews. In short, Walker adduced a couple of brief biblical arguments, but he did so in such a perfunctory manner that it can scarcely be called the mainstay of his tract. Walker did not address pro-slavery passages and he did not seem interested in answering objections or explaining counterexamples.

Frederick Douglass: A Secular Humanist?

Many historians agree that Frederick Douglass (1819–1895) was probably the most important African-American voice of the nineteenth century. Reginald Davis, one of Douglass's main biographers today, calls him a 'precursor of liberation theology'.[7] A brilliant autodidact, Douglass's perspicacious and eloquent writing often outshone even that of the most educated white elite. He eventually rose from a brutal existence as a slave to consul general to Haiti during Benjamin Harrison's presidency (1881–1887).

Important studies of Douglass's views on the Bible and religion have been published by Scott C. Williamson and Sterling Stuckey.[8] These studies show that Douglass, even when viewed as a precursor of liberation theology, had an ambivalent view of the Bible's role in abolition. This ambivalence, or even disinterest, in using the Bible for his abolitionist arguments may be a reason why an anthology devoted to African-American biblical interpretation awards Douglass only one indexed reference.[9]

My own independent study of Douglass's writings shows that, despite his professed love for the Bible, that book formed a very marginal part of his argumentation. On the one hand, Douglass does say that the Bible was the most important book in his life at one time.[10] He approved of the belief that slavery 'was not the fault of the Bible or Christianity'.[11] In 1857, he declared:

---

7. Reginald F. Davis, *Frederick Douglass: A Precursor of Liberation Theology* (Macon, GA: Mercer University Press, 2005). For a standard biography, see William S. McFeeley, *Frederick Douglass* (New York: W.W. Norton, 1995).

8. Scott C. Williamson, *The Narrative Life: The Moral and Religious Thought of Frederick Douglass* (Macon, GA: Mercer University Press, 2002); Sterling Stuckey, '"My Burden Lightened": Frederick Douglass, the Bible, and Slave Culture', in Vincent L. Wimbush (ed.), *African Americans and the Bible: Sacred Texts and Social Textures* (New York: Continuum, 2000), pp. 251-65.

9. Cain Hope Felder (ed.), *Stony the Road we Trod: African American Biblical Interpretation* (Minneapolis: Fortress Press, 1991).

10. Douglass, 'The Bible Opposes Opression, Fraud, and Wrong... 6 January, 1845', in Blassingame, *The Frederick Douglass Papers*, I, p. 128: 'What could be better than the Bible to me, contending against oppression, fraud, and wrong?'

11. Douglass, 'Slavery and the Limits of Non-Intervention...7 December 1859', in Blassingame, *The Frederick Douglass Papers*, III, p. 284.

> It is no evidence that the Bible is a bad book, because those who profess to believe in the Bible are bad. The slaveholders of the South, and many of their wicked allies in the North, claim the Bible for slavery; shall we, therefore, fling the Bible away as a proslavery book? It would be as reasonable to do so as it would be to fling away the Constitution.[12]

On the other hand, he saw an intimate relationship between religiosity and slaveholding. For example, in his *Narrative of the Life*, he remarked that 'of all slaveholders with whom I have met, religious slaveholders are the worst. I have found them the meanest and basest, the most cruel and cowardly, of all others.'[13]

Douglass also reports on the outcome of a visit his master, Thomas Auld, made to a Methodist camp meeting in August of 1832:

> I indulged a faint hope that his conversion would lead him to emancipate his slaves, and that, if he did not do this, it would, at any rate, make him more kind and humane. I was disappointed in both those respects. It neither made him more humane to his slaves, nor emancipate them... Prior to his conversion, he relied on his own depravity to shield and sustain him in his savage barbarity; but after his conversion, he found religious sanction and support for his slaveholding cruelty.[14]

In fact, Douglass adds that Auld would use Lk. 12.47 ('He that knoweth his master's will, and doeth it not, shall be beaten with many stripes') to justify brutally beating a female slave, a 'lacerated young woman tied up in this horrid situation four or five hours at a time'.[15] According to Williamson, Douglass noted 'this passage more than any other'.[16]

Such statements led to Douglass being perceived as so anti-religious that he had to explain himself:

> I have, in several instances, spoken in such a tone and manner, respecting religion, as may possibly lead those unacquainted with my religious views to suppose me an opponent of all religion... What I have said respecting and against religion, I mean strictly to apply to slaveholding religion of this land,

---

12. Douglass, 'The Dred Scott Decision...May 1857', in Blassingame, *The Frederick Douglass Papers*, III, p. 182.

13. Douglass, *Narrative of the Life of Frederick Douglass, an American Slave*, in *Frederick Douglass: Autobiographies* (ed. Henry Louis Gates; New York: The Library of America, 1994), p. 68. All pages cited for Douglass's biographies (*Narrative of the Life of Frederick Douglass, an American Slave*; *My Bondage and my Freedom*; *Life and Times of Frederick Douglass*) are from Gates's edition.

14. Douglass, *Narrative of the Life*, p. 52.

15. Douglass, *Narrative of the Life*, p. 53.

16. Williamson, *The Narrative Life*, p. 86. I have found at least seven other instances, as follows: Blassingame, *The Frederick Douglass Papers*, I, pp. 13, 86, 144, 152, 376, 460, 469.

and with no possible reference to Christianity proper; for, between the Christianity of this land, and the Christianity of Christ, I recognize the widest possible difference... I love the pure, peaceable, and impartial Christianity of Christ.[17]

In other words, Frederick Douglass had a representativist view of the Bible and Christianity. For Douglass, 'pure' Christianity was incompatible with slavery.

Perhaps part of Douglass's ambivalence is rooted in his expressed realization that scriptural interpretation could be arbitrary and used to support slavery. In *My Bondage and my Freedom*, Douglass alluded to the problem of 'representativism' we have discussed:

> Instead of preaching the gospel against this tyranny, rebuke, and wrong, ministers of religion have sought by all and every means, to throw in the background whatever in the bible could be construed into opposition to slavery, and to bring forward that which they could torture into its support. This I conceive to be the darkest feature of slavery, and the most difficult to attack because it is identified with religion, and exposes those who denounce it to the charge of infidelity.[18]

Sometimes, Douglass also seemed unsure about the irrefutability of the idea that the Bible was anti-slavery:

> I do not believe that the Bible sanctions American slavery. I do NOT believe that Christ and his Apostles approved of slave-holding... But here I will say, that should doctors of divinity ever convince me that the Bible sanctions American slavery, that Christ and his apostles justify returning men to bondage, then I will give the Bible to the flames, and no more worship God in the name of Christ. For of what value to men would a religion be which not only permitted, but enjoined upon men the enslavement of each other, and which would leave them to the sway of physical force and permit the strong to enslave the weak?[19]

He went even further in a speech whose theme was the hypocrisy of celebrating the Fourth of July. He remarked that many theologians were using the Bible to promote slavery, and exclaimed '[f]or my part, I would say, welcome infidelity! welcome atheism! welcome anything! in preference to the Gospel as preached by those Divines!'[20]

---

17. Douglass, *Narrative of the Life*, p. 97 (Douglass's italics).
18. Douglass, *My Bondage and my Freedom* (Appendix), p. 406.
19. *Douglass*, 'Slavery's Northern Bulwarks...12 January, 1851', in Blassingame, *The Frederick Douglass Papers*, II, p. 284. Douglass's emphasis.
20. Douglass, 'What to the Slave is the Fourth of July?...5 July, 1852', in Blassingame, *The Frederick Douglass Papers*, II, p. 377.

This ambivalence is further displayed when he registered his opposition to the American and Foreign Anti-Slavery Society's plan to provide Bibles for slaves. His opposition was most forcefully expressed in 1849, when he debated the issue with Reverend Henry Highland Garnet in New York City.[21] Douglass bluntly stated: 'I am not for giving the slave the Bible or anything this side of freedom'.[22] To be fair, Douglass's hesitancy was due to pragmatic concerns that illiterate slaves would simply be fed pro-slavery passages by their masters rather than because he thought the Bible was really pro-slavery.

Otherwise, Douglass's most developed arguments against slavery reveal the absence of any extended biblical exegesis. Unlike David Walker, who had at least a couple of sustained discussions about the superior nature of Egyptian slavery in the biblical records, Douglass's references are usually casual allusions. He mentions a verse here and there, but there is no sustained attention to counterpoints (as we saw with las Casas). In this we agree, only in part, with Williamson, who remarks,

> Douglass referred to better than seventy Biblical passages in speeches during his tenure with the Garrisonians. Most of these references are devoid of any considerable exegetical content. Yet they are not merely passing references.[23]

Williamson, however, does not specify which biblical quotations were more than 'passing references'. My own study of every indexed biblical passage listed in Blassingame's collection of Douglass's documents shows that the vast majority of biblical citations do qualify as 'passing references'. Here are a few examples:

(1) 'We are here to render honor to one to whom honor is due'.[24] An allusion to Rom. 13.7 in a speech honoring Charles Sumner.
(2) 'In few things, perhaps, more than in farming, does one find that there is nothing new under the sun'.[25] An allusion to Eccl. 1.9 in a speech about agriculture.

---

21. For an account of this event, see Joel Schor, 'The Rivalry between Frederick Douglass and Henry Highland Garnet', *Journal of Negro History* 64 (1979), pp. 30-38. See also Callahan, *The Talking Book*, pp. 21-25. It is not clear that Douglass and Garnet faced each other at the same time, thus resembling the debate between las Casas and Sepulveda centuries earlier.

22. Douglass, 'Shalt Thou Steal?...9 May 1849', in Blassingame, *The Frederick Douglass Papers*, II, p. 182.

23. Williamson, *The Narrative Life*, p. 84.

24. Douglass, 'Collection for Funds for Sumner Portrait...11 April, 1873', in Blassingame, *The Frederick Douglass Papers*, IV, p. 356.

25. Douglass, 'Agriculture and Black Progress...18 September 1873', in Blassingame, *The Frederick Douglass Papers*, IV, p. 378.

(3) 'All flesh is grass, and the amount of vegetable matter we obtain from the earth will be a measure of the life and happiness of the men and animals who subsist upon it'.[26] A reference to 1 Pet. 1.24 in a speech about fertilizers.

(4) 'He was often wounded in the house of his friends'.[27] A reference to Zech 13.6 in a speech about Lincoln's critics.

The vast majority of Douglass's allusions to the Bible were similar, and he cited many non-biblical sources as well.

Where Douglass alluded to the Bible for anti-slavery sentiments, he maintained his position by arbitrary exegesis or by ignoring many passages that endorsed slavery. For example, he says that 'there was no such thing known among the Jews as slavery for life, except it was desired on the part of the servant himself'.[28] However, this is not totally correct. While Hebrew slaves could not be enslaved for life, foreigners could certainly be enslaved for life and inherited by descendants in Lev. 25.44-46. Likewise, he accepts that Onesimus was sent back a free man, but gives no detailed defense for that position.[29]

Acts 17.26 is one of the few texts that Douglass explicitly uses to support some of his foundational concepts:

> I want no better basis for my activities and affinities than the broad foundation laid by the Bible itself, that God has made of one blood all nations of men to dwell on all the face of the earth. This comprehends the Fatherhood of God and the brotherhood of man.[30]

But, as used by the author of Acts, the sentiment was meant to show that all people were subject to the same supreme master, the biblical God. Thus, it is not an anti-slavery passage at all, but rather one which suggests universal servitude to the biblical God. Moreover, the author of Acts acknowledges that some non-Christians had the same idea (Acts 17.28: 'even some of your poets have said…').

Douglass's reticence to use the Bible as extensively as some other abolitionists can be explained by his shift toward a deistic or secular humanistic view of the Bible that is still overlooked by some scholars. Thus, Harrill sees

---

26. Douglass, 'Agriculture and Black Progress', IV, p. 390.

27. Douglass, 'The Freedman's Monument to Abraham Lincoln…14 April, 1876', in Blassingame, *The Frederick Douglass Papers*, IV, p. 437.

28. Douglass, 'Baptists, Congregationalists, The Free Church and Slavery…23 December 1845', in Blassingame, *The Frederick Douglass Papers*, I, p. 116.

29. Douglass, 'Baptists, Congregationalists', I, p. 116.

30. Douglass, 'The Nation's Problem…16 April, 1889', in Blassingame, *The Frederick Douglass Papers*, V, p. 413. See other citations of Acts 17.26 in Blassingame, *The Frederick Douglass Papers*, I, p. 493, II, p. 383.

Douglass as opposed to William Lloyd Garrison's 'denial of the authority of Scripture in the slavery question'.[31] Garrison judged the word of God by whether it conformed to self-evident ethical principles. One of Garrison's disciples, Henry C. Wright, even promulgated a radical resolution at the 1850 meeting of the American Anti-Slavery Society in Boston:

> Resolved, That if the Bible sanctions slavery and is thus opposed to the self-evident truth that 'all men are created equal, and have an inalienable right to liberty', the Bible is a self-evident falsehood, and ought to be, and ere long be, regarded as the enemy of Nature and Nature's God, and the progress of the human race in liberty, justice, and goodness.[32]

Nonetheless, Harrill cites items mostly before the late 1860s for evidence of Douglass's stance.

Evidence for Douglass's secularization now comes from the correspondence of Ottilie Assing, the German-born lover of Douglass and a radical atheist. This correspondence came to light in the late 1980s and early 1990s, and so has not been cited by biblical scholars mentioned.[33] A letter, dated 15 May 1871, which Assing wrote to Ludwig Feuerbach (1804–1872), the celebrated German atheist, noted how Douglass's Christianity initially posed a problem between them. So she and Douglass read Feuerbach's *The Essence of Christianity* together. She reported that Feuerbach's ideas 'resulted in a total reversal of his attitudes'.[34] She adds that '[f]or the satisfaction of seeing a superior man won over for atheism [*Geistesfreiheit*]...I feel obliged to you'.[35] Even if Assing is exaggerating (or even if Diedrich's translation is not the best here), it is clear that toward the end of his life, Douglass spoke more like a deist or secular humanist.

---

31. Harrill, 'The Use of the New Testament', p. 161.

32. Quoted in Harrill, 'Use of the New Testament', p. 159. See also comments by Mark A. Noll, *The Civil War as a Theological Crisis* (Chapel Hill: University of North Carolina Press, 2006), pp. 31-32.

33. See Terry H. Pickett, 'The Friendship of Frederick Douglass with the German Ottilie Assing', *Georgia Historical Quarterly* 73 (1989), pp. 88-105; Maria Diedrich, *Love across Color Lines: Ottilie Assing and Frederick Douglass* (New York: Hill & Wang, 1999), pp. xxvi-xxvii.

34. This letter is translated into English in its entirety by Diedrich (*Love across Color Lines*, pp. 259-60, quotation on p. 260). A German edition of the letter is provided in Martin Sass (ed.), *Ausgewählte Briefe von und an Ludwig Feuerbach*, XII–XIII (Stuttgart: Friedrich Frommann, 1964), pp. 365-66. The letter is catalogued as 'Briefe 350'.

35. Diedrich, *Love across Color Lines*, p. 260. Diedrich translates *Geistesfreiheit* as 'atheism'. Diedrich also translates as 'atheism' the German word *Freigeistigkeit*, which is found earlier in the same letter. These words are not as clearly applied to atheism/atheist as other German words available, such as *Atheismus* or *Ungläubig*, which Assing applied to herself ('Wir Ungläubigen') toward the end of the letter.

A good example of this evolution toward humanism is a speech, titled 'It Moves', delivered in Washington, DC, on 20 November 1883. Therein Douglass explains why abolition was successful. He expresses his sympathy with the Higher Criticism of the Bible and new scientific discoveries that cast doubt on the Bible's reliability. Douglass remarks: 'Men are compelled to admit that the Genesis by Moses is less trustworthy as to the time of creating the heavens and the earth than are the rocks and the stars'.[36] Douglass also was irritated with the biblical inerrantist position: 'Better that a thousand errors should remain, it insists, than that the faith of the multitude shall be shocked and unsettled by the discovery of error in what was believed to be infallible and perfect'.[37] Douglass kept a bust of Feuerbach and David Friedrich Strauss, the radical New Testament scholar, in his study.[38]

Toward the end of 'It Moves', Douglass becomes more emphatic that humanity must judge and help themselves:

> It may not be a useless speculation to inquire when[ce] comes the disposition or suggestion of reform; whence that irresistible power that impels men to brave all the hardships and dangers involved in pioneering an unpopular cause? Has it a natural or a celestial origin? Is it human or is it divine, or is it both? I have no hesitation in stating where I stand in respect to these questions. It seems to me that the true philosophy of reform is not found in the clouds, or in the stars, or any where else outside of humanity itself. So far as the laws of the universe have been discovered and understood, they seem to teach that the mission of man's improvement and perfection has been wholly committed to man himself. So is he to be his own savior or his own destroyer. He has neither angels to help him nor devils to hinder him.[39]

Douglass assimilated here some of the most important lessons of the Enlightenment, including the allusion to scientific discoveries and the progress that it augurs for humankind. This could have been said by almost any secular humanist today.

Summary

We can safely state that the Bible was important for perhaps the vast majority of African-American abolitionists in the nineteenth century. But the use of the Bible entailed the same vulnerabilities we have seen in the usage of White abolitionists. The Exodus narrative, for example, could equally be used as a model of liberation, or as an argument that slavery itself was not

---

36. Douglass, 'It Moves…20 November 1883', in Blassingame, *The Frederick Douglass Papers*, V, p. 131.
37. Douglass, 'It Moves', V, p. 136.
38. Diedrich, *Love across Color Lines*, p. 229.
39. Douglass, 'It Moves', V, p. 137.

abolished. After all, God permitted the Hebrews to have slaves in Canaan. The Bible may have inspired many African Americans to pursue liberation, but that was countered by more powerful white masters who could and did use the Bible just as well to serve their ends.

And while we know that important African-American abolitionists used the Bible, most modern historians rarely engage in a close study of that usage. A close study reveals a diverse approach to the Bible in argumentation. Walker used the Bible to subvert the idea that American Christian slavery was better than Egyptian slavery. Douglass had many quotes, but rarely any extensive exegesis of passages. He certainly did not address the pro-slavery passages in depth. Douglass later became more aligned with secular humanism in his thinking, even going so far as to exalt the ethics of Ingersoll, the agnostic, over those of D.L. Moody, the celebrated evangelical leader.[40] In sum, Walker and Douglass certainly should force Christian apologists to clarify what 'using' the Bible meant.

---

40. Douglass, 'We Are Confronted by a New Administration...16 April, 1885', in Blassingame, *The Frederick Douglass Papers*, V, p. 190: 'Infidel though Mr. Ingersoll may be called, he never turned his back upon his colored brothers, as did the evangelical Christians of this city on the occasion of the late visit of Mr. Moody'. For a modern Christian lament on Douglass's liberalization, see William L. Van Deburg, 'The Tragedy of Frederick Douglass', *Christianity Today* 19 (1975), pp. 415-16.

Chapter 16

Explaining Abolition

The present survey emphasizes negative results insofar as it aims to prove that biblical ethics were not mainly responsible for the triumph of abolition. However, I have not explained why abolition became so successful at the time it did. That is to say, why, after thousands of years of persistence, did slavery come to an end in the West between about 1775 and 1900? I cannot claim to have answered this question more satisfactorily than others who have tried before. I can say that there were probably many factors that are at least better candidates than the religious or biblical explanations furnished by Stark and other apologists.

Why Stark's Thesis Is Wrong

In order to understand my more tentative multi-factorial stance on the triumph of abolition, let's return to Stark's contention that Christianity was an essential factor in abolition. As Stark phrased it: 'Just as science arose only once, so, too, did effective moral opposition to slavery. Christian theology was essential to both.'[1] On the other hand, Stark does say that '[a]bolition was not inherent in Christian scripture, it was only a *possible* conclusion and one unlikely to be reached except under favorable circumstances'.[2]

Thus, an inconsistency obtains between Christianity being 'essential' to abolition, and abolition not being 'inherent' in Christian scripture. Stark adds more confusion by saying:

> I do not propose that monotheism or even Christian culture was a *sufficient* basis for deeming slavery to be a sin. Instead, I propose that it was a *necessary* basis, in that only those religious thinkers working within the Christian tradition were able to reach anti-slavery conclusions (with the exception of two Jewish sects)… [T]he *moral potential* for an anti-slavery conclusion lay within Christian thought, but to bring it to fruition probably required exposure to and

1. Stark, *For the Glory of God*, p. 291.
2. Stark, *For the Glory of God*, p. 345 (Stark's italics).

perhaps experience with correlative concepts such as freedom and dignity of the individual—with the general moral and political trends of Western civilization.[3]

More specifically, Stark argues:

> Organized opposition to slavery arose only when and where (1) the appropriate moral predisposition was (2) stimulated by the salience of the phenomenon and (3) was not counteracted by perceived self-interest. The first element explains why indigenous abolitionist movements have yet to appear in non-Christian nations. The second accounts for the fact that abolition movements were limited to places where people felt some direct responsibility for the existence of slavery, as in the United States, Latin America, and those European nations directly involved in colonial slavery. The third element explains why abolition movements did not prosper in the American South or in European colonies.[4]

These reasons can easily be deconstructed because Stark's definitions and premises are demonstrably false or inconsistent.

Briefly, Stark's first element wrongly suggests that an indigenous moral predisposition toward abolition could not exist in non-Christian cultures. But we have seen a moral predisposition against slavery voiced in, among other places, Greece and Rome. In Haiti, mostly non-Christians organized a successful opposition to slavery. Moreover, since nothing in the Bible encourages an organized opposition to slavery itself, it is unclear why biblical ethics would generate the *appropriate moral predisposition* against slavery. If anything, the moral predispositions seen in both the Old Testament and New Testament is that slavery is perfectly compatible with even those moral precepts thought to be fundamental (e.g., the *imago Dei*).

Stark's second element does not explain why abolitionism was strongest in the American North while the 'salience of the phenomenon' was really in the South. This second element leaves unexplained why the British public, which was largely unexposed directly to slavery, had such a strong reaction to slavery, while Christian slaveowners, who were directly seeing the phenomenon, were the fiercest advocates of slavery, especially in the American South.

Stark's third element suggests that abolitionism does not have a perceived self-interest, economic or otherwise, of its own. But even the idea that abolition pleases God denotes self-interest. Pleasing God confers certain benefits, including eternal salvation or God's favor. Moreover, some pro-slavery advocates denied having any direct benefit from slavery. Fred Ross, for instance, said, 'I am not a slave-holder… I merely wish to show I have no selfish motive in giving…the true Southern defense of slavery.'[5]

3. Stark, *For the Glory of God*, p. 345.
4. Stark, *For the Glory of God*, p. 339.
5. Ross, *Slavery Ordained*, p. 34.

Nor does Stark's appeal to the increasing notion of slavery as a 'sin' provide a plausible explanation. According to Stark, slavery was abolished because it came to be seen as a sin against God. However, this theory does not explain why slavery came to be viewed as a sin against God around 1800, given that the Bible had been available for some 1800 years prior to that. The pro-slavery forces, of course, had a reasonable response to the charge that slavery was a sin. Ross simply observed that 'God nowhere says it [slavery] is a sin'.[6]

Not surprisingly, slavery advocates had a different definition of sin. Ross defined it as 'self-will', or the act of going against the will of God, the master of all human beings.[7] For Ross, whatever God commanded could only be reckoned as the right thing to do ('the right as made by God').[8] Ross noted that, when God commanded Adam and Eve to reproduce, their progeny had to commit incest. Yet, it would be absurd to say that God commanded people to sin.[9] The same with slavery. If God commanded and allowed Israelites to enslave non-Israelites, then this alone shows that enslavement itself cannot be a sin.

Given Stark's flawed definitions and assumptions, his explanation for abolition is not very useful. A better explanation of abolition accounts for what was different at the time that abolitionism triumphed. A sound explanation should properly weigh historical constants against variables. The Bible, having been around for thousands of years, cannot be what was different between 1775 and 1900. Something else must be the crucial variable or set of variables. We, therefore, turn our attention to what was different between 1775 and 1900.

Freedom Is Inherent in Slavery

Any explanation of abolition must begin with the fact that slavery has always implied freedom. As Orlando Patterson remarks: 'freedom was generated from the experience of slavery'.[10] Freedom is a weighty historical constant because, unlike the use of the Bible, it is a natural human disposition. Indeed, it is simply natural for slaves to desire freedom. If this were not the case, then no force would have been needed to keep slaves in place. Thus, the seeds of freedom do not need any extensive religious explanation at all. The yearning for freedom will exist even where the Bible does not.

---

6. Ross, *Slavery Ordained*, p. 29.
7. Ross, *Slavery Ordained*, p. 42.
8. Ross, *Slavery Ordained*, p. 52.
9. Ross, *Slavery Ordained*, p. 43.
10. Patterson, *Freedom*, p. xiii.

Most scholars of slavery restrict themselves to Greco-Roman materials or show only superficial knowledge of ancient Near Eastern materials. For example, Orlando Patterson, one of the most influential students of freedom, tells us that 'Freedom...emerged as a supreme value over the course of the sixth and fifth centuries BCE at the very dawn of Western Civilization'.[11] Yet, we have ample evidence that freedom was already being discussed in Mesopotamian materials, which Patterson misrepresented. Again, massive emancipations, even if some are fictional, are recorded in the ancient Near East (e.g., the Egyptians in Exod. 12.31-32; Mesopotamian *misharum* acts).

Economics: Money Matters

Eric Williams, a brilliant doctoral student of history at Oxford and later the first prime minister of Trinidad, ignited a firestorm in 1944 with the publication of his *Capitalism and Slavery*.[12] Williams argued that humanitarian or religious motives were exaggerated by British abolitionist narratives. Such narratives were not only self-serving but also nationalist insofar as the British wanted to promote their own revised version of history in order to make themselves appear better motivated than they were.

Williams argued that the abolitionist movement coincided with the rise of industrial capitalism, which saw it as advantageous to destroy the monopolies at the root of the mercantilist system that kept slavery alive. As Williams phrased it:

> The capitalists had first encouraged West Indian slavery and then helped to destroy it. When British capitalism depended on the West Indies, they ignored slavery or defended it. When British capitalism found the West Indian monopoly a nuisance, they destroyed West Indian slavery as the first step in the destruction of West Indian monopoly.[13]

Williams also notes that the overproduction of British West Indian sugar was creating a surplus that needed subsidies to compete with cheaper sugar from Brazil, and these government subsidies were anathema to capitalists who preferred the free market. Williams says '[o]verproduction in 1807 demanded abolition; overproduction in 1833 demanded emancipation'.[14]

---

11. Patterson, *Freedom*, p. xii.
12. For an overview of Williams's contributions to the study of slavery, see Heather Cateau and Selwyn H.H. Carrington (eds.), *Capitalism and Slavery Fifty Years Later: Eric Eustace Williams—A Reassessment of the Man and his Work* (New York: Peter Lang, 2000). For a more recent contribution to the debate, see Joseph E. Inikori, *Africans and the Industrial Revolution: A Study in International Trade and Economic Development* (Cambridge: Cambridge University Press, 2002).
13. Williams, *Capitalism and Slavery*, p. 169.
14. Williams, *Capitalism and Slavery*, p. 152.

Williams points to the realization that subsidizing the West Indian sugar monopoly meant that 'the production of slavery was more costly than that of free labor'.[15] It was cheaper to hire people for a very low wage because that eliminated the costs of having to feed and clothe workers, not to mention the cost of buying slaves. Another impulse that contributed to abolition was the desire to break the French West Indian economy and promote the British sugar grown in the East Indies. Britain encouraged abolition everywhere so that the French would lose the economic advantage of free labor.

Many scholars have rightly criticized Williams for overextending his explanation. Seymour Drescher and Roger Anstey, among others, have shown that slavery was still very profitable at the time that Britain was encouraging abolition.[16] Drescher notes that 'on the eve of British emancipation slave labour still produced well over nine-tenths of the Atlantic sugar economy'.[17] So why abolish a system that was so integral to the economy at that time? Slave prices were also falling, and so why get rid of something that was becoming less expensive? By 1840 France had developed a capitalist economy as far as Britain had by 1760, but no large-scale abolitionist movement grew in France.[18]

Yet, Philip Gould remarks: '[m]odern antislavery scholarship has undermined the historical accuracy of the Williams thesis, but it also has left in place its essential premise. "Few historians today discount the possibility of some connection between capitalism and antislavery".'[19] Many historians, including Eric Williams, usually credit the origin of such ideas to Adam Smith.[20] Smith, in his famous treatise *The Wealth of Nations* (1776), argued that slave labor, though appearing inexpensive in the short-run, was actually more expensive in the long term.[21] Thus, slavery was eventually destined to fail economically.

15. Williams, *Capitalism and Slavery*, p. 139.
16. Drescher, *Econocide*; Roger T. Anstey, *The Atlantic Slave Trade and British Abolition, 1769-1810* (London: Macmillan, 1975); Stanley L. Engerman and Eugene D. Genovese (eds.), *Race and Slavery in the Western Hemisphere: Quantitative Studies* (Princeton, NJ: Princeton University Press, 1975). For the argument that pre-capitalist and capitalist systems co-existed in the American South, see Elizabeth Fox-Genovese and Eugene Genovese, *Slavery in White and Black: Race and Class in the Southern Slaveholders' New World Order* (New York: Cambridge University Press, 2008). For a look at both sides of the debate about Williams's thesis, see Walter Minchinton, 'Williams and Drescher: Abolition and Emancipation', *Slavery and Abolition* 4 (1983), pp. 81-105.
17. Drescher, *Capitalism and Antislavery*, p. 9.
18. Drescher, *Capitalism and Antislavery*, p. 11.
19. Philip Gould, *Barbaric Traffic: Commerce and Antislavery in the 18th Century Atlantic World* (Cambridge, MA: Harvard University Press, 2003), p. 3, quoting Thomas Bender, 'Introduction', in Bender (ed.), *The Antislavery Debate*, p. 2.
20. Williams, *Capitalism and Slavery*, pp. 4-7.
21. Williams, *Capitalism and Slavery*, p. 6.

The fact is that economic rationales against slavery were known as early as 1624, when the Dutch entrepreneur, William Usselinx, argued against introducing slaves into Swedish colonies because 'their labor would be less profitable than that of Europeans'.[22] As Christopher Brown notes, Malachy Postlewayt, who is often neglected in the histories of abolitionism, provided extensive economic arguments against slavery in his *Britain's Commercial Interests Explained* (1757) and in the 1757 and 1766 editions of his *Universal Trade and Commerce*.[23] Postlewayt had been the head of the Royal Africa Company, and he was a fervent apologist for slavery in the 1740s. He came to understand that slavery disrupted the stability necessary to foster the commercial development of Africa.

Thomas Clarkson, who is usually celebrated for religious motives, was also a leading exponent of the economic benefits of abolition. In 1788, Clarkson wrote *An Essay on the Impolicy of the African Slave Trade*, where he virtually omitted all moral arguments and focused on the potential value of African woods, medicines, and spices.[24] For Clarkson, Britain was ruining Africa, a potential goose that laid the golden egg, by disrupting its basic societal structures through the slave trade.[25] Admittedly, Clarkson believes that he has already proven the immoral aspects of slavery, and so he does not need to do so again in that 1788 *Essay*.[26] Nonetheless, Clarkson's essay shows he did not think biblical ethics were sufficient to ensure the triumph of abolitionism.

Similarly, William Wilberforce, another hero of evangelical abolitionism, helped to found the Sierra Leone colony. According to Stephen Tompkins, Wilberforce and others founded the settlement of Freetown as a 'way of using commerce as a tool for abolition and Christian mission'.[27] This colony was not only supposed to provide former slaves with a livelihood, but also help to defeat the slave trade itself. Greed and the use of 'apprenticeships' eventually meant the virtual re-enslavement of settlers, but that still demonstrates that financial motives, rather than just Christian teachings, helped to determine which direction that colony took in terms of abolition or re-enslavement.

---

22. Mary Stoughton Locke, *Anti-Slavery in America from the Introduction of African Slaves to the Prohibition of the Slave Trade (1619–1808)* (Radcliffe Monographs, 11; Boston: Ginn & Co., 1901), p. 9.

23. Brown, *Moral Capital*, p. 273.

24. Thomas Clarkson, *An Essay on the Impolicy of the African Slave Trade* (London: J. Phillips, 1788).

   25. See further Brown, *Moral Capital*, p. 328.

   26. Clarkson, *Impolicy of the African Slave Trade*, p. 3.

   27. Tomkins, *The Clapham Sect*, p. 92.

Fred Ross, the American pro-slavery minister, was acutely aware of the link between economics and abolition when he remarked:

> God put it into the hearts of many Northern men—especially abolitionists—to believe what Great Britain said,—namely, that free trade would result in slave emancipation. But lo! the slave-holder wanted free trade. So Northern abolitionists helped to destroy the tariff policy, and thus to expand the demand for, and the culture of, cotton.[28]

Ross realized that abolitionists promoted some of the economic policies that perpetuated slavery.

In short, those who point to the flaws of Williams's thesis often miss the fact that many of the abolitionists themselves used economic arguments for abolition. Whether the rise of capitalism actually caused the demise of abolition, therefore, is not always as important as the fact that many of the abolitionists believed that economics could be a tool of abolition. The Sierra Leone experiment alone shows this to be the case. Postlewayt, Wilberforce, Clarkson, and other abolitionists did not see Christian charity by itself as the only motive that would help end slavery. They believed that money mattered, too.

Non-Christian Abolition: Haiti

While Stark and other apologists credit Christian sentiments for abolition, Haiti illustrates a case where non-Christian traditions played a central role in some liberation movements. Some historians have recognized that African religious traditions may have motivated slaves to overthrow slavery as much or more than any Christian abolitionist sentiment.[29] Yet, few Christian biblical scholars and historians pay much attention to it.[30] Religiocentrism and ethnocentrism can explain some of these historiographical oversights.

Haiti provides the only successful slave revolt in history that resulted in a nation controlled by former slaves. Haiti's role in the triumph of abolitionism is acknowledged by Frederick Douglass, who served as minister to Haiti under president Benjamin Harrison. After enumerating the heroes of American and British abolitionism, Douglass remarked: 'Until Haiti struck for

---

28. Ross, *Slavery Ordained*, pp. 73-74.
29. See Odette Menesson-Rigaud, 'Le rôle du Vaudou dans l'independance d'Haiti', *Présence africaine* 17–18 (1958), pp. 43-67; John K. Thornton, '"I am the Subject of the King of Kongo": African Political Ideology and the Haitian Revolution', *Journal of World History* 4 (1993), pp. 181-214.
30. The role of Voodoo in Haiti's revolution is suggested already by Antoine Dalmas, *Histoire de la révolution de Saint Domingue* (2 vols.; Paris: Mame Frères, 1814), I, pp. 116-18.

freedom, the conscience of the Christian world slept profoundly over slavery... Until she [Haiti] spoke no Christian nation had given the world an organized effort to abolish slavery.'[31] More importantly, Stark completely ignores that, at the time of its successful revolt, Haiti was heavily invested in Voodoo, an amalgam of religious tradition that crystallized in Haiti out of the experience of African slaves from Benin (formerly Dahomey) and other neighboring cultures.[32]

Michel S. Laguerre, a widely respected scholar of Voodoo and a professor at the University of California at Berkeley, remarks:

> The singularity of the Haitian revolution stays in part in the religious ardour of the slaves, inflamed by the leaders, who in turn were inspired by Voodoo *loas* [divinities] to exterminate the colonists of Haiti. Revolutionary leaders successfully used Voodoo to make Haiti the first black republic in the New World and the second nation to achieve independence in the western hemisphere and to make the Haitian revolution the first social revolution in the Third World.[33]

In any case, most Christian apologists who exalt Euroamerican abolitionism show no familiarity with these African traditions, which bear 'a moral predisposition' toward freedom.

Demographic Imbalances

Jan Rogozinski, the historian of the Caribbean, claims that 'it was the Jamaican slave rebellion—and not the British antislavery movement—that finally brought slavery to an end'.[34] Rogozinski refers to the Jamaican slave rebellion of 1831 led by Samuel Sharpe (1801–1832), a Baptist lay preacher. This rebellion, involving some 60,000 slaves, left over 200 plantations burnt

---

31. Douglass, 'Haiti and the Haitian People...2 January 1893', in Blassingame, *The Frederick Douglass Papers,* V, p. 529.

32. See Joan Dayan, *Haiti, History and the Gods* (Berkeley: University of California Press, 1995); Alfred Metraux, *Voodoo in Haiti* (New York: Schocken, 1972); Leslie Desmangles, *The Faces of the Gods: Vodou and Roman Catholicism in Haiti* (Chapel Hill: University of North Carolina Press, 1992).

33. Michel S. Laguerre, *Voodoo and Politics in Haiti* (New York: Macmillan, 1989), p. 70. For an appeal to a more complex interaction of factors in the Haitian revolution, see Jeremy D. Popkin, *You Are All Free: The Haitian Revolution and the Abolition of Slavery* (Cambridge: Cambridge University Press, 2010). For the role of African traditions in Cuban resistance, see Matt D. Childs, *The 1812 Aponte Rebellion in Cuba and the Struggle against Atlantic Slavery* (Chapel Hill: University of North Carolina Press, 2006), especially pp. 100-119; Philip A. Howard, *Changing History: Afro-Cuban Cabildos and Societies of Color in the Nineteenth Century* (Baton Rouge: Louisiana State University Press, 1998).

34. Rogozinski, *A Brief History of the Caribbean,* p. 186.

or pillaged.[35] Although the rebellion was suppressed, there is some evidence that this was a crucial event that led to the British emancipations in the 1830s.

Abolitionism, especially between 1784 and 1863, also coincided with the largest imbalances between black/colored slaves and white colonists ever seen in human history. It is true that in Brazil and North America black slaves were never the majority of the population. In the Caribbean, however, where the most successful slave revolts arose, black/colored people numbered seventy-five percent or more of the total population after 1700.[36] In 1791, the population of Haiti included 450,000 slaves, 30,000 free persons of color, and only 40,000 whites.[37] In the Leeward Islands, blacks began to outnumber whites already by 1708, when one finds 23,500 blacks and 7,311 whites.[38] In the British island of St Kitts, we find 4,000 whites and 11,500 slaves in 1724, but only 1,612 whites compared to 15,667 slaves in 1834.[39]

As the population increased, rebellions also increased. Thus, Rogozinski records two major rebellions in Cuba in the 1700s, but some eleven in the 1800s.[40] Even Drescher, who otherwise downplays the significance of slave revolts in abolitionism, observes that 'the incidence rate of resistance rose by over 60 per cent in the period 1790–1832' when compared with the first nine decades of the 1700s.[41] The numbers of rebels also increased dramatically, so that rebels who might have mostly numbered in the hundreds before the middle of the 1700s numbered in the thousands by the late 1700s and in the 1800s.

Fear of rebellion was a documented factor in restricting the slave trade even where blacks did not outnumber whites. In particular, South Carolina introduced legislation, in 1792, to prohibit the importation of slaves. Part of

---

35. For a discussion of the Jamaican revolt, see Michael Craton, *Testing the Chains: British Rebellions in the British West Indies, 1629–1832* (Ithaca, NY: Cornell University Press, 1982), pp. 291-321; Kathleen E.A. Monteith and Glen Richards, *Jamaica in Slavery and Freedom: History, Heritage, and Culture* (Kingston: University of the West Indies, 2002).

36. Blackburn, *The Making of New World Slavery*, p. 332. See also Jeremy D. Popkin, *Facing Racial Revolution: Eyewitness Accounts of the Haitian Insurrection* (Chicago: University of Chicago Press, 2007).

37. Steeve Coupeau, *The History of Haiti* (London: Greenwood Press, 2008), p. 18.

38. Pons, *History of the Caribbean*, p. 67.

39. Rogozinski, *A Brief History of the Caribbean*, p. 114.

40. Rogozinski, *A Brief History of the Caribbean*, pp. 161-63. For the British West Indies, see detailed list in Craton, *Testing the Chains*, pp. 335-39.

41. Drescher, *Capitalism and Antislavery*, p. 103. Drescher's skepticism is countered by Hunt, *Haiti's Influence on Antebellum America*. Historiographically, the role of slave resistance is emphasized by C.L.R. James, *The Black Jacobins: Toussaint L'Ouverture and the San Domingo Revolution* (London: Allison & Busby, 3rd edn, 1980 [1938]). See further Craton, *Testing the Chains*.

the reason was precisely the events in Haiti. The French authorities of St Domingue (now Haiti) had requested the help of South Carolina in fighting the insurrection. After the revolution began, South Carolinians became concerned about having too many blacks and abolitionist Frenchmen in their state. Ralph Izard, a US senator and a federalist from South Carolina, feared that any American alliance with France against Great Britain might bring a 'lower order of Frenchmen to come to this Country who would fraternise with our Democratical clubs & introduce the same horrid tragedies among our Negroes'.[42] In short, we can link restrictions on the slave trade to fear of being overrun by a slave or colored population.

Abolition as a Military Strategy

Yet another impulse towards abolition was military. Giving liberty to slaves in return for military service was a tried and true method of addressing shortages of soldiers from among freemen. As Davis notes: 'even in North America, some Negro slaves won their freedom by serving in the various imperial wars between England and France'.[43] Providing incentives to the slaves of an opponent could help to undermine the authority and viability of the opponent's entire economic or social system.

Adam Hochschild notes that at least a dozen years before Clarkson's appeals to Parliament, British military officials were promising freedom to American slaves who would switch sides to the British in the American Revolutionary War.[44] In April 1773, Lord Dunmore, the royal governor of Virginia, threatened to proclaim liberty for all slaves if American colonists persisted in resistance to British rule.[45] The Emancipation Proclamation of Abraham Lincoln in 1863 was as much a military tactic as it was a humanitarian move.[46] The period between 1775 and the 1830s saw multiple wars that were increasingly global and complex, and that certainly represents more of a change than any major change in Christianity at that time.[47]

42. Izard to Mathias Hutchinson, 26 November 1794, Ralph Izard papers (South Carolinian Library, University of South Carolina, Columbia, SC) as quoted in Patrick S. Brady, 'The Slave Trade and Sectionalism in South Carolina', *Journal of Southern History* 38 (1972), pp. 601-20.
43. See David B. Davis, *The Problem of Slavery in the Age of Revolution 1770–1823* (Ithaca, NY: Cornell University Press, 1975), p. 75.
44. Hochschild, *Bury the Chains*, p. 98.
45. See Davis, *Slavery in the Age of Revolution*, p. 73. See also Peter M. Voelz, *Slave and Soldier: The Military Impact of Blacks in the Colonial Americas* (New York: Routledge, 1993).
46. See Burrus M. Carnahan, 'Military Necessity and the Emancipation Proclamation: Another Look at the Record', *Lincoln Herald* 103 (Spring 2001), pp. 23-29.
47. For the impact of the American revolution on British emancipation, see the detailed treatment in Brown, *Moral Capital*, especially pp. 456-62.

Secularization

Stark is well aware of the fact that the advocacy of slavery co-existed with Christianity and the Bible. In fact, he quotes Francis Asbury (1745–1816), one of the first bishops of the Methodist Episcopal Church in America, to support his observation: 'Methodists, Baptists, Presbyterians...in the highest flights of rapturous piety, still maintain and defend [slavery].'[48] Yet, Stark still claims that 'although many Southern clergy proposed theological defenses of slavery, pro-slavery rhetoric was overwhelmingly secular—references were made to "liberty" and "states' rights", not to "sin" or "salvation"'.[49]

Stark offers no statistical data for this claim other than a very flawed study by John A. Auping.[50] We can find references to 'liberty' and 'states' rights' in abolitionist literature, so that alone does not mean that secularism represents most pro-slavery arguments. After all, Granville Sharp's *A Representation of the Injustice and Dangerous Tendency of Tolerating Slavery* also 'lacks a single religious argument against slavery'.[51] Thomas Paine (1737–1809), a well-known religious skeptic, was also a significant foe of slavery before the first anti-slavery society was formed in America.[52]

It is too easy to say that secularization was the main reason. But secularization is one of the factors that explains abolitionism. For one, some Christian pro-slavery advocates themselves saw abolitionism as inspired by secularization. Note the remarks about the Haitian revolution in *DeBow's Review*, one of the most important antebellum southern periodicals:

> From its discovery by Columbus to the present reign of Solouque, the olive branch has withered under its pestilential breath; and when the atheistical philosophy of revolutionary France added fuel to the volcano of hellish passions which raged in its bosom, the horrors of the island became a narrative which frightened our childhood and still curdles the blood to read.[53]

Of course, many Christians described as 'atheistic' any ideas with which they disagreed. Yet, the statement in *DeBow's Review* shows that atheism could be perceived as liberatory.

---

48. Stark, *For the Glory of God*, p. 345.
49. Stark, *For the Glory of God*, p. 344.
50. Auping, *Religion and Social Justice*. I plan to write a forthcoming detailed critique of Auping's study. Briefly, he uses arbitrary statistics and documentation to provide the impression that experiential religion was preponderant among abolitionists.
51. Brown, *Moral Capital*, p. 174 n. 24.
52. See further Edward H. Davidson and William J. Scheick, *Paine, Scripture and Authority: The Age of Reason as Religious and Political Idea* (Bethlehem, PA: Lehigh University Press, 1994).
53. [Anonymous], 'Hayti and the Haytiens', *DeBow's Review* 16 (January 1854), p. 35.

The Decline of Biblical Authority

The decline of biblical authority is usually ignored by most Christian apologists when explaining abolitionism. One finds such a decline mentioned by some historians of slavery, including David B. Davis and Seymour Drescher, but usually not by Christian apologists.[54] The logical problems with the Bible encountered even by modern apologists explains well the shift away from using the Bible in abolitionist debates. As Caroline Shanks's study of abolitionist exegesis concludes: 'We no longer ask the Bible what it cannot give us'.[55]

Consider, for example, Stark's explanation of why the Bible failed to speak forcefully against slavery:

> The case against slavery is theological, not revelational. Had Moses been given a commandment against slavery, then only heretical Jews and Christians could have owned slaves. Or had Jesus proclaimed that no slave master shall enter heaven, there would have been no ambiguity as to what Christians must do. But theology is based on human interpretations, and therefore sincere and brilliant seekers may reach opposite conclusions.[56]

Stark's argument pivots on a very unclear distinction between 'theological' and 'revelational'. Presumably, a clear prohibition said to be revealed by God qualifies as 'revelational', while something not based on an explicit claim of revelation is merely 'theological'. Similarly, Stark leaves unexplained why revelation cannot also be 'based on human interpretations' of what humans experience.

Indeed, most commandments allowing or endorsing slavery in the Pentateuch are explicitly regarded as a 'revelation' to Moses. Leviticus 25.44 says, 'As for your male and female slaves whom you may have...' But that chapter begins with, 'The LORD said to Moses on Mount Sinai' (Lev. 25.1), which makes it 'revelational', even by Stark's own definition. Given Stark's logic, saying that God is against slavery or that slavery is a sin would make one a heretical Jew or Christian. Violating a 'revelation' is heresy for Stark, and yet all orthodox Christianity is built on disregarding many commandments that were revealed to Moses (see Eph. 2.14-15; Mt. 5.38-40).

In fact, any distinction between 'revelational' and 'theological' arguments could also support slaveholding. After all, the commandment for slaves to obey their slavemaster in Eph. 6.5 is 'revelational' insofar as Christians believe Paul received his Gospel by revelation (Gal. 1.12). Slavery advocates,

---

54. Davis, *Slavery in the Age of Revolution*, pp. 523-56; Drescher, *Capitalism and Antislavery*, p. 20.

55. Caroline L. Shanks, 'The Biblical Anti-Slavery Argument of the Decade 1830–1840', *Journal of Negro History* 15 (1931), p. 156.

56. Stark, *For the Glory of God*, p. 345.

moreover, saw the sanctioning of slavery precisely as 'revelational'. Fred Ross made this very point in a debate against the abolitionist, Albert Barnes: 'They [Moses and Paul] rebuke your pre-judgment of the Almighty when you say if the Bible sanctions slavery, "it neither ought to be nor could be received by mankind as a divine revelation"'.[57] Ross further complained that 'some anti-slavery men have left the light of the Bible, and wandered in to the darkness until they have reached the blackness of the darkness of infidelity'.[58]

Since the Bible is permeated with pro-slavery statements, it was not long before using the Bible became a difficult or losing strategy for abolitionists. As Mark A. Noll observes, '[t]he North...lost the exegetical war'.[59] Abolitionists certainly still used the Bible but they were shifting increasingly to secular humanitarian, legal, and practical arguments that left the Bible out of the debate or consigned it to a secondary role. Harrill remarks:

> The relationship between the moral imperative of anti-slavery and the evolution of biblical criticism resulted in a major paradigm shift away from literalism. This moral imperative fostered an interpretive approach that found conscience to be a more reliable guide to Christian morality than biblical authority.[60]

Douglass follows this trend when he declared: 'It is not what Moses allowed for the hardness of heart, but what God requires, [which] ought to be the rule'.[61]

Ironically, Seymour Drescher, who is not a biblical scholar, also comes to a similar conclusion:

> On the more orthodox side, the more strenuously in favour of the biblical sanction for slavery the more one threatened the relevance of the Bible as a sanction for British liberty. Both the racial and biblical lines of argument were burdened by an implicit delegitimization of contemporary metropolitan norms. Racial, biblical, and classical Aristotelian proslavery arguments occupied a very subordinate place in British political discourse during the eighteenth and early nineteenth centuries.[62]

---

57. Ross, *Slavery Ordained*, p. 98.
58. Ross, *Slavery Ordained*, p. 37.
59. Mark A. Noll, 'The Bible and Slavery', in R.M. Miller, H.S. Stout, and C.R. Wilson (eds.), *Religion and the American Civil War* (New York: Oxford University Press, 1998), p. 66. See also Grant Wacker, 'The Demise of Biblical Civilization', in Nathan O. Hatch and Mark A. Noll (eds.), *The Bible in America: Essays in Cultural History* (New York: Oxford University Press, 1982), pp. 121-38. For an evangelical author who argues that relativizing biblical values is one way to redeem the Bible's stance on slavery, see Kevin Giles, 'The Biblical Argument for Slavery: Can the Bible Mislead? A Case Study in Hermeneutics', *Evangelical Quarterly* 66 (1994), pp. 3-17.
60. Harrill, 'The Use of the New Testament', p. 149.
61. Douglass, 'The Dred Scott Decision...May 1857'.
62. Drescher, *Capitalism and Antislavery*, p. 20.

By 1901, in fact, Mary Stoughton Locke's history of anti-slavery in America noticed that in the late 1700s: '[a]rguments from Scripture which were very prominent in the earlier period now assume a subordinate position'.[63]

In his magisterial treatise on *The Authority of the Bible and the Rise of the Modern World*, Henning Graf Reventlow concluded that, with the Enlightenment,

> [t]he Bible lost its significance for philosophical thought and for the theoretical constitutional foundations of political ideals, and ethical rationalism (with new foundations in Kant's critique) proved to be one of the forces shaping the modern period, which only now can really be said to have begun. Both of these developments were prepared on English soil, so if we are to understand our own cultural situation it is in many ways important to pay attention to that particular historical context.[64]

The mention of the English connection is important because Britain is where the first successful abolitionist movement in Europe took root.

Otherwise, evidence of this shift away from making a case without the Bible is already found in the 1688 petition against slavery by the Mennonites and Quakers of Germantown, Pennsylvania.[65] Not a single biblical text is cited or quoted, though we can infer allusions (e.g., to the Golden Rule). As Brown observes, Sharp's *A Representation of the Injustice and Dangerous Tendency of Tolerating Slavery* 'lacks a single religious argument against slavery'.[66] As already noted, Wilberforce, the evangelical hero of British abolitionism, discouraged any use of the Bible in Parliamentary discussions on slavery. Also, the records of important abolitionist cases (e.g., Somerset) reveal the centrality of legal, not biblical, arguments.[67]

---

63. Locke, *Anti-Slavery in America*, p. 55. For an example of a natural law argument on behalf of abolition from 1709, see Jack P. Greene, '"A Plain and Natural Right to Life and Liberty": An Early Natural Rights Attack on the Excesses of the Slave System in Colonial British America', *William and Mary Quarterly* 57 (2000), pp. 793-808.

64. Hennning Graf Reventlow, *The Authority of the Bible and the Rise of the Modern World* (trans. John Bowden; Philadelphia: Fortress Press, 1985), p. 414. See also Jonathan Sheehan, *The Enlightenment Bible* (Princeton, NJ: Princeton University Press, 2005). Jacques Berlinerblau, *The Secular Bible: Why Nonbelievers Must Take Religion Seriously* (Cambridge: Cambridge University Press, 2005); Jerry W. Brown, *The Rise of Biblical Criticism in America, 1800–1870* (Middletown, CT: Wesleyan University Press, 1969).

65. See Henry J. Cadbury, 'An Early Quaker Anti-Slavery Statement', *Journal of Negro History* 22 (1937), pp. 488-93.

66. Brown, *Moral Capital*, p. 174 n. 24. For a recent treatment of the general rhetorical strategies used, see Srividhya Swaminathan, *Debating the Slave-Trade: Rhetoric of British National Identity, 1759–1815* (Burlington, VT: Ashgate, 2009).

67. See especially, James Oldham, *The Mansfield Manuscripts and the Growth of English Law in the Eighteenth Century* (2 vols.; Chapel Hill: University of North Carolina Press, 1992), especially II, pp. 1221-44.

More importantly, what Hochschild calls the most widely read non-fiction anti-slavery work of all time is Thomas Clarkson's *An Abstract of the Evidence Delivered before a Select Committee of the House of Commons in the Years 1790 and 1791 on the Part of the Petitioners for the Abolition of Slavery*.[68] This work summarized the evidence gathered by Clarkson on the slave trade. Hochschild comments:

> What also makes the *Abstract* feel surprisingly contemporary is what it does not contain. At a time in history when a large portion of all books and pamphlets were theological tracts or sermons, and in a book that quoted several clergymen and witnesses, the *Abstract* had no references to the Bible. Clarkson and his colleagues somehow sensed that they could better evoke sympathy if they stood back and let the evidence speak for itself.[69]

Indeed, the wisdom of Sharp, Clarkson, and Wilberforce, therefore, was precisely in marginalizing the Bible in abolitionist arguments, even if they believed the Bible was abolitionist.

The Afro-British abolitionist, Ottobah Cugoano, also knew the problems of using scripture to defend abolitionism: 'I am aware that some of these arguments will weigh nothing against such men as do not believe in the scriptures themselves nor care to understand; but let him be aware not to make use of these things against us which they do not believe'.[70] Similarly, Frederick Douglass recognized the problem with the Bible when he was hesitant to give Bibles to slaves in 1849. Fred Ross recognized that the use of the Bible had been a grand failure for abolitionists:

> The most consistent abolitionists, affirming the sin of slavery, on the maxim of created equality and unalienable right, after torturing the Bible for a while, to make it give the same testimony, felt they could get nothing from the book. They felt that the God of the Bible disregarded the thumb-screw, the boot, and the wheel; that He would not speak for them but against them. These consistent men have now turned away from the word, in despondency; and are seeking, somewhere, an abolition Bible, an abolition Constitution for the United States, and an abolition God.[71]

Indeed, Ross knew what even most Christian apologists today seem to have forgotten.

---

68. Hochschild, *Bury the Chains*, p. 196. See Thomas Clarkson, *An Abstract of the Evidence Delivered before a Select Committee of the House of Commons in the Years 1790 and 1791 on the Part of the Petitioners for the Abolition of Slavery* (London: James Phillips, 1791).
69. Hochschild, *Bury the Chains*, p. 198.
70. Cugoano, *Thoughts and Sentiments*, p. 135.
71. Ross, *Slavery Ordained*, pp. 96-97.

Summary

I cannot claim to know the precise reason why abolition triumphed when it did. I can say that the Bible and Christian ethics had little to do with the ultimate success of abolition. The Bible and Christian ethics had been available for some 1800–1900 years, and no significant advancements toward abolition were made until the late eighteenth and early nineteenth centuries. If anything, evidence indicates that marginalizing the Bible was increasingly seen as a good idea even by some of the heroes of abolition such as Granville Sharp, William Wilberforce, Thomas Clarkson, and Frederick Douglass.

Chapter 17

CONCLUSION

Biblical and Christian ethics were not a major factor in explaining the triumph of abolitionism between 1775 and 1863 or in any other period. The Bible had been around for some 1800–1900 years before that, and slavery had predominated during that time. The reasons for such a predominance of slavery are repeated in many pro-slavery Christian writings. Consider the resolution against abolitionism passed by the Hopewell Presbytery of South Carolina in 1836:

1. Slavery has existed in the church of God from the time of Abraham to this day. Members of the church of God have held slaves bought with their money and born in their houses; and this relation is not only recognized, but its duties are defined clearly, both in the Old and New Testaments.
2. Emancipation is not mentioned among the duties of the master to his slaves, while obedience, 'even to the froward master' is enjoined upon the slave.
3. No instance can be produced of an otherwise orderly Christian being reproved much less excommunicated from the church, for the single act of holding domestic slaves, from the days of Abraham down to the date of the modern abolitionists.[1]

These reasons, in fact, are repeated throughout all the periods we have studied, and proved so effective that some abolitionists eventually became reluctant to address scripture very extensively.

The usual Christian historiography of slavery applauds the Quakers, and individuals such as William Wilberforce, Granville Sharp, and Thomas Clarkson. Yet, these figures are not representative of the vast majority of Christians who supported slavery in every credible census we have of British or American populations. For every Wilberforce or Clarkson, there were

1. My text is from James G. Birney, *The American Churches: The Bulwarks of American Slavery* (Concord, NH: Parker Pillsbury, 3rd edn, 1885), p. 38. A complete version is found in [Anonymous], 'Resolutions of the Presbyteries in Philadelphia… and Hopewell Concerning Colonization and Slavery', *African Repository and Colonial Journal* 12 (1836), p. 218. See also Bruce Staiger, 'Abolitionism and the Presbyterian Schism of 1837–1838', *Mississippi Valley Historical Review* 36 (1949), pp. 391-414.

hundreds, if not thousands, of divines and ministers who could easily defend the pro-slavery position with the Bible.[2] Such demographics explain the sound conclusion of Locke: 'Except in the case of the Quakers, then, the organized efforts of religious societies must be regarded as a failure'.[3]

What most Christian apologists still overlook is that Christianity is itself modeled on a slave–master paradigm. God is the ultimate slavemaster, and Christians routinely call themselves 'slaves' or 'servants' of God. This reaches back to pre-Christian Jewish traditions enunciated by Philo: 'To be a slave of God is the highest boast of man, a treasure more precious not only than freedom, but than wealth and power and all that mortals cherish' (cf. Lev. 25.42).[4]

Christianity is not anti-imperialist, but rather aims to replace non-Christian empires with its own empire headed by God/Christ. That slave–master paradigm permeates most of Christian history and explains why the popes, as representatives of the universal emperor, were virtually administering that empire as a global slave colony. This inherent Christian imperialism explains why a Pope Alexander VI could allow human kings to conquer and enslave Africans and American Indians. It explains why a Pope Paul III rescinded any enforcement of *Sublimis Deus*, and then declined to make Rome a refuge for slaves in 1548. Any peaceful evangelization injunctions by Christ easily could be interpreted to constitute deferred violence, not anti-violence.

Using a trajectorialist analysis, slavery worsened under Christianity when compared to other pre-Christian cultures. For example, while the Code of Hammurabi had term limits for some slaves and the Old Testament had term limits for Hebrew slaves, no such term limits exist in the New Testament, which enjoined service and obedience even to cruel masters. Ste Croix rightly observes that:

> And if, as by philosophic pagans, Christian masters are briefly enjoined to treat their slaves fairly, the yoke of slavery is fastened even more firmly upon Christian slaves as the emphasis on obedience to their masters becomes even more absolute.[5]

While some pre-Christian groups had outlawed slavery, Christianity continued it and expanded it world-wide. There were probably far more people enslaved (tens of millions) under Christian empires than in all pre-Christian empires combined.

---

2. See Thorton Stringfellow, *Scriptural and Statistical Views in Favor of Slavery* (Richmond, VA: J.W. Randolph, 1856).

3. Locke, *Anti-Slavery in America*, p. 45.

4. Philo, *The Cherubim* 107 (Colson and Whitaker, LCL): τὸ γὰρ δουλεύειν θεῷ μέγιστον αὔχημα καὶ οὐ μόνον ἐλευθερίας ἀλλὰ καὶ πλούτου καὶ πάντων ὅσα τὸ θνητὸν ἀσπάζεται γένος τιμιώτερον.

5. Ste Croix, 'Early Christian Attitudes', pp. 19-20.

17. Conclusion

Christianity often had a pneumatocentric orientation that focused on the liberty and well-being of the soul rather than the body. We can find this in Stoicism, but Christianity certainly continued it (Mt. 10.28; 1 Pet 2.18). Ste Croix rightly argues that:

> it was the exclusive concentration of the early Christian church upon the personal relations between man and man, or man and God, and their complete indifference, as Christians, to the institutions of the world in which they lived, that prevented Christianity from even having much effect for good upon the relations between man and man.[6]

Allied eschatological or other-worldly orientations of early Christianity diminished the problems of a world that was expected to vanish.

Aside from unprecedented geopolitical and demographic developments, the major difference between previous eras of Christianity and the period between 1775 and 1900 was the marginalization of the Bible as a sociopolitical authority. That period witnessed the rise of biblical criticism, which undermined the authority and perceived reliability of the Bible in Europe and America. It was in that period that Americans invested their textual authority in a Constitution made by 'We, the People' instead of by a deity. Influential abolitionists such as Granville Sharp, William Wilberforce, Thomas Clarkson, and Frederick Douglass were part of that shift away from the Bible. Even if they did not all accept the new biblical criticism, they certainly realized the problems that using the Bible posed to abolitionism.

Frederick Douglass, who grew closer to secular humanism toward the end of his life, specifically commented on how Moses, whose laws on slavery posed a great challenge for abolitionists, may not be as reliable as once thought. Douglass kept a bust of D.F. Strauss, a father of modern New Testament criticism, in his study. Douglass exalted the racial ethics of Robert G. Ingersoll (1833–1899), the famed agnostic, above those of Dwight L. Moody (1837–1899), the celebrated evangelical leader.[7] Indeed, Frederick Douglass saw better than most historians today what happened in Christian historiography of slavery:

> Now that slavery is no more, and the multitude are claiming the credit of its abolition, though but a score of years have passed since the same multitude were claiming an exactly opposite credit, it is difficult to realize that an abolitionist was ever an object of popular scorn and reproach in this country.[8]

Many current biblical scholars and historians, such as Rodney Stark, Richard Horsley, and Ben Witherington, simply continue that revisionist historiography of Christian slavery.

---

6. Ste Croix, 'Early Christian Attitudes', p. 36.
7. Douglass, 'New Administration, V, p. 190.
8. Douglass, 'Great Britain's Example is High, Noble, and Grand…6 August, 1885', in Blassingame, *The Frederick Douglass Papers*, V, p. 203.

If there is a 'representative' position in the Bible, it is one that accepts, endorses, or promotes slavery as a justified part of the human condition. Abolition often appealed to reinterpretation, which is not recognized as abandonment of the Bible by most Christian scholars. But it is 'abandonment' because if the original sense of the Bible is changed, then it is no longer the Bible as originally intended. Therefore, abolitionists were not using 'the Bible' but rather a constructed illusion with the same name. That reinterpretation of the Bible's pro-slavery ethics effectively deconstructed biblical authority, one of the greatest pillars of slavery ever seen in human history.

This book began with the premise that, if slavery is regarded as inexcusably wrong, then biblical ethics stands or falls on its attitude toward slavery. Judged by the United Nations Universal Declaration of Human Rights, which expresses the widest consensus available on ethics, the Bible does fail miserably. The Bible's stance on slavery alone is sufficient to confirm the New Atheism's general stance that this collection of books has been one of the greatest obstacles to human ethical progress in history. The Bible is part of a world whose ethics and values are best left in the past. Accordingly, the modern world must completely unshackle itself from using the Bible as any sort of ethical or social authority.

APPENDIX

Synoptic Cultural Table of Concepts and Practices Related to Slavery

This table marks with an × one or more attestations of the concept or practice relating to slavery listed at the left column. Listing an attestation of these concepts or practices does not imply that their opposites did not also exist in these cultures. It is meant to illuminate what is often diminished or not mentioned by Christian apologists or biblical scholars when discussing these cultures.

	Egypt	Mesopotamia	Hittites	Greece	Rome
Abolition of all slavery expressed					
Citizenship available to ex-slaves				×	×
Common origin of humanity		×		×	×
Debt slavery outlawed				×	
Equality of all human beings				×	×
God(s) concerned with interpersonal conduct	×	×	×	×	×
Golden Rule				×	×
Family rights (e.g., marriage; inheritance)	×	×		×	×
Fixed terms of service		×		×	×
Improper enslavement punished by god(s)		×			
Legal contestation by slaves		×	×	×	×
Manumission of individuals		×	×	×	×
Manumission/Emancipation of large groups	×	×			
Mercy to slaves		×	×	×	×
No native/outsider distinctions		×	×		×
Service to God not to Human Masters				×	×
Sheltering fugitive slaves		×		×	×
Slavery not natural state				×	×

BIBLIOGRAPHY

Abusharaf, Rogaia Mustafa, *Female Circumcision: Multicultural Perspectives* (Philadelphia: University of Pennsylvania Press, 2006).

Achenbach, Reinhard, and Martin Arneth (eds.), *'Gerechtigkeit und Recht zu üben' (Gen 18, 19): Studien zur altorientalischen und biblischen Rechtsgeschichte, zur Religionsgeschichte Israels und zur Religionssoziologie* (Festschrift Eckart Otto; Beihefte zur ZABR, 13; Wiesbaden: Harrassowitz, 2010).

Adams, Robert McC., 'Slavery and Freedom in the Third Dynasty of Ur: Implications of the Garshana Archives', *CDLJ* (2010), pp. 1-8. Online: http://cdli.ucla.edu/pubs/cdlj/2010/cdlj2010_002.html.

Albright, William F., *From the Stone Age to Christianity: Monotheism and Historical Progress* (Garden City, NY: Doubleday, 1957).

Aldred, Cyril, *Akhenaten: King of Egypt* (London: Thames & Hudson, 1988).

[Alfonso El Sabio], *Las siete partidas del Rey Don Alfonso el Sabio cotejada con varios codices antiguos por la Real Academia de la Historia* (3 vols.; Madrid: Imprenta Real, 1807).

Allard, Paul, *Les esclaves chrétiens depuis les premiers temps de l'Eglise jusqu'à la fin de la domination romaine en Occident* (repr., Hildesheim/New York: Olms, 1974 [1876]).

Altamira, Rafael, 'El texto de las leyes de Burgos de 1512', *Revista de historia de América* 4 (1938), pp. 5-79.

American Academy of Pediatrics, 'Circumcision Policy Statement', *Pediatrics* 103 (1999), pp. 686-93.

[Anonymous], 'Hayti and the Haytiens', *DeBow's Review* 16 (January 1854), p. 35.

[Anonymous], 'Resolutions of the Presbyteries in Philadelphia...and Hopewell Concerning Colonization and Slavery', *The African Repository and Colonial Journal* 12 (1836), p. 218.

Anstey, Roger T., *The Atlantic Slave Trade and British Abolition, 1760–1810* (London: Macmillan, 1975).

Aquinas, St Thomas, *Summa theologica* (3 vols.; New York: Benziger Brothers, 1947).

—*Summa theologica...a Leone XIII, P. M.* (Rome: Forzani, 1823).

Archer, Gleason, *Encyclopedia of Bible Difficulties* (Grand Rapids: Zondervan, 1982).

Aristotle, *The 'Art' of Rhetoric* (trans. John H. Freese; LCL; Cambridge, MA: Harvard University Press, 1926).

—*The Athenian Constitution, The Eudemian Ethics on Virtues and Vices* (trans. H. Rackham; LCL; Cambridge, MA: Harvard University Press, 1935).

—*Politics* (trans. H. Rackham; LCL; Cambridge, MA: Harvard University Press, 1932).

Armstrong, Karen, *A History of God: The 4000-Year Quest of Judaism, Christianity, and Islam* (New York: Ballantine Books, 1993).

Attwater, Donald, and Catherine Rachel John, *The Penguin Dictionary of Saints* (London: Penguin Books, 1995).

Augustine, *The City of God against the Pagans* (trans. William Chase Greene; LCL; 7 vols.; Cambridge, MA: Harvard University Press, 1960).

Aulén, Gustaf, *Christus Victor: An Historical Study of the Three Main Types of the Idea of the Atonement* (trans. A.G. Hebert; New York: Macmillan, 1969).

Auping, John A., *Religion and Social Justice: The Case of Christianity and the Abolition of Slavery in America* (Mexico City: Universidad Iberoamericana, 1994).

Avalos, Hector, *The End of Biblical Studies* (Amherst, NY: Prometheus, 2007).

—*Fighting Words: The Origins of Religious Violence* (Amherst, NY: Prometheus, 2005).

Baade, Hans W., 'The Bifurcated Romanist Tradition of Law in Louisiana', *Tulane Law Review* 70 (1996), pp. 1481-99.

Bailey, Keith, 'Slavery in the London Area in 1086', *Transactions of the London and Middlesex Archaeological Society* 57 (2006), pp. 69-82.

Bainton, Roland, *Christian Attitudes toward War and Peace: A Historical Survey and Critical Re-evaluation* (repr., Nashville: Abingdon Press, 1989 [1960]).

Baker, J.H., 'Personal Liberty under the Common Law of England, 1200–1600', in R.W. Davies (ed.), *The Origins of Modern Freedom in the West* (Palo Alto, CA: Stanford University Press, 1995), pp. 178-202.

Barclay, John M.G., '"Am I not a man and a brother?" The Bible and the British Anti-Slavery Campaign', *Expository Times* 119 (2007), pp. 3-14.

Barkun, Michael, *Religion and the Racist Right: The Origins of the Christian Identity Movement* (Chapel Hill: University of North Carolina Press, 1994).

Barmash, Pamela, *Homicide in the Biblical World* (Cambridge: Cambridge University Press, 2005).

Barnes, Albert, *An Inquiry into the Scriptural Views on Slavery* (Philadelphia: Parry & McMillan, 1857).

Barney, Stephen A., W.J. Lewis, J.A. Beach, and Oliver Berghof, *The Etymologies of Isidore of Seville* (Cambridge: Cambridge University Press, 2007).

Bartchy, S. Scott, ΜΑΛΛΟΝ ΧΡΗΣΑΙ: *First-Century Slavery and 1 Corinthians 7:21* (Eugene, OR: Wipf & Stock, 1973).

—'Philemon, Epistle to', in *ABD*, V, p. 307.

Barton, John, *Understanding Old Testament Ethics: Approaches and Explorations* (Louisville, KY: Westminster/John Knox Press, 2003).

Batiza, Rodolfo, 'The Louisiana Civil Code of 1808: Its Actual Sources and Present Relevance', *Tulane Law Review* 46 (1971), pp. 4-165.

—'Sources of the Civil Code of 1808, Facts and Speculation: A Rejoinder', *Tulane Law Review* 47 (1972), pp. 628-52.

Beavis, Mary Ann, 'Ancient Slavery as an Interpretive Context for the New Testament Servant Parables with Special Reference to the Unjust Steward (Luke 16:1-8)', *JBL* 111 (1992), pp. 37-54.

Becking, Bob, 'Love thy Neighbour... Exegetical Remarks on Leviticus 19:18, 34', in Achenbach and Arneth (eds.), *Gerechtigkeit und Recht zu üben*, pp. 183-87.

Begg, C. T., 'The Significance of the *Numeruswechsel* in Deuteronomy', *ETL* 55 (1979), pp. 116-24.

Bergsma, John Sietze, *The Jubilee from Leviticus to Qumran: A History of Interpretation* (Supplements to *Vetus Testamentum*, 115; Leiden: E.J. Brill, 2007).

Berlinerblau, Jacques, *The Secular Bible: Why Nonbelievers Must Take Religion Seriously* (Cambridge: Cambridge University Press, 2005).

Berman, Joshua A., *Created Equal: How the Bible Broke with Ancient Political Thought* (New York: Oxford University Press, 2008).

Bernat, David A., *Sign of the Covenant: Circumcision in the Priestly Tradition* (Atlanta: Society of Biblical Literature, 2009).

Betz, Hans Dieter, *Galatians* (Philadelphia: Fortress Press, 1979).

Birch, Bruce C., *Let Justice Roll Down: The Old Testament Ethics and Christian Life* (Louisville, KY: Westminster/John Knox Press, 1991).

Birney, James G., *The American Churches: The Bulwarks of American Slavery* (Concord, NH: Parker Pillsbury, 3rd edn, 1885).

Blackburn, Robin, *The Making of New World Slavery: From the Baroque to the Modern, 1492–1800* (London: Verso, 1997).

Blass, F., A. Debrunner, and Robert Funk, *A Greek Grammar of the New Testament and Other Early Christian Literature* (Chicago: University of Chicago Press, 1975).

Blassingame, John W., and John R. McKivigan (eds.), *The Frederick Douglass Papers: Series One—Speeches, Debates and Interviews* (5 vols.; New Haven: Yale University Press, 1979–92).

Blickle, Peter, *The Revolution of 1525: The German Peasants' War from a New Perspective* (trans. Thomas A. Brady and H.C. Erik Midelfort; Baltimore: The Johns Hopkins University Press, 1985).

Blount, Brian K. (ed.), *True to our Native Land: An African American New Testament Commentary* (Minneapolis: Fortress Press, 2007).

Bodin, Jean, *De la République ou Traité du gouvernement* (repr., New York: Elibron Classics, 2005 [1756]).

—*The Six Bookes of a Commonweale* (ed. Kenneth Douglas McRae; Cambridge, MA: Harvard University Press, 1962).

Bömer, Franz, *Untersuchungen über die Religion der Sklaven in Griechenland und Rom* (4 vols.; Wiesbaden: Akademie der Wissenschaften und Literatur, 1958–63).

Booth, Wayne C., *The Company We Keep: An Ethics of Fiction* (Berkeley: University of California Press, 1988).

Botta, Alejandro, 'Nethinim', in *NIDB*, VI, pp. 260-61.

Bourne, George W. *A Condensed Anti-Slavery Bible Argument; By a Citizen of Virginia* (New York: S.W. Benedict, 1845).

Bouwsma, William J., *John Calvin: A Sixteenth Century Portrait* (New York: Oxford University Press, 1988).

Bowersock, G.W., Peter Brown, and Oleg Grabar (eds.), *Late Antiquity: A Guide to the Postclassical World* (Cambridge, MA: Harvard University Press, 1999).

Bowie, Fiona, *The Anthropology of Religion* (Oxford: Blackwell, 2000).

Boyer, James, 'A Classification of Infinitives: A Statistical Study', *Grace Theological Journal* 6 (1985), pp. 3-27.

Bradley, Keith R., *Slavery and Society at Rome* (Cambridge: Cambridge University Press, 1994).

Brady, Patrick S., 'The Slave Trade and Sectionalism in South Carolina', *Journal of Southern History* 38 (1972), pp. 601-20.

Braxton, Brad R., *No Longer Slaves: Galatians and the African American Experience* (Collegeville, MN: Liturgical Press, 2002).

Breathett, George, 'Catholicism and the Code Noir in Haiti', *Journal of Negro History* 73 (1988), pp. 1-11.
Brett, Stephen F., *Slavery and the Catholic Tradition: Rights in the Balance* (New York: Peter Lang, 1994).
Bright, Pamela (ed.), *Augustine and the Bible* (Notre Dame: University of Notre Dame Press, 1999).
Brooten, Bernadette (ed.), *Beyond Slavery: Overcoming its Religious and Sexual Legacies* (New York: PalgraveMacmillan, 2010).
Brown, Christopher Leslie, *Moral Capital: The Foundations of British Abolitionism* (Chapel Hill: University of North Carolina Press, 2006).
Brown, Jerry W., *The Rise of Biblical Criticism in America, 1800-1870* (Middletown, CT: Wesleyan University Press, 1969).
Brown, Oscar J., 'Aquinas's Doctrine of Slavery in Relation to Thomistic Teaching on Natural Law', *Proceedings of the American Catholic Philosophical Association* 53 (1979), pp. 173-81.
Brown, Peter, *Augustine of Hippo: A Biography* (Berkeley: University of California Press, rev. edn, 2000).
Brueggemann, Walter, *Theology of the Old Testament: Testimony, Dispute, Advocacy* (Minneapolis: Fortress Press, 1997).
Brunt, P.A., and J.M. Moore, *Res gestae Divi Augusti: The Achievements of the Divine Augustus* (London: Oxford University Press, 1967).
Bryce, Trevor, *The Kingdom of the Hittites* (New York: Oxford University Press, 1998).
—*Life and Society in the Hittite World* (New York: Oxford University Press, 2002).
Buell, Denise K., 'Race and Universalism in Early Christianity', *JECS* 10 (2002), pp. 429-68.
Buell, Denise K., and Caroline Johnson Hodge, 'The Politics of Interpretation: The Rhetoric of Race and Ethnicity in Paul', *JBL* 123 (2004), pp. 235-51.
Burkert, Walter, *Greek Religion* (trans. John Raffan; Cambridge, MA: Harvard University Press, 1985).
Butler, Jon, *Awash in a Sea of Faith* (Cambridge, MA: Harvard University Press, 1990).
Buttrick, George A. (ed.), *Interpreter's Dictionary of the Bible* (4 vols.; Nashville: Abingdon Press, 1962).
Byron, John, *Recent Research on Paul and Slavery* (Sheffield: Sheffield Phoenix Press, 2008).
—*Slavery Metaphors in Early Judaism and Pauline Christianity* (Tübingen: Mohr Siebeck, 2003).
Cadbury, Henry J., 'An Early Quaker Anti-Slavery Statement', *Journal of Negro History* 22 (October 1937), pp. 488-93.
Cahill, Thomas, *The Gift of the Jews: How a Desert Tribe of Desert Nomads Changed the Way Everyone Thinks and Feels* (New York: Anchor Books, 1998).
Cairns, David, *The Image of God in Man* (London: Collins, rev. edn, 1973).
Callahan, Allen D., 'Chrysostom on Philemon: A Response to Margaret Mitchell', *HTR* 88 (1995), pp. 149-56.
—*Embassy of Onesimus: The Letter of Paul to Philemon* (Valley Forge, PA: Trinity Press International, 1997).
—'Paul's Epistle to Philemon: Toward an Alternative *Argumentum*', *HTR* 86 (1993), pp. 357-76.

—*The Talking Book: African Americans and the Bible* (New Haven: Yale University Press, 2006).
Callahan, Allen D., Richard A. Horsley, and Abraham Smith (eds.), *Slavery in Text and Interpretation* (Semeia, 83/84; Atlanta, GA: Scholars Press, 1998).
Callender, Dexter, 'Servants of God(s) and Servants of Kings', in Callahan, Horsley, and Smith (eds.), *Slavery in Text and Interpretation*, pp. 67-82.
Calvin, John, *Commentary on Matthew, Mark, and Luke*. Online: http://www.ccel.org/ccel/calvin/calcom32.ii.xxxii.html (accessed 21 June 2010).
Canévet, Mariette, *Grégoire de Nysse et l'herméneutique biblique: Etude des rapports entre le langage et la connaissance de Dieu* (Paris: Etudes augustiniennes, 1983).
Capizzi, Joseph E., 'The Children of God: Natural Slavery in the Thought of Aquinas and Vitoria', *Theological Studies* 63 (2002), pp. 31-52.
Carey, Brycchan, and Peter J. Kitson (eds.), *Slavery and the Cultures of Abolition: Essays Marking the Bicentennial of the British Abolition Act of 1807* (Woodbridge, Suffolk: D.S. Brewer, 2007).
Carmichael, Calum M., 'Three Laws on the Release of Slaves (Exodus 21:2-11; Deuteronomy 15:12-18; Leviticus 25:39-46)', *ZAW* 112 (2000), pp. 509-25.
Carnahan, Burrus M., 'Military Necessity and the Emancipation Proclamation: Another Look at the Record', *Lincoln Herald* 103 (Spring 2001), pp. 23-29.
Carrington, Selwyn H.H., 'The American Revolution and the British West Indies' Economy', *Journal of Interdisciplinary History* 17 (1987), pp. 823-50.
—*The Sugar Industry and the Abolition of the Slave Trade, 1775–1810* (Florida: University Press of Florida, 2002).
Carter, Warren, *Matthew and Empire: Initial Explorations* (Harrisburg, PA: Trinity Press International, 2001).
—*Matthew and the Margins: A Socio-Political and Religious Reading* (New York: T. & T. Clark International, 2004).
Cateau, Heather, and S.H.H. Carrington (eds.), *Capitalism and Slavery Fifty Years Later: Eric Eustace Williams—A Reassessment of the Man and his Work* (New York: Peter Lang, 2000).
Champlin, Edward, *Final Judgment: Duty and Emotion in Roman Wills, 200 B.C.—A.D. 250* (Berkeley: University of California Press, 1991).
Chariton, *Callirhoe* (trans. G.P. Goold; LCL; Cambridge, MA: Harvard University Press, 1995).
Cherniss, Harold, *The Platonism of Gregory of Nyssa* (repr., Berkeley: B. Franklin, 1970 [1939]).
Childs, Matt D., *The 1812 Aponte Rebellion in Cuba and the Struggle against Atlantic Slavery* (Chapel Hill: University of North Carolina Press, 2006).
Chirichigno, Gregory C., *Debt-Slavery in Ancient Israel and the Near East* (JSOTSup, 141; Sheffield: Sheffield Academic Press, 1993).
Church, Frank F., 'Rhetorical Structure and Design in Paul's Letter to Philemon', *HTR* 71 (1978), pp. 17-33.
Cicero, *De oratore* (trans. E.W. Sutton and H. Rackham; LCL; 2 vols.; Cambridge, MA: Harvard University Press, 1942).
—*Letters to Friends* (trans. D.R. Shackleton Bailey; LCL; 3 vols.; Cambridge, MA: Harvard University Press, 2001).
—*On the Republic, On the Laws* (trans. Clinton W. Keyes; LCL; Cambridge, MA: Harvard University Press, 1928).

—*Philippics* (trans. W.C.A. Ker; LCL; Cambridge, MA: Harvard University Press, 1995).

Clark, Elizabeth A., *The Life of Melania the Younger: Introduction, Translation, and Commentary* (Lewiston, NY: Edwin Mellen Press, 1984).

Clark, Emily, *Masterless Mistresses: The New Orleans Ursulines and the Development of a New World Society, 1727–1834* (Chapel Hill: University of North Carolina Press, 2007).

Clarkson, Thomas, *An Abstract of the Evidence Delivered before a Select Committee of the House of Commons in the Years 1790 and 1791 on the Part of the Petitioners for the Abolition of Slavery* (London: James Phillips, 1791).

—*An Essay on the Impolicy of the African Slave Trade* (London: J. Phillips, 1788).

—*An Essay on the Slavery and Commerce of the Human Species, Particularly the African* (London: J. Philips, 1776).

—*The History of the Rise, Progress, and Accomplishment of the Abolition of the African Slave Trade in the British Parliament* (2 vols.; London: John W. Parker, 1839).

Clauss, Manfred, *Kaiser und Gott: Herrscherkult im römischer Reich* (Stuttgart/Leipzig: Teubner, 1999).

Clines, David J.A. (ed.), *Dictionary of Classical Hebrew* (8 vols.; Sheffield: Sheffield Phoenix Press, 1993–2011).

—'Ethics as Deconstruction, and, The Ethics of Deconstruction', in Rogerson, Davies, and Carroll R. (eds.), *The Bible in Ethics*, pp. 77-106.

—'The Image of God in Man', *Tyndale Bulletin* 19 (1968), pp. 53-103.

Coakley, Sarah (ed.), *Re-thinking Gregory of Nyssa* (Malden, MA: Blackwell, 2003).

Cody, Aelred, '*The Didache*: An English Translation', in Jefford (ed.), *The Didache in Context*, pp. 3-14.

Collins, Billie Jean, *The Hittites and their World* (Atlanta: Society of Biblical Literature, 2007).

Columella, *On Agriculture* (trans. Harrison B. Ash; LCL; 3 vols.; Cambridge, MA: Harvard University Press, 1941).

Combes, I.A.H., *The Metaphor of Slavery in the Writings of the Early Church, from the New Testament to the Beginning of the Fifth Century* (Sheffield: Sheffield Academic Press, 1998).

Cone, James H., *A Black Theology of Liberation* (Maryknoll, NY: Orbis Books, twentieth anniversary edn, 1990 [1970]).

Conrad, Robert E., *Children of God's Fire: A Documentary History of Black Slavery in Brazil* (Princeton, NJ: Princeton University Press, 1983).

Conzelmann, Hans, *1 Corinthians* (trans. James W. Leitch; Philadelphia: Fortress Press, 1975).

Coogan, Michael D., 'The Great Gulf between Scholars and the Pew', in Susanne Scholz (ed.), *Biblical Studies Alternatively: An Introductory Reader* (Upper Saddle River, NJ: Prentice–Hall, 2003), pp. 5-12.

Cook, Michael, 'Ibn Qutayba and the Monkeys', *Studia islamica* 89 (1999), pp. 43-74.

Copan, Paul, 'Are Old Testament Laws Evil?', in W.L. Craig and Chad Meister (eds.), *God Is Good: Why Believing in God Is Reasonable and Responsible* (Downers Grove, IL: IVP Books, 2009), pp. 134-54.

—'Is Yahweh a Moral Monster? The New Atheists and the Old Testament', Online. Available: http://www.epsociety.org/library/articles.asp?pid=45. June 5, 2010.

Cortés-Fuentes, D., 'The Least of These my Brothers: Matthew 25:31-46', *Apuntes* 23 (2003), pp. 100-109.

Coupeau, Steeve, *The History of Haiti* (London: Greenwood Press, 2008).
Coupland, Reginald, *Wilberforce: A Narrative* (Oxford: Clarendon Press, 1923).
Craton, Michael, *Testing the Chains: British Rebellions in the British West Indies, 1629–1832* (Ithaca, NY: Cornell University Press, 1982).
Cugoano, Quobna Ottobah, *Thoughts and Sentiments on the Evil of Slavery* (ed. Vincent Carretta; repr., New York: Penguin Books, 1999 [1787]).
Culbertson, Laura (ed.), *Slaves and Households in the Ancient Near East* (Oriental Institute Seminar Series, 6; Chicago: Oriental Institute, 2011).
Dal Lago, Enrico, and Constantina Katsari (eds.), *Slave Systems: Ancient and Modern* (Cambridge: Cambridge University Press, 2008).
Dalmas, Antoine, *Histoire de la révolution de Saint Domingue* (2 vols.; Paris: Mame Frères, 1814).
Dandamaev, Muhammad A., 'Slavery (ANE and Old Testament)', in *ABD*, III, pp. 58-65.
—*Slavery in Babylonia from Nabopolassar to Alexander the Great (626–331 B.C.)* (DeKalb, IL: University of Northern Illinois Press, 1984).
Daniélou, Jean, 'La chronologie des oeuvres de Grégoire de Nysse', *Studia patristica* 7 (1966), pp. 159-79.
—*Platonisme et théologie mystique: essai sur la doctrine spirituelle de Saint Grégoire de Nysse* (Paris: Aubier Editions Montaigne, 1944).
Davenport, Frances Gardiner (ed.), *European Treaties Bearing on the History of the United States and its Dependencies to 1648* (Washington, DC: Carnegie Institution of Washington, 1917).
Davidson, Edward H., and William J. Scheick, *Paine, Scripture and Authority: The Age of Reason as Religious and Political Idea* (Bethlehem, PA: Lehigh University Press, 1994).
Davies, C.S.L., 'Slavery and Protector Somerset: The Vagrancy Act of 1547', *Economic History Review* 19 (1966), pp. 533-49.
Davies, Margaret, 'Work and Slavery in the New Testament: Impoverishment of Traditions', in Rogerson, Davies, and Carroll R. (eds.), *The Bible in Ethics*, pp. 315-47.
Davis, David Brion, *Inhuman Bondage: The Rise and Fall of Slavery in the New World* (New York: Oxford University Press, 2006).
—'The Perils of Doing History by Ahistorical Abstraction: A Reply to Thomas L. Haskell's AHR Forum Reply', in Thomas Bender (ed.), *The Antislavery Debate: Capitalism as a Problem in Historical Interpretation* (Berkeley: University of California Press, 1992), pp. 290-309.
—*The Problem of Slavery in the Age of Revolution 1770–1823* (Ithaca, NY: Cornell University Press, 1975).
—*The Problem of Slavery in Western Culture* (repr., New York: Oxford University Press, 1988 [1966]).
Davis, Reginald F., *Frederick Douglass: A Precursor of Liberation Theology* (Macon, GA: Mercer University Press, 2005).
Davis, Stacy, *This Strange Story: Jewish and Christian Interpretation of the Curse of Canaan from Antiquity to 1865* (Lanham, MD: University Press of America, 2008).
Dawkins, Richard, *The God Delusion* (Boston: Houghton Mifflin, 2006).
Dayan, Joan, *Haiti, History and the Gods* (Berkeley: University of California Press, 1995).

Decret, François, 'Augustin d'Hippone et l'esclavage: problèmes posés par les positions d'un évêque de la Grande Eglise face à une réalité sociale dans l'Afrique de l'antiquité tardive', *Dialogues d'histoire ancienne* 11 (1985), pp. 675-85.

Dennis, T.J., 'The Relationship between Gregory of Nyssa's Attack on Slavery in his Fourth Homily on Ecclesiastes and his Treatise *De Hominis Opificio*', *Studia patristica* 17 (1982), pp. 1065-72.

Dershowitz, Alan, *The Genesis of Justice: Ten Stories of Biblical Injustice that Led to the Ten Commandments and Modern Law* (New York: Warner Books, 2000).

Desmangles, Leslie, *The Faces of the Gods: Vodou and Roman Catholicism in Haiti* (Chapel Hill: University of North Carolina Press, 1992).

Diakonoff, Igor, 'Slave-Labour vs. Non-Slave Labour: The Problem of Definition', in Marvin A. Powell (ed.), *Labor in the Ancient Near East* (New Haven: American Oriental Society, 1987), pp. 1-3.

Dickerson, Debra J., *The End of Blackness: Returning the Souls of Black Folk to their Rightful Owners* (New York: Pantheon Books, 2004).

Didymus the Blind, *Commentary on Zechariah* (trans. Robert C. Hill; The Fathers of the Church, 111; Washington, DC: Catholic University of America Press, 2006).

Diedrich, Maria, *Love across Color Lines: Ottilie Assing and Frederick Douglass* (New York: Hill & Wang, 1999).

Dindorf, Karl Wilhelm (ed.), *Julii Pollucis onomasticon cum annotationibus interpretum* (Leipzig: Kuehn, 1824).

Dion, Paul E., 'Changements sociaux et changements législatifs dans le Deutéronome', *Eglise et théologie* 24 (1993), pp. 343-60.

Divjak, Johannes (ed.), *Epistulae ex duobus codicibus nuper in lucem prolatae* (CSEL, 88; Vienna: Hoelder-Pichler-Tempsky, 1981).

Dolbeau, François (ed.), *Vingt-six sermons au peuple d'Afrique, retrouvé à Mayence* (Collection des Etudes Augustiniennes, Série Antiquité, 147; Paris: Institut d'Etudes Augustiniennes, 1996).

Donnan, Elizabeth (ed.), *Documents Illustrative of the History of the Slave Trade to America* (4 vols.; Washington, DC: The Carnegie Institution of Washington, 1930-35).

Douglass, Frederick, Agriculture and Black Progress...18 September 1873', in Blassingame, *The Frederick Douglass Papers*, IV, p. 378.

—'Baptists, Congregationalists, The Free Church and Slavery...23 December 1845', in Blassingame, *The Frederick Douglass Papers*, I, p. 116.

—'The Bible Opposes Oppression, Fraud, and Wrong... 6 January, 1845', in Blassingame, *The Frederick Douglass Papers*, I, p. 128.

—'Collection for Funds for Sumner Portrait...11 April, 1873', in Blassingame, *The Frederick Douglass Papers*, IV, p. 356.

—'The Dred Scott Decision...May 1857', in Blassingame, *The Frederick Douglass Papers*, III, p. 182.

—'The Freedman's Monument to Abraham Lincoln...14 April, 1876', in Blassingame, *The Frederick Douglass Papers,* IV, p. 437.

—'Great Britain's Example is High, Noble, and Grand...6 August, 1885', in Blassingame, *The Frederick Douglass Papers*, V, p. 203.

—'Haiti and the Haitian People...2 January 1893', in Blassingame, *The Frederick Douglass Papers*, V, p. 529.

—'It Moves...20 November 1883', in Blassingame, *The Frederick Douglass Papers*, V, p. 131.
—'The Nation's Problem...16 April, 1889', in Blassingame, *The Frederick Douglass Papers*, V, p. 413.
—'Our Composite Nationality...7 December 1869', in Blassingame, *The Frederick Douglass Papers*, IV, p. 249.
—'Shalt Thou Steal?...9 May 1849', in Blassingame, *The Frederick Douglass Papers*, II, p. 182.
—'Slavery and the Limits of Non-Intervention...7 December 1859', in Blassingame, *The Frederick Douglass Papers*, III, p. 284.
—'Slavery's Northern Bulwarks...12 January, 1851', in Blassingame, *The Frederick Douglass Papers*, II, p. 284.
—'We Are Confronted by a New Administration...16 April, 1885', in Blassingame, *The Frederick Douglass Papers*, V, p. 190.
—'What to the Slave is the Fourth of July?...5 July, 1852', in Blassingame, *The Frederick Douglass Papers*, II, p. 377.
Doyle, Daniel E., *The Bishop as Disciplinarian in the Letters of St Augustine* (Patristic Studies, 4; New York: Peter Lang, 2002).
Drescher, Seymour, *Capitalism and Antislavery: British Mobilization in Comparative Perspective* (New York: Oxford University Press, 1987).
—*Econocide: British Slavery in the Era of Abolition* (Chapel Hill: University of North Carolina Press, 2nd edn, 2010).
D'Souza, Dinesh, *What's So Great about Christianity* (Washington, DC: Regnery Press, 2007).
Ehrman, Bart, *God's Problem: How the Bible Fails to Answer Our Most Important Question—Why We Suffer* (New York: HarperOne, 2008).
Eilberg-Schwartz, Howard, *God's Phallus and Other Problems for Men and Monotheism* (Boston: Beacon Press, 1994).
Eisenstein, Elizabeth, *The Printing Press as an Agent of Change: Communications and Cultural Transformations in Early-Modern Europe* (2 vols.; New York: Cambridge University Press, 1979).
Elkins, Stanley M., *Slavery: A Problem in American Institutional and Intellectual Life* (Chicago: University of Chicago Press, 1959).
Eltis, David, and David Richardson, *Atlas of the Transatlantic Slave Trade* (New Haven: Yale University Press, 2010).
Engerman, Stanley, and David Eltis, 'Economic Aspects of the Abolition Debate', in Christine Bolt and Seymour Drescher (eds.), *Anti-Slavery, Religion and Reform* (Folkestone, Kent: Wm Dawson & Sons, 1980).
Engerman, Stanley L., and Eugene D. Genovese (eds.), *Race and Slavery in the Western Hemisphere: Quantitative Studies* (Princeton, NJ: Princeton University Press, 1975).
Ennis, Daniel James, *Enter the Press-Gang: Naval Impressment in Eighteenth Century British Literature* (Newark, DE: University of Delaware Press, 2002).
Epictetus (trans. W.A. Oldfather; LCL; 2 vols.; Cambridge, MA: Harvard University Press, 1928).
Epsztein, Léon, *Social Justice in the Ancient Near East and the People of the Bible* (trans. John Bowden; London: SCM Press, 1986).
Everett, Susanne, *History of Slavery* (Edison, NJ: Chartwell Books, 1999).

Exum, J. Cheryl, 'The Ethics of Biblical Violence against Women', in Rogerson, Davies, and Carroll R. (eds.), *The Bible in Ethics*, pp. 248-71.
Falk, Ze'ev W., *Hebrew Law in Biblical Times* (Winona Lake, IN: Eisenbrauns, 2001).
Fee, Gordon, *The First Epistle to the Corinthians* (Grand Rapids: Eerdmans, 1987).
Felder, Cain Hope (ed.), *Stony the Road We Trod: African American Biblical Interpretation* (Minneapolis: Fortress Press, 1991).
Field, Lester I., *Liberty, Dominion and the Two Swords: On the Origins of Western Political Ideology (180–398)* (Publications in Medieval Studies, 28; Notre Dame: University of Notre Dame Press, 1998).
Finke, Roger, and Rodney Stark, *The Churching of America 1776–2005: Winners and Losers in our Religious Economy* (New Brunswick, NJ: Rutgers University Press, 2005).
Finley, Moses I., *Ancient Slavery and Modern Ideology* (ed. Brent D. Shaw; Princeton, NJ: Markus Wiener Publishers, 1998).
Fishbane, Michael, 'Image of the Human in Jewish Tradition', in S. Leroy Rouner (ed.), *Human Rights and the World's Religions* (Notre Dame: University of Notre Dame Press, 1988), pp. 17-32.
Fitzmyer, Joseph A., *The Gospel according to Luke X–XXIV* (AB, 28A; Garden City, NY: Doubleday, 1985).
—*The Letter to Philemon: A New Translation with Introduction and Commentary* (AB, 34C; New York: Doubleday, 2000).
Fleer, David, and Dave Bland (eds.), *Reclaiming the Imagination: The Exodus as Paradigmatic Narrative for Preaching* (St Louis, MO: Chalice Press, 2009).
Flesher, Paul V.M., *Oxen, Women, or Citizens? Slaves in the System of the Mishnah* (Brown Judaic Studies, 143; Atlanta: Scholars Press, 1988).
Fletcher, F.T.H., 'Montesquieu's Influence on Anti-Slavery Opinion in England', *Journal of Negro History* 18 (1933), pp. 414-25.
Fletcher, John, *Studies on Slavery in Easy Lessons, Compiled into Eight Studies, and Subdivided into Short Lessons for the Convenience of Readers* (Natchez, MS: Jackson Warner, 1852).
Fogel, William R., and Stanley L. Engerman, *Time on the Cross: The Economics of American Negro Slavery* (New York: W.W. Norton, 1974).
Ford, Lacy K., *Deliver Us from Evil: The Slavery Question in the Old South* (New York: Oxford University Press, 2009).
Fournet, Pierre A., 'St Bathilde', in *The Catholic Encyclopedia* (New York: Robert Appleton Company, 1907). Online: www.newadvent.org/cathen/02348b.htm (accessed 6 May 2010).
Fox-Genovese, Elizabeth, and Eugene Genovese, *Slavery in White and Black: Race and Class in the Southern Slaveholders' New World Order* (New York: Cambridge University Press, 2008).
Frankfurter, David, 'Things Unbefitting Christians: Violence and Christianization in Fifth Century Panopolis', *JECS* 8 (2000), pp. 273-95.
French, B.F. (ed.), *Historical Memoirs of Louisiana from the First Settlement of the Colony to the Departure of Governor O'Reilly in 1770* (New York: Lamport, Blakeman & Law, 1853).
Frick, Frank S., 'Cui bono?—History in the Service of Political Nationalism: The Deuteronomistic History as Political Propaganda', in Knight (ed.), *Ethics and Politics in the Bible*, pp. 79-92.

Friede, Juan, and Benjamin Keen (eds.), *Bartolomé de las Casas in History: Toward an Understanding of the Man and his Work* (DeKalb, IL: Northern Illinois University Press, 1971).
Furneaux, Robin, *William Wilberforce* (London: Hamish Hamilton, 1974).
Gadamer, Hans-Georg, *Truth and Method* (trans. Joel Weinsheimer and Donald G. Marshall; New York: Crossroad, 2nd edn, 1989).
Gaius, *The Institutes of Gaius* (trans. W.M. Gordon and O.F. Robinson; Ithaca, NY: Cornell University Press, 1988).
Gallay, Allan, 'The Great Sellout: George Whitefield on Slavery', in Winifred B. Moore, Jr, and Joseph F. Tripp (eds.), *Looking South: Chapters in the History of American Religion* (Westport, CT: Greenwood Press, 1989), pp. 21-23.
Galpaz-Feller, Pnina, 'Private Lives and Public Censure: Adultery in Ancient Egypt and Biblical Israel', *Near Eastern Archaeology* 67 (2004), pp. 153-61.
Garnet, Henry Highland, 'An Address to the Slaves of the United States, Buffalo, NY, 1843', Lincoln, NE: Electronic Texts in American Studies, 2007. Online: http://digitalcommons.unl.edu/cgi/viewcontent.cgi?article=1007&context=etas (accessed 4 January 2011).
Garnsey, Peter, *Ideas of Slavery from Aristotle to Augustine* (Cambridge: Cambridge University Press, 1996).
Garr, W. Randall, *In his Own Image and Likeness: Humanity, Divinity, and Monotheism* (Leiden: E.J. Brill, 2003).
Gates, Henry Louis (ed.), *Frederick Douglass: Autobiographies* (New York: The Library of America, 1994).
Gay, Peter, *The Enlightenment: An Interpretation* (New York: W.W. Norton, 1969).
Genovese, Eugene D., *A Consuming Fire: The Fall of the Confederacy in the Mind of the White Christian South* (Mercer University Press Memorial Lecture, 41; Athens: University of Georgia Press, 1998).
Gertz, Jan Christian, 'Hams Sündenfall und Kanaans Erbfluch. Anmerkungen zur kompositiongeschichtlichen Stellung von Gen 9, 18-29', in Achenbach and Arneth (eds.), *Gerechtigkeit und Recht*, pp. 81-95.
Giles, Kevin, 'The Biblical Argument for Slavery: Can the Bible Mislead? A Case Study in Hermeneutics', *Evangelical Quarterly* 66 (1994), pp. 3-17.
Glancy, Jennifer A., 'Early Christianity, Slavery, and Women's Bodies', in Brooten (ed.), *Beyond Slavery*, pp. 143-58.
—*Slavery in Early Christianity* (Minneapolis: Fortress Press, 2006).
Glaude, Eddie S., Jr, *Exodus: Religion, Race, and Nation in Early Nineteenth-Century Black America* (Chicago: University of Chicago Press, 2000).
Glick, Leonard B., *Marked in your Flesh: Circumcision from Ancient Judea to Modern America* (New York: Oxford University Press, 2005).
Glock, Charles Y., and Rodney Stark, *Christian Beliefs and Anti-Semitism* (New York: Harper & Row, 1966).
Godwyn, Morgan, *The Negro's and Indian's Advocate Suing for their Admission into the Church* (repr., Whitefish, MT: Kessinger, 2003 [1680]).
Goldenberg, David M., *The Curse of Ham: Race and Slavery in Early Judaism, Christianity, and Islam* (Princeton, NJ: Princeton University Press, 2003).
Goldman, Ronald, *Questioning Circumcision: A Jewish Perspective* (Boston: Vanguard Publications, 1998).

Gollaher, David L., *Circumcision: A History of the World's Most Controversial Surgery* (New York: Basic Books, 2002).
Gordesian, Lewan, *Zur mykenischen Gesellschaftsordnung* (Tbilisi: Logos-Verlag, 2nd edn, 2002).
Gossett, Thomas F., *Race: The History of an Idea in America* (Dallas, TX: Southern Methodist University Press, 1963).
Gould, Philip, *Barbaric Traffic: Commerce and Antislavery in the 18th Century Atlantic World* (Cambridge, MA: Harvard University Press, 2003).
Grat, Felix, *Etude sur le Motu propio: des origines au début du XVIe siècle* (Melun: Librairie d'Argences, 1945).
Greenberg, Karen L., and Joshua L Dratel, *The Torture Papers: The Road to Abu Ghraib* (Cambridge: Cambridge University Press, 2005).
Greene, Jack P., '"A Plain and Natural Right to Life and Liberty": An Early Natural Rights Attack on the Excesses of the Slave System in Colonial British America', *William and Mary Quarterly* 57 (2000), pp. 793-808.
Greengus, Samuel, 'Some Issues Relating to the Comparability of Laws and Coherence of the Legal Tradition', in Levinson (ed.), *Theory and Method in Biblical and Cuneiform Law*, pp. 60-87.
Gregory of Nyssa, Saint, *Commentary on the Song of Songs* (trans. Casimir McCambley; Brookline, MA: Hellenic College Press, 1987).
Groothuis, Rebecca M., *Good News for Women: A Biblical Picture of Gender Equality* (Grand Rapids: Baker Books, 1997).
Grudem, Wayne A., 'Is Evangelical Feminism the New Path to Liberalism? Some Disturbing Warning Signs', *Journal for Biblical Manhood and Womanhood* 9 (2004), pp. 35-84.
Gurney, Oliver R., *The Hittites* (London: Penguin Books, 1990).
Güzlow, Henneke, *Christentum und Sklaverei in den ersten drei Jahrhunderten* (Bonn: Rudolf Habelt Verlag, 1969).
Hall, George (ed.), *Gregory of Nyssa: Homilies on Ecclesiastes: An English Version with Supporting Studies. Proceedings of the Seventh International Colloquium of Gregory of Nyssa, St Andrews, 5–10 September, 1990* (Berlin: W. de Gruyter, 1993).
Hall, Gwendolyn M., *Databases for the Study of Afro-Louisiana History and Genealogy* (Compact Disk Publication; Baton Rouge: Louisiana State University Press, 2000).
Halpern, Baruch, *David's Secret Demons: Messiah, Murderer, Traitor, King* (Grand Rapids: Eerdmans, 2001).
Hamoto, Azad, *Der Affe in der altorientalischen Kunst* (Münster: Ugarit-Verlag, 1995).
Hanger, Kimberly S., *Bounded Lives, Bounded Places: Free Black Society in Colonial New Orleans, 1769–1803* (Durham, NC: Duke University Press, 1997).
Hanke, Lewis, *All Mankind is One: A Study of the Disputation between Barthlomé de las Casas and Juan Ginés de Sepúlveda in 1550 on the Intellectual and Religious Capacity of American Indians* (DeKalb, IL: Northern Illinois University Press, 1974).
—*Aristotle and the American Indians: A Study in Race Prejudice in the Modern World* (Bloomington: Indiana University Press, 1959).
—'The Requerimiento and its Interpreters', *Revista de historia de América* 1 (1938), pp. 25-34.
—*The Spanish Struggle for Justice in the Conquest of America* (Boston: Little, Brown & Co., 1965).

Hardin, Justin K., *Galatians and the Imperial Cult: A Critical Analysis of the First-Century Social Context of Paul's Letter* (Tübingen: Mohr Siebeck, 2008).
Harrelson, Walter, *The Ten Commandments and Human Rights* (Macon, GA: Mercer University Press, 1997).
Harrill, J. Albert, 'Ignatius ad Polycarp, 4.3 and the Corporate Manumission of Christian Slaves', *JECS* 1 (1993), pp. 107-42.
—*The Manumission of Slaves in Early Christianity* (Tübingen: Mohr Siebeck, 1995).
—'Slavery', in *NIDB*, V, pp. 299-308.
—*Slaves in the New Testament: Literary, Moral, and Social Dimensions* (Minneapolis: Fortress Press, 2006).
—'The Use of the New Testament in the American Slave Controversy: A Case History in the Hermeneutical Tension between Biblical Criticism and Christian Moral Debate', *Religion and American Culture* 10 (Summer 2000), pp. 149-86.
—'The Vice of Slave Dealers in Greco-Roman Society: The Use of a Topos in 1 Timothy 1:10', *JBL* 118 (1999), pp. 97-122.
Harris, Sam, *The End of Faith: Religion, Terror, and the End of Reason* (New York: W.W. Norton, 2005).
Harris, William V., 'Demography, Geography, and the Sources of Roman Slaves', *Journal of Roman Studies* 84 (1994), pp. 67-68.
Hart, David B., 'The "Whole Humanity": Gregory of Nyssa's Critique of Slavery in Light of his Eschatology', *Scottish Journal of Theology* 54 (2001), pp. 51-69.
Haught, John, *God and the New Atheism: A Critical Response to Dawkins, Harris, and Hitchens* (Louisville, KY: Westminster/John Knox Press, 2008).
Haynes, Stephen R., *Noah's Curse: The Biblical Justification of American Slavery* (New York: Oxford University Press, 2002).
Hays, Richard B., *The Moral Vision of the New Testament: A Contemporary Introduction to New Testament Ethics* (New York: HarperOne, 1996).
Healy, Nicholas M., *Thomas Aquinas: Theologian of the Christian Life* (Farnham, Surrey: Ashgate, 2003).
Heidel, Alexander, *The Babylonian Genesis* (Chicago: University of Chicago Press, 1951).
Hempton, David, *The Religion of the People: Methodism and Popular Religion, c. 1750–1900* (London: Routledge, 1996).
Hendricks, Obery, Jr, *The Politics of Jesus: Rediscovering the True Revolutionary Nature of Jesus' Teachings and How They Have Been Corrupted* (New York: Doubleday, 2006).
Hera, Alberto de la, 'El derecho de los indios a la libertad y a la fe', *Anuario de la historia del derecho español* 26 (1956), pp. 89-181.
Hernaez, Francisco Javier, *Colección de bulas, breves y otros documentos relativos a la iglesia de América y Filipinas* (2 vols.; repr., Vaduz: Kraus, 1964 [1879]).
Hess, Hamilton, *The Early Development of Canon Law and the Council of Serdica* (Oxford Early Christian Studies; New York: Oxford University Press, 2002).
Hezser, Catherine, *Jewish Slavery in Antiquity* (New York: Oxford University Press, 2006).
Hiers, Richard H., *Justice and Compassion in Biblical Law* (New York/London: Continuum, 2009).
Hietanen, Mika, *Paul's Argumentation in Galatians: A Pragma-Dialectical Analysis* (New York: T. & T. Clark, 2007).

Hine, Edward, *Identity of the Lost Tribes of Israel with the Anglo-Celto-Saxons* (Boring, OR: CPA Book Publisher, abridged edn, n.d.).
Hirsch, E.D., *Validity in Interpretation* (New Haven: Yale University Press, 1967).
Hitchens, Christopher, *god Is Not Great: How Religion Poisons Everything* (New York: Twelve, 2007).
Hochschild, Adam, *Bury the Chains: Prophets and Rebels in the Fight to Free an Empire's Slaves* (Boston: Houghton Mifflin, 2005).
Hoffner, Harry A., *The Laws of the Hittites: A Critical Edition* (Leiden: E.J. Brill, 1997).
Horsley, Richard A., *1 Corinthians* (Nashville: Abingdon Press, 1998).
—*Jesus and Empire: The Kingdom of God and the New World Disorder* (Minneapolis: Fortress Press, 2003).
—*Jesus and the Spiral of Violence: Popular Jewish Resistance in Roman Palestine* (Minneapolis: Fortress Press, 1993).
—'The Law of Nature in Philo and Cicero', *HTR* 71 (1978), pp. 35-59.
—'The Slave Systems of Classical Antiquity and their Reluctant Recognition by Modern Scholars', in Callahan, Horsley, and Smith (eds.), *Slavery in Text and Interpretation*, pp. 19-66.
Horsley, Richard A. (ed.), *Paul and Empire: Religion, Power and Society in Roman Imperial Society* (Harrisburg, PA: Trinity Press International, 1997).
Horst, Pieter W. van der, 'Chariton and the New Testament', *Novum Testamentum* 25 (1983), pp. 348-55.
Hove, Richard, *Equality in Christ? Galatians 3:28 and the Gender Dispute* (Wheaton, IL: Crossway Books, 1999).
Howard, Philip A., *Changing History: Afro-Cuban Cabildos and Societies of Color in the Nineteenth Century* (Baton Rouge: Louisiana State University Press, 1998).
Hunt, Alfred N., *Haiti's Influence on Antebellum America: Slumbering Volcano in the Caribbean* (Baton Rouge: Louisiana State University Press, 1988).
Hunt, A.S., and C.C. Edgar, *Select Papyri* (LCL; 5 vols.; Cambridge, MA: Harvard University Press, 1934).
Hyson, Leon O., 'Wesley's Thoughts upon Slavery: A Declaration of Human Rights', *Methodist History* 33 (1994), pp. 46-57.
Inikori, Joseph E., *Africans and the Industrial Revolution: A Study in International Trade and Economic Development* (Cambridge: Cambridge University Press, 2002).
Inwood, Brad, *Ethics and Human Action in Early Stoicism* (New York: Oxford University Press, 1985).
Isaac, Benjamin, *The Invention of Racism in Classical Antiquity* (Princeton, NJ: Princeton University Press, 2004).
Isaac, Ephraim, 'Genesis, Judaism, and the "Sons of Ham"', in John Ralph Willis (eds.), *Slaves and Slavery in Muslim Africa* (2 vols.; London: Frank Cass, 1985), I, pp. 75-91.
—'Ham', in *ABD*, III, pp. 31-32.
Jackson, Samuel, *A Comparison of Ancient Near Eastern Law Collections Prior to the First Millennium BC* (Gorgias Dissertation Series, 35; Piscataway, NJ: Gorgias Press, 2008).
James, C.L.R., *The Black Jacobins: Toussaint L'Ouverture and the San Domingo Revolution* (London: Allison & Busby, 3rd edn, 1980 [1938]).
James, Sydney V., *A People among Peoples: Quaker Benevolence in Eighteenth-Century America* (Cambridge, MA: Harvard University Press, 1963).

Jardine, Lisa, *Worldly Goods: A New History of the Renaissance* (New York: Doubleday, 1996).
Jefford, Clayton N. (ed.), *The Didache in Context* (Leiden: E.J. Brill, 1995).
Jones, William R., *Is God a White Racist? A Preamble to Black Theology* (Garden City, NY: Anchor Press, 1973).
Johnson, Luke Timothy, *The Real Jesus: The Misguided Quest for the Historical Jesus and the Truth of the Traditional Gospels* (New York: HarperSanFrancisco, 1996).
Johnson, Sylvester A., 'The Bible, Slavery, and the Problem of Authority', in Brooten (ed.), *Beyond Slavery*, pp. 231-48.
—*The Myth of Ham in Nineteenth-Century American Christianity: Race, Heathens, and the People of God* (New York: Palgrave Macmillan, 2004).
Josephus (trans. H. St. J. Thackeray *et al.*; LCL; 10 vols.; Cambridge, MA: Harvard University Press, 1926–65).
Kaiser, Walter C., *Toward Old Testament Ethics* (Grand Rapids: Zondervan, 1991).
Karras, Ruth Mazo, *Slavery and Society in Medieval Scandinavia* (New Haven: Yale University Press, 1988).
Kawashima, Robert, 'A Revisionist Reading Revisited: On the Creation of Adam and Eve', *VT* 56 (2006), pp. 46-57.
Kendall, Elliott, 'The End of the British Slave Trade', *Epworth Review* 18 (1991), pp. 33-35.
Kennedy, G.A., *The Art of Rhetoric in the Roman World 300 B.C.–A.D. 300* (Princeton, NJ: Princeton University Press, 1972).
—*Classical Rhetoric and its Christian and Secular Tradition from Ancient to Modern Times* (Chapel Hill: University of North Carolina Press, 1980).
—*New Testament Interpretation through Rhetorical Criticism* (Chapel Hill: University of North Carolina Press, 1984).
Kim, Seyoon, *Christ and Caesar: The Gospel and the Roman Empire in the Writings of Paul and Luke* (Grand Rapids: Eerdmans, 2008).
King, Martin Luther, Jr, 'Pilgrimage to Non-Violence', in Staughton Lynd and Alice Lynd (eds.), *Nonviolence in America: A Documentary History* (Maryknoll, NY: Orbis Books, rev. edn, 2002 [1966]), pp. 208-20.
King, Philip J., 'Slavery in Antiquity', in J. David Schloen (ed.), *Exploring the Longue Durée: Essays in Honor of Lawrence E. Stager* (Winona Lake, IN: Eisenbrauns, 2009), pp. 243-49.
Kiple, Kenneth F., *Blacks in Colonial Cuba* (Gainesville: University of Florida Press, 1976).
Kirk, Alan, '"Love Your Enemies", The Golden Rule, and Ancient Reciprocity (Luke 6:27-35)', *JBL* 122 (2003), pp. 667-86.
Kleber, Kristin, 'Neither Slave nor Truly Free: The Status of the Dependents of Babylonian Temple Households', in Culbertson (ed.), *Slaves and Households*, pp. 101-11.
Klein, Richard, 'Gibt es eine Sklavenethik bei Gregor von Nyssa? Anmerkungen zur David R. Stains "*Gregory of Nyssa and the Ethics of Slavery and Emancipation*"', in Hubertus R. Drobner and Albert Viciano (eds.), *Gregory of Nyssa: Homilies on the Beatitudes* (Leiden: E.J. Brill, 2000), pp. 593-604.
Klingberg, Frank J., *The Anti-Slavery Movement in England: A Study in English Humanitarianism* (New Haven: Yale University Press, 1926).

Klingshirn, William E., and Mark Vessey (eds.), *The Limits of Ancient Christianity: Essays on Late Antique Thought and Culture in Honor of R.A. Markus* (Ann Arbor: University of Michigan Press, 1999).

Knight, Douglas A., 'Old Testament Ethics', *Christian Century* 99 (1982), pp. 55-59.

Knight, Douglas A. (ed.), *Ethics and Politics in the Bible* (Semeia, 66; Atlanta: Society of Biblical Literature, 1995).

—*Julius Wellhausen and his Prolegomena to the History of Israel* (Semeia, 25; Chico, CA: Scholars Press, 1983).

Kotlikoff, Laurence J., and Anton J. Rupert, 'The Manumission of Slaves in New Orleans, 1827–1846', *Southern Studies* (1980), pp. 172-81.

Kramer, Samuel Noah, *History Begins at Sumer: Thirty-Nine Firsts in Man's Recorded History* (repr., Philadelphia: University of Pennsylvania Press, 1988 [1956]).

Lactantius, *Institutiones divinae* (CSEL, 19; Vienna: F. Tempsky, 1890).

Ladner, Gerhart B., 'The Philosophical Anthropology of Saint Gregory of Nyssa', *Dumbarton Oaks Papers* 12 (1958), pp. 59-94.

Laertius, Diogenes, *Lives of Eminent Philosophers* (trans. R.D. Hicks; LCL; Cambridge, MA: Harvard University Press, 1925).

Laeuchli, Samuel, *Sexuality and Power: The Emergence of Canon Law at the Council of Elvira* (Philadelphia: Temple University Press, 1974).

Laguerre, Michel S., *Voodoo and Politics in Haiti* (New York: Macmillan, 1989).

Lambdin, Thomas O., *An Introduction to the Gothic Language* (Eugene, OR: Wipf & Stock, 2006).

Lambert, W.G., *Babylonian Wisdom Literature* (Oxford: Clarendon Press, 1960).

Lambert, W.G., and Simon Parker, *Enuma Elish, the Babylonian Creation Epic: The Cuneiform Text* (Oxford: Clarendon Press, 1969).

Lanser, Susan S., '(Feminist) Criticism in the Garden: Inferring Genesis 2–3', *Semeia* 41 (1988), pp. 67-84.

Las Casas, Bartolomé, *In Defense of the Indians* (trans. Stafford Poole; DeKalb, IL: Northern Illinois University Press, 1992).

Lascelles, Edward C.P., *Granville Sharp and the Freedom of Slaves in England* (London: Humphrey Milford, 1928).

Layton, Richard A., *Didymus the Blind and his Circle in Late Antique Alexandria* (Urbana: University of Illinois Press, 2004).

Lebrun, René, *Hymnes et prières hittites* (Louvain-la-Neuve: Centre d'Histoire des Religions, 1980).

Lehman, Winfred, *A Gothic Etymological Dictionary* (Leiden: E.J. Brill, 1986).

Levenson, Jon D, 'Exodus and Liberation', *Horizons in Biblical Theology* 13 (1991), pp. 134-74.

—*The Hebrew Bible, the Old Testament, and Historical Criticism: Jews and Christians in Biblical Studies* (Louisville, KY: Westminster/John Knox Press, 1993).

Levine, Baruch, 'The Netînîm', *JBL* 82 (1963), pp. 207-12.

Levinson, Bernard M., 'The Birth of the Lemma: The Restrictive Reinterpretation of the Covenant Code's Manumission Law by the Holiness Code (Leviticus 25:44-46)', *JBL* 124 (2005), pp. 617-39.

Levinson, Bernard M. (ed.), *Theory and Method in Biblical and Cuneiform Law: Revision, Interpolation, and Development* (Sheffield: Sheffield Academic Press, 1994; repr., Sheffield: Sheffield Phoenix Press, 2006).

Lichtenstadter, Ilse, '"And become ye accursed apes"', *Jerusalem Studies in Arabic and Islam* 14 (1991), pp. 162-75.
Lichtheim, Miriam, *Ancient Egyptian Literature* (3 vols.; Berkeley: University of California Press, 1976).
Lipsius, Justus H., *Das attische Recht und Rechtsverfahren mit Benutzung des attischen Processes* (2 vols.; Leipzig: O.R. Reisland, 1905).
Locke, Mary Stoughton, *Anti-Slavery in America from the Introduction of African Slaves to the Prohibition of the Slave Trade (1619–1808)* (Radcliffe Monographs, 11; Boston: Ginn & Company, 1901).
Loewenisch, Walther von, *Martin Luther: The Man and his Work* (trans. Lawrence W. Denef; Minneapolis: Ausburg, 1982).
Luther, Martin, *Ausgewählte Schriften* (ed. Karin Bornkamm and Gerhard Ebeling; 5 vols.; Frankfurt: Insel Verlag, 1982).
MacMullen, Ramsay, *Christianity and Paganism in the Fourth to Eighth Centuries* (New Haven: Yale University Press, 1997).
—'Late Roman Slavery', *Historia* 36 (1987), pp. 359-82.
Macqueen, J.G., *The Hittites and their Contemporaries in Asia Minor* (London: Thames & Hudson, 1986).
Magdalene, F. Rachel, and Cornelia Wunsch, 'Slavery between Judah and Babylon: The Exilic Experience', in Culbertson (ed.), *Slaves and Households in the Ancient Near East*, pp. 113-34.
Maltby, Richard, *The Reign of Charles V* (New York: Palgrave, 2002).
Malul, Meir, *The Comparative Method in Ancient Near Eastern and Biblical Legal Studies* (Neukirchen–Vluyn: Neukirchener Verlag, 1990).
Mann, Friedhelm (ed.), *Lexicon gregorianum: Wörterbuch zu den Schriften Gregors von Nyssa* (8 vols.; Leiden: E.J. Brill, 1999–).
Mark, Elizabeth Wyner (ed.), *The Covenant of Circumcision: New Perspectives on an Ancient Jewish Rite* (Hanover, NH: University Press of New England/Brandeis University Press, 2003).
Marrietta, Jack D., *The Reformation of American Quakerism 1748–1783* (Philadelphia: University of Pennsylvania Press, 1984).
Marshall, David, *The Truth behind the New Atheism: Responding to the Emerging Challenges to God and Christianity* (Eugene, OR: Harvest House Publishers, 2007).
Martens, Peter W., 'Revisiting the Allegory/Typology Distinction: The Case of Origen', *JECS* 16 (2008), pp. 283-317.
Martin, Dale B., *Slavery as Salvation: The Metaphor of Slavery in Pauline Christianity* (New Haven: Yale University Press, 1990).
Martin, R.P., *Ephesians, Colossians, and Philemon* (Atlanta: John Knox Press, 1991).
Martin, Thomas F., '*Vox Pauli*: Augustine and the Claims to Speak for Paul, An Exploration of Rhetoric in the Service of Exegesis', *JECS* 8 (2000), pp. 237-72.
Maxwell, John Francis, *Slavery and the Catholic Church: The History of Catholic Teaching Concerning the Moral Legitimacy of the Institution of Slavery* (London: Barry Rose Publishers, 1975).
McFeeley, William S., *Frederick Douglass* (New York: W.W. Norton, 1995).
McGukin, John, *Gregory of Nazianzus: An Intellectual Biography* (Crestwood, NY: St Vladimir's Seminary Press, 2001).
McKay, Heather A., *Sabbath and Synagogue: The Question of Sabbath Worship in Ancient Judaism* (Leiden: E.J. Brill, 1994).

McKeown, Niall, *The Invention of Ancient Slavery?* (London: Duckworth, 2007).
Meeks, Wayne A., *The Origins of Christian Morality: The First Two Centuries* (New Haven: Yale University Press, 1993).
Meier, Samuel A., *The Messenger in the Ancient Near East* (HSM, 45; Atlanta: Scholars Press, 1988).
Mendelsohn, Isaac, *Slavery in the Ancient Near East* (New York: Oxford University Press, 1949).
Menesson-Rigaud, Odette, 'Le rôle du Vaudou dans l'independance d'Haiti', *Présence africaine* 17–18 (1958), pp. 43-67.
Meredith, Anthony, *Gregory of Nyssa* (London: Routledge, 1999).
Metraux, Alfred, *Voodoo in Haiti* (New York: Schocken, 1972).
Metzger, Bruce M., *The Canon of the New Testament: Its Origin, Development and Significance* (Oxford: Oxford University Press, 1997).
—*A Textual Commentary on the Greek New Testament* (London: United Bible Societies, 1975).
Metzger, Bruce M., and Bart D. Ehrman, *The Text of the New Testament: Its Transmission, Corruption and Restoration* (New York: Oxford University Press, 4th edn, 2005).
Meyers, Carol, 'Gender and Genesis 3:16', in C.M. Meyers and M. O'Connor (eds.), *The Word of the Lord Shall Go Forth: Essays in Honor of David Noel Freedman in Celebration of his Sixtieth Birthday* (Winona Lake, IN: Eisenbrauns, 1983), pp. 337-54.
Middleton, J. Richard, 'A Liberating Image: Interpreting the *Imago Dei* in Context', *Christian Scholar's Review* 24 (1994), pp. 8-25.
Mikalson, Jon D., *Ancient Greek Religion* (Malden, MA: Blackwell, 2005).
Miles, Jack, *God: A Biography* (New York: Vintage Books, 1996).
Millar, John, *Observations concerning the Distinction of Ranks in Society* (London: John Murray, rev. edn, 1773).
Miller, John W., 'Depatriarchalizing God in Biblical Interpretation: A Critique', *CBQ* 48 (1986), pp. 609-16.
Mills, Mary E., *Biblical Morality: Moral Perspectives in Old Testament Narratives* (Burlington, VT: Ashgate, 2001).
Minchinton, Walter, 'Williams and Drescher: Abolition and Emancipation', *Slavery and Abolition* 4 (1983), pp. 81-105.
Mintz, Steven D., *Sweetness and Power: The Place of Sugar in Modern History* (New York: Penguin Books, 1985).
Mitchell, Margaret A., 'John Chrysostom on Philemon: A Second Look', *HTR* 88 (1995), pp. 135-48.
Mitscherling, Jeffrey A., Tanya DiTommaso, and Aref Nayed, *The Author's Intention* (Lanham, MD: Lexington Books, 2004).
Monteith, Kathleen E.A., and Glen Richards, *Jamaica in Slavery and Freedom: History, Heritage, and Culture* (Kingston: University of the West Indies, 2002).
Morgan, Philip D., *Slave Counterpoint: Black Culture in the Eighteenth Century Chesapeake and Lowcountry* (Chapel Hill: University of North Carolina Press, 1998).
Morgenthau, Hans, *Politics among Nations: The Struggle for Power and Peace* (ed. Kenneth Thompson; Boston: McGraw–Hill, 1993).

Morris, Thomas D., *Southern Slavery and the Law 1619–1860* (Chapel Hill: University of North Carolina Press, 1996).
Morrow, Glenn R., *Plato's Laws of Slavery in its Relation to Greek Law* (repr., New York: Arno Press, 1976 [1939]).
Müller, Gerhard *et al.* (eds.), *Theologische Realenzyklopädie* (36 vols.; Berlin: W. de Gruyter, 1977–2004).
Müller, Peter, *Der Brief an Philemon* (Meyers kritisch-exegetischer Kommentar über das Neue Testament; Göttingen: Vandenhoeck & Ruprecht, in press).
Muraoka, Takamitsu, *Classical Syriac: A Basic Grammar with a Chrestomathy* (Wiesbaden: Harrassowitz, 1997).
Nash, Gary B., 'Slaves and Slaveowners in Colonial Philadelphia', *William and Mary Quarterly* 30 (1973), pp. 223-56.
Nissinen, Martti, C.L. Seow, and Robert K. Ritner, *Prophets and Prophecy in the Ancient Near East* (Atlanta: Society of Biblical Literature, 2003).
Noll, Mark A., 'The Bible and Slavery', in R.M. Miller, H.S. Stout, and C.R. Wilson (eds.), *Religion and the American Civil War* (New York: Oxford University Press, 1998), pp. 43-73.
—*The Civil War as a Theological Crisis* (Chapel Hill: University of North Carolina Press, 2006).
—*The Rise of Evangelicalism: The Age of Edwards, Whitefield and the Wesleys* (Downers Grove, IL: InterVarsity Press, 2003).
Noonan, John T., *A Church That Can and Cannot Change: The Development of Catholic Moral Teaching* (Notre Dame: University of Notre Dame Press, 2005).
Oberman, Heiko A., *Luther: Man between God and the Devil* (trans. Eileen Walliser-Schwarzbart; New York: Image Books, 1992).
Odahl, Charles M., *Constantine and Christian Empire* (New York: Routledge, 2004).
O'Donnell, James J., *Augustine: A New Biography* (New York: HarperCollins, 2005).
Oldham, James, *The Mansfield Manuscripts and the Growth of English Law in the Eighteenth Century* (2 vols.; Chapel Hill: University of North Carolina Press, 1992).
Olsen, Ted, 'The Abolitionist Scandal: William Wilberforce and the Clapham Sect Founded Sierra Leone Then Tolerated a Form of Slavery There, a New Book Reveals', *Christianity Today* 54 (October 2010), pp. 46-49.
Olyan, Saul, *Disability in the Hebrew Bible: Interpreting Mental and Physical Differences* (Cambridge: Cambridge University Press, 2008).
—*Social Inequality in the World of the Text: The Significance of Ritual and Social Distinctions in the Hebrew Bible* (Journal of Ancient Judaism Supplements, 4; Göttingen: Vandenhoeck & Ruprecht, 2011).
Origen, *Homilies on Genesis and Exodus* (trans. Ronald E. Heine; Washington, DC: Catholic University of America Press, 1982).
Orlinsky, Harry M., 'Nationalism-Universalism and Internationalism in Ancient Israel', in Harry Thomas Frank and William L. Reed (eds.), *Translating and Understanding the Old Testament: Essays in Honor of Herbert Gordon May* (Nashville: Abingdon Press, 1970), pp. 206-36.
Ormond, John J., Arthur P. Bagby, and George Goldthwaite, *The Code of Alabama* (Montgomery: Brittan & De Wolf State Printers, 1852).
Osiek, Carolyn, 'Slavery in the Second Testament World', *Biblical Theology Bulletin* 22 (1992), pp. 174-79.

Otto, Eckart, 'Of Aims and Methods in Hebrew Bible Ethics', in Knight (ed.), *Ethics and Politics in the Bible*, pp. 161-71.

—*Theologische Ethik des Alten Testaments* (Stuttgart: Kohlhammer, 1994).

Paget, James Carleton, *The Epistle of Barnabas: Outlook and Background* (Tübingen: J.C.B. Mohr, 1994).

Palafox, Luis Patiño, *Juan Ginés de Sepúlveda y su pensamiento imperialista* (Mexico City: Los Libros de Homero, 2007).

Paley, Ruth, Christina Malcomson, and Michael Hunter, 'Parliament and Slavery 1660 to c. 1710', *Slavery and Abolition* 31 (2010), pp. 257-81.

Palmer, James T., 'Rimbert's *Vita Anskarii* and Scandinavian Mission in the Ninth Century', *Journal of Ecclesiastical History* 55 (2004), pp. 235-56.

Panzer, Joel S., *The Popes and Slavery* (New York: Alba House, 1996).

Parish, Helen-Rand, and Francis Patrick Sullivan (eds.), *Bartolomé de las Casas: The Only Way* (Mahwah, NJ: Paulist Press, 1992).

Parish, Helen-Rand, and Harold E. Weidman, *Las Casas en México: Historia y obra desconocidas* (Mexico, DF: Fondo de cultura ecónomica, 1992).

Park, Eun Chun, *Either Jew or Gentile: Paul's Unfolding Theology of Inclusivity* (Westminster: John Knox Press, 2003).

Parker, Robert, *Miasma: Pollution and Purification in Early Greek Religion* (New York: Oxford University Press, 1983).

Pascal, Robert, 'Sources of the Digest of 1808: A Reply to Professor Batiza', *Tulane Law Review* 47 (1972), pp. 603-27.

Patterson, Orlando, 'The Ancient and Medieval Origins of Modern Freedom', in Stephen D. Mintz and John Stauffer (eds.), *The Problem of Evil: Slavery, Freedom and the Ambiguities of American Reform* (Boston: University of Massachusetts Press, 2007), pp. 31-66.

—*Freedom in the Making of Western Culture* (New York: Basic Books, 1991).

—'Paul, Slavery, and Freedom', in Callahan, Horsley, and Smith (eds.), *Slavery in Text and Interpretation*, pp. 263-79.

—*Slavery and Social Death: A Comparative Study* (Cambridge, MA: Harvard University Press, 1982).

Payne, Philip B., *Man and Woman, One in Christ* (Grand Rapids: Zondervan, 2009).

—'Twelve Reasons to Understand 1 Corinthians 7:21-23 as a Call to Gain Freedom' (2009). Online: www.pbpayne.com/wp-admin/1_Cor_7-21_escape_slavery.pdf (accessed 4 June 2010).

Petersen, Norman R., *Rediscovering Paul: Philemon and the Sociology of Paul's Narrative World* (repr., Eugene, OR: Wipf & Stock, 2008 [1985]).

Pharr, Clyde (ed.), *The Theodosian Code and Novels and the Sirmondian Constitution* (Princeton, NJ: Princeton University Press, 1952).

Philo (trans. F.H. Colson *et al.*; LCL; 11 vols.; Cambridge, MA: Harvard University Press, 1935).

Pickett, Terry H., 'The Friendship of Frederick Douglass with the German Ottilie Assing', *Georgia Historical Quarterly* 73 (1989), pp. 88-105.

Pinn, Anthony B., *Why Lord? Suffering and Evil in Black Theology* (New York: Continuum, 2000).

Plank, Geoffrey, 'The First Person in Antislavery Literature: John Woolman, his Clothes, and his Journal', *Slavery and Abolition* 30 (2009), pp. 67-91.

Plato, *Laws* (trans. R.G. Bury; LCL; 2 vols.; Cambridge, MA: Harvard University Press, 1926).

—*Republic* (trans. Paul Shorey; LCL; 2 vols.; Cambridge, MA: Harvard University Press, 1935).

Plutarch, *Plutarch's Lives* (trans. Bernadotte Perrin; LCL; 11 vols.; Cambridge, MA: Harvard University Press, 1914).

Pons, Frank Moya, *History of the Caribbean* (Princeton, NJ: Markus Wiener Publishers, 2007).

Pope, Marvin H., *Job* (AB, 15; Garden City, NY: Doubleday, 1986).

Popkin, Jeremy D., *Facing Racial Revolution: Eyewitness Accounts of the Haitian Insurrection* (Chicago: University of Chicago Press, 2007).

—*You Are All Free: The Haitian Revolution and the Abolition of Slavery* (Cambridge: Cambridge University Press, 2010).

Preuss, Julius, *Biblical and Talmudic Medicine* (trans. Fred Rosner; repr., London: Jason Aronson, 1994 [1978]).

Price, Robert M., and Julia Sweeney, *The Reason Driven Life: What Am I Here on Earth For?* (Amherst, NY: Prometheus, 2006).

Price, S.R.F., 'Gods and Emperors: The Greek Language of the Roman Imperial Cult', *Journal of Hellenic Studies* 104 (1984), pp. 79-95.

—*Rituals of Power: The Roman Imperial Cult in Asia Minor* (Cambridge: Cambridge University Press, 1985).

Priest, Josiah, *Bible Defence of Slavery and Origin, Fortunes, and History of the Negro Race* (repr., Whitefish, MT: Kessinger, 2007 [1852]).

Propp, William H., 'The Origins of Infant Circumcision in Israel', *Hebrew Annual Review* 11 (1987), pp. 355-70.

Quintilian, *Institutio oratoria* (trans. H.E. Butler; LCL; Cambridge, MA: Harvard University Press, 1920).

Quiroga, Pedro López Barja de, 'Freedmen Social Mobility in Roman Italy', *Historia* 44 (1995), pp. 326-48.

Ramelli, Illaria L.E., 'Luke 16:16: The Good News for God's Kingdom Is Proclaimed and Everyone Is Forced into It', *JBL* 27 (2008), pp. 737-58.

Ramsay, James, *An Essay on the Treatment and Conversion of African Slaves in the British Sugar Colonies* (London: James Phillips, 1784).

Rebillard, Eric, 'A New Style of Argument in Christian Polemic: Augustine and the Use of Patristic Citations', *JECS* 8 (2002), pp. 559-78.

Redford, Donald B., *Akhenaten: The Heretic King* (Princeton, NJ: Princeton University Press, 1984).

Reed, Jeffrey E., 'The Epistle', in Stanley E. Porter (ed.), *Handbook of Classical Rhetoric in the Hellenistic Period, 330 B.C.–A.D. 400* (Leiden: E.J. Brill, 2001), pp. 171-93.

Reis, João José, *Slave Rebellion in Brazil: The Muslim Uprising of 1835 in Bahia* (trans. Arthur Brakel; Baltimore: The Johns Hopkins University Press, 1993).

Reventlow, Henning Graf, *The Authority of the Bible and the Rise of the Modern World* (trans. John Bowden; Philadelphia: Fortress Press, 1985).

Riesener, Ingrid, *Der Stamm* עבד *im Alten Testament: Eine Wortuntersuchung unter Berücksichtigung neuerer sprachwissenschaftlicher Methoden* (BZAW, 149; Berlin: W. de Gruyter, 1979).

Roach, Joseph, 'Body of Law: The Sun King and the Code Noir', in Sara E. Meltzer and Kathryn Norberg (eds.), *From the Royal to the Republican Body: Incorporating the*

Political in Seventeenth- and Eighteenth-Century France (Berkeley: University of California Press, 1998), pp. 113-30.

Robertson, A.T., *A Grammar of the Greek New Testament in Light of Historical Research* (Nashville: Broadman Press, 1934).

Robinson, Charles H., *Anskar, Apostle of the North, 801–865, Translated from the Vita Anskarii by Bishop Rimbert his Fellow Missionary and Successor* (London: Society for the Propagation of the Gospel in Foreign Parts, 1921).

Rogers, Nicholas, 'Vagrancy, Impressment, and the Regulation of Labour in Eighteenth Century Britain', *Slavery and Abolition* 15 (1994), pp. 207-26.

Rogers, Tommy W., 'Dr F.A. Ross and the Presbyterian Defense of Slavery', *Journal of Presbyterian History* 45 (1967), pp. 112-24.

Rogerson, John W., Margaret Davies, and M. Daniel Carroll R. (eds.), *The Bible in Ethics: The Second Sheffield Colloquium* (JSOTSup, 207; Sheffield: Sheffield Academic Press, 1995).

Rogozinski, Jan, *A Brief History of the Caribbean: From the Arawak and the Carib to the Present* (New York: Penguin Putnam, 1999).

Rollins, W.G., 'Slavery in the New Testament', in *IDBSup*, pp. 831-32.

Ross, Fred A., *Slavery Ordained of God* (repr., New York: Negro University Press, 1969 [1859]).

Roth, Martha T., *Law Collections from Mesopotamia* (Atlanta: Scholars Press, 2nd edn, 1997).

Rozbicki, Michal J., 'To Save Them from Themselves: Proposals to Enslave the British Poor, 1698–1755', *Slavery and Abolition* 22 (2001), pp. 29-50.

Rupprecht, Arthur A., 'Attitudes on Slavery', in Richard N. Longenecker and Merrill C. Tenney (eds.), *New Dimensions in New Testament Study* (Grand Rapids: Zondervan, 1974), pp. 261-77.

Sala-Molins, Louis, *Le Code noir ou le calvaire de Canaan* (Paris: Presses universitaires de France, 2003).

Salzman, Michele R., 'The Evidence for Conversion of the Roman Empire to Christianity in Book 16 of the "Theodosian Code"', *Historia* 42 (1993), pp. 362-78.

Samoral, Manuel Lucena, 'El Código negro español tambien llamado carolino: comentario y texto', *Estudios de historia social y económica de América* 12 (1995), pp. 267-324.

Sampson, Ross, 'Rural Slavery, Inscriptions, Archaeology and Marx: A Response to Ramsay MacMullen's "Late Roman Slavery"', *Historia* 38 (1989), pp. 99-110.

Sandiford, Keith A., *Measuring the Moment: Strategies of Protest in Eighteenth-Century Afro-English Writing* (Selingrove, PA: Susquehanna University Press, 1988).

Sandt, Huub van de, and David Flusser, *The Didache: Its Jewish Sources and its Place in Early Judaism and Christianity* (Assen: Van Gorcum, 2002).

Sass, Gerhard, 'Zur Bedeutung von *doulos* bei Paulus', *Zeitschrift für die neutestamentliche Wissenschaft* 40 (1941), pp. 24-32.

Sass, Martin (ed.), *Ausgewählte Briefe von und an Ludwig Feuerbach*, XII–XIII (Stuttgart: Friedrich Frommann, 1964).

Sawyer, Philip H., *Kings and Vikings: Scandinavia and Europe AD 700–1100* (New York: Methuen, 1982).

Schafer, Judith Kelleher, *Slavery, the Civil Law and the Supreme Court of Louisiana* (Baton Rouge: Louisiana State University Press, 1994).

Schellenberg, Annette, *Der Mensch, das Bild Gottes? Zum Gedanken einer Sonderstellung des Menschen im Alten Testament und in weiteren altorientalischen Quellen* (Göttingen: Vandenhoeck & Ruprecht, in press).

—'Humankind as the "Image of God"', *Theologische Zeitschrift* 65 (2009), pp. 97-115.

Schenker, Adrian, 'The Biblical Legislation on the Release of Slaves: The Road from Exodus to Leviticus', *JSOT* 78 (1998): 23-41.

Scherer, Lester B., *Slavery and the Churches in Early America* (Grand Rapids: Eerdmans, 1976).

Schlaifer, Robert, 'Greek Theories of Slavery from Homer to Aristotle', *Harvard Studies in Classical Philology* 47 (1936), pp. 165-204.

Schmidt, Alvin J., *How Christianity Changed the World* (Grand Rapids: Zondervan, 2004).

Schnackenburg, Rudolf, *The Moral Teaching of the New Testament* (trans. J. Holland-Smith and W.J. O'Hara; London: Burns & Oates, 1975).

Schneider, Tammi J., *Sarah: Mother of Nations* (New York: Continuum International, 2004).

Schor, Joel, 'The Rivalry between Frederick Douglass and Henry Highland Garnet', *Journal of Negro History* 64 (1979), pp. 30-38.

Schuler, Einar von, *Hethitische Dienstanweisungen für höhere Hof- und Staatsbeamte: Ein Beitrag zum antiken Recht Kleinasiens* (Graz: Archiv für Orientforschung, 1957).

Schulz, Siegfried, *Gott ist kein Sklavenhalter: Die Geschichte einer verspäteten Revolution* (Zurich: Flamberg, 1972).

Schwab, Günther, *Echtheitskritische Untersuchungen zu den vier kleineren Paulusbriefe. I/A: Der Philemonbrief, Beobachtungen zur Sprache des Philipper und des Galaterbriefs* (Norderstedt: Books on Demand, 2011).

Seibert, Eric A., *Disturbing Divine Behavior: Troubling Old Testament Images of God* (Minneapolis: Fortress Press, 2009).

Sen, Amartya, *Inequality Reexamined* (New York: Oxford University Press, 1992).

Seneca, *Epistles 1–65* (trans. Richard M. Gummere; LCL; Cambridge, MA: Harvard University Press, 1917).

Sensbach, Jon F., *A Separate Canaan: The Making of an Afro-Moravian World in North Carolina, 1763–1840* (Chapel Hill: University of North Carolina Press, 1998).

Sepulveda, Juan Ginés de, *Democrates segundo o de las justas causas de la guerra contra los Indios* (ed. Angel Losada; Madrid: Consejo Superior de Investigaciones Cientificas, 1951).

Serfass, Adam, 'Slavery and Pope Gregory the Great', *JECS* 14 (2006), pp. 77-103.

Sewall, Samuel, *The Selling of Joseph: A Memorial* (Boston: Bartholomew Green & John Allen, 1700).

Shanks, Caroline L., 'The Biblical Anti-Slavery Argument of the Decade 1830–1840', *Journal of Negro History* 15 (1931), pp. 132-57.

Shaw, Brent D., 'A Wolf by the Ears: M.I. Finley's *Ancient Slavery and Modern Ideology* in Historical Context', in Finley, *Ancient Slavery and Modern Ideology*, pp. 3-78.

Sheehan, Jonathan, *The Enlightenment Bible* (Princeton, NJ: Princeton University Press, 2005).

Shtaerman, Elena M., and M.K. Trofimova, *La schiavitù nell' Italia imperiale: I–III secolo* (Rome: Editori Riuniti, 1982).

Shyllon, Folarin, *James Ramsay: The Unknown Abolitionist* (Edinburgh: Canongate, 1977).
Sider, Ronald, *Christ and Violence* (repr., Eugene, OR: Wipf & Stock, 2001 [1979]).
Skehan, Patrick, and Alexander A. Di Lella, *The Wisdom of Ben Sira* (AB, 39; New York: Doubleday, 1987).
Sloat, William A., 'George Whitefield, African-Americans and Slavery', *Methodist History* 20–23 (1994), pp. 3-13.
Smith, J. Payne (ed.), *A Compendious Syriac Dictionary Founded on the Thesaurus of R. Payne Smith* (repr., Winona Lake, IN: Eisenbrauns, 1998 [1903]).
Smith, Ruth, *Handel's Oratorios and Eighteenth-Century Thought* (Cambridge: Cambridge University Press, 1996).
Soden, Wolfram von, *The Ancient Orient: An Introduction to the Study of the Ancient Near East* (trans. Donald G. Schley; Grand Rapids: Eerdmans, 1994).
Soderlund, Jean R., *Quakers and Slavery: A Divided Spirit* (Princeton, NJ: Princeton University Press, 1988).
Sollberger, E., 'The Cruciform Monument', *Jaarberich van het Vooraziatisch-Egyptisch Genootschap 'Ex Oriente Lux'* 20 (1967–68), pp. 50-70.
Solow, Barbara L., 'Capitalism and Slavery in the Exceedingly Long Run', *Journal of Interdisciplinary History* 17 (1987), pp. 711-37.
Spear, Jennifer M., *Race, Sex, and Social Order in New Orleans* (Baltimore: The Johns Hopkins University Press, 2009).
Sprinkle, Joe M., *Biblical Law and its Relevance: A Christian Understanding and Ethical Application for Today of the Mosaic Regulations* (Lanham, MD: University Press of America, 2006).
Staiger, C. Bruce, 'Abolitionism and the Presbyterian Schism of 1837–1838', *Mississippi Valley Historical Review* 36 (1949), pp. 391-414.
Stark, Rodney, *For the Glory of God: How Monotheism Led to Reformations, Science, Witch-Hunts and the End of Slavery* (Princeton, NJ: Princeton University Press, 2003).
—*One True God: Historical Consequences of Monotheism* (Princeton, NJ: Princeton University Press, 2001).
—*The Victory of Reason: How Christianity Led to Freedom, Capitalism, and Western Success* (New York: Random House, 2005).
Ste Croix, G.E.M. de, 'Early Christian Attitudes toward Property and Slavery', in Derek Baker (ed.), *Church Society and Politics: Papers Read at the Thirteenth Summer Meeting and the Fourteenth Winter Meeting of the Ecclesiastical History Society* (Oxford: Blackwell, 1975), pp. 1-38.
Stein, Stephen J., 'George Whitefield on Slavery: Some New Evidence', *Church History* 42 (1973), pp. 243-56.
Stendahl, Krister, 'Biblical Studies', in Paul Ramsey and John F. Wilson (eds.), *The Study of Religion in Colleges and Universities* (Princeton: Princeton University Press, 1970), pp. 23-39.
—'Biblical Theology, Contemporary', in *IDB*, I, pp. 418-32.
Stern, Philip, *The Biblical Ḥerem: A Window on Israel's Religious Experience* (Atlanta: Scholars Press, 1991).
Stowers, Stanley K., *Letter Writing in Greco-Roman Antiquity* (Philadelphia: Westminster Press, 1986).

—'Paul and Slavery: A Response', in Callahan, Horsley, and Smith (eds.), *Slavery in Text and Interpretation*, pp. 295-311.
Stramara, Daniel F., 'Gregory of Nyssa: An Ardent Abolitionist?', *St Vladimir's Theological Quarterly* 41 (1997), pp. 37-60.
Strickland, Debra H., *Saracens, Demons, and Jews: Making Monsters in Medieval Art* (Princeton, NJ: Princeton University Press, 2003).
Stringfellow, Thorton, *Scriptural and Statistical Views in Favor of Slavery* (Richmond, VA: J.W. Randolph, 1856).
Stuart, Charles, *A Memoir of Granville Sharp, to Which is Added the Law of Passive Obedience or Christian Submission to Personal Injuries* (New York: American Anti-Slavery Society, 1836).
Stuart, Moses, *Conscience and the Constitution: With Remarks on the Recent Speech of the Hon[orable] Daniel Webster in the Senate of the United States on the Subject of Slavery* (Boston: Crocker & Brewster, 1850).
Stuckey, Sterling, '"My Burden Lightened": Frederick Douglass, the Bible, and Slave Culture', in Vincent L. Wimbush (ed.), *African Americans and the Bible: Sacred Texts and Social Textures* (New York: Continuum, 2000), pp. 251-65.
Swaminathan, Srividhya, *Debating the Slave-Trade: Rhetoric of British National Identity, 1759–1815* (Burlington, VT: Ashgate, 2009).
Tackach, James, *The Abolitionist Movement* (Detroit: Thompson/Gale, 2005).
Tannenbaum, Frank, *Slave and Citizen* (repr., Boston: Beacon Press, 1992 [1946]).
Tappert, Theodore G., *Selected Writings of Martin Luther 1517–1546* (4 vols.; Philadelphia: Fortress Press, 1967).
Tawil, Hayim ben Yosef, *An Akkadian Lexical Companion for Biblical Hebrew: Etymological and Idiomatic Equivalents with Supplement in Biblical Aramaic* (Jersey City, NJ: Ktav, 2009).
Taylor, Michelle Ellis, 'Numbers', in Hugh R. Page (ed.), *The Africana Bible: Reading Israel's Scriptures from Africa and the African Diaspora* (Minneapolis: Fortress Press, 2010), pp. 94-99.
Thayer, Joseph Henry, *A Greek–English Lexicon of the New Testament* (repr., Grand Rapids: Zondervan, 1974 [1889]).
Theissen, Gerd, *The Religion of the Earliest Churches: Creating a Symbolic World View* (Minneapolis: Fortress Press, 1999).
Thiselton, Anthony C., *Hermeneutics: An Introduction* (Grand Rapids: Eerdmans, 2009).
Thomas, Hugh, *The Slave Trade: The Story of the Atlantic Slave Trade 1440–1870* (New York: Simon & Schuster, 1997).
Thorley, John, 'Aktionsart in New Testament Greek: Infinitive and Imperative', *Novum Testamentum* 31 (1989), pp. 290-315.
Thornton, John K., '"I Am the Subject of the King of Kongo": African Political Ideology and the Haitian Revolution', *Journal of World History* 4 (1993), pp. 181-214.
Thucydides (trans. C.F. Smith; LCL; Cambridge, MA: Harvard University Press, 1975).
Thurston, H., 'Bulls and Briefs', in *The Catholic Encyclopedia* (New York: Robert Appleton Company, 1908). Online: www.newadvent.org/cathen/03052b.htm (accessed 5 June 2010).
Tierney, Brian, *The Idea of Natural Rights: Studies on Natural Rights, Natural Law and Church Law 1150–1625* (Atlanta: Scholars Press, 1997).
Tolmie, D. Francois, *Philemon in Perspective: Interpreting a Pauline Letter* (Berlin: W. de Gruyter, 2010).

Tomkins, Stephen, *The Clapham Sect: How Wilberforce's Circle Transformed Britain* (Oxford: Lion Hudson, 2010).
—'Wilberforce Was Complicit in Slavery', *The Guardian* (3 August 2010). Online: http://www.guardian.co.uk/commentisfree/belief/2010/aug/03/wilberforce-slavery-sierra-leone.
—*William Wilberforce: A Biography* (Grand Rapids: Eerdmans, 2007).
Tov, Emanuel, *Textual Criticism of the Hebrew Bible* (Minneapolis: Fortress Press; Assen: Royal Van Gorcum, 2001).
Traboulay, David M., *Columbus and Las Casas: The Conquest and Christianization of America, 1492–1566* (Lanham, MD: University Press of America, 1994).
Trible, Phyllis, *God and the Rhetoric of Sexuality* (Philadelphia: Fortress Press, 1978).
—*Texts of Terror: Literary-Feminist Readings of Biblical Narratives* (Philadelphia: Fortress Press, 1984).
The Triglot Bible Comprising the Holy Scriptures of the Old and New Testaments in the Original Tongues also the Septuagint, the Syriac (of the New Testament) and the Vulgate Versions (London: Richard Dickinson, 1897).
Tsevat, Matitiahu, 'The Hebrew Slave according to Deuteronomy 15:12-18: His Lot and Value of his Work, with Special Attention to the Meaning of מִשְׁנֶה', *JBL* 113 (1994), pp. 587-95.
United Nations, The Universal Declaration of Human Rights, 1948. Online: http://www.un.org/en/documents/udhr/ (accessed 25 March 2010).
Van Deburg, William L., 'The Tragedy of Frederick Douglass', *Christianity Today* 19 (1975), pp. 415-16.
Varro, *On Agriculture* (trans. W.D. Hooper and Harrison B. Ash; LCL; Cambridge, MA: Harvard University Press, 1934).
Vaux, Roland de, *Ancient Israel: Its Life and Institutions* (trans. John McHugh; London: Darton, Longman & Todd, 1961).
—*Ancient Israel: Social Institutions* (New York: McGraw–Hill, 1965).
Vercoutter, Jean et al. *The Image of the Black in Western Art* (2 vols.; Cambridge, MA: Harvard University Press, 1976–79).
Verlinden, Charles, *L'esclavage dans l'Europe médiévale* (2 vols.; Brugge: Rijksuniversiteit te Gent, 1955).
Vial, Theodore M., and Mark A. Hadley, *Ethical Monotheism, Past and Present: Essays in Honor of Wendell S. Dietrich* (Brown Judaic Studies, 329; Providence, RI: Brown Judaic Studies, 2001).
Vickery, Paul, *Bartolomé de las Casas: Great Prophet of the Americas* (New York: Paulist Press, 2006).
Vitoria, Francisco de, *Relectio de Indis o Libertad de los Indios* (ed. L. Pereña and J.M. Perez Prendes; Madrid: Consejo Superior de Investigaciones Científicas, 1967).
Voelz, Peter M., *Slave and Soldier: The Military Impact of Blacks in the Colonial Americas* (New York: Routledge, 1993).
Wacker, Grant, 'The Demise of Biblical Civilization', in Nathan O. Hatch and Mark A. Noll (eds.), *The Bible in America: Essays in Cultural History* (New York: Oxford University Press, 1982), pp. 121-38.
Waitz, G., *Vita Anskarii auctore Rimberto* (Hanover: Hahn, 1884).
Wajdenbaum, Philippe, *Argonauts of the Desert: Structural Analysis of the Hebrew Bible* (Sheffield: Equinox, 2011).

Walker, David, *David Walker's Appeal to the Coloured Citizens of the World but in Particular and very Expressly, to Those in the United States of America* (repr., Baltimore: Black Classic Press, 1993 [1830]).
Wallon, Henri, *Histoire de l'esclavage dans l'antiquité* (Paris: Librairie Hachette, 2nd edn, 1879 [1847]).
Walvin, James, *The Quakers: Money and Morals* (London: John Murray, 1999).
Walzer, Michael, *Exodus and Revolution* (New York: Basic Books, 1985).
Watson, Alan, *Roman Slave Law* (Baltimore: The Johns Hopkins University Press, 1987).
Wattles, Jeffrey, *The Golden Rule* (New York: Oxford University Press, 1996).
Watts, William, 'Seneca on Slavery', *Downside Review* 90 (1972), pp. 183-95.
Weaver, P.R.C., *Familia Caesaris: A Social Study of the Emperor's Freedmen and Slaves* (Cambridge: Cambridge University Press, 1972).
Weinfeld, Moshe, *Social Justice in Ancient Israel and in the Ancient Near East* (Jerusalem: Magnes Press, 1995).
Wellhausen, Julius, *Prolegomena to the History of Ancient Israel* (repr., Gloucester, MA: Peter Smith, 1983 [1883]).
Wendel, François, *Calvin: The Origins and Development of his Religious Thought* (trans. Philip Mairet; repr., Grand Rapids: Baker Books, 1997 [1963]).
Wenham, Gordon J., *Story as Torah: Reading Old Testament Narrative Ethically* (Grand Rapids: Baker Academic, 2000).
Westbrook, Raymond (ed.), *A History of Ancient Near Eastern Law* (2 vols.; Leiden: E.J. Brill, 2003).
—'International Law in the Amarna Age', in Raymond Cohen and Raymond Westbrook (eds.), *Amarna Diplomacy: The Beginnings of International Relations* (Baltimore: The Johns Hopkins University Press, 2000), pp. 28-41.
—*Property and the Family in Biblical Law* (Sheffield: Sheffield Academic Press, 1991).
—*Studies in Biblical and Cuneiform Law* (Paris: J. Gabalda, 1988).
Westermann, Claus, ' *'ebed*, servant', in *TLOT*, II, pp. 819-32.
Westermann, William L., *The Slave Systems of Greek and Roman Antiquity* (Philadelphia: The American Philosophical Society, 1955).
White, Joel, 'Anti-Imperial Subtexts in Paul: An Attempt at Building a Firmer Foundation', *Biblica* 90 (2009), pp. 305-33.
Whitford, David M., *The Curse of Ham in the Early Modern Era: The Bible and the Justifications for Slavery* (St Andrews Studies in Reformation History; Burlington, VT: Ashgate, 2009).
Whitlock, Keith (ed.), *The Renaissance in Europe: A Reader* (New Haven: Yale University Press, 2000).
Whybray, R. Norman, 'The Immorality of God: Reflections on Some Passages in Genesis, Job, Exodus and Numbers', *JSOT* 21 (1996), pp. 89-120.
—' "Shall not the judge of the earth do what is just?" God's Oppression of the Innocent in the Old Testament', in David Penchansky and Paul L. Redditt (eds.), *Shall Not the Judge of the Earth Do What Is Right? Studies in the Nature of God in Tribute to James L. Crenshaw* (Winona Lake, IN: Eisenbrauns, 2000), pp. 1-19.
Wiedemann, Thomas, *Greek and Roman Slavery* (London: Croom Helm, 1981).
Wilberforce, William, *An Appeal to the Religion Justice and Humanity of the Inhabitants of the British Empire in Behalf of the Negro Slaves in the West Indies* (London: J. Hatchard & Son, 1823).

Williams, Eric, *Capitalism and Slavery* (ed. Colin A. Palmer; Chapel Hill: University of North Carolina Press, 1994 [1944]).
Williams, Peter J., 'The Meaning of the Word *'ebed*' (unpublished paper delivered at the Annual Meeting of the Society of Biblical Literature, Lexicography Section, Atlanta, GA, 20 November 2010).
Williamson, Scott C., *The Narrative Life: The Moral and Religious Thought of Frederick Douglass* (Macon, GA: Mercer University Press, 2002).
Wills, Richard W., *Martin Luther King, Jr and the Image of God* (New York: Oxford University Press, 2009).
Wilson, Andrew, 'The Pragmatics of Politeness and Pauline Epistolography: A Case Study of the Letter to Philemon', *JSNT* 48 (1992), pp. 107-19.
Wilson, John A., *The Culture of Ancient Egypt* (Chicago: University of Chicago Press, 1951).
Wink, Walter, *Jesus and Nonviolence: A Third Way* (Minneapolis: Fortress Press, 2003).
Wise, Steven M., *Though the Heavens May Fail: The Landmark Trial That Led to the End of Slavery* (Cambridge, MA: Da Capo Press, 2005).
Wiseman, D.J., *The Vassal-Treaties of Esarhaddon* (London: The British School of Archaeology in Iraq, 1958).
Witherington III, Ben, *The Indelible Image: The Theological and Ethical Thought World of the New Testament* (2 vols.; Downers Grove, IL: IVP Academic Press, 2010).
—*The Letters to Philemon, the Colossians, and Ephesians: A Socio-Rhetorical Commentary on the Captivity Epistles* (Grand Rapids: Eerdmans, 2007).
—'Was Paul a Pro-Slavery Chauvinist? Making Sense of Paul's Seemingly Mixed Moral Messages', *BR* 20 (April 2004), pp. 8, 44.
Wölfel, Dominik Josef, 'La curia romana y la corona de España en la defensa de los aborígenes canarios', *Anthropos* 25 (1930), pp. 1011-83.
Wolff, Hans Walter, 'Masters and Slaves: On Overcoming Class-Struggle in the Old Testament' (trans. Gary Stansell), *Interpretation* 27 (1973), pp. 259-72.
Woolman, John, *Considerations on the Keeping of Negroes; Recommended to the Professors of Christianity of Every Denomination* (Philadelphia: The Tract Association of Friends, 1754).
Wright III, Benjamin G., ''EBED/DOULOS—Terms and Social Status in the Meeting of Hebrew Biblical and Hellenistic-Roman Culture', in Callahan, Horsley, and Smith (eds.), *Slavery in Text and Interpretation*, pp. 83-111.
—*Praise Israel for Wisdom and Instruction: Essays on Ben Sira and Wisdom, the Letter of Aristeas and the Septuagint* (SJSJ, 131; Leiden: E.J. Brill, 2008).
Wright, David P., *God's Law: How the Covenant Code of the Bible Used and Revised the Code of Hammurabi* (New York: Oxford University Press, 2009).
—'"She shall not go free as male slaves do": Developing Views about Slavery and Gender in the Laws of the Hebrew Bible', in Brooten (ed.), *Beyond Slavery*, pp. 125-42.
Wright, Joseph, *A Grammar of the Gothic Language* (Oxford: Clarendon Press, 1910).
Wyatt, David, *Slaves and Warriors in Medieval Britain and Ireland, 800–1200* (Leiden: E.J. Brill, 2009).
Wyatt, Nick, 'Circumcision and Circumstance: Genital Mutilation in Ancient Israel and Ugarit', *JSOT* 33 (2009), pp. 405-31.

Wyrick, Jed, *The Ascension of Authorship: Attribution and Canon Formation in Jewish, Hellenistic, and Christian Traditions* (Cambridge, MA: Harvard University Department of Comparative Literature, 2004).
Xenophon, *Scripta minora, Pseudo-Xenophon, Constitution of the Athenians* (trans. E.C. Marchant and G.W. Bowersock; LCL; Cambridge, MA: Harvard University Press, 1968).
Yoder, John Howard, *The Politics of Jesus* (Grand Rapids: Eerdmans, 1972).
Zagal Arreguin, Hector, 'Aquinas on Slavery: An Aristotelian Puzzle', *Atti del Congresso Internazionale su l'umanesimo cristiano nel III millennio: la prospettiva di Tommaso d'Aquino, 21–25 Settembre, 2003* 3 (2006), pp. 323-32.
Zawadizki, S., 'A Contribution to the Understanding of *širkûtu* in the Light of a Text from the Ebabbar Archive', *AoF* 24 (1997), pp. 226-30.
Zerbe, Gordon M., *Non-Retaliation in Early Jewish and New Testament Texts: Ethical Themes and Social Contexts* (Sheffield: JSOT Press, 1993).
Zimmerli, Walther, 'Slavery in the Old Testament', in *IDBSup*, pp. 829-30.

INDEXES

INDEX OF REFERENCES

HEBREW BIBLE/
OLD TESTAMENT
Genesis
1	66
1.26-27	88
1.26-28	66
1.26	36, 65
2.5	66
2.15	58, 66
2.19	66
2.23	67
3.16	54, 67
3.22-23	66
9	69, 70, 161
9.18-27	69
9.19-27	69
9.22-27	35
10.6-8	246
12.1-3	88
12.3	88
12.6	88
12.7	110
15.13	110
16	70
16.9	71
17.9-14	71
17.12	71
17.23	72, 220
19.24	211
21.10-12	64
21.10	82
21.12	82
24.1	73
34.22	72
41.44	60
41.45	60
42.22	255
52	253

Exodus
1–15	73
12.31-32	272
12.43	87
20.5	39
20.10	75
21	87, 225
21.1-6	76
21.2-11	63, 94
21.5	245
21.6	72, 86, 257
21.16	77, 79, 89, 255, 256
21.17 LXX	256
21.20-21	80
21.20	80
21.21	81, 151
21.26-27	80
33.19	151

Leviticus
18.29	206
19.18	204, 205
19.33-34	254
20.4-5	205
24.17	256
25	85, 87
25.1	280
25.8-17	245
25.8-13	85
25.14	258
25.29-44	86
25.29-31	245
25.35-43	84
25.39-55	94
25.39-46	49, 86
25.39	257
25.42	83, 286
25.44-46	64, 86, 246, 257, 265
25.44	256, 257, 280
25.45	64
25.46	64, 86
25.52	240
25.55	73, 91, 145
29.35-43	85

Numbers
12.10	35
31.17-18	78
31.41	78

Deuteronomy
5.12-15	75
5.14	94
5.29	145
7	10
7.6	146
10	25
10.9	254
10.12-22	24, 25
10.14	25
15	87
15.3	87
15.12-15	56, 87
15.12	255, 256
18.15	92
18.20	146
20	10
20.10-14	206
20.15	206
23	10
23.3	87

Index of References

Deuteronomy (cont.)		Ezra		Zechariah	
23.15-16	45, 88	2.64-65	92, 93	13.6	265
23.15	88	6.14	92		
23.20	87	7.25-26	92	**APOCRYPHA/**	
24.7	79, 246, 256			**DEUTERO-CANONICAL**	
		Nehemiah		*Wisdom of Solomon*	
24.14	254	5.7	84	12.3-7	205
28	42				
28.15-68	145	*Job*		*Ecclesiasticus*	
29.10-13	64	31.13-15	94	8.4	50
32.29	255			33.24-31	209
32.43	153	*Psalms*		33.30-31	130
		8	88	34	209
Joshua		33.10 LXX	149	34.18-22	209
6.21	78	34.9	149		
6.24	78	72.11	213	**NEW TESTAMENT**	
7.16-26	207	105.23	70	*Matthew*	
7.24-25	207			5.17	138
9.23-27	246	*Proverbs*		5.38-41	79
		11.29	54	5.38-40	280
Judges		22.19	45	5.38-39	46
21.17-24	79	22.20	44	5.39	45
		24.21	149	5.44	153
1 Samuel		25.21-22	143	7.12	96
8	90			7.16-17	197
8.7	90	*Ecclesiastes*		10	211
8.11	90	1.9	264	10.5-15	210
8.16-17	90	2.8	146	10.5	211
8.17	93, 145	7.7	253	10.8-12	211
9.16	91			10.12	210
		Isaiah		10.13-16	211
2 Samuel		3.9	34	10.15	211
24	116	14.1-2	28, 88	10.28	155, 287
		53	36	10.34-37	136-38
1 Kings		61.1-2	85	10.34	137, 198, 211
5.13	93				
		Jeremiah		10.37	142
2 Kings		1.5	146	12.12	104
10.5	65	27.6-11	91	12.46-50	153
				13.3	105
1 Chronicles		*Daniel*		13.24	150
9.2	84	7.18	149	13.45-46	150
29.3	146			14.5	128
		Joel		15.22	246
2 Chronicles		2.28-29	94	18.6-9	155
12.7-9	145	2.29	146	18.23	150
28.8-11	170				

Index of References

18.35	150	*John*		*1 Corinthians*	
19.12	155	13.36	104	2.1-4	123
19.19	115, 129, 204	15.12-18	155	4.21	117, 146
		15.12-15	155	5	130
19.21	217	15.19	156	5.12-13	214
20	150			5.12	215
20.1-16	149	*Acts*		6.1-6	106
20.1	150	2.16-18	94	6.2-3	215
20.8-16	150	2.30	142	6.7	106
20.15	151	5.29	115	6.8-9	130
22.1-14	147	9.3-9	147	6.9-10	134
22.2	150	9.3-7	213	6.19-20	148
22.12-13	212	10.7	260	7	100, 105
24.44-51	154	10.34-35	260	7.10	105
24.51	154	12.12-14	119	7.11	105
25.31-34	152	14	134	7.15	105
25.40	152	15.37	104	7.17-24	100
25.41-46	153	17.5-9	141	7.20-25	98
25.41-45	143, 153	17.7	136	7.21	12, 96, 98-103, 105-107, 115, 238, 240
25.41	153	17.26-28	98		
25.42-43	44	17.26	58, 97, 253, 265		
25.45	152, 153				
28.10	153	17.28	98, 265	7.28	105
28.19-20	198	26.10-11	212	7.29-31	147
				7.31	147
Mark		*Romans*		11	66
3.4	104	1.20-26	206	12.3	109
3.35	142	6.22	144	12.12-31	54
4.3	105	7.23	176	14.34	110
6.34-42	141	8.18-25	147	15.20-28	147
6.45	212	9.6-8	34	15.23-28	142
8.1-10	141	9.15	151		
		9.20-22	151	*2 Corinthians*	
Luke		11.25-26	147	4.3	103
4.18-21	86	12.14	143	4.16	103
6.9	105	12.19	143	7.8	103
12.47	262	12.20	143	10.9-11	122
14.5	57	13.1-10	143		
14.16-24	211	13.1-5	106	*Galatians*	
14.22-23	203	13.1-4	92	1.12	280
14.23	211-14	13.1-2	148	3.2	109
14.26	35, 142	13.1	115	3.3-6	109
16.16	212	13.7	264	3.7-9	109
21.3	100	13.9	204	3.16-18	110
21.21-24	143	14.18	144	3.16-17	110
21.27	143			3.16	110
				3.24-28	109

Galatians (cont.)		*1 Thessalonians*		1.24	265
3.26-28	108	2.6	128	2.18-20	215
3.26	110	3.13	149	2.18	97, 112, 114, 215, 240, 244, 246, 255, 260
3.28	108, 109, 111-15, 161, 215	4.14-18	147		
		2 Thessalonians			
4.6-8	112	2.10	130		
4.7	112, 114	3.14	129	3.5-6	69
4.30	82	3.15	129	3.7	54, 66
4.31	114			287	287
		1 Timothy			
Ephesians		1.9-10	125	*Revelation*	
1.15-16	124	1.10	124-26	7.3	145
2.14-15	280	2	111	19.16	141
3.1	124	6	126, 176, 182, 246		
5	111			PHILO	
5.23	54	6.1-8	240	*The Cherubim*	
5.24	68, 111	6.1-4	126	107	286
6.5	97, 110-12, 114-16, 215, 221, 240, 244, 246, 255, 280	6.1	164, 176, 240, 244	*Joseph*	
		6.2	241	67	149
		Titus		*Every Good Man Is Free*	
		2.10	240	17	55
6.9	164			19–20	92
		Philemon		19	54
Philippians		8–14	133	79	137
2.4-11	106	12	132	148	90
2.4-6	116	14	133, 134		
2.6-8	117	15	129	*On the Virtues*	
3.20-21	148	16–17	132	124	90
3.20	148	16	128, 129		
3.21	148	16a	128	JOSEPHUS	
		17–22	132	*Antiquities*	
Colossians		17	128, 129	8.161-162	84
1.4	124	21	132, 133	13.45	153
1.29	122			18.243	101, 102
3.2	240	*James*		18.336	134
3.6-8	122	2.4	118		
3.18–4.1	26, 119, 120	2.17	197	*Against Apion*	
				2.282-83	75
3.22-23	240	*1 Peter*			
3.22	164	1.2	114	*Jewish War*	
4.1	52, 110, 118	1.14	114	2.367-69	115
		1.22	114	4.175-79	115

Index of References

CHRISTIAN LITERATURE
Aquinas, St Thomas
Summa theologica
I, q. 92, a. 1, ad 2   179
I, q. 96, a. 4   179
I, q. 96, a. 4, ad 3   180
I-II, q. 94, a. 5,
  ad 3   174
I-II, q. 94, a. 6,
  ad 2   175
II-II, q. 57, a. 3,
  ad 2   174
II-II, q. 66, a. 8,
  ad 2   207
II-II, q. 104, a. 5,
  Ob 3   175
II-II, q. 104, a. 6,
  ad 1   176

Augustine
City of God
19.15   163
19.16   163
19.21   61

In Johannis Evangelium
6.25   162

Letters
93.5   213
173.10   213

Chalcedon
Canon 4   161

Chrysostom
*Homilies on
First Corinthians*
40.6   161

*Constitutiones
Apostolorum*
2.62.4   160

Cyprian
Ad Demetrianum
8   163

Didache
4.11   160

Epistle of Barnabas
19.7   160

Gregory of Nyssa
The Great Catechism
22   167
23   167

*Homily IV on
Ecclesiastes*   165

*Homily IV on the
Song of Songs*   166

Gregory of Nazianzus
Exemplum Testamenti
202   163

Gregory, Pope
Regulae Pastoralis Liber
3.5   164

Isidore of Seville
Etymologies
9.4.41   179

Lactantius
Institutiones divinae
15.14.15-16   59

Theodosian Code
4.7.6   89
9.9.1   164

Vita Anskarii
38   169

GREEK AND LATIN
AUTHORS
Antiphon
5.48   52

Aristotle
Eudemian Ethics
7.10.8-9   54

Aristotle
Politics
1.2.3   112
1.2.7-8   53, 54
1.2.12   54

Rhetoric
1.2.3   121

Chariton
Callirhoe
2.1.7-8   125

Cicero
De amicitia
13.44   122
19.69   124
20.71   124
20.74   124

De oratore
2.77.310   121
2.77.313-314   132
2.79.324   131

Laws
1.7.24   98

Letters to Friends
5.12   122
7.11.3   133
7.14.2   133
9.21.1   120, 132
15.21.4   121

Philippics
8.11.32   107

Columella
On Agriculture
1.8.15-16   118

Diodorus Siculus
Historia
13.20-27   217

Diogenes Laertius
6.63   58

Epictetus			Seneca		Code of Lipit-Ishtar	
The Discourses			*Epistles*		Law 14	43
1.13.4-5	58, 94		3.4	122		
			47.10-11	56	*Enuma elish*	
Plato			47.10	98	1.16	58
Laws			47.11-12	56, 97	6.33	58
6.776e	50		47.11	26		
6.777d	50		47.13-15	156	*Hittite Law Code*	
6.777d-e	53		47.15	57	Law 24	46
6.778a	50				Law 166	46
7.794B	50		Thucydides		Law 167	46
9.865	50		4.19.1-4	97		
9.865d	53				*Laws of Eshunna*	
9.868	50		Varro		6	77
9.872	50		*On Agriculture*		24	77
9.872c	53		1.7.6	118		
9.881c	53				*Laws of Ur Nammu*	
9.882	50		Xenophon		18–19	47
9.882a-b	51		*The Polity of the*			
11.914	50		*Athenians*		OTHER	
11.936	50		1.10	81	CIL	
12.955a	126		1.11-12	48, 112	13.7119	118
Republic			INSCRIPTIONS		*Code Noir*	
5.16	210		AND TABLETS		2	229
5.469b-c	49		*Code of Hammurabi*		3	229
5.469e-470a	216		Law 14	78	13	229
			Laws 15–20	88	17	229
Plutarch's Lives, Solon			Law 16	89	27	228
15.4	48		Law 16		38	228, 229
			section	45	39	228
Pollux			Law 117	40, 76, 225		
Onomasticon			Law 126	89	*Las siete partidas*	
3.78	125		Law 146	70	4.5.1	178
			Laws 170-171	81	4.21.1	177, 179
Quintilian			Law 170	63, 82		
Institutio Oratorio			Law 171	82, 229		
6.1.52	132		Law 175	164		
			Law 196	47		

INDEX OF AUTHORS

Abusharaf, R.M. 71
Adams, R.M. 7
Albright, W.F. 9
Aldred, C. 44
Allard, P. 13
Altamira, R. 207
Anonymous 279, 285
Anstey, R.T. 273
Archer, G. 27
Armstrong, K. 9
Attwater, D. 168
Aulén, G. 167
Auping, J.A. 15, 279
Avalos, H. 3, 35, 78, 139, 155

Baade, H.W. 230, 231
Bagby, A.P. 6
Bailey, K. 180, 223, 224
Bainton, R. 137, 217
Baker, J.H. 243
Barclay, J.M.G. 249
Barkun, M. 33, 34
Barmash, P. 81
Barnes, A. 14
Barney, S.A. 179
Bartchy, S.S. 8, 26, 99, 100, 103, 104, 107, 127
Barton, J. 4, 8
Batiza, R. 231
Beach, J.A. 179
Beavis, M.A. 154
Becking, B. 204
Begg, C.T. 257
Bender, S. 273
Berghof, O. 179
Bergsma, J.S. 85
Berlinerblau, J. 282
Berman, J.A. 64

Bernat, D.A. 71
Betz, H.D. 48, 108-11
Birch, B.C. 4
Birney, J.G. 285
Blackburn, R. 60, 223, 277
Bland, D. 73
Blass, F. 137, 138
Blassingame, J.W. 13, 262
Blickle, P. 220
Blount, B.K. 113
Bodin, J. 222-25
Booth, W.C. 2
Bömer, F. 50
Botta, A. 84
Bourne, G.W. 128, 255-57
Bouwsma, W.J. 221
Bowersock, G.W. 159
Bowie, F. 9
Boyer, J. 104
Bradley, K.R. 55
Brady, P.S. 278
Braxton, B.R. 112, 113
Breathett, G. 227
Brett, S.F. 172, 177, 179, 180, 183
Bright, P. 162
Brown, C.L. 237-39, 274, 278, 279, 282
Brown, J.W. 282
Brown, O.J. 174
Brown, P. 159, 162
Brueggemann, W. 24-26, 124
Brunt, P.A. 141, 152
Bryce, T. 45
Buell, D.K. 108, 161
Burkert, W. 50
Butler, J. 251
Buttrick, G.A. 8
Byron, J. 13, 127, 130

Cadbury, H.J. 282
Cahill, T. 11
Cairns, D. 57
Callahan, A.D. 7, 10, 12, 73, 127-30, 133, 134, 161, 259, 264
Callender, D. 90, 93
Calvin, J. 214
Canévet, M. 167
Capizzi, J.E. 180, 192
Carey, B. 238
Carmichael, C.M. 85
Carnahan, B.M. 278
Carrington, S.H.H. 199, 238, 272
Carter, W. 150, 151
Cateau, H. 272
Champlin, E. 153
Cherniss, H. 167
Childs, M.D. 276
Chirichigno, G.C. 84
Church, F.F. 130
Clark, E. 234, 235
Clark, E.A. 169
Clarkson, T. 237, 239, 242-45, 274, 283
Clauss, M. 141
Clines, D.J.A. 23, 57
Coakley, S. 167
Cody, A. 160
Collins, B.J. 45
Combes, I.A.H. 6, 56, 116-18, 145, 146, 155
Cone, J.H. 73
Conrad, R.E. 60
Conzelmann, H. 106
Coogan, M.D. 28
Cook, M. 35
Copan, P. 45, 46, 81, 84, 85, 87, 88
Cortés-Fuentes, D. 153
Coupland, R. 237
Craton, M. 277
Cugoano, Q.O. 245, 246, 283

D'Souza, D. 11
Dal Lago, E. 7
Dalmas, A. 275
Dandamaev, M.A. 10, 39

Daniélou, J. 165, 167
Davenport, F.G. 184, 186-89, 191, 192
Davidson, E.H. 279
Davies, C.S.L. 243
Davies, M. 136, 138, 150
Davis, D.B. 6, 9, 14, 40, 49, 50, 56, 163, 164, 218, 237, 248, 278, 280
Davis, R.F. 261
Davis, S. 69, 166
Dawkins, R. 16
Dayan, J. 276
Debrunner, A. 137, 138
Decret, F. 162
Dennis, T.J. 166, 243
Dershowitz, A. 39
Desmangles, L. 276
Di Lella, A.A. 209
DiTommaso, T. 30
Diakonoff, I. 65
Dickerson, D.J. 113
Diedrich, M. 266
Dindorf, K.W. 125
Dion, P.E. 87
Divjak, J. 162
Dolbeau, F. 162
Donnan, E. 199
Douglass, F. 60, 261-65, 267, 268, 276, 281, 287
Doyle, D.E. 213
Dratel, J.L. 228
Drescher, S. 237, 273, 277, 280, 281

Edgar, C.C. 51
Ehrman, B. 16, 103
Eilberg-Schwartz, H. 72
Eisenstein, E. 184
Elkins, S.M. 227
Eltis, D. 15, 199
Engerman, S.L. 175, 273
Ennis, D.J. 243
Epsztein, L. 8, 9, 40
Everett, S. 28
Exum, J.C. 26

Falk, Z.W. 84
Fee, G. 102, 104
Felder, C.H. 261
Field, L.I. 198
Finke, R. 11
Finley, M.I. 7, 27, 55
Fishbane, M. 64
Fitzmyer, J.A. 127, 128, 133, 212
Fleer, D. 73
Flesher, P.V.M. 7, 39, 42, 56
Fletcher, F.T.H. 250
Fletcher, J. 170
Flusser, D. 160
Fogel, W.R. 175
Ford, L.K. 14
Fournet, P.A. 169
Fox-Genovese, E. 273
Frankfurter, D. 159
French, B.F. 230
Frick, F.S. 25
Friede, J. 200
Funk, R. 137, 138
Furneaux, R. 247

Gadamer, H.-G. 30
Gallay, A. 251
Galpaz-Feller, P. 44
Garnet, H.H. 260
Garnsey, P. 160
Garr, W.R. 57, 66
Gay, P. 227
Genovese, E.D. 69, 273
Gertz, J.C. 70
Giles, K. 281
Glancy, J.A. 13, 55, 71, 101, 114,
    135, 148, 154, 155
Glaude, E.S., Jr 73
Glick, L.B. 72
Glock, C.Y. 11
Godwyn, M. 59
Goldenberg, D.M. 35, 70, 69, 161
Goldman, R. 72
Goldthwaite, G. 6
Gollaher, D.L. 71
Gordesian, L. 146
Gossett, T.F. 33
Gould, P. 273

Grabar, O. 159
Grat, F. 197
Greenberg, K.L. 228
Greene, J.P. 282
Greengus, S. 46
Groothuis, R.M. 108, 111
Grudem, W.A. 27, 111
Gurney, O.R. 47
Güzlow, H. 94, 99

Hadley, M.A. 9
Hall, G. 166, 232
Hall, G.M. 232
Halpern. B. 2
Hamoto, A. 35
Hanger, K.S. 232-35
Hanke, L. 53, 200-202, 207, 216-18
Hardin, J.K. 141
Harrelson, W. 75, 76
Harrill, J.A. 7, 8, 12, 23, 26, 99-101,
    103, 105, 125, 160, 266, 281
Harris, W.V. 55
Hart, D.B. 166
Haught, J. 16
Haynes, S.R. 69, 108, 166
Hays, R.B. 4
Healy, N.M. 172, 173
Heidel, A. 58
Hempton, D. 251
Hendricks, O., Jr 139, 140, 142, 149,
    150, 152
Hera, A. de la 195
Hernaez, F.J. 189, 190, 193
Hess, H. 160
Hezser, C. 82
Hiers, R.H. 9
Hietanen, M. 109
Hine, E. 34
Hirsch, E.D. 29
Hitchens, C. 16
Hochschild, A. 242, 278, 283
Hodge, C.J. 108
Hoffner, H.A. 46
Horsley, R.A. 2, 7, 10, 59, 99-103,
    105, 106, 114, 126, 127, 135,
    138, 139, 140, 144, 145, 147-49
Horst, P.W. van der 125

Hove, R. 109
Howard, P.A. 276
Hunt, A.N. 231, 233, 234, 277
Hunt, A.S. 51
Hunter, M. 243
Hyson, L.O. 251

Inikori, J.E. 272
Inwood, B. 55, 166
Isaac, B. 181
Isaac, E. 9-10, 70

Jackson, S. 39
James, C.L.R. 277
James, S.V. 252
Jardine, L. 183
Jefford, C.N. 160
John, C.R. 168
Johnson, L.T. 3
Johnson, S.A. 69, 70, 75
Jones, W.R. 75

Kaiser, W.C. 81
Karras, R.M. 170
Katsari, C. 7
Kawashima, R. 67
Keen, B. 200
Kendall, E. 251
Kennedy, G.A. 123
Kim, S. 136, 139, 143
King, M.L., Jr 35
King, P.J. 63
Kiple, K.F. 232
Kirk, A. 96
Kitson, P.J. 238
Kleber, K. 84
Klein, R. 165, 167
Klingberg, F.J. 237
Klingshirn, W.E. 159
Knight, D.A. 4, 9
Kotlikoff, L.J. 233
Kramer, S.N. 39

Ladner, G.B. 166
Laeuchli, S. 160
Laguerre, M.S. 276
Lambdin, T.O. 103

Lambert, W.G. 42, 43, 58
Lanser, S.S. 67
Las Casas, B. 203-206, 208, 209, 211, 213-15, 229
Lascelles, E.C.P. 239
Layton, R.A. 181
Lebrun, R. 47
Lehman, W. 103
Levenson, J.D. 31-34, 36, 73
Levine, B. 84
Levinson, B.M. 86
Lewis, W.J. 179
Lichtenstadter, I. 35
Lichtheim, M. 44, 45
Lipsius, J.H. 90
Locke, M.S. 274, 282, 286
Loewenisch, W. von 219
Luther, M. 220

MacMullen, R. 51, 159
Macqueen, J.G. 45
Magdalene, F.R. 38
Malcolmson, C. 243
Maltby, R. 195
Malul, M. 39
Mann, F. 166
Mark, E.W. 72
Marrietta, J.D. 252
Marshall, D. 16
Martens, P.W. 113
Martin, D.B. 117, 118, 144, 147
Martin, R.P. 135
Martin, T.F. 30
Maxwell, J.F. 164, 165, 166, 177, 183, 197
McFeeley, W.S. 261
McGukin, J. 163
McKay, H.A. 75
McKeown, N. 7, 24, 55
McKivigan, J.R. 13
Meeks, W.A. 159
Meier, S.A. 146
Mendelsohn, I. 9, 10, 12, 40-42, 76, 82, 83, 88, 89, 94
Menesson-Rigaud, O. 275
Meredith, A. 165
Metraux, A. 276

Index of Authors

Metzger, B.M. 97, 103, 160
Meyers, C. 68
Middleton, J.R. 57
Mikalson, J.D. 50
Miles, J. 9
Millar, J. 12
Miller, J.W. 67
Mills, M.E. 2
Minchinton, W. 273
Mintz, S.D. 199
Mitchell, M.A. 161
Mitscherling, J.A. 30
Monteith, K.E.A. 277
Moore, J.M. 141, 152
Morgan, P.D. 51
Morgenthau, H. 140
Morris, T.D. 6, 7, 52
Morrow, G.R. 50-53, 56, 77, 137
Müller, G. 165
Müller, P. 127
Muraoka, T. 103

Nash, G.B. 252
Nayed, A. 30
Nissinen, M. 65, 95, 146
Noll, M.A. 251, 252, 266, 281
Noonan, J.T. 183, 194

O'Donnell, J.J. 162
Oberman, H.A. 219
Odahl, C.M. 159
Oldham, J. 282
Olsen, T. 247
Olyan, S. 5, 71
Orlinsky, H.M. 204
Ormond, J.J. 6
Osiek, C. 138
Otto, E. 4

Paget, J.C. 160
Palafox, L.P. 203
Paley, R. 243
Palmer, J.T. 168
Panzer, J.S. 12, 171, 177-79, 185-88, 190-92, 194, 195, 197
Parish, H.-R. 195, 196, 201, 202
Park, E.C. 58

Parker, R. 209
Parker, S. 58
Pascal, R. 231
Patterson, O. 6, 10, 40, 56, 93, 271, 272
Payne, P.B. 100, 104, 108, 115
Petersen, N.R. 130, 144, 147
Pharr, C. 89, 164
Pickett, T.H. 266
Pinn, A.B. 75
Plank, G. 252
Pons, F.M. 199, 277
Pope, M.H. 94
Popkin, J.D. 276, 277
Preuss, J. 35
Price, R.M. 16,
Price, S.R.F. 141, 142
Priest, J. 175
Propp, W.H. 71

Quiroga, P.L.B. de 118

Ramelli, I.L.E. 212
Ramsay, J. 238, 239
Rebillard, E. 162
Redford, D.B. 44
Reed, J.E. 120, 121
Reis, J.J. 224, 225
Rengstorf, K. 100
Reventlow, H.G. 282
Richards, G. 277
Richardson, D. 199
Riesener, I. 63, 80
Ritner, R.K. 65, 95
Roach, J. 227
Robertson, A.T. 104, 129
Robinson, C.H. 168-70
Rogers, N. 243
Rogers, T.W. 14
Rogozinski, J. 199, 236, 237, 276, 277
Rollins, W.G. 8
Ross, F.A. 14, 28, 66-68, 71, 73, 79, 119, 270, 271, 275, 281, 283
Roth, M.T. 41-43, 64, 76-78, 82, 89, 94, 164
Rozbicki, M.J. 243

Rupert, A.J. 233
Rupprecht, A.A. 15

Sala-Molins, L. 227-29
Salzman, M.R. 164
Samoral, M.L. 230
Sampson, R. 159
Sandiford, K.A. 245
Sandt, H. van de 160
Sass, G. 117
Sass, M. 266
Sawyer, P.H. 170
Schafer, J.K. 227, 231
Scheick, W.J. 279
Schellenberg, A. 57, 58
Schenker, A. 87
Scherer, L.B. 136, 251
Schlaifer, R. 49
Schlier, H. 100
Schmidt, A.J. 11
Schnackenburg, R. 1
Schneider, T.J. 70
Schor, J. 264
Schuler, E. von 47
Schulz, S. 12
Schwab, G. 127
Seibert, E.A. 3
Sen, A. 5
Sensbach, J.F. 51
Seow, C.L. 65, 95
Sepulveda, J.G. de 189, 203-207, 210, 211, 213-16
Serfass, A. 164
Sewall, S. 255
Shanks, C.L. 280
Shaw, B.D. 162
Sheehan, J. 282
Shtaerman, E.M. 14
Shyllon, F. 238
Sider, R. 140
Skehan, P. 209
Sloat, W.A. 251
Smith, A. 7, 10
Smith, J.P. 103
Smith, R. 35
Soden, W. von 39
Soderlund, J.R. 252

Soggin, J.A. 68
Sollberger, E. 83
Solow, B.L. 199
Spear, J.M. 230-33
Sprinkle, J.M. 77
Staiger, C.B. 285
Stark, R. 9, 11, 15, 40, 42, 43, 49, 55, 56, 59, 61, 80, 81, 88, 93, 95, 152, 167-69, 170, 172-74, 176, 177, 183-85, 194, 197, 198, 221, 222, 224, 226-36, 242, 252, 253, 258, 269, 270, 271, 275, 276, 279, 280, 287
Ste Croix, G.E.M. de 14, 160, 216, 286, 287
Stein, S.J. 251
Stendahl, K. 29, 30
Stern, P. 78
Stowers, S.K. 10, 120, 144
Stramara, D.F. 166
Strickland, D.H. 180, 181
Stringfellow, T. 286
Stuart, C. 239-41
Stuart, M. 256
Stuckey, S. 261
Sullivan, F.P. 202
Swaminathan, S. 282
Sweeney, J. 16

Tackach, J. 251
Tannenbaum, F. 227
Tappert, T.G. 220
Tawil, H. ben Y. 65
Taylor, M.E. 74
Thayer, J.H. 129
Theissen, G. 139
Thiselton, A.C. 24
Thomas, H. 168, 199, 226
Thorley, J. 104, 105
Thornton, J.K. 275
Thurston, H. 184
Tierney, B. 53
Tolmie, D.F. 127
Tomkins, S. 247, 274
Tov, E. 62
Traboulay, D.M. 202
Trible, P. 67, 68

Trofimova, M.K. 14
Tsevat, M. 85

Van Deburg, W.L. 268
Vaux, R. de 93
Vercoutter, J. 181
Verlinden, C. 168, 173, 181
Vessey, M. 159
Vial, T.M. 9
Vickery, P. 200
Vitoria, F. de 192, 193
Voelz, P.M. 278

Wacker, G. 281
Waitz, G. 168, 169
Wajdenbaum, P. 49
Walker, D. 60, 260
Wallon, H. 13
Walvin, J. 252
Walzer, M. 31
Watson, A. 107
Wattles, J. 97
Watts, W. 57
Weaver, P.R.C. 142, 153
Weidman, H.E. 195, 196, 201, 202
Weinfeld, M. 83
Wellhausen, J. 9
Wendel, F. 221
Wenham, G.J. 8
Westbrook, R. 39, 79, 80, 85, 90
Westermann, C. 62
Westermann, W.L. 14
White, J. 139

Whitford, D.M. 70, 180
Whitlock, K. 183
Whybray, R.N. 3
Wiedemann, T. 90, 225, 231
Wilberforce, W. 248, 249
Williams, E. 15, 272, 273
Williams, P.J. 64
Williamson, S.C. 261, 262, 264
Wills, R.W. 57
Wilson, A. 131
Wilson, J.A. 45
Wink, W. 140
Wise, S.M. 237, 239
Wiseman, D.J. 146
Witherington III, B. 10, 26, 30, 52, 114, 115, 119-21, 130-33, 135
Wölfel, D.J. 185
Wolff, H.W. 63
Woolman, J. 253-55
Wright III, B.G. 83
Wright, D.P. 12, 13, 38, 41
Wright, J. 103
Wunsch, C. 38
Wyatt, D. 180
Wyatt, N. 71
Wyrick, J. 30

Yoder, J.H. 140

Zagal Arreguin, H. 176
Zawadizki, S. 84
Zerbe, G.M. 144
Zimmerli, W. 8